Ultimate PowerShell Automation for System Administration

Streamline Automation and Administration Tasks with Advanced PowerShell Techniques and Expert Insights

Prashanth Jayaram

Rajendra Gupta

www.orangeava.com

First published: June 2024

Published by: Orange Education Pvt Ltd, AVA™

Address: 9, Daryaganj, Delhi, 110002, India

275 New North Road Islington Suite 1314 London,
N1 7AA, United Kingdom

ISBN: 978-81-97396-526

www.orangeava.com

Dedicated To

Teachers, Parents, Family, and Friends

- Prashanth Jayaram

My Beloved Parents:

Shri Shyam Sunder Gupta
Smt. Krishna Gupta

and

My wife Kashish and My kids Akshita and Vanshil

- Rajendra Gupta

About the Authors

Prashanth Jayaram is an experienced professional in data and data science, with diverse expertise and roles spanning over 18 years. He excels in designing innovative database solutions and has hands-on experience with cutting-edge Next-Gen database technologies. He has authored and published over 500 articles and several books on SQL, NoSQL, PowerShell, Python, SQL on Linux, Azure, AWS, MongoDB, Graph Database, Ansible, and Azure DevOps.

His contributions to the SQL Server community have been recognized through prestigious awards such as ABOVE and BEYOND. He was honored as the Best SQL Author in 2018.

He is the author of multiple books, including *PowerShell 6.0 Linux Administration Cookbook*, *Introduction to SQL*, *The SQL Workshop*, *Administering Relational Databases on Microsoft Azure: A Detailed Paradigm to Support SQL on Azure Cloud and DP 300 Study Guide*, and *PowerShell Essential Guide: Master the Fundamentals of PowerShell Scripting and Automation*.

Rajendra Gupta is a distinguished Technical Architect and Database Consultant, boasting an impressive 17-year track record of immersive involvement in the realm of database technologies. With a remarkable accolade to his name, Rajendra has clinched the esteemed Best Author of the Year award from SQLShack not once but thrice consecutively.

An authoritative figure in the field, Rajendra has authored an extensive collection of over 600+ articles on SQLSHACK, MSSQLTIPS, QUEST, DZONE, and CodingSight that span across the expansive domains of SQL Server, Azure, MySQL, Linux, Power BI, Performance Tuning, AWS/Amazon RDS, Git, and various related technologies. His insightful compositions have garnered an impressive readership, with over 15 million avid readers engaging with his content to date. He is also the co-author of the books *The Essential PowerShell Handbook* and *Administering Relational Databases on Microsoft Azure*.

About the Technical Reviewer

Shubham Chauhan is a seasoned IT professional with a B.Tech degree in Electronics and Communication from the College of Technology, Pantnagar. With a fervent dedication to innovation and excellence, he has forged a successful career marked by continuous growth and adaptability.

Beginning his journey in the IT realm, he diligently honed his expertise in system administration, playing a pivotal role in maintaining IT infrastructure stability and security. His proficiency in endpoint administration allowed him to streamline operations and enhance productivity.

Expanding upon this foundation, he propelled himself to master software deployment, OS management, and troubleshooting processes, setting new standards of excellence. Additionally, Shubham excels in PowerShell automation, creating scripts and applications that revolutionize intricate tasks, leading to significant efficiency gains and operational improvements.

Recognized for his adeptness in diverse technologies, including Window/MacOS/iOS/Linux administration, Terraform for infrastructure provisioning, and Azure VDI management, Shubham is a main stakeholder in creating system policies and collaborates closely with the security team to enforce policies aimed at safeguarding the IT infrastructure.

Furthermore, Shubham shares his expertise by training individuals on these tech stacks, empowering them to excel in the ever-evolving IT landscape. His commitment to professional development and keen eye for emerging technologies keep him at the forefront of IT advancements, driving positive change and making invaluable contributions to organizational success.

Acknowledgements

Jumping out of the comfort zone is never easy. Embracing that challenge and seizing the opportunity has brought us to the brink of releasing this book. As I stand on this milestone, I am reminded of my teachers' invaluable guidance and support.

I want to thank the noble soul of my mathematics professor, the late Mrs. Pushpalatha S Sukatankar, for her enduring influence.

My deepest love to my daughters, Prarthana and Pravitha, whose journey from premature babies to blossoming, loving kids inspires me daily. Their motivation and small steps in life motivate me in every way.

I sincerely thank my beloved wife, Ambika SG, for her endless love, care, and unwavering support. I am forever thankful for her companionship on this journey.

I want to thank my parents, R Jayaram and Indira, and my siblings, Balu Jayaram, and Gopi Jayaram, for being there and giving meaning to everything I do.

- Prashanth Jayaram

Throughout the journey of crafting this book, numerous hands have guided and supported me. I extend my heartfelt gratitude to each of you.

Thank you, God, Shyam Baba, for illuminating my path and blessing me with the ability to share these words.

I want to express my deepest appreciation to my family – my parents, my spouse, and my children – whose unwavering support and understanding have been my anchor through the highs and lows of this creative endeavor.

I would like to thank my publisher for believing in this book and making its publication possible. I extend my gratitude to the readers – it is for you that these words were written. Your curiosity, engagement, and support are the driving force behind every word penned on these pages.

- Rajendra Gupta

Preface

The trend of automation has been gaining momentum lately. Over the past decade, PowerShell has become the preferred tool for automation and has become popular among administrators, automation engineers, and cloud engineers. Its versatility enables it to automate almost all tasks within the Microsoft ecosystem, making it a valuable tool for IT professionals.

Nowadays, IT professionals and administrators are required to manage and automate complex tasks across various platforms. Given its incredible versatility and features, PowerShell has emerged as the ultimate tool to achieve this goal.

This book is designed to be your comprehensive companion on becoming a PowerShell expert. It is divided into three parts, each focusing on different aspects of PowerShell to guide you through a progressive journey in PowerShell automation. This book will provide you with the knowledge and practical skills to handle various tasks, from Windows administration to cloud operations and everything in between.

Part 1: Fundamentals of PowerShell

This guide is a comprehensive PowerShell introduction covering everything from the basics to advanced techniques. The first three chapters are designed to equip you with the fundamental knowledge and skills required to start your journey with PowerShell, whether you are a novice seeking to automate your first task or an experienced expert exploring the latest features.

PowerShell is a powerful tool for automating tasks, and Part 1 (**Chapters 1-3**) covers the essentials of using it. You will learn how to install and set up PowerShell, run PowerShell commands, and introduce yourself to PowerShell modules. Additionally, you will delve into PowerShell Core, which is a robust scripting solution that provides an environment for automation tasks. You will learn the differences between PowerShell Core and Windows PowerShell and how to install and run PowerShell Core commands. You will also learn how to configure variables, allowing for precise control and data manipulation within your scripts. Finally, you will master PowerShell pipelines, enabling you to select output columns strategically, work with properties and methods using the Select-Object cmdlet, and gain insights into controlling the quantity of your script's output.

Chapter 1: This chapter introduces you to the fundamental knowledge and skills required to start your journey with PowerShell. Whether you are a novice seeking to automate your first task or an experienced expert exploring the latest features, this chapter will provide you with the necessary resources to succeed in PowerShell.

Chapter 2: This chapter serves as an indispensable guide, offering a thorough exploration of the robust scripting solution that is PowerShell Core. As a cross-platform tool, PowerShell Core transcends traditional boundaries, providing users a dynamic and versatile environment for automation tasks.

Chapter 3: This chapter equips you with the skills to configure variables, allowing for precise control and data manipulation within your scripts. The heart of PowerShell efficiency lies in its pipelines, and we will empower you to master this concept. Learn to select output columns strategically, work with properties and methods using the Select-Object cmdlet, and gain insights into controlling the quantity of your script's output.

Part 2: PowerShell Scripting and Automation

This part of the book covers **Chapters 4-7**, which delve deeper into the intricacies of PowerShell scripting and automation.

This part is a crucial part of our journey through programming in PowerShell. In these chapters, you'll learn how to work with data control, arrays, conditional statements, loops, and hash tables, which are essential for unlocking the true potential of PowerShell. Additionally, you'll explore advanced functions and scripting techniques, including parameter validation, pipeline support, script blocks, switch parameters, and navigating through function parameters. Furthermore, you'll learn about code signing, which enhances the integrity and authenticity of your scripts, creating a more secure execution environment. Finally, you'll become familiar with the essential tools and techniques to manage and automate tasks efficiently in diverse system environments, including managing user accounts, monitoring system resources, and configuring network settings.

Overall, Part 2 of the book is a must-read for anyone who wants to become proficient in PowerShell scripting and automation. By the end of these chapters, you'll have a solid understanding of the advanced features of PowerShell and how to use them to automate tasks and improve productivity.

Chapter 4: This chapter is the pivotal chapter of our journey through the intricacies of programming. Here, we dive headfirst into the realm of data control and arrays, where the mastery of conditional statements, loops, and hash tables unlocks the true potential of a PowerShell.

Chapter 5: This chapter delves into the world of code signing, unraveling the process of designing a self-signed certificate for code signing. Discover how code signing enhances the integrity and authenticity of your scripts, fostering a secure execution environment.

Chapter 6: This chapter provides an in-depth discussion of PowerShell Advanced Functions and Scripting Techniques. It explores the intricacies of crafting advanced functions in PowerShell, covering topics such as parameter validation, pipeline support, utilizing script blocks, switch parameters, navigating through function parameters, and leveraging common parameters. Learn how to create functions that are not only powerful but also adaptable to various scenarios. Additionally, we touch upon the significance of adequate documentation, providing a comprehensive guide to mastering PowerShell scripting.

Chapter 7: This chapter explores the essential tools and techniques that empower Windows administrators to manage and automate tasks efficiently in diverse system environments. As PowerShell has become the de facto scripting language for Windows, mastering its capabilities is crucial for administrators looking to streamline administrative workflows and enhance productivity.

Part 3: PowerShell Advanced Topics

We delve deeper into PowerShell's advanced features in Part 3, consisting of **Chapters 8 through 11**. We cover background jobs, remoting, cloud computing, and integration with Microsoft technologies. This section is particularly useful for those looking to increase their productivity and efficiency when working with PowerShell. Using PowerShell's advanced features, users can automate complex tasks, freeing up valuable time for more important work. For example, background jobs allow users to run resource-intensive operations in parallel, while remoting enables users to execute commands on remote systems without leaving their workstations. Additionally, PowerShell's integration with cloud computing and DevOps practices enables users to automate infrastructure management and deployment, streamlining workflows and reducing the risk of errors.

Chapter 8: This chapter delves deep into PowerShell background jobs, a crucial aspect for mastering implementation at an advanced level. Background jobs refer to discreetly executed tasks in the background of an application or system, allowing users to focus on other tasks. They are especially useful for resource-intensive or time-consuming operations, such as extensive data processing or automated email dispatches.

Chapter 9: This chapter discusses about remoting. PowerShell Remoting is a feature that empowers administrators to execute commands on remote systems, enabling seamless management of machines without physically accessing them. This functionality allows the administrator's local PowerShell session to connect to a remote session on a different machine. Commands entered in the local system are transmitted to the remote computer and executed as if the administrator were physically present. The results are then sent back to the local system. PowerShell Remoting relies on the Windows Remote Management (WinRM) framework and Windows Management Instrumentation (WMI) within the WinRM framework. It occurs over TCP, HTTP, and HTTPS protocols.

Chapter 10: This chapter explores the convergence of cloud computing and automation through the lens of PowerShell. As organizations increasingly rely on cloud services for their infrastructure, these topics will help you navigate and orchestrate your cloud operations.

Chapter 11: This chapter explores how PowerShell seamlessly integrates with various Microsoft technologies and ecosystems. This integration enables administrators and developers to automate diverse tasks more efficiently across databases, cloud infrastructure, and DevOps practices.

Get a Free eBook

We hope you are enjoying your recently purchased book! Your feedback is incredibly valuable to us, and to all other readers looking for great books.

If you found this book helpful or enjoyable, we would truly appreciate it, if you could take a moment to leave a short review with a 5 star rating on Amazon. It helps us grow, and lets other readers discover our books.

As a thank you, we would love to send you a free digital copy of this book, and a **30%** discount code on your next cart value on our official websites:

www.orangeava.com

www.orangeava.in (For Indian Subcontinent)

☑ **Here's how:**

Leave a review for the book on Amazon.

Take a screenshot of your review, and send an email to **info@orangeava.com** (it can be just the confirmation screen).

Once, we receive your screenshot, we will send you the digital file, within 24 hours.

Thank you so much for your support – it means a lot to us!

Downloading the code bundles and colored images

Please follow the links or scan the QR codes to download the **_Code Bundles and Images_** of the book:

https://github.com/ava-orange-education/Ultimate-PowerShell-Automation-for-System-Administration

The code bundles and images of the book are also hosted on **_https://rebrand.ly/jto31bo_**

In case there's an update to the code, it will be updated on the existing GitHub repository.

Errata

We take immense pride in our work at **Orange Education Pvt Ltd,** and follow best practices to ensure the accuracy of our content to provide an indulging reading experience to our subscribers. Our readers are our mirrors, and we use their inputs to reflect and improve upon human errors, if any, that may have occurred during the publishing processes involved. To let us maintain the quality and help us reach out to any readers who might be having difficulties due to any unforeseen errors, please write to us at :

errata@orangeava.com

Your support, suggestions, and feedback are highly appreciated.

DID YOU KNOW

Did you know that Orange Education Pvt Ltd offers eBook versions of every book published, with PDF and ePub files available? You can upgrade to the eBook version at **www.orangeava.com** and as a print book customer, you are entitled to a discount on the eBook copy. Get in touch with us at: **info@orangeava.com** for more details.

At **www.orangeava.com**, you can also read a collection of free technical articles, sign up for a range of free newsletters, and receive exclusive discounts and offers on AVA™ Books and eBooks.

PIRACY

If you come across any illegal copies of our works in any form on the internet, we would be grateful if you would provide us with the location address or website name. Please contact us at **info@orangeava.com** with a link to the material.

ARE YOU INTERESTED IN AUTHORING WITH US?

If there is a topic that you have expertise in, and you are interested in either writing or contributing to a book, please write to us at **business@orangeava.com**. We are on a journey to help developers and tech professionals to gain insights on the present technological advancements and innovations happening across the globe and build a community that believes Knowledge is best acquired by sharing and learning with others. Please reach out to us to learn what our audience demands and how you can be part of this educational reform. We also welcome ideas from tech experts and help them build learning and development content for their domains.

REVIEWS

Please leave a review. Once you have read and used this book, why not leave a review on the site that you purchased it from? Potential readers can then see and use your unbiased opinion to make purchase decisions. We at Orange Education would love to know what you think about our products, and our authors can learn from your feedback. Thank you!

For more information about Orange Education, please visit **www.orangeava.com**.

Table of Contents

Part 1
Fundamentals of PowerShell

CHAPTER 1
Introduction to PowerShell

Introduction

In this chapter, you will gain the foundational knowledge and skills to embark on your PowerShell journey. Whether you are a beginner looking to automate your first task or a seasoned pro exploring the latest features, this chapter will equip you with the essential tools to succeed in PowerShell.

The emphasis on automation is prevalent nowadays. In the last decade, PowerShell has propelled in every manner in the automation arena. Within the realm of automation, PowerShell has thrived and transformed into a powerhouse. From its inception, PowerShell became the *de facto* primary tool for automation for Windows administrators. Its capabilities span the automation spectrum, enabling the execution of virtually any task within the extensive Microsoft ecosystem. This underscores its pivotal role in the complex landscape of automation solutions. Moreover, its newfound cross-platform capability enhances the breadth and depth of its utilization, further solidifying its significance in the field.

Over the past decade, many product vendors have conducted extensive explorations into the realm of automation, deploying a spectrum of tools that offer a seamless and robust framework for resource management. PowerShell has emerged as a stalwart in this landscape, renowned for its exceptional prowess in handling a diverse array of components, ranging from on-premises to cloud services.

Structure

In this chapter, we will discuss the following topics:

- Understanding PowerShell
- PowerShell Evolution
- Learning PowerShell

- Getting Started with PowerShell 7
- Automating IT Administration Tasks
- Using PowerShell to Automate IT Administration Tasks
- A Technical Exploration
- Getting Started with Installation and Setup
  - Installing PowerShell 6.2.7
  - Installing the Latest Version: PowerShell 7.4
  - Navigating PowerShell Integrated Scripting Environment (ISE)

Understanding PowerShell

The adoption of PowerShell is driven by its multifaceted advantages. PowerShell stands out due to its accessibility, making it an ideal choice for beginners and seasoned users alike. Its integration into the Windows Operating System ensures a smooth entry as a simple search in the Windows menu provides instant access to the PowerShell.

Beyond its accessibility, PowerShell empowers users with a robust automation framework. With many cmdlets, it is a versatile tool for creating and sharing custom cmdlets. This capability allows users to automate tasks, ranging from simple to complex, fostering efficiency and consistency in system management.

Moreover, PowerShell offers scalable management capabilities. Tasks requiring multiple mouse clicks in a graphical user interface can be executed swiftly and efficiently through PowerShell. This scalability extends to a wide array of administrative functions, enabling users to manage diverse aspects of their systems in a streamlined manner.

The strength of Powershell, which is often overlooked, lies in its ability to provide comprehensive access to information. PowerShell facilitates navigation through the file system as a command-line interface (CLI). Additionally, integrating PowerShell with a wide range of products provides a platform to manage and administer the products, and this information might be challenging to reach through traditional means.

PowerShell Evolution

PowerShell, a dynamic shell and scripting language developed by Microsoft, stands as a pivotal tool in the toolkit of IT professionals. Its evolution over time has solidified its position as a robust and flexible solution for system administrators and IT specialists.

Invented by Microsoft, PowerShell's inception and development were spearheaded by Jeffrey Snover, a Technical Fellow at the company. The genesis of PowerShell dates back to the early 2000s when Snover and his team embarked on its creation. The inaugural version, named Monad, was released in 2006, marking the commencement of PowerShell's journey as a powerful automation and configuration management framework.

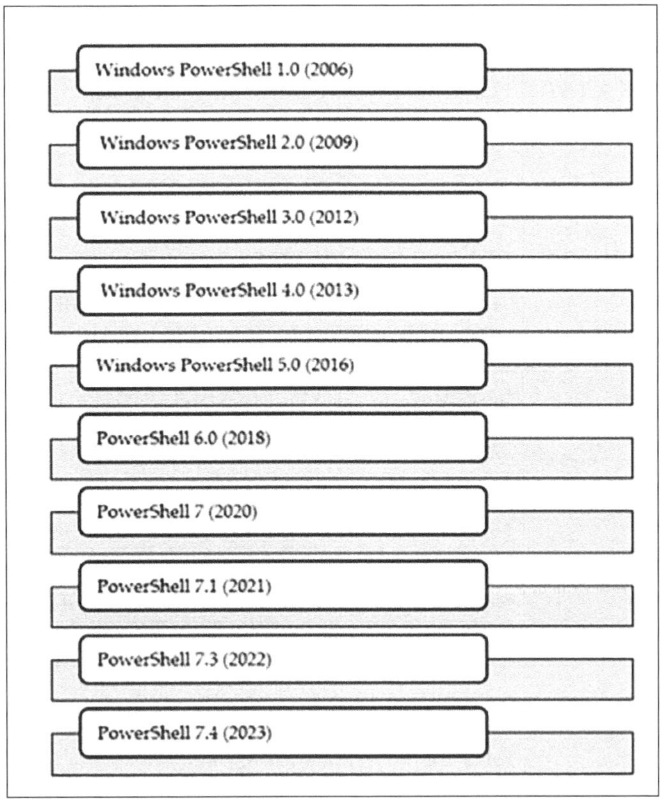

Figure 1.1: *Evolution of PowerShell*

The following table displays Powershell's release history:

Version	**Release Date**	**Notes**
PowerShell 1.0	Nov-2006	Optional component of Windows Server 2008
Windows PowerShell 2.0	Jul-2009	Integrated with Windows 7 Integrated with Windows Server 2008 R2 WMF 2.0
Windows PowerShell 3.0	Oct-2012	Integrated with Windows 8 Integrated with Windows Server 2012 WMF 3.0

Version	Release Date	Notes
Windows PowerShell 4.0	Oct-2013	Integrated with Windows 8.1 Integrated with Windows Server 2012 R2 WMF 4.0
Windows PowerShell 5.0	Feb-2016	Released in Windows Management Framework (WMF) 5.0
Windows PowerShell 5.1	Aug-2016	Released during Windows 10 Anniversary Update Integrated with Windows Server 2016 WMF 5.1
PowerShell 6.0	Jan-2018	First release, built on .NET Core 2.0. Installable on Windows, Linux, and macOS
PowerShell 6.1	Sep-2018	Built on .NET Core 2.1
PowerShell 6.2	Mar-2019	Built on .NET Core 2.1
PowerShell 7.0 (LTS)	Mar-2020	Built on .NET Core 3.1 (LTS)
PowerShell 7.1	Nov-2020	Built on .NET 5.0
PowerShell 7.2 (LTS-previous)	Nov-2021	Built on .NET 6.0 (LTS-previous)
PowerShell 7.3	Nov-2022	Built on .NET 7.0
PowerShell 7.4 (LTS-current)	Nov-2023	Built on .NET 8.0.0

***Table 1.1**: PowerShell release history*

Learning PowerShell

Its deep integration into the Microsoft ecosystem underscores the imperative to learn PowerShell. As many Microsoft products, including cloud platforms, pivot towards PowerShell-centric interfaces, navigating and commanding this environment becomes a critical skill. The shift from traditional graphical user interfaces (GUIs) to PowerShell-based interfaces means that proficiency in PowerShell is a gateway to effective system administration.

Automation stands out as a core strength of PowerShell. The capacity to automate multiple tasks enhances efficiency and positions individuals as adept administrators capable of managing complex environments. Beyond mere automation, PowerShell facilitates seamless interaction between products and platforms. Whether managing an entire network or orchestrating tasks across diverse platforms, PowerShell serves as a unifying force in system administration.

Furthermore, the prevalence of PowerShell in Microsoft certification exams underscores its significance. Specific PowerShell-related questions have become a standard feature in these exams, making PowerShell proficiency an essential component of professional certifications.

In essence, learning PowerShell is not merely a practical choice; it's a strategic investment in staying relevant and effective in an evolving IT landscape.

Getting Started with PowerShell 7

PowerShell 7 represents a significant leap forward, introducing several key enhancements. First and foremost, it embraces cross-platform functionality, breaking free from the constraints of its predecessors. This cross-platform capability ensures that PowerShell 7 is not bound by specific operating systems, expanding its utility to a broader audience.

Built on the foundation of .NET Core 3 and above, PowerShell 7 exhibits improved performance and compatibility. Departing from the traditional .NET framework, this version is optimized for modern computing environments, offering advantages in speed, resource utilization, and compatibility with newer technologies.

Another pivotal aspect of PowerShell 7 is its transition to an open-source model. This marks a departure from previous versions and encourages community participation. Users now can contribute, provide feedback, and even make direct changes to enhance the functionality and versatility of PowerShell.

Beyond these advancements, PowerShell 7 addresses a critical need for improved backward compatibility. Bridging the gap between Windows PowerShell and PowerShell 7 cmdlets, this version ensures a smoother transition for users familiar with earlier iterations. This commitment to compatibility makes PowerShell 7 a viable choice for organizations with diverse environments, minimizing disruptions during the adoption phase.

Automating IT Administration Tasks

Automation in IT administration isn't just a convenience – it's a strategic imperative. Let's explore the compelling reasons why organizations and IT professionals are fervently embracing the automation of IT administration tasks:

For Beginners:

Why should we consider automating IT administration tasks, especially if you are just starting in the field? automation is a time-saving superhero. You free up valuable time and energy by Automating repetitive and time-consuming tasks. As a beginner, you can focus on learning and mastering more complex tasks that require your unique input and expertise.

Automation is also your ally in reducing errors. Let's face it – everyone makes mistakes, especially when tasks become monotonous. Automating tasks minimizes the chances of errors, ensuring that your IT systems operate smoothly and reliably. It's like having a safety net that catches potential slip-ups before they become more significant.

Speaking of reliability, automation contributes significantly to the stability of IT systems. Consistency is vital; automation ensures that tasks are executed uniformly, following predefined rules. This reduces the risk of configuration drift and other inconsistencies that can crop up when tasks are handled manually.

And let's remember scalability. Even as a beginner, you will quickly realize that managing larger and more complex IT environments is a real challenge. Automation makes it possible to efficiently handle numerous systems and devices simultaneously, which would only be practical with automation tools.

For Experts:

For seasoned IT professionals, automating IT administration tasks is a strategic move with many benefits. Beyond the time-saving aspect, automation allows you to channel your expertise into high-impact activities requiring human intervention. Instead of drowning in routine tasks, you can tackle more complex challenges and contribute strategic value to your organization.

Error reduction remains a critical advantage. As an expert, your work carries higher stakes, and even minor errors can have significant consequences. Automation provides a reliable mechanism to execute tasks precisely, minimizing the chances of costly mistakes.

The consistency brought by automation is paramount in large-scale operations. It becomes a linchpin for maintaining uniformity across diverse systems, reducing the risk of configuration discrepancies. This is especially crucial in environments where compliance and adherence to standard operating procedures are non-negotiable.

Scalability takes on new dimensions for experts managing expansive IT landscapes. Automation becomes the linchpin for efficiently orchestrating a multitude of devices and systems. This scalability saves time and positions you as a force multiplier within your organization.

From a compliance standpoint, automation becomes a compliance enforcer. It ensures that industry and regulatory standards are met consistently. This is vital for experts navigating the complex web of rules governing IT operations, providing peace of mind and minimizing regulatory risks.

And, of course, there is the financial aspect. For experts, automation translates into significant cost savings. By reducing the need for manual labor, minimizing downtime, and enhancing overall operational efficiency, automation becomes a strategic tool for optimizing IT budgets and resource allocation.

Using PowerShell to Automate IT Administration Tasks

For beginners and experts, PowerShell is a powerful choice for automating IT administration tasks. Its advantages are threefold:

Built for Windows and Beyond:

PowerShell is tailor-made for Windows environments, seamlessly integrating with Microsoft products and services. This native compatibility makes it an ideal tool for automating tasks specific to Windows-based systems.

PowerShell was initially designed for Windows, but with the introduction of PowerShell Core (also known as PowerShell 6 and later), Microsoft extended its reach to cross-platform environments. This cross-platform version is an open-source, community-driven project that brings PowerShell to various operating systems, including Windows, Linux, and macOS.

Key points about PowerShell's cross-platform capabilities are as follows:

PowerShell Core:

- PowerShell Core is a cross-platform edition of PowerShell.
- It is open source and hosted on GitHub.
- It supports Windows, Linux, and macOS.

Compatibility with Windows PowerShell:

While PowerShell Core expands to non-Windows platforms, the traditional Windows PowerShell (5.1 and earlier) is still available and widely used only on Windows systems.

Wide Range of Functionality:

PowerShell offers a comprehensive suite of automation tools, encompassing command-line interfaces, scripting, and automation frameworks. Its support for various data formats, including XML, JSON, and CSV, adds versatility, making it suitable for multiple automation tasks.

User-Friendly and Accessible:

PowerShell's user-friendly syntax makes it easy to learn and use, even for IT administrators with minimal programming experience. Extensive documentation and a vibrant community provide a supportive environment where users share tips, tricks, and best practices. This accessibility makes PowerShell an excellent choice for beginners and experts looking to automate daily tasks effectively.

A Technical Exploration

PowerShell emerges as a formidable language in IT, where efficiency is vital. Whether an IT pro or a developer, diving into PowerShell brings many capabilities to your IT infrastructure. Let's delve into the reasons why embracing PowerShell is a game-changer:

Figure 1.2 displays the key capabilities of PowerShell that makes it a versatile and powerful tool for administrators and IT professionals:

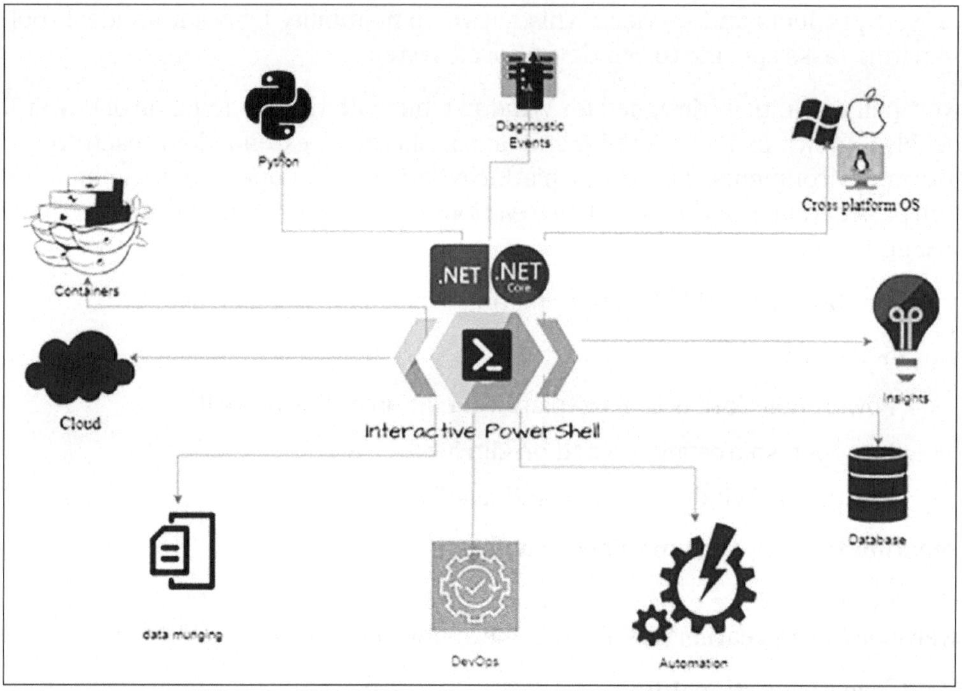

***Figure 1.2**: PowerShell integrations*

Note: *In this section, you will see concise and illustrative examples that showcase the simplicity and effectiveness of PowerShell in different scenarios. Brief snippets or explanations are provided to demonstrate various use cases. As this is the introduction chapter, readers are encouraged to take their time with all the coding samples. We will dive further into these topics in the later chapters.*

PowerShell as an Interactive Shell

The interactive shell provides a dynamic environment where you can explore, experiment, and execute commands in real-time, making it a powerful tool for both beginners and experienced users.

Open PowerShell:

Open PowerShell on your Windows machine. You can do this by searching for "*PowerShell*" in the `Start` menu or using the "`Run`" dialog (*Win* + R and type PowerShell).

Basic Commands:

In the PowerShell window, you can start by running simple commands. For example:

```
Get-Process
```

This command retrieves information about processes that are currently running on your system.

Variable Assignment:

You can assign values to variables and use them in subsequent commands:

```
$name = "Prashanth Jayaram"
$age = 40
Write-Host "Hello, my name is $name, and I am $age years old."
```

Exploration and Discovery:

PowerShell provides commands for exploration and discovery. For instance:

```
Get-Command -Module Microsoft.PowerShell.Management | select -First 10
```

This command lists all available cmdlets in `Microsoft.PowerShell.Management` module.

Working with Files:

You can interact with files and directories:

```
Get-ChildItem -Path C:\Windows
```

This command lists items in the C:\Windows directory.

User Interaction:

PowerShell allows for user interaction. For example:

```
$inputName = Read-Host -Prompt "What is your name?"
Write-Host "Hello, $inputName! Welcome to the interactive shell."
```

Custom Functions:

You can define custom functions interactively:

```
function SayHi{
    param (
```

```
        [string]$name
    )
    Write-Host "Hello, $name!"
}

# Call the function
SayHi -name "Prashanth Jayaram"
```

Exiting the Shell:

To exit the PowerShell session, you can use the Exit command or close the PowerShell window.

Object-Oriented Approach

In PowerShell, the Object-Oriented Approach is the building block for script development. Embracing this paradigm, PowerShell treats everything as an object, whether a service, a process, or a server.

Cmdlets and Consistent Syntax:

PowerShell introduces cmdlets with a standardized Verb-Noun syntax, providing a consistent and readable approach to command execution.

Object-Oriented Nature:

Treating everything as objects simplifies the combination and manipulation of commands, making it more intuitive than traditional plain-text environments.

Discovery and Exploration:

Simple commands like **`Get-Command`**, **`Get-Help`**, and **`Get-Member`** facilitate learning and discovering PowerShell features.

Here is a simple example of using classes in PowerShell:

```
# Define a simple Person class
class Person {
    [string]$Name
    [int]$Age

    Person([string]$name, [int]$age) {
        $this.Name = $name
        $this.Age = $age
```

```
    }

    [string] GetInfo() {
        return "Name: $($this.Name), Age: $($this.Age)"
    }
}

# Create an instance of the Person class
$person = [Person]::new("Prashanth", 40)

# Access properties
Write-Host $person.GetInfo()
```

In this example, we define a Person class with properties (**Name** and **Age**), a constructor, and a method (**GetInfo**). We create an instance of the Person class with the name "**Prashanth**" and age **40**, and then call the **GetInfo** method to display information about the person.

Object-Oriented Approach and Cmdlets Example

For example, if you want to retrieve information about the processes, you can use the **Get-Process** cmdlet. The output of **Get-Process** is a collection of process objects, and each object has properties representing information about a specific process.

```
# Using Get-Process cmdlet to get information about running processes
$processes = Get-Process

# Displaying properties of the first process in the collection
$firstProcess = $processes[0]

# Accessing specific properties (e.g., Name, ID, CPU usage)
Write-Host "Process Name: $($firstProcess.Name)"
Write-Host "Process ID: $($firstProcess.Id)"
Write-Host "CPU Usage: $($firstProcess.CPU)"
```

In this example, the **Get-Process** cmdlet is used to retrieve information about the running processes on the system.

The output of **Get-Process** is a collection of process objects. Each object represents a specific process and has properties like Name, Id, and CPU.

You can access specific properties of the process objects (for example, **Name**, **Id**, **CPU**), treating them as objects.

.Net and PowerShell

.NET classes in PowerShell scripts expand the scripting capabilities by leveraging the rich functionality provided by .NET. This allows users to perform advanced programming operations directly within their PowerShell scripts. Here is a brief overview and examples using .NET classes:

Using .NET's System.Math Class in PowerShell

In this example, **[System.Math]::PI** accesses the PI property of the **System.Math** class, providing the value of PI.

```
# Accessing properties of System.Math
$piValue = [System.Math]::PI
Write-Host "Value of Pi: $piValue"
```

Using .NET's DateTime Class

In this example, **[System.DateTime]::Now** retrieves the current date and time, and **.ToString("yyyy-MM-dd HH:mm:ss")** formats it to a specific string representation.

```
# Using .NET's DateTime class
$currentDateTime = [System.DateTime]::Now
Write-Host "Current Date and Time: $currentDateTime"
# Formatting DateTime
$formattedDateTime = [System.DateTime]::Now.ToString("yyyy-MM-dd HH:
mm:ss")
Write-Host "Formatted Date and Time: $formattedDateTime"
```

Using .NET's System.IO Namespace for File Operations

In this example, **[System.IO.File]::ReadAllText and [System.IO.File]::ReadAllLines** are used for reading the content of a text file.

```
# Using .NET's System.IO for file operations
$fileContent = [System.IO.File]::ReadAllText("C:\Path\To\File.txt")
Write-Host "File Content: $fileContent"

$fileLines = [System.IO.File]::ReadAllLines("C:\Path\To\File.txt")
```

```
Write-Host "Number of Lines in File: $($fileLines.Count)"
```

Data Format Flexibility

PowerShell excels in handling a variety of data formats, including CSV, HTML, XML, and JSON, making it effective for handling diverse data sources encountered in administrative and scripting tasks.

Structured Data Processing:

PowerShell's object-oriented nature extends its ability to process and manipulate structured data efficiently. This facilitates seamless interaction with databases, REST APIs, and other data sources.

Custom Object Creation:

Administrators can create custom objects, allowing for the structured representation of data within PowerShell scripts. This feature is handy for creating custom reports or manipulating data before further processing.

Data Transformation and Reporting:

PowerShell's rich data transformation and reporting capabilities empower administrators to generate custom reports, analyze trends, and derive insights from various data sources.

Let's go through a simple example in PowerShell that demonstrates data format flexibility, specifically focusing on handling CSV (Comma-Separated Values) data:

CSV Handling Example:

Suppose you have a CSV file named "**`example.csv`**" with the following content:

```
Name, Age, City
Prashanth, 40, New York
Jane, 38, New Jersey
Haris, 28, Chicago
```

Now, let's use PowerShell to read and manipulate this CSV data:

```
# Path to the CSV file
$csvFilePath = "C:\Ultimate PowerShell Automation\example.csv"
# Import the CSV file into a variable
$data = Import-Csv -Path $csvFilePath
# Display the imported data
$data
```

```
PS C:\Users\pjayaram> # Path to the CSV file
$csvFilePath = "C:\Ultimate PowerShell Automation\example.csv"

# Import the CSV file into a variable
$data = Import-Csv -Path $csvFilePath

# Display the imported data
$data

Name       Age City
----       --- ----
Prashanth  40  New York
Rajendra   38  New Jersey
Haris      28  Chicago
```

Figure 1.3: *PowerShell for manipulating CSV data*

```
# Accessing specific elements

Write-Host "First person: $($data[0].Name), Age $($data[0].Age), City $($data[0].City)"


# Filtering data based on a condition (e.g., age greater than 28)

$filteredData = $data | Where-Object { $_.Age -gt 28 }

# Converting the output data to JSON

$filteredData |ConvertTo-Json
```

```
PS C:\Users\pjayaram> # Accessing specific elements
Write-Host "First person: $($data[0].Name), Age $($data[0].Age), City $($data[0].City)"

# Filtering data based on a condition (e.g., age greater than 28)
$filteredData = $data | Where-Object { $_.Age -gt 28 }
# Converting the output data to JSON
$filteredData |ConvertTo-Json
First person: Prashanth, Age 40, City New York
[
    {
        "Name":  "Prashanth",
        "Age":  "40",
        "City":  "New York"
    },
    {
        "Name":  "Rajendra",
        "Age":  "38",
        "City":  "New Jersey"
    }
]
```

Figure 1.4: *PowerShell example for data format flexibility*

The Import-Csv cmdlet is used to import the data from the CSV file into the $data variable. The imported data is displayed, showing the structure of the CSV data in a tabular format. Specific elements of the data, such as the name, age, and city of the first person, are accessed and displayed. Next, the data is filtered to include only those individuals whose age is greater than 28, and the filtered data is converted to JSON.

Scripting and Automation

PowerShell's ubiquitous scripting capabilities are essential for scripting and automation tasks:

ARM-Based Templates

PowerShell seamlessly integrates with Azure Resource Manager (ARM) templates, empowering administrators to define and deploy Azure resources using declarative templates.

ARM-based scripting allows for the automated provisioning and configuration of complex infrastructure in Microsoft Azure.

```
# Azure PowerShell module
Connect-AzAccount


# Variables
$resourceGroupName = "YourResourceGroup"
$location = "East US"
$templateUri = "https://raw.githubusercontent.com/Azure/azure-quick-start-templates/master/101-storage-account-create/azuredeploy.json"


# Deploy Azure resources
New-AzResourceGroupDeployment -ResourceGroupName $resourceGroupName -TemplateUri $templateUri
```

In this script:

- The **`Connect-AzAccount`** cmdlet is used to authenticate and connect to your Azure account.
- The **`$resourceGroupName`** and **`$location`** variables define the resource group name and location.
- The **`$templateUri`** variable specifies the URI of the ARM template. In this example, it's pointing to the raw GitHub content of the Azure Quickstart Templates repository.
- **`New-AzResourceGroupDeployment`** is then used to deploy the Azure resources based on the specified template URI.
- This script will deploy an Azure Storage Account using the provided ARM template. Remember to replace **"YourResourceGroup"** with your desired resource group name.

Note: *You can explore more ARM templates in the Azure Quickstart Templates repository on GitHub.*

REST API Integration

PowerShell's native support for REST APIs facilitates automation for platforms and services that expose RESTful interfaces.

Administrators can interact with a wide range of web services, enabling seamless integration and automation of tasks through RESTful API endpoints.

The script is an example of interacting with a REST API using PowerShell's **`Invoke-RestMethod`** cmdlet. This script makes a GET request to the "**`https://jsonplaceholder.typicode.com/posts`**" API endpoint and then outputs the **`API response`**:

```
# Example interacting with a REST API

# Use Invoke-RestMethod to make API requests

$response = Invoke-RestMethod -Uri "https://jsonplaceholder.typicode.
com/posts" -Method Get

Write-Host "API Response: $($response | ConvertTo-Json -Depth 5)"
```

Ubiquitous Scripting

PowerShell's fully fledged scripting language, combined with its command-line interface, provides a consistent and powerful environment for automation.

Ubiquitous scripting allows administrators to automate diverse tasks, ranging from system configuration to cloud resource management, directly from the command line.

This script automates the process of copying files from one location to another. It demonstrates how PowerShell can be used to perform routine tasks directly from the command line:

```
# PowerShell script to copy files from one location to another


# Source and destination paths

$sourcePath = "C:\Path\To\Source"

$destinationPath = "C:\Path\To\Backup"


# Copy files

Copy-Item -Path $sourcePath\* -Destination $destinationPath -Recurse
-Force
```

Script-Based Configuration Management

PowerShell scripting allows administrators to define and enforce configuration management practices, ensuring consistency and compliance across servers and applications.

Let us see a PowerShell script that takes parameters and manipulates an XML file by replacing specific values:

```
$XML='C:\Ultimate PowerShell Automation\webconfig.XML'

Get-Content $XML
```

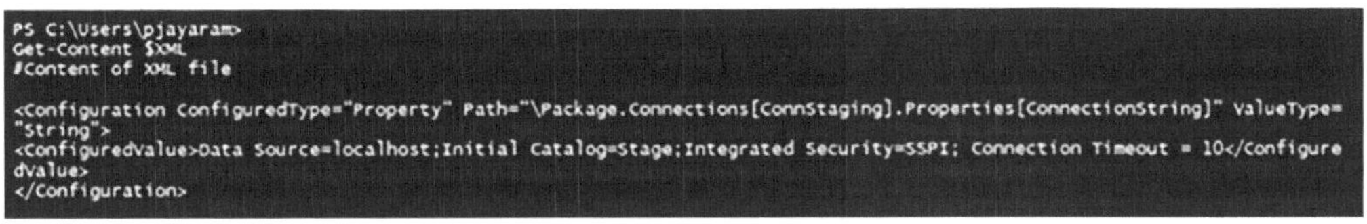

Figure 1.5: *PowerShell for script-based configuration management*

```
# Define parameters for the script
PARAM(
    [String]$XML='C:\Ultimate PowerShell Automation\webconfig.XML',
    [String]$DatabaseName='TargetDB',
    [String]$DatabaseServer='DataCenterDB01'
)

# Create strings to be used for replacement
[string]$db = 'Catalog='+ $DatabaseName
[string]$dbs = 'Source='+ $DatabaseServer

# Read the content of the XML file
(Get-Content $XML) |
Foreach-Object {
    # Replace "Catalog=..." with the specified database name
    # Replace "Source=..." with the specified database server
    $_ -replace "Catalog=([A-Za-z0-9_]+)", $db -replace "Source=([A-Za-z0-9_]+)", $dbs
} | Set-Content $XML
```

```
PS C:\Users\pjayaram>
Param(
[String]$XML='C:\Ultimate PowerShell Automation\webconfig.XML',
[String]$DatabaseName='TargetDB',
[String]$DatabaseServer='DataCenterDB01')
[string]$db = 'Catalog='+ $DatabaseName
[string]$dbs = 'Source='+ $DatabaseServer
(Get-Content $XML) |
Foreach-Object {
$_ -replace "Catalog=([A-Za-z0-9_]+)", $db -replace "Source=([A-Za-z0-9_]+)", $dbs } | Set-Content $XML
```

Figure 1.6: *Defining parameters*

Get-Content **`$XML`**

```
PS C:\Users\pjayaram>
Get-Content $XML
#Content of XML file

<Configuration ConfiguredType="Property" Path="\Package.Connections[ConnStaging].Properties[ConnectionString]" ValueType=
"String">
<ConfiguredValue>Data Source=DataCenterDB01;Initial Catalog=TargetDB;Integrated Security=SSPI; Connection Timeout = 10</C
onfiguredValue>
</Configuration>

PS C:\Users\pjayaram>
```

Figure 1.7: *Read the content of the XML file*

This script is helpful for dynamically updating values in an XML configuration file based on the parameters provided when running the script. It's commonly used for tasks such as configuring connection strings in **`web.config`** files dynamically.

- **`PARAM` block**: Defines parameters that can be passed to the script when it is executed. The parameters include the path to the XML file (**`$XML`**), the database name (**`$DatabaseName`**), and the database server (**`$DatabaseServer`**).
- **Replacement Strings**: Creates strings (**`$db`** and **`$dbs`**) that will be used for replacement in the XML file.
- **`Get-Content ($XML)`**: Reads the XML file content specified by the $XML parameter.
- **`Foreach-Object`**: Processes each line of the XML content.
- **String Replacement:** Uses the **`-replace`** operator to replace occurrences of "**`Catalog=...`**" with the specified database name and "**`Source=...`**" with the specified database server.
- **`Set-Content ($XML)`**: Writes the modified content back to the same XML file, effectively updating it with the new values.

Scripting for Hybrid Environments

PowerShell's versatility extends to hybrid environments, enabling administrators to script and automate tasks seamlessly across on-premises and cloud-based infrastructure.

```
# On-Premises PowerShell

# Variables
$onPremisesSqlServer = "YourOnPremisesSqlServer"
$azureSqlServer = "YourAzureSqlServer"
$databaseName = "YourDatabase"

# Query data from on-premises SQL Server
$onPremisesQueryResult = Invoke-Sqlcmd -ServerInstance $onPremisesSqlS-
erver -Database $databaseName -Query "SELECT * FROM YourTable"

Write-Host "On-Premises Query Result:"
$onPremisesQueryResult

# Query data from Azure SQL Database
$azureQueryResult = Invoke-Sqlcmd -ServerInstance $azureSqlServer -Data-
base $databaseName -Query "SELECT * FROM YourTable"

Write-Host "Azure Query Result:"
$azureQueryResult
```

This example demonstrates how PowerShell's versatility enables administrators to script and automate tasks seamlessly across on-premises and cloud-based infrastructure, making it a powerful tool for managing hybrid environments. Adjust the scripts based on your specific on-premises and cloud configurations.

Versatility and Modernization

PowerShell's versatility across platforms and the collaborative strength of its community contribute to its modernization, making it a dynamic and responsive tool for administrators and IT professionals in contemporary IT landscapes.

Compatibility Across Platforms

PowerShell Core, the cross-platform version of PowerShell, extends its reach beyond the traditional Windows environment. This cross-platform support enables users to leverage PowerShell on macOS and Linux, fostering a unified scripting and automation experience across diverse operating systems.

```
# Checking PowerShell Core version and platform
$psVersion = $PSVersionTable.PSVersion
Write-Host "PowerShell Core Version: $($psVersion.Major).$($psVersion.
Minor).$($psVersion.Build)"
Write-Host "Platform: $($env:OS)"
```

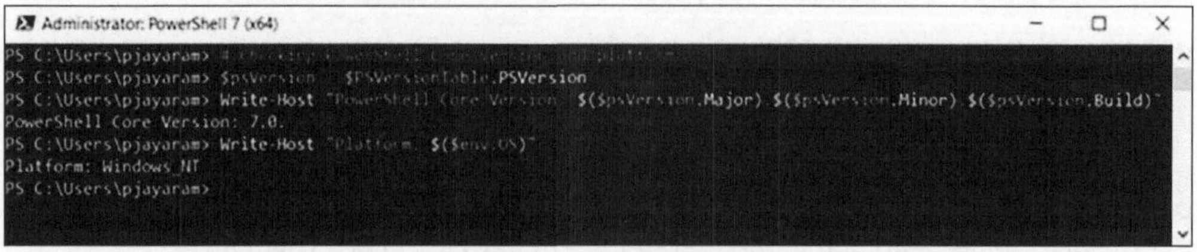

***Figure 1.8**: Checking PowerShell Core version and platform*

Community-Driven Modules

The PowerShell community plays a pivotal role in expanding its functionality. The PowerShell Gallery is a repository where community members contribute modules, scripts, and functions, enriching the PowerShell ecosystem. This collaborative effort addresses various needs, from system administration to specialized tasks.

```
# Installing a community-contributed module from the PowerShell Gallery
Install-Module -Name "ModuleName"
```

Unified Scripting and Automation

PowerShell's cross-platform compatibility and community-contributed modules create a unified scripting and automation experience.

Whether managing Windows servers, Linux machines, or cloud resources, administrators can use a consistent set of PowerShell commands and modules, streamlining their workflows.

```
# Example of using a module for Azure automation (Azure PowerShell module)
# Connect to Azure
Connect-AzAccount

# Manage Azure resources
Get-AzResourceGroup
New-AzStorageAccount -ResourceGroupName "MyResourceGroup" -AccountName
"mystorageaccount" -SkuName Standard_LRS -Location "East US"
```

In this example, the Azure PowerShell module connects to Azure and manages resources. This showcases the unified experience of using PowerShell for automation tasks, regardless of the platform used.

Data Store Management

PowerShell's provider model enables the management of data stores, allowing consistent techniques for managing data alongside files and folders.

Provider Model

The PowerShell provider model is a powerful feature that allows users to interact with various data stores using a consistent set of commands and techniques, similar to how you manage files and folders in a file system. Providers in PowerShell abstract different types of data stores, making it easier for users to manage diverse resources in a unified manner.

```
# PowerShell script to configure registry settings


# Registry path and key
$registryPath = "HKLM:\Software\MyApp"
$registryKey = "ConfigSetting"
$registryValue = "Enabled"


# Set registry value
New-Item -Path $registryPath -Force
Set-ItemProperty -Path $registryPath -Name $registryKey -Value $regis-
tryValue


Get-ItemProperty -Path  "HKLM:\Software\MyApp"
```

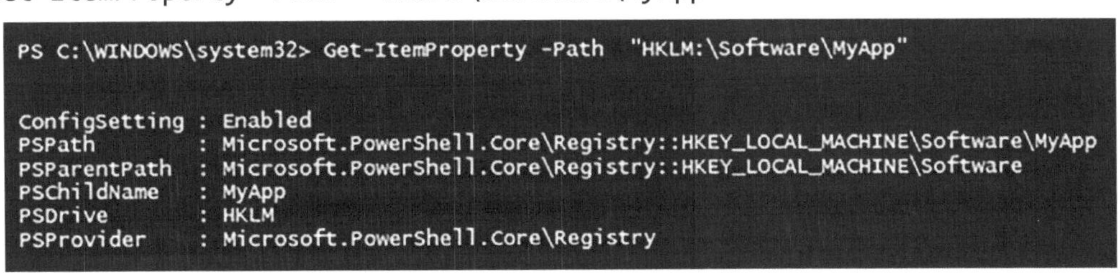

Figure 1.9: *PowerShell script to configure registry settings*

Security and Compliance

PowerShell execution policies and security best practices are a prudent and valuable approach. Addressing security considerations in PowerShell is crucial, especially in production environments.

Controlled Execution

Controlled execution is a crucial aspect of PowerShell's security features. It ensures that potentially harmful scripts or commands are not executed without explicit consent. PowerShell achieves this through its execution policies.

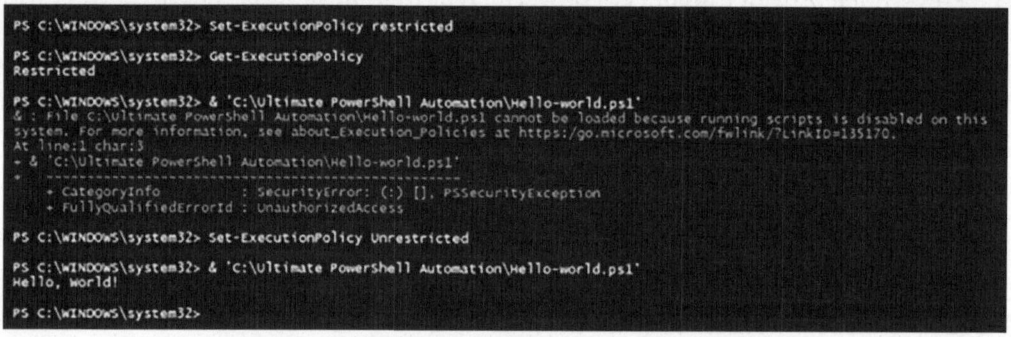

Figure 1.10: *Execution Policy for controlled execution*

Note: *Setting the execution policy to* "`Unrestricted`" *might pose security risks in a production environment because it allows the execution of all scripts without any restrictions. In a more secure setting, you might consider using a policy like* "`RemoteSigned`" *or* "`AllSigned`," *which allows only signed scripts to run.*

User Interaction

PowerShell's design emphasizes an administrator-centric approach, balancing powerful scripting capabilities and a flexible, real-time command entry experience. This design choice acknowledges the need for human interaction in certain scenarios.

```
# Prompting for user input
$UserName = Read-Host "Enter your username"
$Password = Read-Host -AsSecureString "Enter your password"
```

The **`Read-Host`** cmdlet is used to interactively prompt the user for input, such as a username and password. The **`-AsSecureString`** parameter ensures that sensitive information such as passwords is securely entered.

Compliance

PowerShell also plays a role in maintaining compliance by providing logging and auditing capabilities. Administrators can track and review actions performed using PowerShell for compliance purposes.

```
# Enable PowerShell script block logging

Enable-PSRemoting -Force

# Review PowerShell script block logs

Get-WinEvent -LogName "Windows PowerShell" -FilterXPath "*[System[(Even-
tID=4104)]]"
```

PowerShell remoting is enabled in this example, and script block logs can be reviewed using the **`Get-WinEvent`** cmdlet. This logging capability contributes to compliance efforts by allowing administrators to monitor and audit PowerShell activity.

Cloud Administration

Let's delve into the dimension of cloud administration within the context of PowerShell:

Unified Cloud Management:

Integration with major cloud providers (Azure, AWS, GCP) allows administrators to manage cloud resources directly from PowerShell.

Azure PowerShell Module:

A dedicated module for Azure empowers administrators to script and automate tasks related to Azure resources.

AWS Tools for PowerShell:

PowerShell seamlessly interacts with AWS services through dedicated cmdlets, enabling AWS resource management.

Google Cloud SDK for PowerShell:

The Google Cloud SDK for PowerShell facilitates the management of Google Cloud resources from the PowerShell environment.

In this example, we will install and use PowerShell modules for Google Cloud Platform (GCP) and Microsoft Azure. These modules allow users to manage cloud resources using PowerShell scripts, providing a convenient and familiar interface for cloud-related tasks.

```
# Install the Google Cloud PowerShell Module

Install-Module GoogleCloud
```

Figure 1.11: *Installing Google Cloud PowerShell Module*

```
# Install the Azure PowerShell Module
Install-Module -Name Az -AllowClobber -Scope AllUsers
```

These modules streamline the interaction with Google Cloud Platform and Microsoft Azure, allowing users to manage resources, execute commands, and automate tasks using PowerShell scripts.

DevOps Integration

DevOps Automation:

PowerShell plays a pivotal role in DevOps practices, enabling automation of deployment, configuration management, and continuous integration tasks.

CI/CD Pipelines:

Integration with CI/CD (Continuous Integration/Continuous Deployment) pipelines allows for seamlessly incorporating PowerShell scripts into automated build and deployment processes.

Infrastructure as Code (IaC):

PowerShell scripts facilitate Infrastructure as Code (IaC) practices, allowing administrators and DevOps teams to define and manage infrastructure in a code-centric manner.

Integration with Configuration Management Tools:

PowerShell integrates with popular configuration management tools, such as Ansible and Chef, supporting the automation of configuration tasks across diverse environments.

The versatility of PowerShell in Azure DevOps allows you to perform a wide range of tasks, making it a powerful tool for automation and orchestration in your CI/CD pipelines. While the "`Hello, world!`" example is simple, it serves as a starting point to showcase the execution of PowerShell tasks in an Azure DevOps pipeline. As you become more familiar with PowerShell and Azure DevOps, you can leverage its capabilities to perform more advanced actions.

Figure 1.12: *Integration with Configuration Management Tools*

To begin, create an inline PowerShell script to demonstrate "`Hello World`" output.

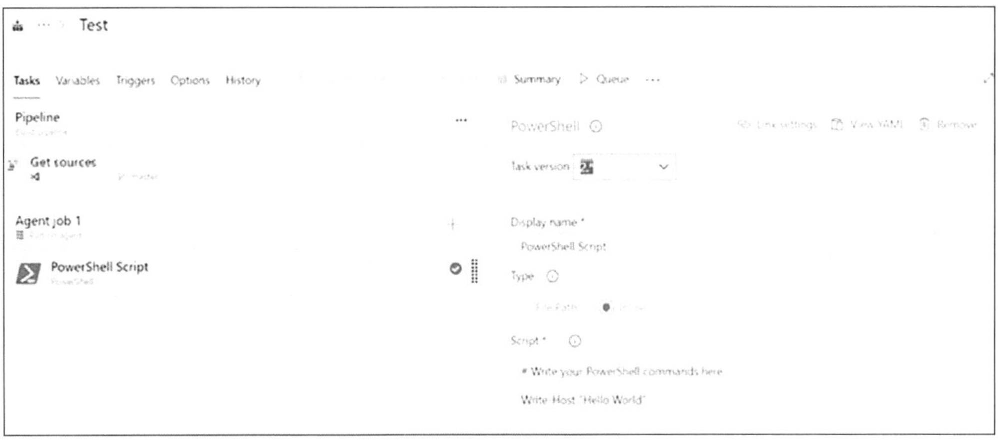

Figure 1.13: *Write sample script*

Next, execute the pipeline, with the log file logging the output of the PowerShell task.

Figure 1.14: *Execute the pipeline*

Getting Started with Installation and Setup

In PowerShell, the **`$PSVersionTable`** automatic variable provides information about the version of PowerShell that is currently running. This variable contains various properties, and the **`PSVersion`** property specifically indicates the version number of PowerShell.

Launch Windows PowerShell and type the command - **`$PSVersionTable.PSVersion`**. The output displays the major, minor, build, and revision numbers of the installed PowerShell version:

- **`Major`**: The major version number of PowerShell
- **`Minor`**: The minor version number
- **`Build`**: The build number
- **`Revision`**: The revision number

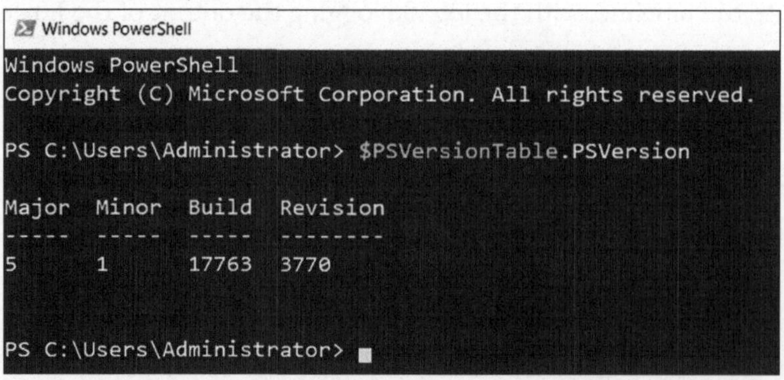

Figure 1.15: *Check PowerShell version and build number*

You can use the following script to display the PowerShell version in a user-friendly way:

```
# Check PowerShell version

$psVersion = $PSVersionTable.PSVersion

# Display version information

Write-Host "PowerShell Version: $($psVersion.Major).$($psVersion.Mi-
nor).$($psVersion.Build).$($psVersion.Revision)"
```

The PowerShell script checks the version of PowerShell and then displays detailed version information:

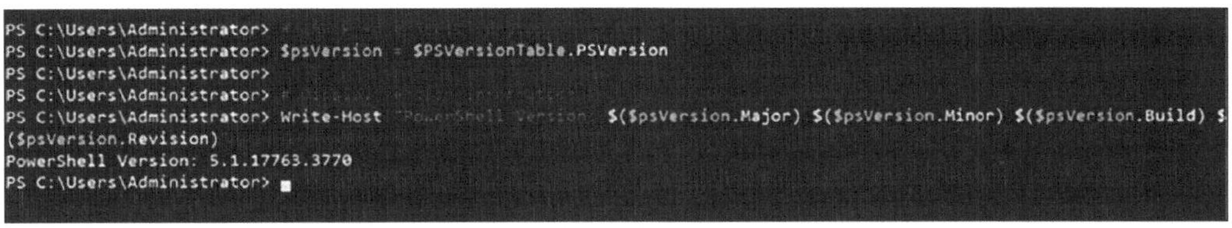

Figure 1.16: *Script to check PowerShell version*

Sometimes, you write a PowerShell script that requires a minimum version of PowerShell. In such cases, you can use the **$PSVersionTable** automatic variable to put the conditional statement. For example, let's say you require a minimum PowerShell version 6 for the script and your current PowerShell version is 5.1.17763, the conditional check would fail, as follows:

```
# Minimum required version

$minRequiredVersion = [Version]'6.0.0'

# Check if the installed version meets the requirement

if ($PSVersionTable.PSVersion -ge $minRequiredVersion) {

    Write-Host "PowerShell version is sufficient to run the script."

} else {

    Write-Host "PowerShell version does not meet the minimum requirement.
Please upgrade PS version."

}
```

The PowerShell script you provided checks whether the installed version of PowerShell meets a minimum required version

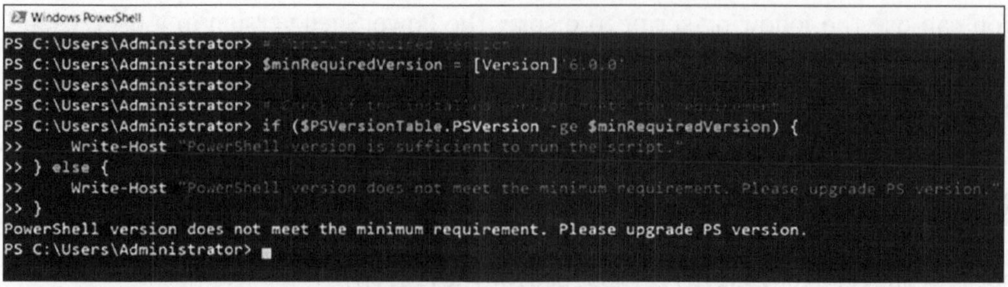

***Figure 1.17**: Conditional check*

Installing PowerShell 6.2.7

Navigate to Microsoft's GitHub repository for PowerShell Core https://github.com/PowerShell/PowerShell/releases/tag/v6.2.7

Download the PowerShell MSI - **`PowerShell-6.2.7-win-x64.msi`** for the Windows:

***Figure 1.18:** Download the PowerShell package*

Double-click the downloaded MSI to launch the installer, and follow the on-screen instructions (with default options) to install PowerShell 6.2.7.

After installation, launch PowerShell 6 (x64) from the Start and run the script to validate the minimum version.

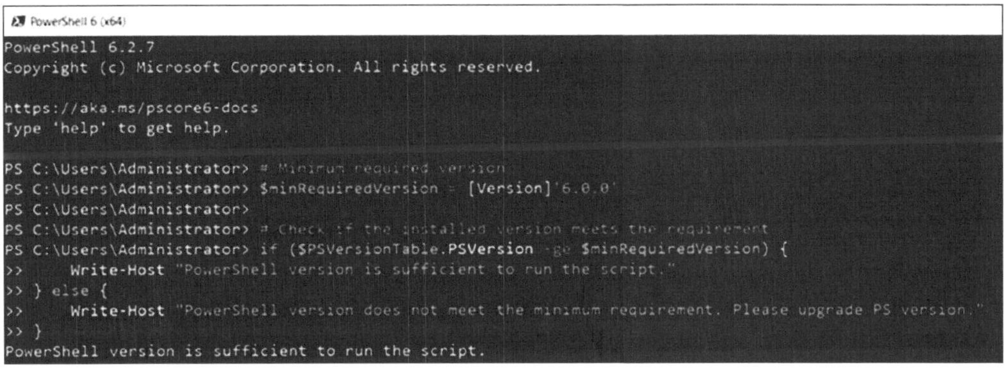

Figure 1.19: *Validate the PowerShell version*

Installing PowerShell 7.4 (Latest) version

The latest PowerShell version is `7.4.0` (as of 2023-11-16).

Navigate to the PowerShell GitHub Release Page at https://github.com/PowerShell/PowerShell/releases and check the latest release version.

Figure 1.20: *List the PowerShell 7.4 version*

Download the installer file from the Assets section and launch the installer.

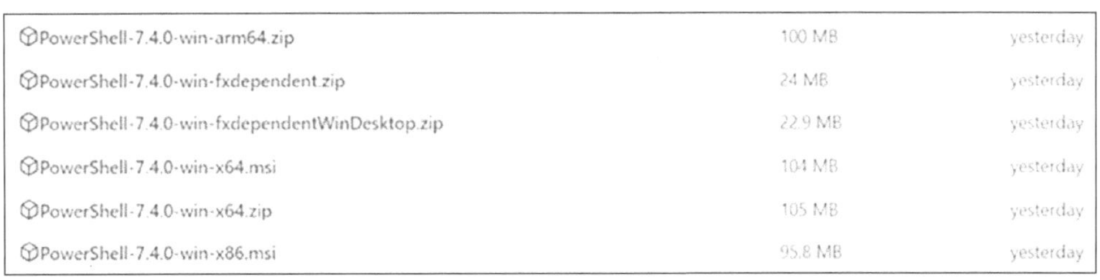

Figure 1.21: *Download the latest PowerShell module*

After installation, launch PowerShell 7 from the `Start` menu and verify the version.

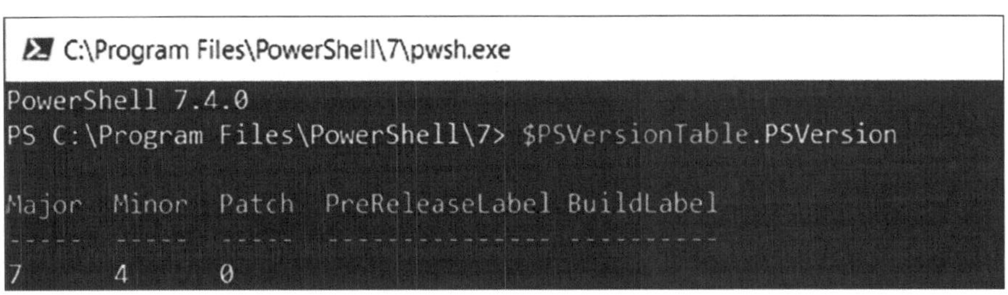

Figure 1.22: *Check PowerShell version*

Navigating PowerShell ISE

PowerShell Integrated Scripting Environment (ISE) is a graphical user interface (GUI) tool provided by Microsoft for PowerShell scripting. It offers features like syntax highlighting, tab completion, and debugging capabilities. Here is an essential guide on navigating PowerShell ISE:

Opening PowerShell ISE

You can open PowerShell ISE by searching for it in the Start menu or on the Start screen of your Windows computer. It is usually named "*Windows PowerShell* ISE."

Alternatively, you can open it from a PowerShell console by typing `` `powershell_ise` `` and pressing *Enter*.

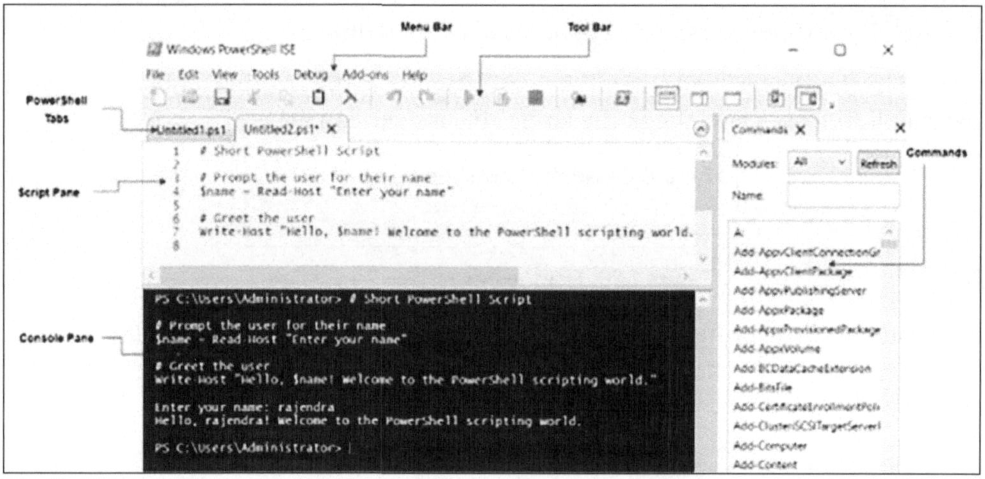

Figure 1.23: *Navigate PowerShell ISE*

User Interface

- **Menu Bar**: The menu bar is at the top and it contains menus like **`File`**, **`Edit`**, **`View`**, and more.
- **Toolbar**: The toolbar includes buttons for common actions such as opening, saving, and running scripts.
- **Scripting Pane**: This is where you write and edit your PowerShell scripts. It supports syntax highlighting for better readability.
- **Output Pane**: The output pane displays the results of executed commands or scripts.

- **Console Pane**: This pane provides an interactive PowerShell console where you can enter and execute commands directly.
- **Command Pane**: Allows you to enter and execute commands quickly.
- **Running Scripts**: To run a script, click the "`Run Script`" button on the toolbar or use the keyboard shortcut `` `F5` ``.
- **Tabs**: PowerShell ISE supports tabs, allowing you to work on multiple scripts or PowerShell sessions simultaneously. You can open a new tab using `*Ctrl* + T`.
- **Debugging**: PowerShell ISE includes debugging features. You can set breakpoints, step through code, and inspect variables during script execution. The debugging options are available in the toolbar.
- **Console Integration**: The console pane at the bottom allows you to interact with PowerShell directly. You can execute commands and see the results in real time.
- **Script Pane Shortcuts**: Various keyboard shortcuts can enhance your scripting experience. For example, `*Ctrl* + *Space*` provides auto-completion suggestions.
- **Saving and Opening Scripts**: Use the "`Save`" and "`Open`" options in the File menu to save and load your PowerShell scripts.
- **Getting Help**: The "`Help`" menu provides access to PowerShell help documentation, including cmdlet references.
- **Options and Settings**: You can customize various settings and preferences through the "`Options`" menu.

Note: *PowerShell ISE is primarily used for scripting and automation tasks. If you are working on newer systems, consider using the cross-platform Visual Studio Code (VSCode) with the PowerShell extension for an enhanced scripting experience.*

Conclusion

In the ever-evolving landscape of Information Technology, the decision to automate IT administration tasks emerges as a transformative force – a strategic shift from conventional practices to a future-oriented paradigm. As we navigate the complexities of modern technology ecosystems, the significance of IT automation becomes abundantly clear.

The journey through PowerShell automation unveils a multitude of benefits – fostering consistency, scalability, and operational cost savings. Automation reshapes the role of IT professionals, transcending the mundane by tackling routine and intricate tasks equally.

The precision of automated processes minimizes the risk of errors and safeguards against configuration drift, aligning organizations with regulatory standards and ensuring compliance.

IT automation is a beacon in pursuing operational efficiency, offering a proactive approach to problem resolution and predictive IT management.

PowerShell becomes a potent tool – a conduit for efficiency, scalability, and cross-platform harmony. Whether navigating the intricacies of Windows, Linux, or the vast landscapes of cloud environments, automation provides a common language and a unified approach.

PowerShell's capabilities span a broad spectrum, from its object-oriented approach and compatibility across platforms to its integration with cloud providers, modern scripting and automation capabilities, and a robust community ecosystem. These dimensions collectively position PowerShell as a versatile and essential tool for administrators in diverse IT landscapes.

As we delve into the next chapter, we explore PowerShell Core, a pivotal evolution in the PowerShell landscape. PowerShell Core represents a significant leap forward, extending its capabilities beyond the confines of Windows to embrace a cross-platform paradigm.

Points to Remember

- **PowerShell Scripting**

  PowerShell transcends mere scripting; it's a powerful shell and an environment for interactive commands. Move beyond the limits of traditional scripting and enter a realm where commands come to life.

- **Bulk Operations Mastery**

  Scripting often involves repetitive tasks. With PowerShell, you can perform these tasks on multiple servers – thousands even – streamlining work and ensuring consistency without the manual labor of GUI navigation.

- **Bridging the Windows-Linux Gap**

  It provides an interactive shell experience tailored for Windows environments for Linux users new to PowerShell. Command it to perform tasks, fetch information, and configure settings interactively.

- **Task Automation**

  PowerShell excels in automating diverse tasks, especially server configurations. Take it a step further with desired state configuration, allowing precise control over server states and automated corrections when configurations drift.

- **Object-Oriented**

  PowerShell treats every element as an object, whether it's a service, process, or server. Dive into the world of nouns, where PowerShell describes, configures, and works seamlessly with these objects.

- **.Net Framework**

  Built on the dot net framework, PowerShell is a treasure trove for developers. Witness the integration of dot net functionality in PowerShell command-lets, making it a go-to tool for developers in everyday coding.

- **Consistent Repeatable Tasks: The Heart of PowerShell Usage**

  PowerShell is your ally for tasks that demand consistency. For tasks repeated across servers, PowerShell ensures efficiency without needing to manually visit each server.

- **Built-In Providers**

  Built-in providers complement PowerShell's interactive shell. These providers allow you to ask questions and interact with elements like Active Directory, the registry, and WMI using natural language.

- **Aliasing**

  A bridging language Gap with shortcuts that leverage aliases to bridge language gaps. Whether you are accustomed to **`DIR`**, **`LS`**, or **`Get-ChildItem`**, PowerShell's aliases make the language transition smoother, offering a familiar touch.

- **PowerShell Integration**

  PowerShell isn't just a standalone language; it's deeply ingrained in Microsoft products and is a shipping requirement. It extends its reach into third-party products like VMware and Citrix, making it a go-to tool for IT professionals.

- **Version Evolution**

  Witness the evolution of PowerShell, now in its fifth version. Adapted and embraced by IT professionals, PowerShell continues to grow, offering new possibilities and enhanced capabilities.

Multiple Choice Questions

1. Who led the initial design and development of PowerShell at Microsoft?

   a. Bill Gates

   b. Satya Nadella

   c. Jeffrey Snover

   d. Steve Ballmer

2. In which year was the first version of PowerShell, initially known as "*Monad,*" released?
   a. 2002
   b. 2006
   c. 2010
   d. 2015
3. Which version of PowerShell marked a significant shift by becoming open-source and cross platform?
   a. PowerShell 5.0
   b. PowerShell 6.0
   c. PowerShell 7.0
   d. PowerShell 7.4
4. What does the abbreviation "LTS" stand for in the context of PowerShell releases?
   a. Long-Term Support
   b. Latest Technology Standards
   c. Legacy Technology System
   d. Lightweight Task Scheduler
5. What is the primary use case of PowerShell in Azure DevOps?
   a. Graphic Design
   b. Video Editing
   c. Task Automation
   d. 3D Modeling

Answers

1. c
2. b
3. b
4. a
5. c

Questions

- What is the purpose of the pipeline operator (|) in PowerShell?
- How does the output of cmdlets differ from the traditional text-based output in PowerShell?
- What is the significance of chaining cmdlets in a PowerShell pipeline?
- Which cmdlet is commonly used to filter data in a PowerShell pipeline?
- What kind of data does a PowerShell cmdlet typically output in a pipeline?

Key Terms

- **PowerShell:**

  Microsoft developed a shell and scripting language for task automation and configuration management.

- **Cmdlet:**

  A lightweight command used in PowerShell, typically following the verb-noun naming convention (for example, `Get-Process`).

- **Pipeline:**

  A "*pipeline*" refers to the mechanism by which the output of one cmdlet (command) is passed as input to another cmdlet

- **Task Automation:**

  The process of automating repetitive tasks and procedures to improve efficiency and reduce manual intervention.

- **Open-Source:**

  Software or tools with source code made available to the public allow users to view, modify, and distribute the code.

- **Cross-Platform:**

  The ability of a software or tool to run on multiple operating systems, such as Windows, Linux, and macOS.

Chapter 2
Introduction to PowerShell Core

Introduction

This chapter serves as an indispensable guide, offering a thorough exploration of the robust scripting solution that is PowerShell Core. PowerShell Core transcends traditional boundaries as a cross-platform tool, providing users with a dynamic and versatile environment for automation tasks.

One significant aspect covered in this chapter is the installation process of PowerShell Core on Ubuntu, showcasing the tool's adaptability to Linux environments.

This chapter elucidates the key differences between PowerShell and PowerShell Core, clarifying how the latter is more advanced and improved. This comparative analysis aids users in making informed decisions regarding their choice of scripting solution based on specific needs and requirements.

This chapter sheds light on modules unsupported in PowerShell Core. By elucidating these nuances, users gain insights into potential limitations and workarounds, ensuring a smooth transition to PowerShell Core while being aware of any feature disparities.

Furthermore, the chapter facilitates a comparative exploration of Bash and PowerShell commands, elucidating the strengths and capabilities of each. This comparative analysis equips users with the knowledge needed to make strategic choices in their automation journey, recognizing each scripting language's distinctive advantages in various scenarios.

Ultimately, this chapter serves as a gateway to the future of automation with PowerShell. By comprehensively covering key aspects, from installation procedures to feature differentials and cross-platform compatibility, it empowers users to navigate the dynamic landscape of scripting solutions. Whether you are a seasoned IT professional or a budding enthusiast, this chapter is a vital resource for unlocking the full potential of PowerShell Core and embracing a new era of seamless and efficient automation.

Structure

In this chapter, we will discuss the following topics:

- Introduction to PowerShell Core
- Features of PowerShell Core
- A Brief Note on .Net Core
- Installing PowerShell 7 on Ubuntu
- Understanding the Difference Between PowerShell and PowerShell Core
- Knowing about Unsupported Modules
- Comparing the Commands - Bash and PowerShell

Introduction to PowerShell Core

PowerShell Core is a cross-platform, open-source automation and scripting framework developed by Microsoft. It is designed to be a powerful and flexible command-line shell and a scripting language that facilitates the automation of various tasks, particularly in system administration and configuration management. PowerShell Core is an evolution of Windows PowerShell, with the key distinction that it is designed to run on platforms including Windows, Linux, and macOS.

Here's a concise history of PowerShell Core:

- **2006**: Introduction of Windows PowerShell, designed for Windows system administration.
- **2016**: PowerShell Core (6.0) released as an open-source, cross-platform version running on Windows, Linux, and macOS.

Features of PowerShell Core

Here are some key features and aspects of PowerShell Core:

- **Cross-Platform Compatibility**: PowerShell Core is designed to run on Windows, Linux, and macOS. Therefore, it is a versatile choice for managing systems in mixed environments.
- **Open Source**: Unlike its predecessor, Windows PowerShell, which is tightly integrated with the Windows operating system, PowerShell Core is open source and available on GitHub. This allows the community to contribute to its development and helps Microsoft continuously improve the tool.
- **Cmdlets**: PowerShell Core uses **"cmdlets"** (pronounced command-lets) as its core components. Cmdlets are small, single-function commands that follow a verb-noun naming convention (for example, **`Get-Process`**, **`New-Item`**,

`Remove-Item`). PowerShell Cmdlets can be combined to perform complex tasks through the pipeline.

- **Object-Oriented Pipeline**: One of the powerful features of PowerShell Core is its object-oriented pipeline. Instead of passing plain text between commands, PowerShell passes objects. This allows for richer data manipulation and transformation.
- **Scripting Language**: PowerShell Core is a command-line shell and a scripting language. It supports variables, loops, conditional statements, functions, and other programming constructs, making it suitable for writing scripts and automation workflows.
- **Module System**: PowerShell Core uses a module system to organize and distribute functionality. Modules are collections of cmdlets, functions, scripts, and other resources. Users can create or install existing modules to extend PowerShell Core's capabilities.
- **Remoting**: PowerShell Core includes robust remoting capabilities, allowing administrators to manage and automate tasks on remote systems. Remoting can be used to execute commands on remote machines as if they were local.
- **Integration with .NET**: PowerShell Core is built on the .NET Core runtime, enabling seamless integration with .NET libraries. It provides access to various functionalities and allows users to leverage existing .NET assemblies.
- **Interactive Shell**: PowerShell Core provides an interactive shell, making it easy for users to experiment with commands, test scripts, and explore the tool's capabilities.

To start with PowerShell Core, you can download it from the official GitHub repository, install it on your preferred platform, and explore its features and capabilities. Whether you are managing Windows servers, Linux machines, or a combination of both, PowerShell Core provides a consistent and powerful automation platform.

A Brief Note on .Net Core

.NET Core is an open-source, cross-platform framework developed by Microsoft for building modern, scalable, high-performance applications. Here's a concise overview:

- **Cross-Platform Compatibility**: .NET Core is designed to run on operating systems, including Windows, Linux, and macOS, offering flexibility in application deployment.
- **Open Source**: It is an open-source framework developed on GitHub. This encourages community contributions, transparency, and rapid development cycles.
- **Modular Design**: .NET Core follows a modular design and allows developers

to include only the necessary components for their specific application. This helps reduce the application's footprint and improves performance.

- **High Performance**: .NET Core is optimized for high performance, featuring features like Just-In-Time (JIT) compilation for efficient code execution.
- **Unified Platform**: With the introduction of .NET 5 (later renamed .NET), Microsoft unified the .NET platform, bringing together the best features of .NET Core, .NET Framework, and Xamarin. This simplifies development and supports a broader range of application types.
- **Modern Workloads**: .NET Core is well-suited for modern development scenarios, including cloud-native and containerized applications using technologies like Docker, microservices architecture, and serverless computing.
- **Cross-Language Interoperability**: .NET Core supports multiple programming languages, including C#, F#, and Visual Basic. It allows developers to choose the language that best suits their preferences and project requirements while still leveraging the capabilities of the .NET platform.
- **Tooling and Development Experience**: .NET Core comes with a rich set of development tools, including Visual Studio Code, Visual Studio, and command-line interface (CLI) tools, providing developers with flexibility in their development environment.
- **ASP.NET Core**: ASP.NET Core, built on top of .NET Core, is a cross-platform, high-performance framework that can build modern web applications and services.
- **Entity Framework Core**: Entity Framework Core, a lightweight and cross-platform version of Entity Framework, allows developers to interact with databases using .NET objects.

The following figure (source: https://dotnet.microsoft.com/en-us/platform/support/policy/dotnet-core) gives the currently supported .NET core details:

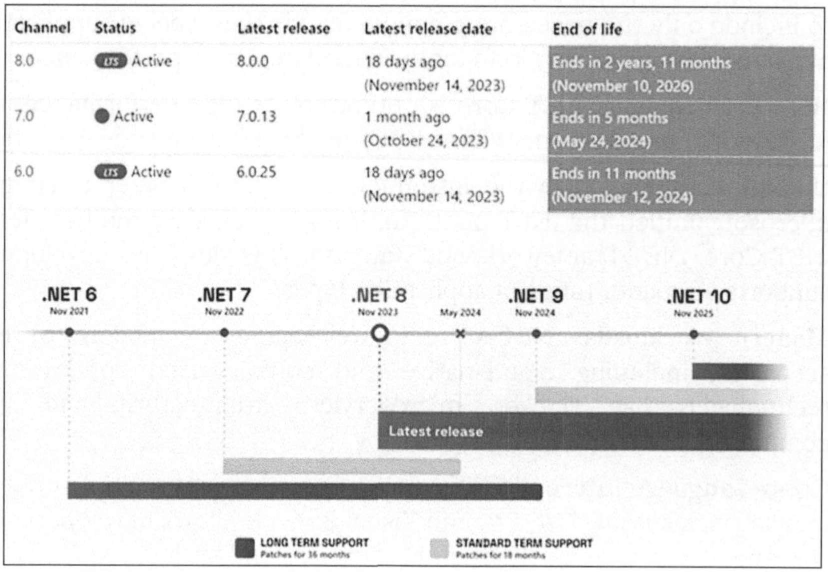

Figure 2.1: .Net Core supported versions

Understanding the Difference Between PowerShell and PowerShell Core

The primary differences between PowerShell and PowerShell Core lie in their platforms, architecture, and development. Here's a breakdown of the key distinctions:

Feature	**Windows PowerShell**	**PowerShell Core**
Platform Compatibility	Historically, PowerShell was designed exclusively for Windows operating systems. It integrated tightly with Windows technologies and had limited cross-platform capabilities	PowerShell Core is designed to be cross-platform, running on Windows, Linux, and macOS. This allows users to use PowerShell Core in heterogeneous environments with different operating systems
Open Source vs. Closed Source	The original PowerShell (Windows PowerShell) is a closed-source solution developed by Microsoft	PowerShell Core is open source and hosted on GitHub. This open nature encourages community contributions and transparency in the development process
Runtime Architecture	Windows PowerShell is built on the full .NET Framework, which is closely tied to the Windows operating system	PowerShell Core is built on the more modular and cross-platform .NET Core runtime. It can run on both .NET Core and .NET 5 (and later) versions, allowing it to operate on various platforms

Cmdlet Compatibility	Some cmdlets in Windows PowerShell may be specific to Windows technologies or features unavailable on other platforms	While efforts have been made to provide cross-platform compatibility, some Windows-specific cmdlets or features might not be available or may have platform-specific behavior in PowerShell Core
Versioning	Versions of PowerShell were closely tied to Windows releases, and the latest versions were often shipped with new Windows versions	PowerShell Core introduced a separate versioning scheme. It started with version 6.0 and continued independently of Windows releases. However, with the unification of the .NET platform, PowerShell is now referred to simply as "*PowerShell*," and the versioning aligns with .NET (for example, PowerShell 7.x aligns with .NET 5, 6, and more)
Integration with .NET	Windows PowerShell tightly integrates with the full .NET Framework	PowerShell Core is built on the more modular and cross-platform .NET Core, providing greater flexibility and compatibility with different platforms
Package Management	Windows PowerShell uses the `PowerShellGet` module for package management, which is closely tied to thc Windows environment	PowerShell Core uses the cross-platform module, `PowerShellGet`, allowing package management across diverse operating systems

Table 2.1: Difference between PowerShell and PowerShell Core

Compatibility Module:

The Compatibility Module, specifically **`WindowsCompatibility`**, is a crucial bridge between PowerShell Core and traditional Windows PowerShell.

The primary aim of the **`WindowsCompatibility`** module is to create a more seamless experience for users transitioning from Windows PowerShell to PowerShell Core. By maintaining familiar cmdlet names and behaviors, the module minimizes the learning curve associated with adapting to the cross-platform environment.

The following code snippets demonstrate installing a module named **`"WindowsCompatibility"`** and retrieving the commands available in that module:

```
PS C:\Users\pjayaram> Install-Module -Name WindowsCompatibility
PS C:\Users\pjayaram> Get-Command -Module WindowsCompatibility
```

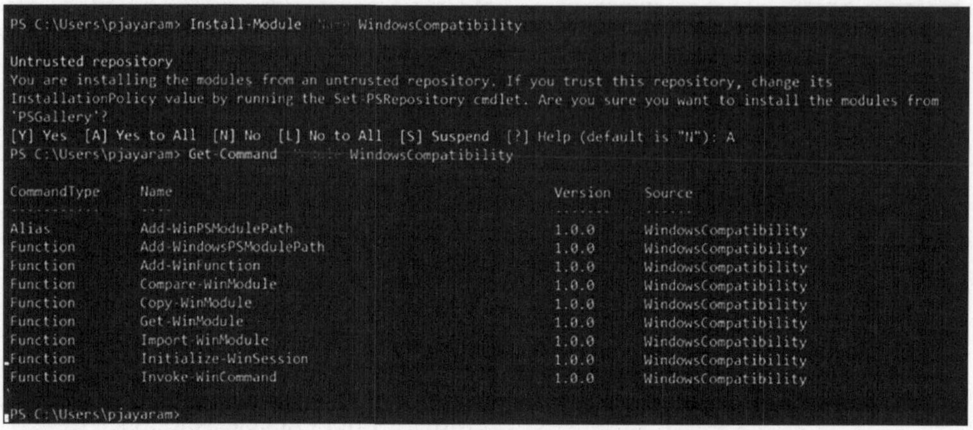

***Figure 2.2**: List compatibility module in PowerShell Core*

The following command uses the **`Invoke-WinCommand`** cmdlet to execute a Windows command within a PowerShell session. It retrieves the latest 10 events from the "**`Application`**" event log using the **`Get-EventLog`** cmdlet:

```
PS C:\Users\pjayaram> Invoke-WinCommand {Get-EventLog -Log Application
-New 10 }
```

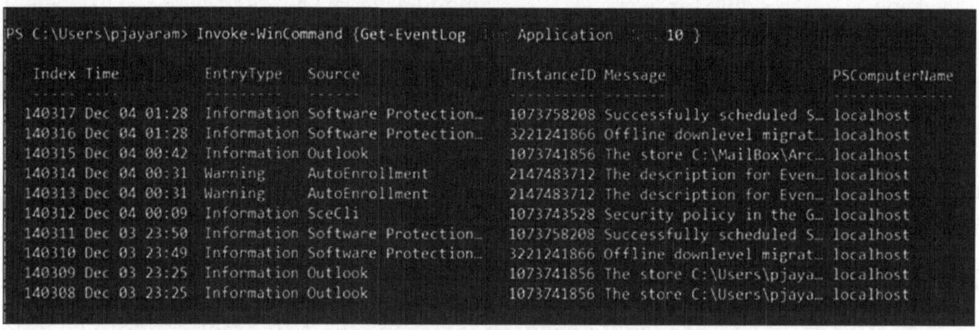

***Figure 2.3**: Run PowerShell compatibility commands in PowerShell Core*

The following PowerShell commands demonstrate the importation of **`Microsoft.Powershell.Management`** module and the subsequent retrieval of the latest 10 events from the "**`Application`**" event log:

```
PS C:\Users\pjayaram> Import-WinModule Microsoft.Powershell.Management
PS C:\Users\pjayaram> Get-EventLog -Log Application -New 10
```

```
PS C:\Users\pjayaram> Import-WinModule Microsoft.Powershell.Management
PS C:\Users\pjayaram> Get-EventLog Application 10

   Index Time          EntryType   Source                 InstanceID Message
   ----- ----          ---------   ------                 ---------- -------
  140317 Dec 04 01:28  Information Software Protection…   1073758208 Successfully scheduled Software Protection servic…
  140316 Dec 04 01:28  Information Software Protection…   3221241866 Offline downlevel migration succeeded.
  140315 Dec 04 00:42  Information Outlook                1073741856 The store C:\MailBox\Archive_data.pst has detecte…
  140314 Dec 04 00:31  Warning     AutoEnrollment         2147483712 The description for Event ID '-2147483584' in Sou…
  140313 Dec 04 00:31  Warning     AutoEnrollment         2147483712 The description for Event ID '-2147483584' in Sou…
  140312 Dec 04 00:09  Information SceCli                 1073743528 Security policy in the Group policy objects has b…
  140311 Dec 03 23:50  Information Software Protection…   1073758208 Successfully scheduled Software Protection servic…
  140310 Dec 03 23:49  Information Software Protection…   3221241866 Offline downlevel migration succeeded.
  140309 Dec 03 23:25  Information Outlook                1073741856 The store C:\Users\pjayaram\OneDrive - Commvault\…
  140308 Dec 03 23:25  Information Outlook                1073741856 The store C:\Users\pjayaram\AppData\Local\Microso…
```

Figure 2.4: *Load Microsoft.PowerShell.Management module*

In summary, PowerShell Core is an evolution of Windows PowerShell, designed to be cross-platform, open-source, and more modular. It extends the capabilities of PowerShell beyond the Windows ecosystem, making it a versatile tool for automation and scripting in heterogeneous environments. With the unification of the .NET platform, the differences between PowerShell and PowerShell Core are becoming less pronounced.

Detecting Your PowerShell Environment: Windows PowerShell vs. PowerShell Core

1. **Check the PowerShell Edition**: Use the command **`$PSVersionTable.PSEdition`** to check whether the PowerShell environment is Desktop (Windows PowerShell) or PowerShell Core.

   Windows PowerShell

   ```
   PS C:\Users\rajendragupta> $PSVersionTable.PSEdition
   Desktop
   ```

   Figure 2.5: *PowerShell edition*

   PowerShell Core

   ```
   PS C:\Users\rajendragupta> $PSVersionTable.PSEdition
   Core
   ```

   Figure 2.6: *PowerShell Core edition*

2. **Check the PowerShell version**: Use the command **`$PSVersionTable.PSVersion`** to get the PowerShell version. If it is 5, it's Windows PowerShell; version 6 or later is for PowerShell Core.

   Windows PowerShell

   ```
   PS C:\Users\rajendragupta> $PSVersionTable.PSVersion

   Major  Minor  Build  Revision
   -----  -----  -----  --------
   5      1      22621  2506
   ```

   Figure 2.7: *Windows PowerShell version*

PowerShell Core

```
PS C:\Users\rajendragupta> $PSVersionTable.PSVersion

Major  Minor  Patch  PreReleaseLabel BuildLabel
-----  -----  -----  --------------- ----------
7      2      16
```

***Figure 2.8**: PowerShell Core version*

3. **Check the Shell Executable**: In PowerShell Core, the executable is usually named "**pwsh.exe**" or "**pwsh**" (on Unix-like systems). In Windows PowerShell, it's typically "**powershell.exe.**"

Windows PowerShell

In Windows PowerShell, the command Get-Command PowerShell retrieves information about the "**powershell**" command, providing details about its type, definition, and other related information. The name "**powershell.exe**" specifically indicates that it is the executable for Windows PowerShell:

```
Get-Command powershell
```

```
PS C:\Users\rajendragupta> Get-Command powershell

CommandType     Name
-----------     ----
Application     powershell.exe
```

***Figure 2.9**: Indicates Windows PowerShell*

PowerShell Core

The name "**pwsh.exe**" specifically indicates that it is the executable for PowerShell Core:

```
Get-Command pwsh
```

```
PS C:\Users\rajendragupta> Get-Command pwsh

CommandType     Name
-----------     ----
Application     pwsh.exe
```

***Figure 2.10**: Indicates PowerShell Core*

4. **Check the directory**: Check the location of the PowerShell executable to determine the PowerShell or PowerShell Core directory.

On Windows PowerShell, running **(Get-Command powershell.exe).Source** command lists the the location of the Windows PowerShell installation directory:

```
C:\WINDOWS\System32\WindowsPowerShell\v1.0\powershell.exe
```

Figure 2.11: *List the Installation Windows PowerShell directory*

Note: *This path corresponds to the installation directory for Windows PowerShell, and the version number (v1.0) may vary based on the specific version of Windows PowerShell installed on your system.*

PowerShell Core is typically located in the following directory:

```
C:\Program Files\PowerShell\7\pwsh.exe
(Get-Command pwsh.exe).Source
```

Figure 2.12: *List the Installation PowerShell Core directory*

The Transition from PowerShell ISE to Visual Studio Code for Enhanced Scripting

The PowerShell Integrated Scripting Environment (ISE) was a dedicated scripting environment provided by Microsoft for Windows PowerShell. It offered features such as script editing, debugging, and execution in a user-friendly graphical interface.

Microsoft would no longer actively develop the PowerShell ISE. Instead, they recommended using Visual Studio Code (VSCode) as PowerShell's preferred scripting and development environment. Visual Studio Code is a lightweight, cross-platform code editor that supports various languages, including PowerShell.

Here are a few reasons why Microsoft shifted focus from PowerShell ISE to Visual Studio Code:

- **Cross-Platform Support**: Visual Studio Code is available on multiple platforms (Windows, macOS, and Linux), making it more versatile for users who work in heterogeneous environments.
- **Extended Language Support**: Visual Studio Code supports many languages and extensions, providing a more comprehensive development environment.
- **Active Community and Extension Ecosystem**: Visual Studio Code has a vibrant community and a vast ecosystem of extensions, including those specifically designed for PowerShell development.
- **Regular Updates**: Visual Studio Code receives regular updates and improvements, ensuring users can access the latest features and enhancements.

While PowerShell ISE is still available in Windows for compatibility reasons, Microsoft recommends using Visual Studio Code for an enhanced and modern scripting experience. If you are working with PowerShell, you might find Visual Studio Code a powerful and feature-rich alternative to PowerShell ISE.

To download the Visual Studio Code, visit the URL **https://code.visualstudio.com/download** and download the package as per the operating system.

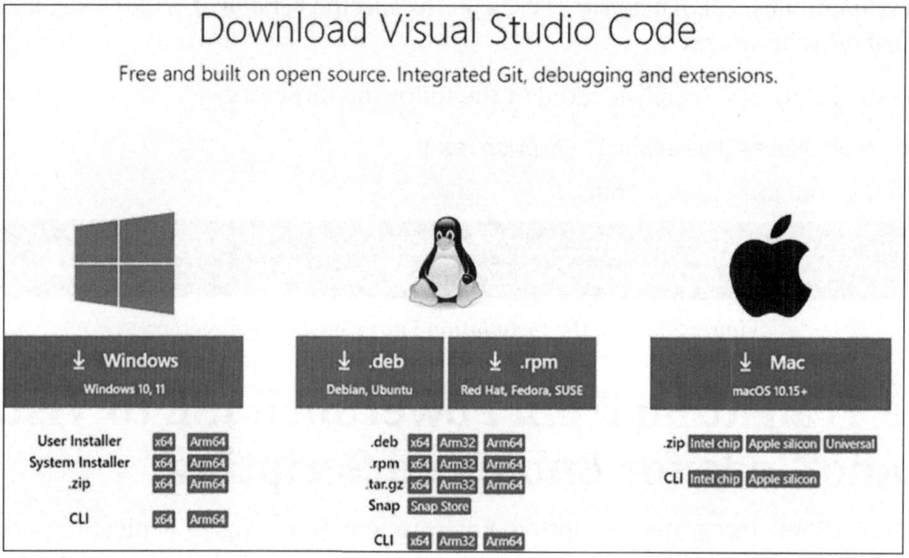

***Figure 2.13**: Download the Visual Studio Code*

Installing PowerShell 7 on Ubuntu

Here are two ways to install PowerShell 7 on Ubuntu:

Using the Microsoft Apt Repository

Follow these steps to install PowerShell 7 on Ubuntu using the Microsoft APT repository:

Step 1: Launch the terminal and update the list of packages:

```
sudo apt-get update
```

Step 2: Install pre-requisite packages for PowerShell:

```
sudo apt-get install -y wget apt-transport-https software-
properties-common
```

Step 3: Download the Microsoft repository keys as per the Ubuntu version:

```
source /etc/os-release

wget -q
```

https://packages.microsoft.com/config/ubuntu/$VERSION_ID/packages-microsoft-prod.deb

Step 4: Register the Microsoft repository keys:

```
sudo dpkg -i packages-microsoft-prod.deb
```

Step 5: Update the list of packages after adding the PowerShell package:

```
sudo apt-get update
```

Step 6: Install PowerShell:

```
sudo apt-get install -y powershell
```

Using the Universal Package

You can use the universal package to install PowerShell from PowerShell 7.2. The latest PowerShell 7.4 universal package location is: https://github.com/PowerShell/PowerShell/releases/download/v7.4.0/powershell_7.4.0-1.deb_amd64.deb

To use the universal package, follow the steps outlined here:

Step 1: Launch the terminal and update the list of packages:

```
sudo apt-get update
```

Step 2: Install pre-requisite packages for PowerShell:

```
sudo apt-get install -y wget
```

Step 3: Download the PowerShell package file from GitHub:

```
wget
```

https://github.com/PowerShell/PowerShell/releases/download/v7.4.0/powershell_7.4.0-1.deb_amd64.deb

Step 4: Install the PowerShell deb package:

```
sudo dpkg -i powershell_7.4.0-1.deb_amd64.deb
```

Step 5: Resolve missing dependencies and finish the installation (if necessary):

```
sudo apt-get install -f
```

Knowing About Unsupported Modules

The compatibility of cmdlets between Windows PowerShell and PowerShell Core can be affected by several factors. While efforts have been made to make PowerShell Core as cross-platform as possible, there are some key reasons why specific cmdlets may not work in PowerShell Core:

- **Platform-Specific Functionality**: Some cmdlets are designed to interact with features or components specific to the Windows operating system. For example, cmdlets related to Windows Management Instrumentation (WMI) or Active Directory may not have equivalent functionality on non-Windows platforms.
- **Dependency on Windows APIs**: Certain cmdlets rely on Windows APIs and features that are unavailable or have different implementations on Linux or macOS. Cmdlets interacting with specific Windows subsystems may not be fully supported in cross-platform environments.
- **Windows PowerShell Modules**: Some modules are tightly integrated with Windows PowerShell and may not be fully compatible with the cross-platform nature of PowerShell Core. It includes modules related to Windows-specific technologies.
- **.NET Framework Dependencies**: Cmdlets with dependencies on features available only in the full .NET Framework may not work seamlessly in PowerShell Core, which is built on the more modular and cross-platform .NET Core runtime.
- **Cross-Platform Design Considerations**: PowerShell Core was developed with a focus on cross-platform compatibility, and as a result, some cmdlets or features might have different behavior or limitations on non-Windows platforms.
- **Development and Testing**: Some cmdlets or modules might not be thoroughly tested or optimized for cross-platform use. While Microsoft and the community strive to enhance compatibility, there might be cases where certain functionalities are prioritized for Windows.
- **Community Contributions**: The PowerShell community plays a role in enhancing cross-platform support. While many modules are actively maintained and updated for compatibility, others may not receive the same attention.
- **Version Differences**: PowerShell Core and Windows PowerShell have evolved independently, and some features may differ between versions. New features and improvements in PowerShell Core may not be present in older Windows PowerShell versions and vice versa.

It's important to note that the PowerShell team at Microsoft is continually working to improve cross-platform compatibility, and the ecosystem is evolving. Users are encouraged to check the official documentation, community forums, and GitHub repositories for updates and report any issues or limitations.

PowerShell Core 6.1 contains a property - PSEdition to indicate whether the PowerShell module is supported by PowerShell Core, Windows PowerShell (Desk), or both editions:

```
Get-Module -ListAvailable
```

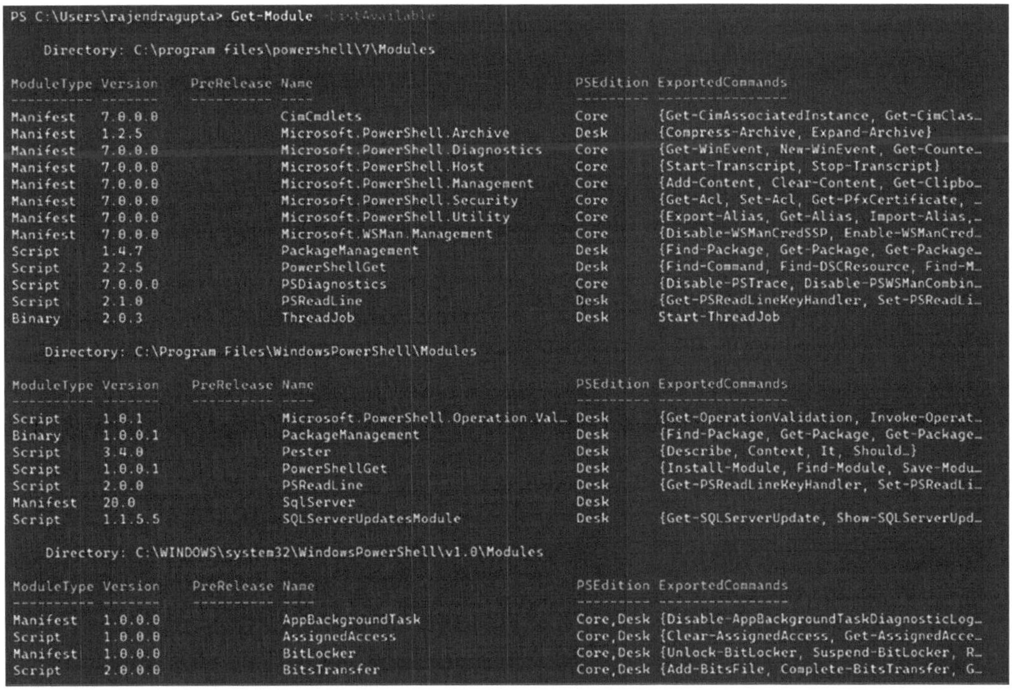

***Figure 2.14**: List the module*

A few examples of unsupported modules in PowerShell Core are as follows:

1. Active Directory Module
2. Group Policy Module
3. Remote Desktop Service Module

Comparing the Commands - Bash and PowerShell

Bourne Again SHell or Bash is a widely-used shell and scripting language primarily associated with Unix and Unix-like operating systems. It serves as the default shell for many Linux distributions and macOS. Bash is an enhanced version of the original Bourne Shell (sh), providing a command-line interface (CLI) for interacting with the operating system.

Key Features:

- **Scripting Language**: Bash is a command-line shell and a scripting language. It allows users to write shell scripts to automate tasks and create complex workflows.
- **Pipelines and Redirection**: Bash supports powerful features like pipelines

(|) for connecting commands and redirection (>, <) for managing input and output streams.

- **Extensibility**: Users can extend Bash functionality through custom scripts, functions, and aliases.
- **Environment Variables**: Bash uses environment variables to store information about the environment, configuration, and user preferences.

Usage:

Bash is used for system administration tasks, automation, and general command-line interaction in Unix and Linux environments.

It is often the default shell for interactive sessions and scripts on Linux and macOS.

Bash and PowerShell are two different command-line interfaces with distinct syntax and features.

Here's a basic comparison of Bash and PowerShell in tabular form:

	Bash	**PowerShell**
Purpose	Developed for Unix/Linux environments	Developed for Microsoft for Windows
Script File Extension	`.sh`	`.ps1`
Scripting Environment	Scripts are written in a text editor (for example, Vim, Nano)	Scripts are often created and edited in the PowerShell ISE or Visual Studio Code
Interactive Shell	Bash	PowerShell provides an interactive command-line shell
Compatibility	Native on Unix/Linux	Native on Windows, cross-platform with PowerShell Core
Syntax	It is primarily based on traditional Unix commands and syntax	The syntax follows a verb-noun structure, with cmdlets often resembling natural language
Variables	Variables are created and referenced using the `$` symbol	The `$` symbol denotes variables, and variable names are case-insensitive
File Paths	It uses forward slashes (/) for paths	It uses backslashes (\) for Windows paths and forward slashes (/) on Unix-like systems
Error Handling	It uses trap for signal handling and set `-e` for exiting on error	It uses try, catch, and, finally blocks for error handling
Job Scheduling	Utilizes `cron` for scheduling tasks	It uses `ScheduledTasks` cmdlets (`New-ScheduledTask`, `Get-ScheduledTask`)

***Table 2.2**: Comparison of Bash and PowerShell*

Here's a basic comparison of some commonly used commands in Bash and PowerShell in tabular form:

Navigation	`cd /path/to/directory` `ls`	`Set-Location C:\path\to\directory Get-ChildItem`

File Manipulation	`touch filename`
	`mv file1.txt file2.txt`
	`cp file.txt /path/to/destination/`
	`rm file.txt`
		`New-Item -ItemType File -Name filename`
		`Move-Item file1.txt file2.txt`
		`Copy-Item file.txt -Destination C:\path\to\destination\`
		`Remove-Item file.txt`

File Content	`cat file.txt` `grep pattern file.txt`	`Get-Content file.txt` `Select-String -Pattern pattern -Path file.txt`
Process Management	`ps aux` `kill PID`	`Get-Process` `Stop-Process -Id PID`
Environment Variables	`export VARNAME=value` `echo $VARNAME`	`$env:VARNAME = "value"` `echo $env:VARNAME`

Conditional Statements	`if [ $condition ]; then`
	`    echo “True”`
	`else`
	`    echo “False”`
	`fi`
		`if ($condition) {`
		`    Write-Output "True"`
		`} else {`
		`    Write-Output "False"`
		`}`

Looping	`for i in {1..5}; do`
	`    echo $i`
	`done`
		`foreach ($i in 1..5) {`
		`    Write-Output $i`
		`}`

Pipeline	`command1 | command2`	`command1 | command2`
Comments	`# This is a comment`	`# This is a comment`
Running Scripts	`./myscript.sh`	`.\myscript.ps1`

***Table 2.3**: List commands in Bash and PowerShell*

Conclusion

At an advanced level of comprehension, it is imperative that PowerShell's exceptional integration with the .NET Framework, affords developers and administrators using PowerShell the ability to manage and automate a wide spectrum of computer tasks. Originally designed exclusively for Windows, Windows PowerShell was intricately woven into the complete .NET Framework, incorporating numerous dependencies specific to the Windows environment.

However, with the introduction of PowerShell Core, a cross-platform iteration, the Microsoft PowerShell team faced the intricate task of reengineering PowerShell components to align with .NET Core. This framework, compatible with Windows, Linux, and macOS, represents a streamlined version of the .NET Framework – the ultimate aim of Microsoft is to provide an utterly platform-agnostic experience across both Windows and Linux.

For those transitioning from Windows PowerShell to PowerShell Core, disparities become apparent, ranging from experiential differences to the absence of familiar functionalities. Additionally, the cmdlet set in PowerShell Core is more constrained compared to its Windows PowerShell counterpart.

Microsoft persistently endeavors to bridge the gap between Windows PowerShell and PowerShell Core, aspiring to achieve parity. However, this process is dynamic and continuously evolves over time.

The upcoming chapter on PowerShell Building Blocks and Pipelines will delve into the fundamental components that form the backbone of PowerShell scripting. Exploring the intricacies of pipelines, we will discover how these powerful tools enable seamless command chaining and data manipulation, unlocking new possibilities for efficient and streamlined automation in PowerShell.

Multiple Choice Questions

1. What is PowerShell Core?
    a. The latest version of Windows PowerShell
    b. A cross-platform and open-source version of PowerShell
    c. A graphical user interface for managing servers
    d. A scripting language exclusive to Linux

2. Which operating systems does PowerShell Core support?
    a. Windows only
    b. Linux and macOS only
    c. Windows, Linux, and macOS
    d. Windows and Android
3. What is the primary purpose of PowerShell Core?
    a. Web development
    b. Data analysis
    c. System administration and automation
    d. Game development
4. How does PowerShell Core differ from Windows PowerShell?
    a. PowerShell Core is only for Windows, while Windows PowerShell is cross-platform
    b. Windows PowerShell is open-source, while PowerShell Core is proprietary
    c. PowerShell Core is cross-platform and open-source, while Windows PowerShell is exclusive to Windows
    d. There is no difference; the terms are used interchangeably
5. Which scripting language is used in PowerShell Core?
    a. Python
    b. JavaScript
    c. C#
    d. PowerShell scripting language
6. What is the file extension for PowerShell script files?
    a. `.ps1`
    b. `.script`
    c. `.power`
    d. `.sh`

7. Which command lists all available cmdlets in PowerShell Core?
   a. `Get-Help`
   b. `Show-Commands`
   c. `Get-Command`
   d. `List-Cmdlets`
8. What is the purpose of the `` `Get-Help` `` cmdlet in PowerShell Core?
   a. Retrieves information about available updates
   b. Displays help information for PowerShell cmdlets
   c. Retrieves help desk contact information
   d. Gets information about the current user
9. What is NOT a benefit of using PowerShell Core?
   a. Cross-platform support
   b. Open-source nature
   c. Integration with Visual Studio only
   d. Extensive automation capabilities

Answers

1. b
2. c
3. c
4. c
5. d
6. a
7. d
8. b
9. c

Key Terms

- **PowerShell Core**: An open-source, cross-platform automation and scripting language that allows IT professionals to automate tasks and manage configurations.
- **Cmdlet**: A lightweight command used in PowerShell, typically designed to perform a specific function. Cmdlets follow a Verb-Noun naming convention.
- **Open Source**: Software for which the source code is freely available and may be redistributed and modified.
- **Cmdlet Parameter**: Additional information or options can be passed to a cmdlet to modify its behavior.
- **Get-Help**: A cmdlet used to retrieve information about the usage and syntax of other cmdlets.
- **Pipeline**: A mechanism in PowerShell that allows the output of one cmdlet or command to be used as the input for another, creating a flow of data between commands.
- **Module**: A collection of cmdlets, providers, functions, workflows, aliases, and scripts bundled in a package for easy distribution and management.
- **Integrated Scripting Environment (ISE)**: A graphical user interface in PowerShell that provides a convenient environment for writing, testing, and executing scripts.

CHAPTER 3
PowerShell Building Blocks and Pipelines

Introduction

Welcome to the immersive exploration of *PowerShell Building Blocks and Pipelines*, a chapter designed to deepen your understanding and proficiency in PowerShell scripting. We start our journey by unraveling the universe of cmdlets, uncovering their significance and diverse applications. Moving forward, we guide you through the meticulous management of PowerShell modules, enabling you to harness modularity for enhanced script organization and efficiency.

As we navigate the chapter, we will equip you with the skills to configure variables, allowing for precise control and data manipulation within your scripts. The heart of PowerShell efficiency lies in its pipelines, and we will empower you to master this concept. Learn to select output columns strategically, work with properties and methods using the Select-Object cmdlet, and gain insights into controlling the quantity of your script's output.

Venture into advanced techniques such as expanding nested properties, and explore the art of filtering, grouping, and sorting data with finesse. Elevate your scripting capabilities by performing dynamic actions on output data and harnessing pipeline-enabled parameters for greater flexibility.

Our journey concludes with a focus on importing data seamlessly using pipelines, demonstrating how to integrate external information effortlessly into your scripts. Get ready to unlock the full potential of PowerShell, transforming your scripting endeavors into robust, efficient, and dynamic automation solutions.

Structure

In this chapter, we will cover the following topics:

- PowerShell Building Blocks and Pipelines

- Cmdlets
- Variables
- Parameters
- Operators
- Script Blocks

- Pipelines
  - Importing Data Using Pipelines
  - Harnessing Pipeline-Enabled Parameters
- Composable Commands
- Managing PowerShell Modules
- Understanding PowerShell Providers
- Selecting Output Columns
- Grouping and Sorting Data

PowerShell Building Blocks and Pipelines

PowerShell building blocks are the fundamental components and elements for writing scripts using the PowerShell scripting language. They provide the essential tools for performing tasks, managing data, and controlling the logic flow within PowerShell scripts. These building blocks include:

- Cmdlets (Command-lets)
- Parameters
- Variables
- Operators
- Script Blocks

Let's explore each building block in detail with examples.

Cmdlets (Command-lets)

Cmdlets are small, lightweight commands that perform specific tasks in the PowerShell. It follows a consistent naming convention, using a Verb-Noun pair, which makes it easy to discover and remember. For example, `Get-Process` is a cmdlet that retrieves information about running processes.

Here are key characteristics and aspects of cmdlets:

- **Verb-Noun Naming Convention**: Cmdlet names consist of two parts: a verb and a noun, separated by a hyphen (for example, `Get-Service`, `Start-Process`).

The Verb indicates the action or operation the cmdlet performs, and the Noun specifies the action's target or object.

- **Focused Functionality**: Cmdlets are designed to perform specific and well-defined tasks.
- **Built-In and Extensible**: PowerShell has a rich set of built-in cmdlets covering many system administration tasks. Additionally, users can create their custom cmdlets or install additional modules that extend PowerShell's functionality.
- **Pipeline Support**: Cmdlets work seamlessly with the PowerShell pipeline. Output from one cmdlet can be directly passed as input to another, enabling the creation of powerful one-liners and efficient data processing.
- **Common Parameters**: Cmdlets share a set of standard parameters, such as `-Verbose`, `-Debug`, `-ErrorAction`, and `-ErrorVariable`, which provide consistent control over cmdlet behavior.
- **Output Formatting**: Cmdlets typically output objects rather than plain text. The objects can be easily manipulated and formatted, carrying metadata for subsequent pipeline stages.
- **Help System**: Cmdlets come with detailed help information, accessible using the `Get-Help` cmdlet. Users can learn about a cmdlet's syntax, parameters, and examples through the help system.

For example, the **Get-Help** cmdlet is helpful for finding information about commands, functions, workflows, aliases, providers, and scripts.

Run the following command to get information about the cmdlet **Get-Process**:

```
Get-Help Get-Process
```

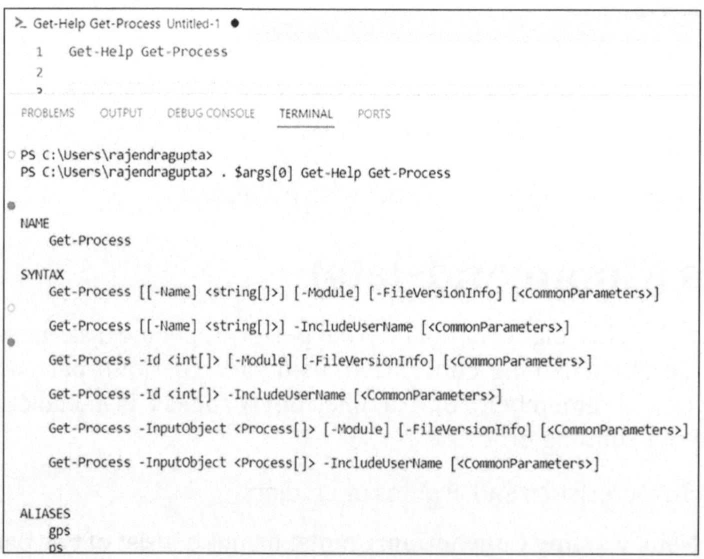

Figure 3.1: *Get-Help cmdlet*

Let's explore a few valuable cmdlets and their usage.

Cmdlet	Description	Example Code	Remarks
`Get-Process`	Retrieves information about processes	`Get-Process`	A list of running processes, including their process names, IDs, and memory usage
`Start-Process`	Launches a specified application\process	`Start-Process notepad`	Opens a new instance of the Notepad application
`Get-Service`	Retrieves information about services	`Get-Service`	A list of installed services, including their status, startup type, and display name
`New-Item`	Creates a new item (file or directory)	`New-Item -Path C:\Temp\NewFile.txt -ItemType File`	Creates a new file in the `C:\Temp` directory
`Set-ItemProperty`	Sets the properties of an item	`Set-ItemProperty -Path C:\Temp\NewFile.txt -Name "ReadOnly" -Value $true`	
`Remove-Item`	Deletes an item	`Remove-Item -Path C:\Temp\OldFile.txt`	Removes the file "`OldFile.txt`" from `C:\Temp`
`Get-Help`	Displays help information	`Get-Help Get-Process`	
`Get-Command`	Gets all commands in the current session	`Get-Command -Verb Get`	A list of available cmdlets and their descriptions
`Get-EventLog`	Gets events in the event log	`Get-EventLog System -Newest 10`	Displays the 10 most recent events from the System event log
`ForEach-Object`	Performs operation on each item	`Get-Process | ForEach-Object { $_.Name }`	It retrieves a list of all running processes on the local computer and then filters the results only to include the process names

Get-Item	Gets an item (file or directory)	Get-Item -Path C:\Temp\ExistingFile.txt	Retrieves a file named ExistingFile.txt from the C:\Temp directory
Start-Service	Starts a service	Start-Service -Name Spooler	Starts the spooler service
Stop-Service	Stops a service	Stop-Service -Name Spooler	Stops the spooler service

***Table 3.1**: Different examples of useful cmdlets*

Discovering Cmdlets

PowerShell has an extensive collection of cmdlets that help in performing various tasks. Knowing which cmdlet to use for a specific task becomes a challenging task. Therefore, PowerShell provides multiple ways to discover cmdlets and their capabilities. Here are some methods:

- **`Get-Command` cmdlet:** The `Get-Command` cmdlet allows the discovery of cmdlets, functions, workflows, aliases, and scripts available in a PowerShell session. It can filter the results based on a module, Noun, or Verb. The following code returns all cmdlet's names, versions, and sources:

```
Get-Command -CommandType Cmdlet
```

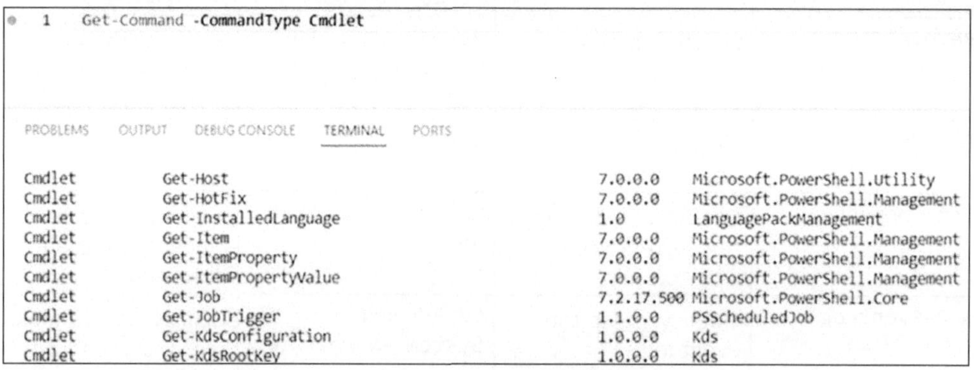

***Figure 3.2**: PowerShell cmdlet to discover cmdlets*

If you want to get information about cmdlets related to the process, filter records with the following command:

```
Get-Command -Noun Process
```

```
Get-Command -Noun Process

PROBLEMS   OUTPUT   DEBUG CONSOLE   TERMINAL   PORTS

PS C:\Users\rajendragupta>
PS C:\Users\rajendragupta> . $args[0] Get-Command -Noun Process

CommandType     Name                                               Version    Source
-----------     ----                                               -------    ------
Cmdlet          Debug-Process                                      7.0.0.0    Microsoft.PowerShell.Management
Cmdlet          Get-Process                                        7.0.0.0    Microsoft.PowerShell.Management
Cmdlet          Start-Process                                      7.0.0.0    Microsoft.PowerShell.Management
Cmdlet          Stop-Process                                       7.0.0.0    Microsoft.PowerShell.Management
Cmdlet          Wait-Process                                       7.0.0.0    Microsoft.PowerShell.Management
```

***Figure 3.3**: Filter result sets in Get-Command cmdlet using Noun*

Similarly, it allows searching specific cmdlet action (Verb) to get to a particular cmdlet. For example, if you want to get cmdlets related to starting processes, use the following command:

```
Get-Command -Noun Process -Verb Start
```

```
Get-Command -Noun Process -Verb Start

PROBLEMS   OUTPUT   DEBUG CONSOLE   TERMINAL   PORTS

PS C:\Users\rajendragupta>
PS C:\Users\rajendragupta> . $args[0] Get-Command -Noun Process -Verb Start

CommandType     Name                                               Version    Source
-----------     ----                                               -------    ------
Cmdlet          Start-Process                                      7.0.0.0    Microsoft.PowerShell.Management
```

***Figure 3.4**: Filter result sets in Get-Command cmdlet using Verb*

PowerShell supports the wildcards with **`Get-Command`** to find cmdlets based on partial names or patterns.

For example, you can use the following command to search cmdlets starting with **`Get-Phy*`**:

```
Get-Command -Name Get-Phy*
```

```
Get-Command -Name Get-Phy*

PROBLEMS   OUTPUT   DEBUG CONSOLE   TERMINAL   PORTS

PS C:\Users\rajendragupta>
PS C:\Users\rajendragupta> . $args[0] Get-Command -Name Get-Phy*

CommandType     Name                                               Version    Source
-----------     ----                                               -------    ------
Alias           Get-PhysicalDiskSNV                                2.0.0.0    Storage
Alias           Get-PhysicalDiskSNV                                1.0.0.0    VMDirectStorage
Function        Get-PhysicalDisk                                   2.0.0.0    Storage
Function        Get-PhysicalDiskStorageNodeView                    2.0.0.0    Storage
Function        Get-PhysicalExtent                                 2.0.0.0    Storage
Function        Get-PhysicalExtentAssociation                      2.0.0.0    Storage
```

***Figure 3.5**: Filter results using Wildcard search*

Similarly, search the keyword (Noun) for the cmdlets related to the service using the following command:

```
Get-Command -Noun *Service*
```

```
1    Get-Command -Noun "Service"

PROBLEMS    OUTPUT    DEBUG CONSOLE    TERMINAL    PORTS

PS C:\Users\rajendragupta>
PS C:\Users\rajendragupta> . $args[0] Get-Command -Noun "Service"

CommandType     Name                                Version    Source
-----------     ----                                -------    ------
Function        Get-NetFirewallServiceFilter        2.0.0.0    NetSecurity
Function        Set-NetFirewallServiceFilter        2.0.0.0    NetSecurity
Cmdlet          Get-Service                         7.0.0.0    Microsoft.PowerShell.Management
Cmdlet          New-Service                         7.0.0.0    Microsoft.PowerShell.Management
Cmdlet          Remove-Service                      7.0.0.0    Microsoft.PowerShell.Management
Cmdlet          Restart-Service                     7.0.0.0    Microsoft.PowerShell.Management
Cmdlet          Resume-Service                      7.0.0.0    Microsoft.PowerShell.Management
Cmdlet          Set-Service                         7.0.0.0    Microsoft.PowerShell.Management
Cmdlet          Start-EditorServices                3.13.0     PowerShellEditorServices
Cmdlet          Start-Service                       7.0.0.0    Microsoft.PowerShell.Management
Cmdlet          Stop-Service                        7.0.0.0    Microsoft.PowerShell.Management
Cmdlet          Suspend-Service                     7.0.0.0    Microsoft.PowerShell.Management
```

Figure 3.6: *Search keyword with Wildcard*

- **`Get-Help` cmdlet**: The **`Get-Help`** cmdlet provides detailed information about cmdlets, including their syntax, parameters, examples, and related topics. It's an excellent way to learn how to use a cmdlet.

If you want to know details about the **`Get-Process`** cmdlet, you can use the following command:

```
Get-Help Get-Process
```

It gives the following output fields:

- Cmdlet Name
- Syntax
- Alias
- Remarks

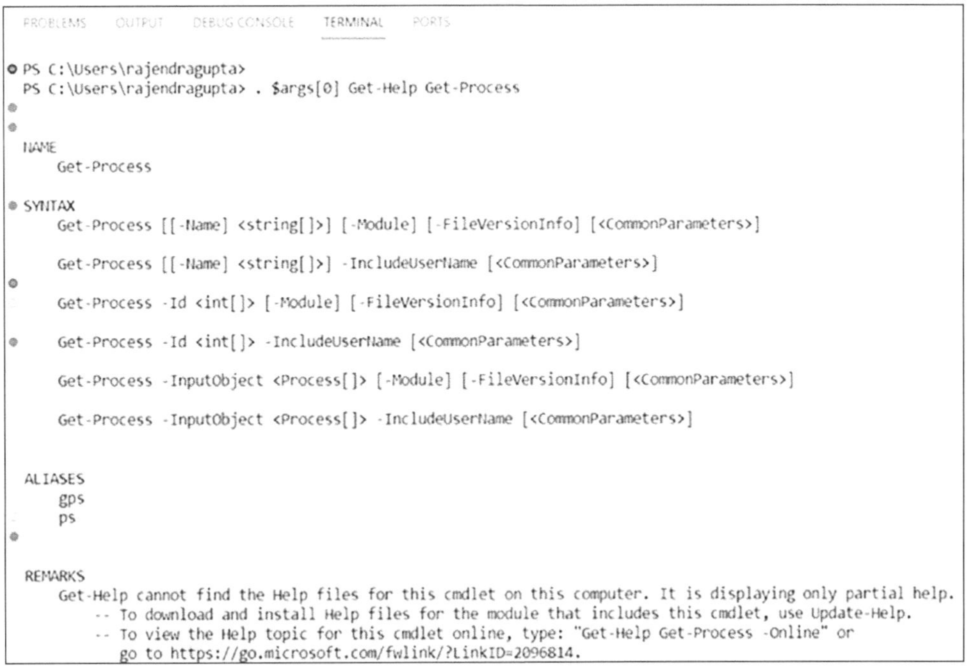

***Figure 3.7**: Get-Help cmdlet information*

You can control the information returned from the **`Get-help`** cmdlet using two parameters: Detailed and Full.

- The **`Detailed`** parameter displays the help article›s detailed view, including parameter descriptions and examples.
- The **`Full`** parameter displays the help article›s full view, including parameter descriptions, examples, input and output object types, and additional notes.

The following command returns the information about a cmdlet using **`-Full`** parameter:

```
Get-Help Get-Process -Full
```

```
1    Get-Help Get-Process -Full

PROBLEMS    OUTPUT    DEBUG CONSOLE    TERMINAL    PORTS

PS C:\Users\rajendragupta> . $args[0] Get-Help Get-Process -Full

NAME
    Get-Process

SYNTAX
    Get-Process [[-Name] <string[]>] [-Module] [-FileVersionInfo] [<CommonParameters>]

    Get-Process [[-Name] <string[]>] -IncludeUserName [<CommonParameters>]

    Get-Process -Id <int[]> [-Module] [-FileVersionInfo] [<CommonParameters>]

    Get-Process -Id <int[]> -IncludeUserName [<CommonParameters>]

    Get-Process -InputObject <Process[]> [-Module] [-FileVersionInfo] [<CommonParameters>]

    Get-Process -InputObject <Process[]> -IncludeUserName [<CommonParameters>]


PARAMETERS
    -FileVersionInfo

        Required?                    false
        Position?                    Named
        Accept pipeline input?       false
        Parameter set name           Name, Id, InputObject
        Aliases                      FV, FVI
        Dynamic?                     false
        Accept wildcard characters?  false

    -Id <int[]>

        Required?                    true
        Position?                    Named
        Accept pipeline input?       true (ByPropertyName)
        Parameter set name           Id, IdWithUserName
        Aliases                      PID
        Dynamic?                     false
        Accept wildcard characters?  false
```

***Figure 3.8**: Get-Help result with -Full parameter*

- **Modules:** PowerShell modules are collections of cmdlets, functions, aliases, and scripts for specific tasks. You can discover available modules and their cmdlets using **`Get-Module`** and **`Get-Command`**.

The **`Get-Module`** cmdlet returns the information about the modules and cmdlets. It also returns the **`PSEdition`** as Core or Desk, as follows:

```
Get-Module -ListAvailable
```

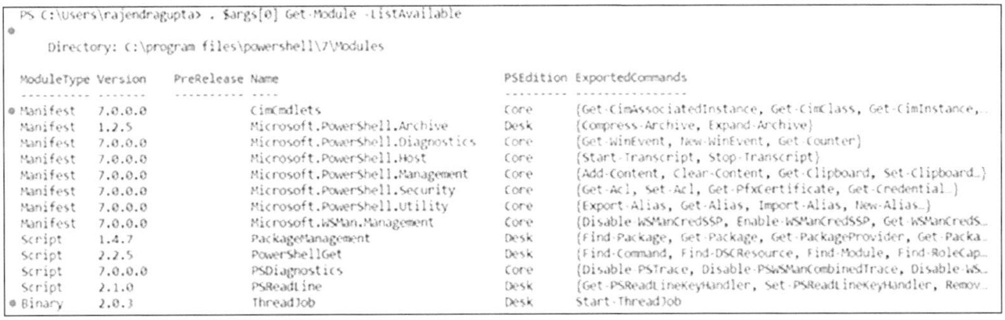

Figure 3.9: *Get a list of PowerShell modules*

Use the **`Get-Command`** cmdlet to get the cmdlet list for a specific module. For example, the following script returns the cmdlets from the **`SqlServer`** module:

```
Get-Command -Module SqlServer
```

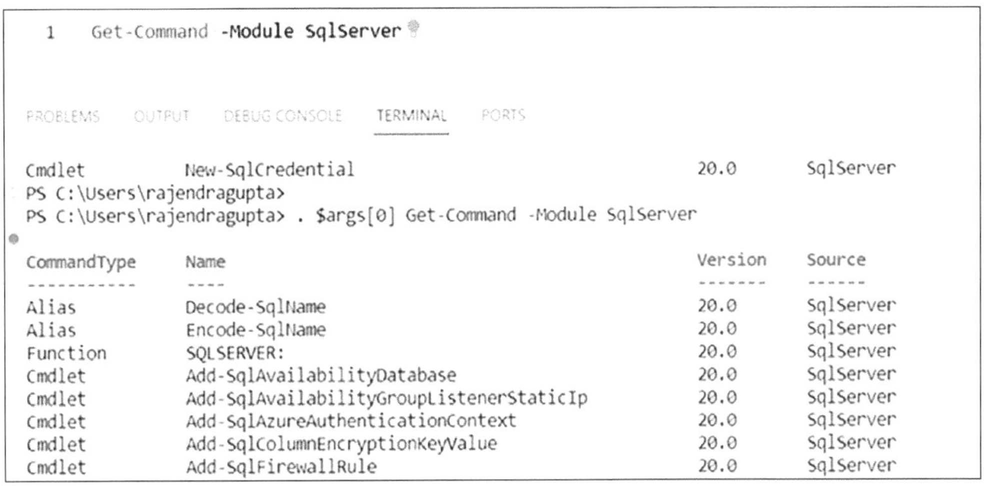

Figure 3.10: *Get a list of commands in the SqlServer module*

- **Online Resources**: Explore online documentation and resources to discover cmdlets and their use cases. The official Microsoft Docs PowerShell Documentation (https://learn.microsoft.com/en-us/powershell/) is a comprehensive resource.

Variables

PowerShell variables can store and manage data temporarily in a script. Variable names in PowerShell start with a dollar sign (**$**). They provide a mechanism for referencing and reusing data, making scripts more efficient and organized. The value assigned to a variable can be of any data type, including strings, numbers, Booleans, arrays, or even custom objects.

- **Define variables**: Variables are created using the dollar sign (**$**) symbol followed by the variable name. For instance, to create a variable named Files and assign it the path to a file, you would use the following code:

```
$Files = "C:\Temp\myfile.txt"
```

- **Accessing variables**: To access the value of a variable, use the variable name preceded by the dollar sign, such as **`$Files`**.

You can also use the cmdlet Write-Output to print its value to the console:

```
Write-Output $Files
```

Various Usage of Variables in PowerShell

Let's look at a few examples of using variables in the script.

- **Mathematical operations using variables**: The following code defines two variables named **`$firstNumber`** and **`$secondNumber`**. Later, we perform the sum on these variables:

```
# Assign numbers to variables
$firstNumber = 10
$secondNumber = 25
# Perform a mathematical operation
$sum = $firstNumber + $secondNumber
# Display the result
Write-Output "The sum is: $sum"
```

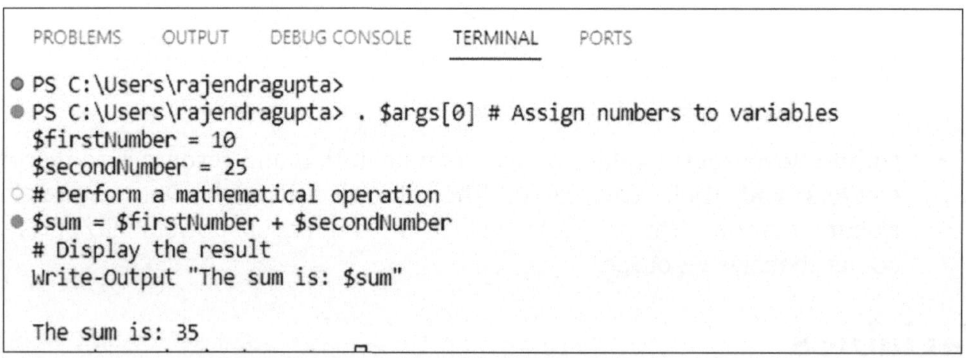

***Figure 3.11**: Mathematical operations using variables*

- **Variables in the cmdlets:** Variables are useful for working with the cmdlets to provide inputs to various parameters. For example, the following script inputs in the **`Get-ChildItems`** cmdlet to input the path:

```
# Assign a directory path to a variable
$folderPath = "C:\temp\PowerShell"
# List the contents of the directory using the variable
Get-ChildItem -Path $folderPath
```

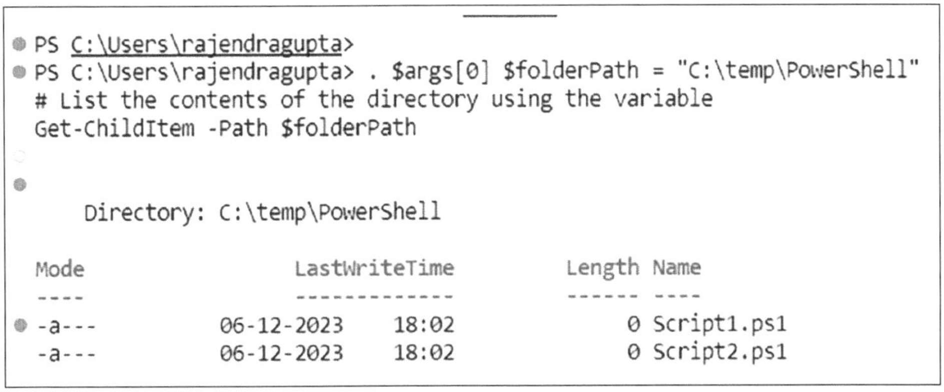

Figure 3.12: *Variables in the cmdlets*

- **Dynamic Variable Names**: The PowerShell variables can also be dynamic (based on certain conditions). In the following script, dynamic variable names are created and manipulated using the values of **`$fruitName`** and **`$quantity`**:

```
$fruitName = "Apple"
$quantity = 5
# Create a dynamic variable name
$MyDynamicvariable = "${fruitName}Count"
# Assign the quantity value to the dynamic variable
Set-Variable $MyDynamicvariable -Value $quantity
# Retrieve the value of the dynamic variable and access its Value property
$fruitCount = Get-Variable $MyDynamicvariable | Select-Object -ExpandProperty Value
# Display the value of the fruit count
Write-Output "$fruitName count is $fruitCount"
```

```
PS C:\Users\rajendragupta>
PS C:\Users\rajendragupta> . $args[0] $fruitName = "Apple"
$quantity = 5

# Create a dynamic variable name
$MyDynamicvariable = "${fruitName}Count"

# Assign the quantity value to the dynamic variable
Set-Variable $MyDynamicvariable -Value $quantity

# Retrieve the value of the dynamic variable and access its Value property
$fruitCount = Get-Variable $MyDynamicvariable | Select-Object -ExpandProperty Value

# Display the value of the fruit count
Write-Output "$fruitName count is $fruitCount"

Apple count is 5
```

Figure 3.13: *Dynamic variables*

Environment Variables

Environment variables play a crucial role in storing and retrieving information that can be utilized across different scripts and sessions. They store information that affects system and process execution, offering numerous benefits. The environment variables can be accessed using the **$env** prefix.

Environment variable	Sample command	Description
`$env:USERNAME`	`Write-Host "Current User: $env:USERNAME"`	Display the current username
`$env:COMPUTERNAME`	`Write-Host "Computer Name: $env:COMPUTERNAME"`	Output the computer name
`$env:USERPROFILE`	`Write-Host "User Profile: $env:USERPROFILE"`	Show the user's profile directory
`$env:TEMP`	`Write-Host "Temporary Directory: $env:TEMP"`	Display the temporary directory paths
`$env:PATH`	`Write-Host "System Path: $env:PATH"`	View the system's executable paths
`$env:PSModulePath"`	`Write-Host "PowerShell Module Paths: $env:PSModulePath"`	Check the PowerShell module paths

$env:OS	Write-Host "Operating System: $env:OS"	Output the operating system information
$env:PROCESSOR_ARCHITECTURE	Write-Host "Processor Architecture: $env:PROCESSOR_ARCHITECTURE"	Display the processor architecture

***Table 3.2**: PowerShell environment variables*

Let's look at a few examples of using environment variables in PowerShell scripting:

- **Use environment variables in file path**: The following script uses the **$env:USERPROFILE** environment variable to create the "**Documents**" folder path based on logged-in user:

  ```
  $userDocuments = Join-Path $env:USERPROFILE "Documents"
  Write-Output "User Documents Path: $userDocuments"
  ```

- **Use conditional statements to run scripts on specific OS**: To build a PowerShell script that runs code based on the Windows Linux operating system, the environment variable **$env:OS** can be helpful:

  ```
  #Example code:
  if ($env:OS -eq "Windows_NT") {
      Write-Output "Running on Windows"
  } else {
      Write-Output "Not running on Windows"
  }
  ```

In another example, the PowerShell function **Get-SystemInformation** accepts OS as the parameter, executes OS-specific code, and returns values:

```
# Determine the operating system
$operatingSystem = $env:OS

# Function to get system information based on the OS
function Get-SystemInformation {
    param (
        [string]$os
    )

    switch ($os) {
```

```
        "Windows_NT" {
            $systemInfo = Get-WmiObject Win32_ComputerSystem
            $architecture = $env:PROCESSOR_ARCHITECTURE
            $installedMemory = $systemInfo.TotalPhysicalMemory / 1GB

            Write-Output "Operating System: Windows"
            Write-Output "Architecture: $architecture"
            Write-Output "Installed Memory: $installedMemory GB"
        }
        "Linux" {
            $kernelVersion = (Get-Command uname).ScriptBlock.
InvokeReturnAsIs()
            $homeDirectory = $env:HOME

            Write-Output "Operating System: Linux"
            Write-Output "Kernel Version: $kernelVersion"
            Write-Output "Home Directory: $homeDirectory"
        }
        "Darwin" {
            $macVersion = (Get-Command sw_vers).ScriptBlock.
InvokeReturnAsIs()

            Write-Output "Operating System: macOS"
            Write-Output "Version: $macVersion"
        }
        default {
            Write-Output "Unsupported Operating System: $os"
        }
    }
}

# Display system information based on the detected OS
Get-SystemInformation -os $operatingSystem
```

In the demo Windows system, the output is as follows:

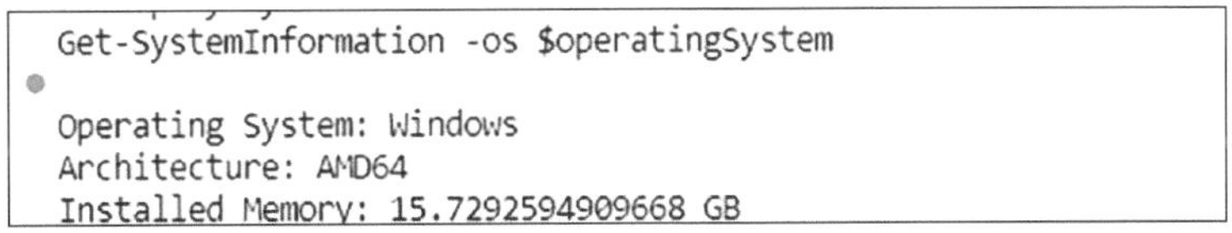

Figure 3.14: *Environment variables for getting OS information*

- Custom Environment Variables: PowerShell also allows defining custom environment variables in the script. For example, let's set a custom variable **`$env:mydatabase`**.

```
# Set a custom environment variable for the current session
$env:mydatabase = "AdventureWorks2022"
# Display the custom environment variable
Write-Output "Custom Variable: $($env:mydatabase)"
```

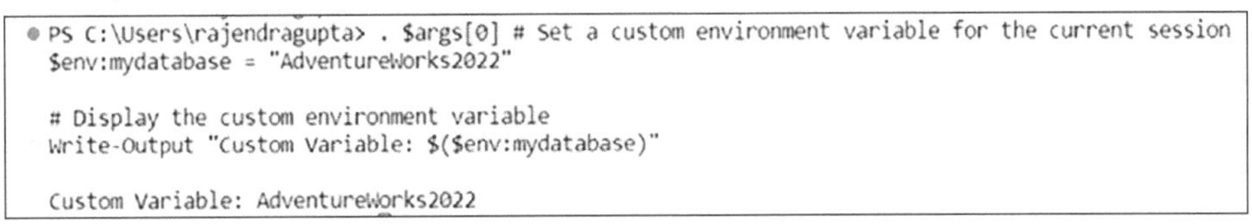

Figure 3.15: *Custom environment variable*

The custom variable can be referenced in the script as follows:

```
$env:mydatabase = "AdventureWorks2022"
$databaseName = $env:mydatabase
Write-Output "Executing  script on database: $databaseName"
```

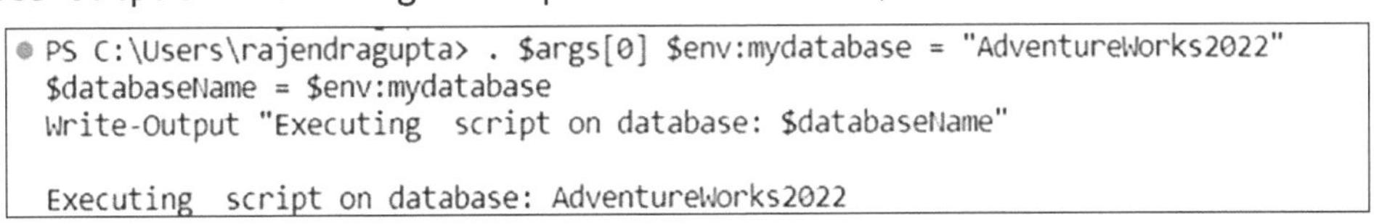

Figure 3.16: *Use of custom environment variable*

Variable Scopes

Variables scope determines the range of visibility of a variable within a script. PowerShell has three main variable scopes:

Scope	Where Variables are Created	Where Variables are Visible
Local	Inside functions or script blocks	Inside the function or script block where they are created

Script	Outside of functions or script blocks	Throughout the entire script
Global	Using the global keyword	Throughout all PowerShell sessions

Table 3.3: *Variables scopes*

Let's look at the following code, which has global and local variables:

```
# Global variable
$globalVariable = "I am global"

function Test-Scope {
    # Local variable
    $localVariable = "I am local"

    # Access local and global variables
    Write-Output "Local Variable: $localVariable"
    Write-Output "Global Variable: $globalVariable"
}

# Call the function
Test-Scope

# Attempt to access the local variable outside the function:
Write-Output "Trying to access local variable outside the function:
$localVariable"
```

In the script, we have variables as follows:

`$globalVariable` is a global variable defined outside the function.

`$localVariable` is a local variable defined inside the Test-Scope function.

When the function is called, it outputs the values of the local and global variables as per their scopes. PowerShell treats it as an empty value if you attempt to access an undefined local variable outside its scope (Outside function).

```
# Attempt to access the local variable outside the function (will result in an error)
Write-Output "Trying to access local variable outside the function: $localVariable"

Local Variable: I am local
Global Variable: I am global
Trying to access local variable outside the function:
```

Figure 3.17: *Examples of variable scopes*

Parameters

Parameters are inputs provided to a cmdlet, function, or script. These parameters include a name and their data type, such as string or number. It helps to make code flexible and reusable by allowing the user to input when the function or cmdlet is called.

- Each parameter has a name you reference in your command.
- A script can specify a value for the parameter, like a string enclosed in quotes or a number.
- Some parameters can accept pipeline input, meaning you can send data from other commands directly to them.

Let's take an example of cmdlet **`Get-ChildItem`**. It uses a parameter **`-Path`**, where the user can specify the input directory enclosed within double quotes:

```
Get-ChildItem -Path "C:\temp\"
```

You can check the parameters in a PowerShell cmdlet using the **`Get-Help`**:

```
Get-Help Get-ChildItem -Parameter *
```

```
PS C:\Users\rajendragupta> . $args[0] Get-Help Get-ChildItem -Parameter *


-Attributes <FlagsExpression[FileAttributes]>

    Required?                    false
    Position?                    Named
    Accept pipeline input?       false
    Parameter set name           (All)
    Aliases                      None
    Dynamic?                     true
    Accept wildcard characters?  false


-Depth <uint>

    Required?                    false
    Position?                    Named
    Accept pipeline input?       false
    Parameter set name           (All)
    Aliases                      None
    Dynamic?                     false
    Accept wildcard characters?  false
```

Figure 3.18: *Parameters in the PowerShell*

- Defining parameters in PowerShell:

To define a parameter in PowerShell script or function, use the keyword **param** followed by opening and closing parentheses. The **param** block can contain one or multiple variables. PowerShell uses the following format for defining parameters. Here, it declares a parameter inside the **param** block.

```
param(
    $Parameter1
)
```

It is always a good practice to assign a data type with the parameter to avoid issues with input of invalid data types. The following script defines a parameter **$Parameter1** that accepts input data type String:

```
param(
     [Parameter()]
     [string]$Parameter1
 )
```

PowerShell script can have multiple parameter declarations in a script, as follows:

```
param(
     [Parameter()]
     [string]$P1,
     [Parameter()]
     [string]$P2
 )
 Write-Host "Parameter 1 value is $P1"
 Write-Host "Parameter 2 value is $P2"
```

Different Attributes for a Parameter in PowerShell

A PowerShell script can use the following attributes for a parameter in PowerShell:

Attributes	Details
-Required	It specifies whether the parameter is a must for running the function or script. PowerShell raises an error if no inputs are provided for the parameter with the -Required attribute

`-Position`	Positional parameters are those whose position is specified by a positive integer. Using parameter names is optional when employing such parameters, but the parameter values must be specified in the correct order. If the position value is set to 0, the parameter name is not mandatory, but its value should be the first to follow the cmdlet's name. When the position setting is omitted, it can be defined at any point within the cmdlet
`-Type`	It denotes the parameter type, such as string, int, switches, and more
`-Default Value`	It signifies the parameter's default value without a specified value externally. In the case of a mandatory parameter, a default value is non-existent, and the user is always required to provide one. Numerous optional parameters often lack default values, as these parameters typically hold less significance
`-Accepts Multiple Values`	It indicates whether a parameter can accept multiple values. If multiple values are permissible, they can be entered in a comma-separated format and passed directly, or the values can be stored in a variable in a comma-separated manner, with the variable then provided as the parameter's value
`-Accepts Pipeline Input`	It indicates whether the parameter can accept input from the pipeline. A false value signifies that the parameter does not allow it
`-Accepts Wildcard Characters`	It indicates whether the parameter can employ wildcards to match characters
`switch`	The switch parameter is for binary or Boolean values

***Table 3.4**: Different attributes for a parameter in PowerShell*

Let's look at a few examples of parameters to understand it:

Define a mandatory parameter	`Param(`
	`[Parameter(Mandatory=$true)] ] [String] $UId`
	`)`

Define the parameter in a function	`function Say-Hello {`
	`    param (`
	`        [string]$Name`
	`    )`
	`    Write-Output "Hello, $Name!"`
	`}`
	`# Usage`
	`Say-Hello -Name "John"`

<table>
<tr><td>Assign a default value to the parameter</td><td><pre>function Get-Square {
    param (
        [int]$Number = 5
)
    $Square = $Number * $Number
    Write-Host "The square of $Number is
$Square."
}
# Usage
Get-Square -Number 3</pre></td></tr>
<tr><td>Assign multiple parameters in a function</td><td><pre>function Get-Sum {
    param (
        [int]$Number1,
        [int]$Number2
)
    $Sum = $Number1 + $Number2
    Write-Output "The sum is $Sum."
}
# Usage
Get-Sum -Number1 5 -Number2 7</pre></td></tr>
<tr><td>Assign a default value to the parameter</td><td><pre>function Example-Function {
    param (
        [string]$Name = "Guest"
)

    Write-Host "Hello, $Name!"
}

Calling the function without specifying the
$Name parameter
Example-Function</pre></td></tr>
</table>

<table>
<tr><td>Accept pipeline input</td><td><pre><code>function Get-Total {
    param (
        [Parameter(ValueFromPipeline=$true)]
        [int]$Value
)
    process {
        $Total += $Value
    }
    end {
        Write-Output "Total: $Total"
    }
}
# Usage
1, 2, 3 | Get-Total</code></pre></td></tr>
<tr><td>Wildcard matching</td><td><pre><code>function Get-Files {
    param (
        [string]$Pattern
)
    Get-ChildItem -Path "C:\Temp" -Filter $Pattern
}
# Usage
Get-Files -Pattern "*.txt"</code></pre></td></tr>
<tr><td>Validate inputs from pre-defined values</td><td><pre><code>function Get-ColorInfo {
    param (
        [Parameter(Mandatory=$true)]
        [ValidateSet("Red", "Green", "Blue")]
        [string]$Color
)

    switch ($Color) {
        "Red"   { Write-Host "You selected the color Red." }
        "Green" { Write-Host "You selected the color Green." }
        "Blue" { Write-Host "You selected the color Blue." }
    }
}
# Usage
Get-ColorInfo -Color "Green"</code></pre></td></tr>
</table>

<table>
<tr><td>Using Switch parameter</td><td><pre>function Start-ProcessWithLogging {
    param (
        [string]$ProcessName,
        [switch]$EnableLogging
)

    if ($EnableLogging) {
        Write-Host "Logging is enabled.
Starting process: $ProcessName with
logging..."
        # Code to start the process with
logging
    } else {
        Write-Host "Logging is not enabled.
Starting process: $ProcessName..."
        # Code to start the process without
logging
    }
}
# Usage with logging enabled
Start-ProcessWithLogging -ProcessName "MyApp"
-EnableLogging
Usage without logging
Start-ProcessWithLogging -ProcessName "MyApp"</pre></td></tr>
</table>

***Table 3.5**: Different examples of PowerShell parameters*

Parameter Splatting

Splatting allows passing a collection of parameter values to a command as a single unit using a hashtable. It makes code more readable and maintainable, especially when dealing with commands with many parameters.

Let's understand the following code using the Parameter splatting:

`$directoryParams` is a hashtable that contains parameters for the **`New-Item`** cmdlet.

`@directoryParams` is used to splat the parameters to the **`New-Item`** cmdlet, creating a new directory at the specified path with the specified options.

```
# Define parameters using a hashtable
$directoryParams = @{
    Path         = 'C:\Temp\MyPD'
    ItemType     = 'Directory'
```

```
    Force       = $true
    Confirm     = $false
}

# Use splatting to pass parameters to the New-Item cmdlet
New-Item @directoryParams
```

This approach can be beneficial when you have many parameters or when the parameter values are determined dynamically. It keeps the command invocation clean and easy to understand, allowing for more flexibility in building and modifying the parameter set as needed.

Operators

PowerShell uses various operators to manipulate data and control program flow. These operators are crucial in constructing complex expressions and facilitating data manipulation and flow in PowerShell scripts.

These operators fall into several categories, as follows:

Category	**Operator**	**Description**	**Example**
Arithmetic Operators	`+`	Addition	`$sum = 1 + 2; Write-Output $sum`
	`-`	Subtraction	`$difference = 5 - 3; Write-Output $difference`
	`*`	Multiplication	`$product = 4 * 5; Write-Output $product`
	`/`	Division	`$quotient = 10 / 2; Write-Output $quotient`
	`%`	Modulus	`$remainder = 11 % 3; Write-Output $remainder`
	`++`	Increment	`$count++; Write-Output $count`
	`--`	Decrement	`$counter--; Write-Output $counter`
Comparison Operators	`-eq`	Equal to	`if ($age -eq 25) { Write-Output "You are 25 years old." }`
	`-ne`	Not equal to	`if ($name -ne "John") { Write-Output "Your name is not John." }`
	`-gt`	Greater than	`if ($temperature > 30) { Write-Output "It is hot outside." }`
	`-lt`	Less than	`if ($price < 10) { Write-Output "The item is on sale." }`

	-ge	Greater than or equal to	if ($grade >= 90) { Write-Output "You received an A." }
	-le	Less than or equal to	if ($inventory <= 5) { Write-Output "We need to reorder." }
Logical Operators	-and	Logical AND	if ($isEligible -and $hasPassedTest) { Write-Output "You are qualified." }
	-or	Logical OR	if ($isMember -or $hasDiscount) { Write-Output "You receive a discount." }
	-not	Logical NOT	if (-not $isAvailable) { Write-Output "The item is out of stock." }
String Operators	-like	Matches a wildcard pattern	$files = Get-ChildItem -Path C:\MyData -Filter "*.txt"
	-match	Matches a regular expression	if ($text -match "\d+") { Write-Output "The text contains a number." }
	-contains	Checks if a string contains another string	if ($message -contains "error") { Write-Output "An error occurred." }
	-replace	Replaces part of a string with another string	$replacedString = $originalString -replace "old", "new"
	+	Concatenates strings	$fullName = $firstName + " " + $lastName
Array Operators	@	Creates an array	$fruits = @("Apple", "Banana", "Orange")
	,	Adds elements to an array	$fruits += "Mango"
	[ ]	Accesses elements in an array	$firstFruit = $fruits[0]
Special Operators	-?	Conditional operator (ternary operator)	$result = $age >= 18 ? "Adult" : "Minor"
	-in	Checks if a value is in a list	if ($color -in @("red", "green", "blue")) { Write-Output "Valid color." }
	-notin	Checks if a value is not in a list	if ($number -notin 1..10) { Write-Output "Number is outside the range." }

***Table 3.6**: PowerShell operators*

Conditional Command Execution in PowerShell

One of the primary objectives of employing PowerShell is the creation of reusable scripts that can be leveraged consistently. Furthermore, these scripts should be transferable to other individuals or organizations seeking to utilize them. When constructing such scripts, the emphasis lies on optimizing them for efficiency and readability. The intention is not merely to present an extensive codebase but to offer a streamlined and comprehensible solution. This involves the reduction of unnecessary code, as crafting PowerShell scripts can easily lead to the generation of extensive lines of code. Explaining mechanisms for concatenating commands is imperative, exemplified by the frequent utilization of the pipe command.

In PowerShell, the `&&` (logical AND) and `||` (logical OR) operators can be used to combine commands conditionally based on the success or failure of previous commands. Here are some examples:

- **Using && (Logical AND):** This command retrieves the "**explorer**" process, and if it exists (**Get-Process** succeeds), it proceeds to stop the process (**Stop-Process**).

  ```
  Get-Process -Name "explorer" && Stop-Process -Name "explorer"
  ```

- **Using || (Logical OR):** This command attempts to retrieve a service named "**NonexistentService**," and if it doesn't exist (**Get-Service** fails), it executes the command to write a message to the console.

  ```
  Get-Service -Name "NonexistentService" || Write-Host "Service not
  found."
  ```

- **Combining Multiple Commands:** This example checks if the directory "**C:\Temp**" exists (**Test-Path**). It removes all items in the directory (**Get-ChildItem** and **Remove-Item**) if it does. If the directory doesn't exist, it writes a message to the console.

  ```
  Test-Path -Path "C:\Temp" && (Get-ChildItem -Path "C:\Temp" |
  Remove-Item -Force) || Write-Host "Directory does not exist."
  ```

- **Using semicolon (;) to Combine Commands Unconditionally:** Here, two commands are combined using **;**. The second command (**Write-Host**) executes regardless of the success or failure of the first command.

  ```
  Get-Process -Name "explorer"; Write-Host "Command completed."
  ```

Script Blocks

A script block is a code enclosed within curly braces **{}**. Script blocks group statements together and can be treated as a single execution unit. Script blocks are commonly used in various scenarios, such as defining functions, creating delegates, and passing code as parameters to cmdlets or functions.

Script blocks offer several benefits, as follows:

- **Improved readability and organization**: By grouping related commands, your scripts become more accessible to read and understand.
- **Reusability**: You can define and reuse script blocks throughout your scripts, reducing redundancy and improving efficiency.
- **Dynamic execution**: Script blocks can be passed as arguments to other commands or functions, allowing for dynamic and flexible script execution.

Let's explore script blocks using examples:

- **Single-line script block**: These are simple blocks enclosed in curly braces, containing only one command.

  ```
  { Get-Process Notepad }
  ```

- **Multi-line script blocks**: These are used for more complex scenarios and can contain multiple commands.

  ```
  PowerShell
  {
    Get-ChildItem -Path C:\MyData
    Get-ItemProperty -Path C:\MyData\myfile.txt
  }
  ```

Script Block Usages

The PowerShell script can use the script blocks in various ways, as follows:

- It can serve as an argument to other commands. For example, the following script runs the script specified in the script block on the computer named **server1**:

  ```
  Invoke-Command -ComputerName server1 -ScriptBlock { Get-Process }
  ```

The script block is used in the following functions:

```
function Get-SystemInfo {
  {
    Get-Process | Select-Object Name, CPU, Memory
    Get-Service | Where-Object { $_.Status -eq "Running" }
  }
}
```

- Script blocks with conditional statements:

```
if ({ Get-Process notepad -ErrorAction SilentlyContinue }) {
  Write-Output "Notepad is running."
}
Script blocks with loops
foreach ($file in Get-ChildItem -Path C:\MyData) {
  {
    Write-Output "File name: $file.Name"
    Write-Output "File size: $file.Length"
  }
}
```

- Script block as a parameter:

```
function Perform-Operation {
    param (
        [scriptblock]$operation
    )

    Write-Host "Executing the provided operation:"
    &$operation
}

# Usage
Perform-Operation -operation {
    $result = 5 * 8
    Write-Host "The result of the operation is: $result"
}
```

Pipelines

Pipelines are one of the most powerful and fundamental features of PowerShell. They allow you to chain together commands, sending the output of one command as the input to the next. It enables you to perform complex tasks concisely and efficiently.

Concept:

- Each command separated by the | (pipe) operator forms a pipeline.

- The first command's output becomes the second's input, and so on.
- Commands can be combined to filter, manipulate, and format data.

Benefits:

- Reduced code: Complex tasks accomplished with fewer lines.
- Readability: Code structure is more precise and more accessible to follow.
- Efficiency: Commands share objects, minimizing data processing overhead.

Let's look at a few examples to understand the pipelines in PowerShell:

- Filtering processes and stopping them:

```
Get-Process | Where-Object {$_.Name -like "notepad"} | Stop-Process
```

The preceding code does the following:

1. It gets a list of all running processes using **`Get-Process`**.
2. Filters the list only to include processes with the "**`notepad`**" name using **`Where-Object`**.
3. Stops the filtered processes using **`Stop-Process`**.

- Formatting and exporting data:

```
Get-ChildItem | Format-Table Name, LastWriteTime | Export-Csv
-Path "C:\files.csv"
```

1. Gets a list of all files and folders in the current directory using **`Get-ChildItem`**.
2. Formats the list to display only the "**`Name`**" and "**`LastWriteTime`**" properties using **`Format-Table`**.
3. Exports the formatted data to a CSV file named "**`files.csv`**" using **`Export-Csv`**.

- Combining cmdlets with complex filtering:

```
Get-EventLog -LogName System | Where-Object {$_.EntryType -eq
"Error"} | Select-Object -ExpandProperty Message | Out-File
-FilePath "C:\system_errors.txt"
```

This pipeline:

1. Gets all events from the "**`System`**" event log using **`Get-EventLog`**.
2. Filters the events only to include those with the "**`Error`**" entry type using **`Where-Object`**.
3. Extract the **`message`** property from each event and combine them into a single string using **`Select-Object -ExpandProperty`**.

4. Writes the combined message string to a file named "**system_errors.txt**" using **Out-File**.

Importing Data Using Pipelines

Importing data using pipelines is a common technique in PowerShell. The pipeline (|) allows you to pass the output of one cmdlet or command as input to another. It is advantageous when dealing with large datasets or performing data processing steps.

Example 1: Importing data from a CSV file and filtering results

In the first example, data is imported from a CSV file, and then the **Where-Object** cmdlet filters the results based on a specified condition:

```
Import-Csv 'C:\Path\To\Data.csv' | Where-Object { $_.Category -eq
'Technology' }
```

Example 2: Importing data from a text file and sorting results

In the second example, data is imported from a text file using **Get-Content**, and the **Sort-Object** cmdlet is used to sort the lines of text:

```
Get-Content 'C:\Path\To\TextFile.txt' | Sort-Object.
```

Example 3: Combining cmdlets using pipelines

In the third example, a series of steps are combined using pipelines. It retrieves a list of processes using Get-Process, filters those with a working set greater than 100 megabytes using **Where-Object**, sorts them based on CPU usage using **Sort-Object**, and selects specific properties using **Select-Object**:

```
Get-Process | Where-Object { $_.WorkingSet -gt 100MB } | Sort-Object
-Property CPU | Select-Object -Property ProcessName, CPU
```

The following example script retrieves entries from the Security event log using **Get-WinEvent**. The pipeline (|) then sends the output to **Where-Object**, which filters the entries only to include those with a log level of '**Error**':

```
Get-WinEvent -LogName Security | Where-Object { $_.Level -eq 'Error' }
```

The following command retrieves a list of services using Get-Service. The pipeline then filters the services to include only those with a status of '**Running**' using **Where-Object**. The filtered list is then sorted alphabetically by display:

```
Get-Service | Where-Object { $_.Status -eq 'Running' } | Sort-Object
-Property DisplayName | Select-Object -Property DisplayName, Status
```

Another example script command remotely executes the **Get-Process** cmdlet on a computer named '**Server01**' using **Invoke-Command**. The pipeline then filters the process objects returned to only include those with more than 1000 handles using **Where-Object**:

```
Invoke-Command -ComputerName Server01 -ScriptBlock { Get-Process } |
Where-Object { $_.Handles -gt 1000 }
```

Harnessing Pipeline-Enabled Parameters

Pipeline-enabled parameters allow a cmdlet or function to accept input directly from the pipeline. It enables a more seamless and efficient workflow by allowing the output of one command to serve as input for another. When a parameter is pipeline-enabled, PowerShell automatically binds the incoming pipeline data to that parameter.

Let's consider a simple example where a function calculates the square of a given number, and the parameter is pipeline-enabled:

```
function Get-Square {
    param (
        [Parameter(Position = 0, ValueFromPipeline = $true)]
        [int]$Number
    )
    process {
        $Square = $Number * $Number
        Write-Output "The square of $Number is $Square."
    }
}
# Usage with pipeline input
1, 2, 3 | Get-Square
```

In this example:

- The Number parameter is pipeline-enabled with the attribute **`[ValueFromPipeline = $true]`**.
- The process block is used to define the script block that will be executed for each item in the pipeline.
- When you use the pipeline (|) to send a list of numbers (1, 2, 3) to **`Get-Square`**, the function automatically processes each number and calculates its square.

Another example involves multiple pipeline-enabled parameters and some advanced filtering and processing:

```
function Get-EvenOddSum {
    param (
        [Parameter(Position = 0, ValueFromPipeline = $true)]
```

```
        [int]$Number,

        [Parameter(Position = 1, ValueFromPipeline = $true)]
        [string]$Category
    )

    begin {
        $evenSum = 0
        $oddSum = 0
    }

    process {
        if ($Number % 2 -eq 0) {
            $evenSum += $Number
        } else {
            $oddSum += $Number
        }
    }

    end {
        Write-Output "Category: $Category, Even Sum: $evenSum, Odd Sum:
$oddSum"
    }
}

# Usage with pipeline input
1..5 | ForEach-Object { $_ } | Get-EvenOddSum -Category 'Numbers'
2..6 | ForEach-Object { $_ } | Get-EvenOddSum -Category 'MoreNumbers'
```

In this example:

- There are two pipeline-enabled parameters: **`$Number`** and **`$Category`**.
- The begin block initializes variables for tracking the sum of even and odd numbers.
- The process block checks if each number is even or odd and updates the corresponding sum.

- The end block outputs the total sum for even and odd numbers and the specified category.

Composable Commands

Both PowerShell and Bash embrace the concept of pipelines, enabling the seamless transfer of output from one command to another. In Bash, this functionality is realized using the "|" symbol. Similarly, PowerShell utilizes the same "|" symbol in its pipeline, aligning with a comparable notion. Whenever a command generates output, the pipeline character serves as a conduit, directing that output as input to a subsequent command.

The PowerShell command **`Get-Service ssh* | Stop-Service`** is an example of a composable command, leveraging the concept of pipelines. In PowerShell, pipelines use the | symbol to pass the output of one command as input to another. It allows for the creation of powerful compositions by chaining together multiple commands.

The following PowerShell command exemplifies the use of composable commands through pipelines:

```
Get-ChildItem -Path C:\Files\* | Where-Object { $_.LastWriteTime -lt
(Get-Date).AddDays(-30) } | Remove-Item -Force
```

In this single command, **`Get-ChildItem -Path C:\Files*`** initiates by retrieving all child items, such as files and directories, within the specified path "**C:\Files**." The obtained items are seamlessly directed through the pipeline (|) to the **`Where-Object`** cmdlet, which filters them based on a condition – specifically, selecting items whose last written time exceeds 30 days. The filtered items are then seamlessly transferred to the subsequent command in the pipeline, **`Remove-Item -Force`**, executing a forceful removal of the identified items.

Managing PowerShell Modules

PowerShell modules extend the core functionality of the shell by providing additional cmdlets, functions, and providers. Effectively managing your modules is crucial for keeping your environment organized and efficient.

Here are some everyday tasks for managing PowerShell modules:

1. **Listing Installed Modules**: To list the modules currently installed on your system, you can use the **`Get-Module`** cmdlet:

```
# List all installed modules
Get-Module -ListAvailable
```

2. **Installing Modules**: You can install modules from the PowerShell Gallery or other sources using the **`Install-Module`** cmdlet:

```
# Install a module from the PowerShell Gallery
Install-Module -Name ModuleName
```

3. **Updating Modules**: To update a module to the latest version, use the **`Update-Module`** cmdlet:

```
# Update a module
Update-Module -Name ModuleName
```

4. **Removing Modules**: To remove an installed module, use the **`Uninstall-Module`** cmdlet:

```
# Uninstall a module
Uninstall-Module -Name ModuleName
```

5. **Importing Modules**: To use the functionality of a module in your PowerShell session, you need to import the module using **`Import-Module`**:

```
# Import a module
Import-Module -Name ModuleName
```

6. **Viewing Module Contents**: You can view the functions, cmdlets, and aliases provided by a module using the **`Get-Command`** cmdlet:

```
# List cmdlets provided by a module
Get-Command -Module ModuleName
```

7. **Automatically Loading Modules**: You can configure PowerShell to load specific modules automatically when you start a new session by adding the **`Import-Module`** command to your PowerShell profile (**`$Profile`**).

8. **Discovering Modules**: Use the **`Find-Module`** cmdlet to discover modules available in the PowerShell Gallery:

```
# Find modules in the PowerShell Gallery
Find-Module -Name ModuleName
```

9. **Handling Module Versioning**: When working with multiple versions of the same module, you may need to specify the version explicitly using the **`-RequiredVersion`** parameter.

```
# Import a specific version of a module
Import-Module -Name ModuleName -RequiredVersion 1.2.3
```

The intricacies of managing PowerShell modules will be thoroughly explored in subsequent chapters.

Understanding PowerShell Providers

PowerShell providers are the secret sauce that makes interacting with diverse data sources in Windows (and other platforms) so seamless. They act as bridges, translating commands designed for the file system into operations understandable by different data stores. Using familiar file system commands allows you to manage and manipulate data in the registry, Active Directory, WMI, cloud storage, and even custom data sources.

Benefits of Using Providers:

- Unified Interface: Interact with various data stores using familiar file system commands and cmdlets.
- Simplified Management: Complex tasks become more straightforward with powerful provider-specific cmdlets.
- Automation Potential: Automate routine tasks with scripts using provider capabilities.
- Improved Consistency: Work with different data stores using a standardized approach.

Key Components of Providers:

- Data Store: The actual source of information (for example, registry entries, WMI objects).
- Provider: A program that exposes the data store as a virtual drive within PowerShell.
- Drive: A virtual representation of the data store accessible through a path or drive letter (for example, HKLM for the registry).
- Cmdlets: Commands specific to the provider for interacting with the data.
- Understanding Specific Providers:

File System Provider	Exposes the local file system as a virtual drive (`C:`)	`Get-ChildItem C:\` lists all files and folders in the C drive
Registry Provider	Exposes the Windows registry as a virtual drive (HKLM, HKCU)	`Get-Item HKLM:\System\CurrentControlSet\Control` retrieves the current Control set values
WMI provider	Exposes WMI objects as virtual drives (**`root\cimv2`**)	`Get-WmiObject Win32_Process` retrieves information about all running processes
Certificate Provider	Exposes certificate stores as virtual drives (**`Cert:`**)	`Get-ChildItem Cert:\LocalMachine\My` lists all certificates in the local machine's "My" store

Active Directory Provider	Exposes Active Directory objects as a virtual drive (`AD:`)	`Get-ADUser -Filter * -Properties Name, EmailAddress` retrieves all users with their email addresses

Table 3.7: *Key providers*

Here are some of the useful cmdlets to work with the providers:

- **`Get-PSProvider`**: Lists all available providers and their drives.
- **`Set-Location`**: Navigates within a provider's virtual drive using its drive letter or path.
- **`Get-ChildItem`**: Lists items within the current location of the provider.
- **`Get-Item`**: Retrieves specific items within the provider's virtual drive.
- **`Where-Object`**: Filters items based on specific properties.
- **`Select-Object`**: Selects specific properties of items for display.

Selecting Output Columns

The **`Select-Object`** cmdlet is a powerful tool in PowerShell for filtering and displaying specific properties of objects. It allows you to control which data you want to see and customize its presentation.

Purpose:

- Select specific properties from objects in a pipeline.
- Create new objects containing only the desired properties.
- Control the order in which properties are displayed.

Basic Syntax:

```
Select-Object [-Property] <Property1>, <Property2>, ...
```

- **`-Property`**: Optional parameter to explicitly specify the **`PropertyName`** parameter set.
- **`<Property1>, <Property2>, ...`**: List property names to include in the output.

Consider the following example to retrieve a list of processes and select only columns - **`ProcessName`**, Id, and CPU - for display:

```
Get-Process | Select-Object -Property ProcessName, Id, CPU
```

The command accepts parameters such as **`-First`**, **`-Last`**, and **`-Unique`** with the **`Select-object`** cmdlet.

Example	Description
`Get-Process | Select-Object -First 5`	Selects the first 5 processes from the list
`Get-Process | Select-Object -Last 3`	Selects the last 3 processes from the list
`Get-Service | Select-Object -Unique`	Selects unique values of the `Status` property from the list of services

***Table 3.8**: Cmdlet example*

The **`Select-Object`** can be used to select specific properties, including a computed property. The result will display a table with columns for **`DisplayName`**, **`Status`**, and the computed **`StartType`**:

```
Get-Service -Name wuauserv | Select-Object -Property DisplayName,
Status, @{Name='StartType'; Expression={$_.StartType -as [string]}}
```

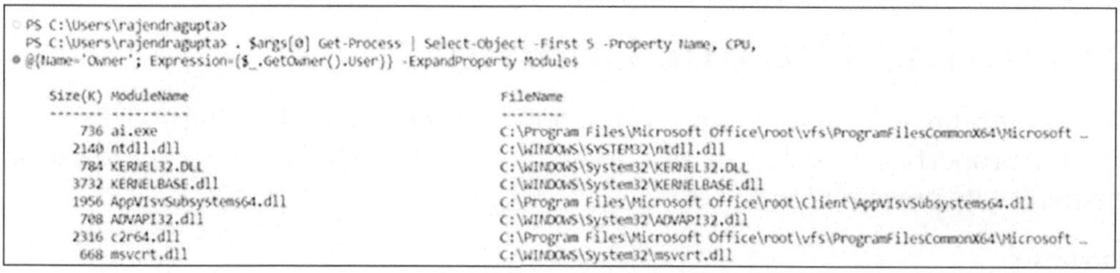

***Figure 3.19**: Selecting output columns using Select-Object*

The breakdown of the preceding code is as follows:

- **`Get-Service -Name wuauserv`**: Retrieves information about the **`wuauserv`** service (Windows Update).
- **`Select-Object -Property DisplayName, Status, @{Name='StartType'; Expression={$_.StartType -as [string]}}`**: Selects the **`DisplayName`** and **`Status`** properties directly. It also creates a computed property named **`StartType`**, which converts the numeric start type (**`StartType`**) to a string representation.

Adding a Calculated Column

A calculated column typically refers to a column in a data structure, such as a table or an object, where the values are derived or calculated based on expressions or computations rather than being directly stored in the underlying data source.

For example, when working with objects or tables in PowerShell, you might create a calculated column using the **`Select-Object`** cmdlet. Here's a simple illustration:

```
# Get process information and add a calculated column
Get-Process | Select-Object -Property ProcessName, CPU, @{Name='Memory
(MB)'; Expression={$_.WorkingSet/1MB}}, @{Name='CPU Percentage';
Expression={($_.CPU * 100) / (Get-WmiObject -Class Win32_ComputerSystem
| Select-Object -ExpandProperty NumberOfLogicalProcessors)}}
```

In this example:

`ProcessName`, **`CPU`**, and **`Memory (MB)`** are existing properties.

The CPU Percentage column is a calculated column. It calculates the CPU percentage based on the process's CPU usage and the total number of logical processors.

Using Excluding Property

The excluding parameter lets you specify the properties you want to exclude from the selected output. For example, the service startup type is excluded from the properties displayed for each process in the following query.

The following PowerShell code uses **`ExcludeProperty`** to exclude the service startup type in the output:

```
Get-Service -Name wuauserv  | Select-Object -Property DisplayName, Sta-
tus -ExcludeProperty StartType
```

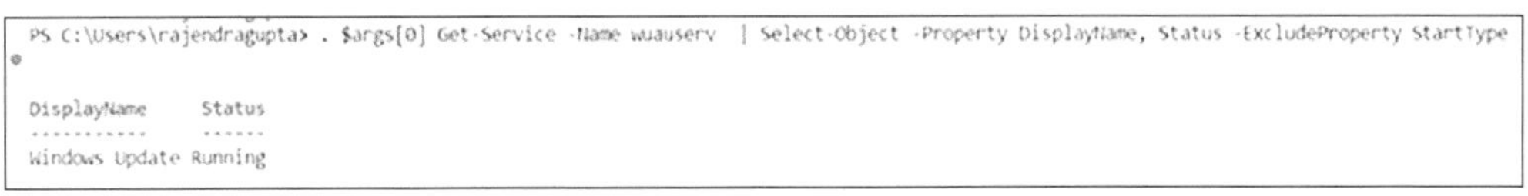

Figure 3.20: *Select-Object with ExcludeProperty*

Exploring the Formatted Output for a Specific Pattern

PowerShell's versatile filtering tools, such as the **`Where-Object`** cmdlet, typically target specific properties within incoming objects. However, a straightforward text-based filtering approach can be beneficial when searching for text within the formatted output of an object or when uncertain about which property contains the relevant text.

Retrieve information about services, convert the output to a string format, and then search for occurrences of the term "**`remote`**" within the formatted output:

```
Get-Service | Out-String -Stream | Select-String remote
```

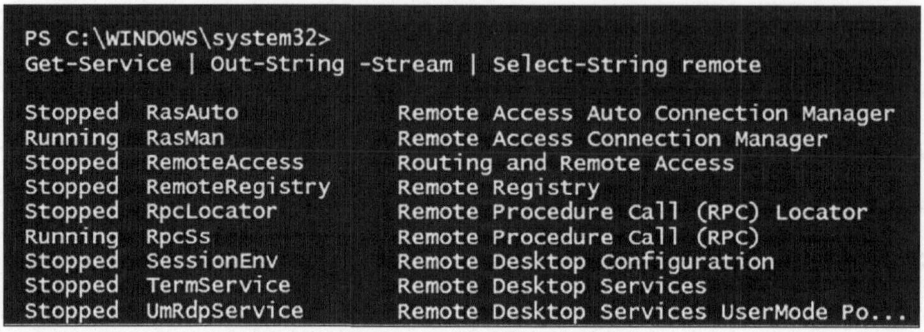

Figure 3.21: *Explore the formatted output*

Expanding Nested Properties

In PowerShell, you can use the **ExpandProperty** parameter with **Select-Object** to expand and display the values of nested properties. It is useful when dealing with objects that have properties containing nested objects or collections. Here's an example:

```
# Example with Get-Process to illustrate nested properties
Get-Process | Select-Object -Property Name, CPU, @{Name='Owner';
Expression={$_.GetOwner().User}} -ExpandProperty Modules
```

Explanation:

- **Get-Process**: Retrieves information about running processes.
- **Select-Object -Property Name, CPU, @{Name='Owner'; Expression={$_.GetOwner().User}} -ExpandProperty** Modules:
  - Select the **Name** and **CPU** properties directly.
  - Create a computed property named Owner that retrieves the user owning the process.
  - Use -**ExpandProperty** Modules to expand and display the Modules property, a nested property containing information about loaded modules.

The result will display information about processes, including the expanded Modules property.

Let's look at another example of creating a custom object with nested properties:

- It creates a custom object **$myObject** with properties **Name**, **Department**, and a nested property **Manager** that itself has properties **Name** and **Email**.
- **Select-Object** is used to select the properties **Name** and **Department** directly.
- **-ExpandProperty Manager** is for expanding all properties within the **Manager** property.

- The **Write-Host** expands the property and prints the manager's name and email.

```
$myObject = [PSCustomObject]@{
    Name = "David"
    Department = "IT"
    Manager = @{
        Name = "Jane Doe"
        Email = "jane.doe@example.com"
    }
}
# Select "Name", "Department", and all properties within "Manager"
$expandedProperties = $myObject | Select-Object Name, Department,
Manager* -ExpandProperty Manager

# Access expanded properties directly
Write-Host "Manager Name:", $expandedProperties.Manager.Name
Write-Host "Manager Email:", $expandedProperties.Manager.Email

# Output:
# Manager Name: Jane Doe
# Manager Email: jane.doe@example.com
```

Grouping and Sorting Data

Grouping and Sorting are fundamental operations for organizing and analyzing data. You can combine grouping and sorting in powerful ways to analyze your data.

Grouping

Grouping involves dividing your data into sets based on shared characteristics. These characteristics can be any property of your data objects, such as file extensions, server names, or user IDs. The **Group-Object** cmdlet groups objects based on a specified property or expression. It creates groups of things that share a common value in the specified property.

Syntax:

```
Group-Object -Property PropertyName
```

The following example uses **Group-Object** to group the objects based on their status property:

```
# Sample data representing tasks
$tasks = @(
    @{ TaskName = "TaskA"; Status = "InProgress" },
    @{ TaskName = "TaskB"; Status = "Completed" },
    @{ TaskName = "TaskC"; Status = "InProgress" },
    @{ TaskName = "TaskD"; Status = "Pending" },
    @{ TaskName = "TaskE"; Status = "Completed" }
)
# Grouping tasks by Status
$groupedTasks = $tasks | Group-Object -Property Status


# Displaying grouped tasks
foreach ($group in $groupedTasks) {
    Write-Host "Tasks with Status $($group.Name):"
    foreach ($task in $group.Group) {
        Write-Host "  - $($task.TaskName)"
    }
}
```

The output shows the grouped objects:

```
Tasks with Status Completed:
  - TaskB
  - TaskE
Tasks with Status InProgress:
  - TaskA
  - TaskC
Tasks with Status Pending:
  - TaskD
```

***Figure 3.22:** Output*

Sorting

Sorting arranges data in a specific order. This order can be ascending (smallest to largest), descending (largest to smallest), or based on customized criteria. The **Sort-Object** cmdlet sorts objects based on one or more properties. It arranges the objects in ascending or descending order. The default sorting order is Ascending.

```
# Sample data representing books
$books = @(
    @{ Title = "BookA"; Year = 2010 },
    @{ Title = "BookB"; Year = 2005 },
    @{ Title = "BookC"; Year = 2015 },
    @{ Title = "BookD"; Year = 2000 },
    @{ Title = "BookE"; Year = 2020 }
)
# Sorting books by Year in ascending order
$sortedBooks = $books | Sort-Object -Property Year

# Displaying sorted books
Write-Host "Sorted Books by Year (Ascending):"
$sortedBooks | ForEach-Object {
    Write-Host ("Title: {0,-10} Year: {1,-4}" -f $_.Title, $_.Year)
}
```

Output:

```
Sorted Books by Year (Ascending):
Title: BookD      Year: 2000
Title: BookB      Year: 2005
Title: BookA      Year: 2010
Title: BookC      Year: 2015
Title: BookE      Year: 2020
```

***Figure 3.23**: Output*

To sort data in descending order, add the keyword **`-Descending`** as follows:

```
# Sample data representing books
$books = @(
    @{ Title = "BookA"; Year = 2010 },
    @{ Title = "BookB"; Year = 2005 },
    @{ Title = "BookC"; Year = 2015 },
    @{ Title = "BookD"; Year = 2000 },
    @{ Title = "BookE"; Year = 2020 }
)
```

```
# Sorting books by Year in descending order
$sortedBooks = $books | Sort-Object -Property Year -Descending

# Displaying sorted books
Write-Host "Sorted Books by Year (Descending):"
$sortedBooks | ForEach-Object {
    Write-Host ("Title: {0,-10} Year: {1,-4}" -f $_.Title, $_.Year)
}
```

Output in descending order:

```
Sorted Books by Year (descending):
PS C:\Users\rajendragupta> $sortedBooks | ForEach-Object {
>>     Write-Host ("Title: {0,-10} Year: {1,-4}" -f $_.Title, $_.Year)
>> }
Title: BookE      Year: 2020
Title: BookC      Year: 2015
Title: BookA      Year: 2010
Title: BookB      Year: 2005
Title: BookD      Year: 2000
```

***Figure 3.24**: Output*

PowerShell can combine grouping and sorting together in a script. This script groups employees by department and sorts employees within departments by salary in descending order:

```
# Sample data representing employees
$employees = @(
    @{ EmployeeName = "Alice"; Department = "HR"; Salary = 90000 },
    @{ EmployeeName = "Bob"; Department = "IT"; Salary = 85000 },
    @{ EmployeeName = "Charlie"; Department = "HR"; Salary = 55000 },
    @{ EmployeeName = "David"; Department = "IT"; Salary = 80000 },
    @{ EmployeeName = "Eva"; Department = "Finance"; Salary = 70000 }
)

# Grouping employees by Department
$groupedEmployees = $employees | Group-Object -Property Department

# Sorting employees within each department by Salary in descending order
$sortedEmployees = $groupedEmployees | ForEach-Object {
```

```
    $_ | Sort-Object -Property { $_.Salary } -Descending
}

# Displaying grouped and sorted employees
foreach ($group in $sortedEmployees) {
    Write-Host "Department: $($group.Name)"
    foreach ($employee in $group.Group) {
        Write-Host "  - $($employee.EmployeeName), Salary: $($employee.
Salary)"
    }
    Write-Host ""
}
```

Output:

```
Department: Finance
  - Eva, Salary: 70000

Department: HR
  - Alice, Salary: 90000
  - Charlie, Salary: 55000

Department: IT
  - Bob, Salary: 85000
  - David, Salary: 80000
```

***Figure 3.25**: Output*

- **Adding a New Property Using `Add-Member`**

In this example, a custom object is created with the properties "**`Name`**" and "**`Age`**." The **`Add-Member`** cmdlet is then used to add a new property named "**`Occupation`**" with the value "**`Software Engineer`**" to the existing object. Finally, the updated object is displayed, showing the added property.

```
# Creating a custom object
$customObject = [PSCustomObject]@{
    Name = "Prashanth Jayaram"
    Age = 40
}
```

```
# Adding a new property using Add-Member
$customObject | Add-Member -MemberType NoteProperty -Name "Occupation"
-Value "Software Engineer"

# Displaying the updated object
$customObject |Get-Member
```

Conclusion

In a nutshell, *PowerShell Building Blocks and Pipelines* has equipped you with foundational skills – from cmdlets and module management to dynamic data interactions. Mastering pipelines, selecting columns, and advanced data manipulation techniques will empower you to create precise and adaptable scripts. As you navigate the PowerShell landscape, these tools provide a solid foundation for efficient and innovative automation solutions.

The next chapter explores data control, array operations, conditional statements, loops, and hashtables. Mastering these elements enhances your ability to create efficient and sophisticated automation solutions. As you navigate the PowerShell landscape, these skills will prove invaluable. Happy scripting, and may your PowerShell journey be filled with continued success!

Multiple Choice Questions

1. What is the primary function of cmdlets in PowerShell?
    a. Display system information
    b. Manage PowerShell modules
    c. Perform specialized tasks
    d. Configure user profiles
2. How can you assign a default value to a parameter in a PowerShell function?
    a. Using the **`-DefaultValue`** parameter
    b. Specifying it after the function declaration
    c. Utilizing the **`$Default`** keyword
    d. Using the equals sign in the parameter definition
3. Which PowerShell feature is used for organizing and modularizing scripts?
    a. PowerShell Profiles
    b. Cmdlets

   c. Providers
   d. Modules
4. What is the purpose of a calculated column in PowerShell?
   a. It stores fixed values in a data structure
   b. It dynamically computes values based on expressions
   c. It manages PowerShell profiles
   d. It controls the quantity of script output
5. How do you control the quantity of script output in a PowerShell pipeline?
   a. Using the **-Quantity** parameter in the pipeline
   b. Configuring the **$OutputQuantity** variable
   c. Employing the **Select-Object** cmdlet
   d. Adjusting the pipeline buffer size
6. In PowerShell, what is the purpose of a PowerShell provider?
   a. It manages PowerShell modules
   b. It interacts with different data stores
   c. It controls script output quantity
   d. It organizes variables within scripts
7. What is the significance of the `` `Select-Object` `` cmdlet in PowerShell pipelines?
   a. It filters data based on specified criteria
   b. It controls the quantity of script output
   c. It works with properties and methods of objects
   d. It manages PowerShell profiles
8. What does the `` `$Profile` `` variable represent in PowerShell?
   a. The default output profile for scripts
   b. The user's profile information
   c. The current PowerShell session profile
   d. A reserved variable for managing modules

9. Which PowerShell feature allows you to work with properties and methods of objects in a pipeline?
   a. `Select-Object` cmdlet
   b. `Configure-Property` cmdlet
   c. `Invoke-Method` cmdlet
   d. `Extract-Property` cmdlet
10. How can you dynamically compute a property value in a PowerShell pipeline?
   a. Using the `-ComputeProperty` parameter in `Select-Object`
   b. Utilizing the `Calculate-Property` cmdlet
   c. Employing a script block in the calculated property definition
   d. Configuring the `$DynamicProperty` variable

Answers

1. c
2. d
3. d
4. b
5. c
6. b
7. c
8. c
9. a
10. c

Questions

- Share examples of cmdlets you frequently use in your PowerShell scripts and explain how they contribute to automation tasks.
- Share instances where configuring variables in your scripts provided precise control and manipulation of data.
- In what ways has mastering PowerShell pipelines improved the efficiency and readability of your scripts? Can you provide examples?

- Share specific scenarios where strategically selecting output columns enhances output readability and relevance in your scripts.
- Describe practical examples of how you have used the Select-Object cmdlet to work with properties and methods in a PowerShell pipeline.
- Provide examples of how you have applied techniques like expanding nested properties, filtering, grouping, and sorting data in your PowerShell scripts.
- Share a scenario where harnessing pipeline-enabled parameters increased the flexibility and adaptability of your PowerShell scripts.

Key Terms

- **Cmdlets**: Specialized commands in PowerShell that perform specific tasks and operations.
- **PowerShell Modules**: Self-contained and reusable scripts or functions that can be organized and imported into PowerShell sessions.
- **PowerShell Providers**: Components that allow PowerShell to interact with different data stores, making various resources accessible as if they were part of a file system.
- **PowerShell Profiles**: Customized configurations that define the environment and behavior of a PowerShell session.
- **Variables**: Storage locations in PowerShell are used to store and manipulate data, providing flexibility and dynamic behavior in scripts.
- **Pipelines:** A sequence of commands in which the output of one command is passed as the input to the next, allowing efficient and streamlined scripts to be created.
- **Select-Object Cmdlet**: A cmdlet used to select specific properties from objects, allowing users to control and customize the output in a PowerShell pipeline.
- **Calculated Column**: A column in a data structure, such as a table or object, where values are computed based on expressions or calculations.
- **Nested Properties**: Properties within properties allow for hierarchical data structure organization.
- **Filtering, Grouping, and Sorting**: Techniques used to refine and organize data output in PowerShell scripts based on specific criteria.
- **Pipeline-Enabled Parameters**: Parameters in a function or cmdlet that accept pipeline input enhance script flexibility and adaptability.

Part 2

PowerShell Scripting and Automation

CHAPTER 4

Data Control and Arrays Using Conditional Statements, Loops, and Hashtables

Introduction

Welcome to a pivotal chapter in our journey through the intricacies of programming. In this chapter, we will explore the realm of data control and arrays, where the mastery of conditional statements, loops, and hashtables unlocks the true potential of a PowerShell.

Navigating Decision-Making with Conditional Statements:

Our journey begins with conditional statements – a programmer's compass in navigating the myriad decision-making paths. Uncover the power of if statements, else statements, and the art of nesting as we dissect the fundamental constructs that shape the flow of your code.

Efficient Repetition with Loops:

Next, we venture into the world of loops, the unsung efficiency heroes. Whether traversing arrays with for loops, dynamically iterating with while loops, or ensuring execution at least once with do-while loops, loops are the heartbeat of repetitive tasks. Learn to wield loop control statements to tune your program's rhythm finely.

Harnessing the Power of Hashtables:

Our exploration culminates in the domain of hashtables. These dynamic data structures, driven by potent hash functions, revolutionize data organization and retrieval. Delve into collision resolution strategies, witness hashtables in action, and grasp their transformative applications in the real world.

As we embark on this chapter, brace yourself for a journey that will equip you with the technical prowess of data control and sparks the creativity to sculpt elegant solutions. This chapter will deepen your understanding, providing hands-on experiences to cement your newfound knowledge. So, let's embark on this expedition into the heart of data control and arrays, where the true artistry of programming unfolds.

Structure

In this chapter, we will discuss the following topics:

- Implementing if-else Conditions
- Utilizing switch-case Statements
- Working with Delays
- Creating Looping Structures
- Exploring Arrays
- Exploring Hashtables

Implementing `if-else` Conditions

Conditional statements like **`if-else`** are fundamental to programming languages like PowerShell. They allow you to control the flow of your script based on certain conditions. The basic syntax for an **`if-else`** statement in PowerShell is as follows:

```
if (condition) {
    # Code to execute if the condition is true
} elseif (anotherCondition) {
    # Code to execute if the first condition is false, but this one is
true
} else {
    # Code to execute if none of the conditions are true
}
```

Here's a breakdown of the components:

- **`If`** statement: Checks a specified condition. If **`true`**, the associated block of code is executed.
- **`elseif`** statement: Allows you to check additional conditions if the previous ones were **`false`**. You can have multiple elseif blocks.
- **`Else`** statement: Executes a code block if none of the preceding conditions are **`true`**.

Conditions are typically expressed using comparison operators (for example, **`-eq`** for equality, **`-lt`** for less than) and logical operators (for example, **`-and`**, **`-or`**) to create complex conditions.

Let's understand **`If-else`** conditions using examples.

- **Example: Checking if a Number is Positive, Negative, or Zero**

```
$number = Read-Host "Enter a number"
$number = [int]$number


if ($number -gt 0) {
    Write-Host "The number is positive."
} elseif ($number -lt 0) {
    Write-Host "The number is negative."
} else {
    Write-Host "The number is zero."
}
```

Explanation:

- Prompt for User Input:

`$number = Read-Host "Enter a number"`: This line prompts the user to enter a number. The entered value is stored in the variable **`$number`**.

- Convert Input to Integer:

`$number = [int]$number`: The entered value is converted to an integer using **`[int]`**. This ensures that the variable **`$number`** contains an integer value.

- **`If-Else`** Conditions:
    - **`if ($number -gt 0) { ... }`**: Checks if the number is greater than 0. If true, it executes the code block inside the curly braces and prints "*The number is positive.*"

- **`elseif ($number -lt 0) { ... }`**: If the previous condition is false, this block checks if the number is less than 0. If true, it executes the code block inside the curly braces and prints "*The number is negative.*"
- **`else { ... }`**: If none of the previous conditions are **`true`**, this block is executed and prints "*The number is zero.*"

Example Execution:

If the user enters 5, the output will be "`The number is positive.`"

If the user enters -3, the output will be "`The number is negative.`"

If the user enters 0, the output will be "`The number is zero.`"

- **Example: Checking if a File Exists**

```
$filePath = "C:\Path\to\Your\File.txt"
if (Test-Path $filePath) {
    Write-Host "The file exists at $filePath."
} else {
    Write-Host "The file does not exist at $filePath."
}
```

Example Execution:

If the file at the specified path (C:\Path\to\Your\File.txt) exists, the output will be "`The file exists at C:\Path\to\Your\File.txt.`"

If the file does not exist, the output will be "`The file does not exist at C:\Path\to\Your\File.txt.`"

- **Example: Using `if-else` in a PowerShell Function to Check for Palindromes**

```
function Test-Palindrome($inputString) {
    # Remove spaces and convert to lowercase for case-insensitive
comparison
    $cleanedString = $inputString -replace '\s', '' -replace '\W', ''
    $cleanedString = $cleanedString.ToLower()

    # Reverse the string
    $reversedString = $cleanedString.ToCharArray() -join ''

    if ($cleanedString -eq $reversedString) {
        Write-Host "$inputString is a palindrome."
```

```
    } else {
        Write-Host "$inputString is not a palindrome."
    }
}
```

Explanation:

- Function Definition:

`Function Test-Palindrome($inputString) { ... }`: Defines a PowerShell function named Test-Palindrome that takes a single parameter **`$inputString`**.

- String Cleaning:

`$cleanedString = $inputString -replace '\s', '' -replace '\W', ''`: Removes spaces (**`\s`**) and non-alphanumeric characters (**`\W`**) from the input string. This cleaning step helps ensure a more accurate palindrome check. The result is stored in **`$cleanedString`**.

- **`$cleanedString = $cleanedString.ToLower()`**: Converts the cleaned string to lowercase for case-insensitive comparison.
- String Reversal:

`$reversedString = $cleanedString.ToCharArray() -join ''`: Converts the cleaned string into an array of characters, reverses the array, and then joins it back into a string. This creates the reversed version of the cleaned string.

- Palindrome Check:

`if ($cleanedString -eq $reversedString) { ... }`: Compares the cleaned string with its reversed version. If they are equal, the input string is a palindrome.

- Output Messages:

`Write-Host "$inputString is a palindrome."`: If the input string is a palindrome, this message is displayed.

`else { Write-Host "$inputString is not a palindrome." }`: This message is displayed if the input string is not a palindrome.

Example Usage:

```
# Test the function with different input values
Test-Palindrome "radar"
Test-Palindrome "hello"
Test-Palindrome "A man a plan a canal Panama"
```

```
# Test the function with different input values
Test-Palindrome "radar"
Test-Palindrome "hello"
Test-Palindrome "A man a plan a canal Panama"

radar is a palindrome.
hello is a palindrome.
A man a plan a canal Panama is a palindrome.
```

Figure 4.1: *If-Else conditions in a function*

Utilizing `switch-case` Statements

`switch-case` statements in PowerShell provide an elegant way to perform multi-way branching based on the value of an expression. It allows you to compare a variable or an expression against multiple values and execute different code blocks depending on the match.

Benefits of Switch Statements:

- **Readability**: Switch statements improve code readability, especially when dealing with multiple conditions.
- **Maintainability**: Adding or modifying cases is straightforward, making the code easy to maintain.
- **Performance**: Switch statements can be more efficient than a series of nested if-else statements, especially when dealing with many cases.
- **Flexibility**: Switch statements support matching options, including exact matches, wildcards, and conditions.

Anatomy of a Switch Statement:

```
switch ($variable) {
    "value1" {
        # Code to execute if $variable equals "value1"
    }
    "value2" {
        # Code to execute if $variable equals "value2"
    }
    "value3" {
        # Code to execute if $variable equals "value3"
    }
    Default {
```

```
        # Code to execute if $variable doesn't match any specified values
    }
}
```

- **`$variable`**: The expression or variable whose value is being tested against multiple cases.
- **`Case Blocks`**: Each value to be tested is enclosed in curly braces, and the code to be executed if there is a match is placed inside these blocks.
- **`Default`**: The **`Default`** block is optional and is executed if none of the specified cases match the value of the expression.

Let's look at the following example that creates a simple function that classifies a day of the week based on its name:

```
# Function: Classify-Day
function Classify-Day($day) {
    switch ($day) {
        "Monday" {
            Write-Host "It's the start of the workweek."
        }
        "Tuesday" {
            Write-Host "It's the second day of the week."
        }
        "Wednesday" {
            Write-Host "It's hump day!"
        }
        "Thursday" {
            Write-Host "It's almost the weekend."
        }
        "Friday" {
            Write-Host "TGIF! It's the end of the workweek."
        }
        Default {
            Write-Host "It's the weekend or an unrecognized day."
        }
    }
}
```

Explanation:

- Function Definition:

`Function Classify-Day($day) { ... }`: Defines a PowerShell function named **`Classify-Day`** that takes a single parameter **`$day`**.

- Switch Statement:

`switch ($day) { ... }`: Initiates a switch statement based on the value of the **`$day`** parameter.

- Case Blocks:

`"Monday" { Write-Host "It's the start of the workweek." }`: Defines a case block for the value "**`Monday`**." If the value of **`$day`** is "**`Monday`**," it executes the code block inside the curly braces.

- Default Case:

`Default { Write-Host "It's the weekend or an unrecognized day." }`: Provides a default case that executes if none of the specified cases match the value of $day.

```
# Test the function with different days

Classify-Day "Monday"

Classify-Day "Wednesday"

Classify-Day "Saturday"
```

```
# Test the function with different days
Classify-Day "Monday"
Classify-Day "Wednesday"
Classify-Day "Saturday"

It's the start of the workweek.
It's hump day!
It's the weekend or an unrecognized day.
```

***Figure 4.2**: Example of Switch-Case statements*

Switch with Conditions:

Here's an example of using a **`switch`** statement with conditions to classify numbers into different ranges:

```
function Classify-Number($number) {

    switch ($number) {

        { $_ -lt 0 } {

            Write-Host "$number is negative."

        }
```

```
        { $_ -ge 0 -and $_ -lt 10 } {
            Write-Host "$number is in the range 0 to 9."
        }
        { $_ -ge 10 -and $_ -lt 20 } {
            Write-Host "$number is in the range 10 to 19."
        }
        Default {
            Write-Host "$number is in an unrecognized range."
        }
    }
}

# Test the function with different numbers
Classify-Number -5
Classify-Number 7
Classify-Number 15
Classify-Number 25
```

Switch with Wildcard Matches:

Here's an example of using a switch statement with wildcard matches to identify file types based on their extensions:

```
function Check-FileType($filePath) {
    switch -Wildcard ($filePath) {
        "*.txt" {
            Write-Host "Text file detected: $filePath"
        }
        "*.csv" {
            Write-Host "CSV file detected: $filePath"
        }
        "*.pdf" {
            Write-Host "PDF file detected: $filePath"
        }
        Default {
            Write-Host "File type not recognized for: $filePath"
```

```
        }
    }
}

# Test the function with different file paths
Check-FileType "C:\Documents\example.txt"
Check-FileType "C:\Data\data.csv"
Check-FileType "C:\Reports\report.pdf"
Check-FileType "C:\Images\photo.jpg"
```

In this example:

- The **Check-FileType** function takes a parameter **$filePath**.
- The **switch** statement uses the **-Wildcard** option to enable wildcard matching.
- Each case uses a wildcard pattern to match file extensions (*.txt, *.csv, *.pdf).
- The Default case is executed if none of the wildcard patterns match.

Working with Delays

Working with delays or introducing pauses in your PowerShell scripts can be helpful in various scenarios, such as waiting for a process to complete, introducing a delay between commands, or implementing timed actions. PowerShell provides several ways to handle delays. Here are a few methods:

Start-Sleep

The **Start-Sleep** cmdlet allows you to introduce a delay by specifying the number of seconds to sleep.

```
Write-Host "Executing command 1..."
Start-Sleep -Seconds 5
Write-Host "Executing command 2..."
```

This example introduces a 5-second delay between the execution of "**Command 1**" and "**Command 2**."

You can use a for loop in conjunction with **Start-Sleep** for repetitive delays:

```
# Example: Repeatedly execute a command with a delay
for ($i = 1; $i -le 3; $i++) {
```

```
    Write-Host "Executing command $i..."
    Start-Sleep -Seconds 3
}
```

Consider a real-time example where you want to perform a periodic action, such as checking a folder for new files every 10 seconds. In this example, **`Start-Sleep`** will be used to introduce a delay between iterations of the loop:

```
# Example: Checking a Folder for New Files Every 10 Seconds

function Check-ForNewFiles {
    $folderPath = "C:\Path\To\Your\Folder"

    while ($true) {
        $newFiles = Get-ChildItem -Path $folderPath -File | Where-Object
{ $_.CreationTime -gt (Get-Date).AddMinutes(-1) }

        if ($newFiles.Count -gt 0) {
            Write-Host "New files detected:"
            $newFiles | ForEach-Object { Write-Host "- $_" }
        } else {
            Write-Host "No new files detected."
        }

        Write-Host "Waiting for 10 seconds before checking again..."
        Start-Sleep -Seconds 10
    }
}

# Test the function
Check-ForNewFiles
```

Code Explanation:

In this example:

1. The **`Check-ForNewFiles`** function continuously checks a specified folder for new files.

2. It uses a while (**`$true`**) loop to run indefinitely.
3. Inside the loop, it checks for files created within the last minute (**`-gt (Get-Date).AddMinutes(-1)`**).
4. If new files are found, it prints their names.
5. If no new files are found, it prints a message indicating so.
6. After each iteration, it waits 10 seconds before re-checking using **`Start-Sleep -Seconds 10`**.

Wait-Event

It **`Waits`** until a particular event is raised before continuing to run. You can use Wait-Event to wait for a specific event to occur, with the ability to set a timeout.

Let's consider an example where we want to wait for a user to press a key before proceeding with the script. We can use **`Wait`**-Event to wait for a key press event:

```
# Example: Wait for User Keypress


function Wait-ForKeypress {
    Write-Host "Press any key to continue..."

    # Wait for a key press using [System.Console]::KeyAvailable
    while (-not [System.Console]::KeyAvailable) {
        Start-Sleep -Milliseconds 100  # Introduce a short delay
    }

    # Consume the key event
    [System.Console]::ReadKey() | Out-Null
}

# Test the function
Wait-ForKeypress
Write-Host "You pressed a key. Continuing with the script..."
```

Code Explanation:

- **Function Definition**: function `Wait-ForKeypress { ... }`: Defines a PowerShell function named `Wait-ForKeypress`.
- **Prompt User**: `Write-Host "Press any key to continue..."`: Displays a message to prompt the user to press any key.
- **Waiting for Keypress**: while `(-not [System.Console]::KeyAvailable) { Start-Sleep -Milliseconds 100 }`: Uses a while loop to check if a key is available using `[System continuously.Console]::KeyAvailable`. The loop continues until a key is pressed.
- `Start-Sleep -Milliseconds 100`: Introduces a short delay of 100 milliseconds between each iteration of the loop to avoid excessive CPU usage.
- Consume Key Event:

  `[System.Console]::ReadKey() | Out-Null`: Once a key is available, the script uses `[System.Console]::ReadKey()` to consume the key event. The | Out-Null part is used to discard the key press information, as we are only interested in waiting for the key press event.
- Continuation Message:

  `Write-Host "You pressed a key. Continuing with the script..."`: Displays a message indicating that a key has been pressed, and the script continues.

Creating Looping Structures

In PowerShell, you can create looping structures to execute a code block repeatedly. Different loops are available, including **`for`**, **`foreach`**, **`while`**, and **`do-while`**. Each type of loop has its own use case. Let's explore each type:

For Loop

A **`for`** loop is a control flow statement that allows you to execute a block of code repeatedly for a specified number of times or for each item in a collection. It's a fundamental tool for automating repetitive tasks and processing data efficiently.

This example prints "**`Iteration 1`**" through "**`Iteration 5`**" using a for loop:

```
# Example: For Loop
for ($i = 1; $i -le 5; $i++) {
    Write-Host "Iteration $i"
}
```

Let's consider another example to simulate a countdown timer using a for loop with a delay:

```
# Example: Simulate a Countdown Timer

function Start-Countdown {
    $durationInSeconds = 10

    for ($i = $durationInSeconds; $i -gt 0; $i--) {
        Write-Host "Time left: $i seconds"
        Start-Sleep -Seconds 1
    }

    Write-Host "Countdown completed!"
}

# Test the function
Start-Countdown
Write-Host "Task after countdown."
```

Foreach Loop

A **foreach** loop is used to iterate over elements in a collection, such as an array. For example, look at the following code using a foreach loop for array elements:

```
# Example: Foreach Loop
$fruits = @("Apple", "Banana", "Orange")
foreach ($fruit in $fruits) {
    Write-Host "Current fruit: $fruit"
}

#Code Output:
Current fruit: Apple
Current fruit: Banana
Current fruit: Orange
```

Code Explanation:

- **Array Initialization**:

`$fruits = @("Apple", "Banana", "Orange")`: Creates an array named **`$fruits`** with three elements - "**`Apple`**", "**`Banana`**", and "**`Orange`**".

- **Foreach Loop**:

`foreach ($fruit in $fruits) { ... }`: Initiates a foreach loop that iterates over each element in the $fruits array. The loop variable $fruit represents the current element in each iteration.

- Code Block Inside the Loop:

`Write-Host "Current fruit: $fruit"`: Inside the loop, this line of code writes the current fruit to the console using **`Write-Host`**. The **`$fruit`** variable contains the current element's value in the array.

Let's consider a real-time example where you have a list of employee names and want to perform an action for each employee. In this example, we will use a **`foreach`** loop to iterate over the list of employees and display a personalized message for each one:

```
# Example: Perform Action for Each Employee


# List of employee names

$employees = @("Alice", "Bob", "Charlie", "David")


# Use foreach loop to iterate over each employee

foreach ($employee in $employees) {

    Write-Host "Processing employee: $employee"

    # Add your custom action here for each employee

}


Write-Host "Processing completed for all employees."
```

While Loop

A **`while`** loop is used when the number of iterations is not known in advance but is determined by a condition.

```
# Example: While Loop

$counter = 1

while ($counter -le 3) {
```

```
    Write-Host "Iteration $counter"
    $counter++
}
```

Let's consider a real-time example where you want to simulate a simple interactive game where the user is prompted to guess a number. The game continues until the user correctly guesses the number. We will use a **while** loop to achieve this.

```
# Example: Number Guessing Game with While Loop

# Generate a random number between 1 and 10
$correctNumber = Get-Random -Minimum 1 -Maximum 11

Write-Host "Welcome to the Number Guessing Game!"
Write-Host "Try to guess the correct number between 1 and 10."

# Initialize variables
$guessedNumber = 0

# Use a while loop until the correct number is guessed
while ($guessedNumber -ne $correctNumber) {
    # Prompt user for input
    $guessedNumber = Read-Host "Enter your guess"

    # Try to convert the input to an integer
    if ($guessedNumber -as [int]) {
        $guessedNumber = $guessedNumber -as [int]

        # Validate the range
        if ($guessedNumber -ge 1 -and $guessedNumber -le 10) {
            # Compare user's guess with the correct number
            if ($guessedNumber -eq $correctNumber) {
                Write-Host "Congratulations! You guessed the correct 
number: $correctNumber"
            } else {
```

```
                Write-Host "Try again. Incorrect guess."
            }
        } else {
            Write-Host "Invalid input. Please enter a number between 1 
and 10."
        }
    } else {
        Write-Host "Invalid input. Please enter a valid number."
    }
}

Write-Host "Game Over."
```

Do-While Loop

A **do-while** loop is similar to a **while** loop, but it always executes the block of code at least once before checking the condition.

The following code prints "**Iteration 1**" through "**Iteration 3**" using a **do-while** loop:

```
# Example: Do-While Loop
$counter = 1
do {
    Write-Host "Iteration $counter"
    $counter++
} while ($counter -le 3)
```

Difference between **While** and **Do-While** loop:

Feature	**While Loop**	**Do-While Loop**
Structure	`while (condition) { ... }`	`do { ... } while (condition)`
Execution Flow	Condition is evaluated before the loop block	A loop block is executed at least once, and then the condition is evaluated
Execution Control	It may not execute the loop block if the initial condition is false	Always executes the loop block at least once

Example	`PowerShell $counter = 1 while ($counter -le 3) { Write-Host "Iteration $counter" $counter++ }`	`PowerShell $counter = 1 do { Write-Host "Iteration $counter" $counter++ } while ($counter -le 3)`
Output	`Iteration 1 Iteration 2 Iteration 3`	`Iteration 1 Iteration 2 Iteration 3`

***Table 4.1**: Comparison between While and Do-While loop*

`ForEach-Object` Loop (Pipeline)

The `**ForEach-Object**` loop in PowerShell is used in the context of the pipeline (`|`) to iterate over each item in a collection or stream of objects. It's commonly used to process objects coming from the output of a cmdlet or as part of a pipeline. Here's an explanation of how the `**ForEach-Object**` loop works:

Structure:

```
<cmdlet or expression> | ForEach-Object {
    # Code to be executed for each object in the pipeline
}
```

Explanation:

- Cmdlet or Expression: The cmdlet or expression on the left side of the pipeline (`|`) generates a collection of objects or data.
- **`ForEach-Object`** Loop: The `**Foreach-Object**` cmdlet is used to iterate over each object in the collection.
- Code Block Inside the Loop: The code block inside the loop contains the instructions to be executed for each object in the pipeline.
- **- $_** is a special variable inside the `**ForEach-Object**` loop that represents the current object being processed

Example: Using ForEach-Object to Iterate Over a Collection:

```
1..5 | ForEach-Object {
    Write-Host "Current number: $_"
}
### Output:
Current number: 1
Current number: 2
Current number: 3
```

```
Current number: 4
Current number: 5
```

In this example:

- The range operator `1..5` generates a collection of numbers from 1 to 5.
- The pipeline passes each number to the `ForEach-Object` loop.
- Inside the loop, `Write-Host "Current number: $_"` is executed for each number, displaying the current number in the console.

Let's consider a real-time example where you have a list of file names, and you want to check and display information about each file using **ForEach-Object**:

```
# Example: Using ForEach-Object to Check File Information
# List of file names
$fileNames = @("C:\Path\To\file1.txt", "C:\Path\To\file2.txt", "C:\Path\To\file3.txt")

# Use ForEach-Object to iterate over each file name
$fileNames | ForEach-Object {
    $fileName = $_

    # Check if the file exists
    if (Test-Path $fileName -PathType Leaf) {
        # Display information about the file
        $fileInfo = Get-Item $fileName
        Write-Host "File: $fileInfo.FullName"
        Write-Host "Size: $($fileInfo.Length) bytes"
        Write-Host "Last Modified: $($fileInfo.LastWriteTime)”
        Write-Host "-----"
    } else {
        Write-Host "File not found: $fileName"
    }
}
```

PowerShell ForEach vs. ForEach-Object

Here is a summarized list of key differences between the **foreach** statement and the **ForEach-Object** cmdlet in PowerShell:

Feature	foreach Statement	ForEach-Object Cmdlet
Syntax	`foreach ($item in $collection) { ... }`	`` `$collection ``
Input Source	Directly iterates over an enumerable collection	Processes objects from the pipeline
Performance	Generally performs better with arrays	Can be slower due to pipeline object processing
Usage	Preferred for working with arrays or collections	Preferred when processing objects from cmdlets
Scope	Used within script blocks or functions	Typically used in the context of a pipeline
Output to Pipeline	No direct output to the pipeline	Outputs processed objects to the pipeline
Input Object ($_)	Not applicable	Represents the current object in the pipeline
Common Use Case	Enumerating through a known collection	Processing objects from cmdlets or pipeline

Table 4.2*: Comparison between foreach and ForEach-Object*

Let's look at an example of how scripting differs for each and **ForEach-Object** in PowerShell.

Suppose you have a CSV file, **MyData.csv**, with the following contents in the **C:\Temp\PowerShell** directory:

```
Name,Age,Occupation
Rajendra,25,Principal Engineer
Prashanth,30,Solution Architect
Vanshil,28,Doctor
```

The following code uses PowerShell **ForEach** loop to read data in CSV file:

Let's use a PowerShell **ForEach** Loop to read through a CSV file row:

```
# Import CSV file
$CSVData = Import-Csv -Path "C:\Temp\PowerShell\MyData.csv"


# Loop through each row in the CSV
ForEach ($user in $CSVData) {
```

```
    Write-Output ("Name: $($user.Name), Age: $($user.Age), Occupation: $($user.Occupation)")
}
```

The code iterates through each row in CSV file and prints it as follows:

```
PS C:\Users\rajendragupta>
PS C:\Users\rajendragupta> . $args[0] # Import CSV file
$CSVData = Import-Csv -Path "C:\Temp\PowerShell\MyData.csv"

# Loop through each row in the CSV
ForEach ($user in $CSVData) {
    Write-Output ("Name: $($user.Name), Age: $($user.Age), Occupation: $($user.Occupation)")
}

Name: Rajendra, Age: 25, Occupation: Principal Engineer
Name: Prashanth, Age: 30, Occupation: Solution Architect
Name: Vanshil, Age: 28, Occupation: Doctor
PS C:\Users\rajendragupta>
```

***Figure 4.3**: ForEach example*

The **ForEach-Object** PowerShell code to read CSV files uses the pipeline input, as follows:

```
# Import CSV file
$csvData = Import-Csv -Path "C:\Temp\PowerShell\MyData.csv"


# Loop through each row in the CSV
$CSVData | ForEach-Object {
    Write-Output ("Name: $($_.Name), Age: $($_.Age), Occupation: $($_.Occupation)")
}
```

```
PS C:\Users\rajendragupta>
PS C:\Users\rajendragupta> . $args[0] # Import CSV file
$csvData = Import-Csv -Path "C:\Temp\PowerShell\MyData.csv"

# Loop through each row in the CSV
$CSVData | ForEach-Object {
    Write-Output ("Name: $($_.Name), Age: $($_.Age), Occupation: $($_.Occupation)")
}


Name: Rajendra, Age: 25, Occupation: Principal Engineer
Name: Prashanth, Age: 30, Occupation: Solution Architect
Name: Vanshil, Age: 28, Occupation: Doctor
PS C:\Users\rajendragupta>
```

***Figure 4.4**: ForEach-Object PowerShell code to read CSV files*

Break ForEach Loop and ForEach-Object Cmdlet in PowerShell

The **break** keyword can be used to exit the loop before it has completed its normal iteration. Suppose you have an array of numbers, and you want to find the first even number in the array. Once you find it, you want to break out of the loop. Here's how you might achieve this with a foreach loop:

```
$numbers = 3, 7, 1, 4, 9, 5, 6

foreach ($number in $numbers) {
    Write-Output "Checking number: $number"

    if ($number % 2 -eq 0) {
        Write-Output "Found the first even number: $number"
        break
    }
}
```

In this example, the loop iterates through each number in the array, and when it finds the first even number (in this case, 4), it prints a message and breaks out of the loop.

Similarly, Let's consider a scenario where you want to list all the running processes on a computer until you find a process with a specific name. Once you find that process, you want to stop listing the processes. Here's how you might use **ForEach-Object** with the break keyword:

```
$targetProcessName = "explorer"

Get-Process | ForEach-Object {
    Write-Output "Process Name: $($_.ProcessName), ID: $($_.Id)"

    if ($_.ProcessName -eq $targetProcessName) {
        Write-Output "Found the target process: $targetProcessName"
        break
    }
}
```

In this example, the pipeline processes each running process, and when it finds the process with the specified name (in this case, "explorer"), it prints a message and breaks out of the pipeline.

Skipping an Element with `Continue` Keyword in PowerShell `ForEach` and `ForEach-Object` Methods

The **`continue`** keyword is used to skip the rest of the current iteration of a loop (either a foreach loop or the **`ForEach-Object`** cmdlet) and move to the next iteration. It allows you to skip certain code within the loop or pipeline for a particular condition without exiting the entire loop.

Suppose you have an array of numbers, and you want to print only the odd numbers. You can use the continue keyword to skip the even numbers. Here's an example:

```
$numbers = 1, 2, 3, 4, 5, 6, 7, 8, 9

foreach ($number in $numbers) {
    if ($number % 2 -eq 0) {
        # Skip even numbers
        continue
    }

    Write-Output "Odd Number: $number"
}
```

In this example, when the loop encounters an even number, the **`continue`** keyword is used to skip the **`Write-Output`** statement, and the loop moves on to the next iteration.

Similarly, suppose you have a collection of strings representing file names, and you want to display the length of each file name, excluding those that start with the letter **`"a"`**. The **`ForEach-Object`** cmdlet with the continue keyword can be used for this task:

```
$fileNames = "apple.txt", "banana.doc", "cherry.jpg", "orange.txt",
"grape.doc"

$fileNames | ForEach-Object {
    # Skip file names that start with the letter "a"
    if ($_ -like "a*") {
        continue
    }
```

```
    Write-Output "File Name: $_, Length: $($_.Length)"
}
```

In this example, the pipeline processes each file name in the collection. The **continue** keyword is used to skip file names that start with the letter "a", and the **Write-Output** statement is executed only for file names that don't meet this condition.

Exploring Arrays

An array in PowerShell is a data structure that stores a collection of elements, each identified by an index or a key. Arrays are used to organize and work with data in a structured way. An item can be a string, an integer, an object, or even another array, and one array can contain any combination of these items. Each item in an array has an index position starting with index 0. So, the first array element has an index of 0, the second is indexed as 1, and so on.

The Command to create the blank array is **@()** in PowerShell. To add the items, we can run the following command. This array has three elements.

```
$fruit = @('Apples','Oranges','Bananas')
```

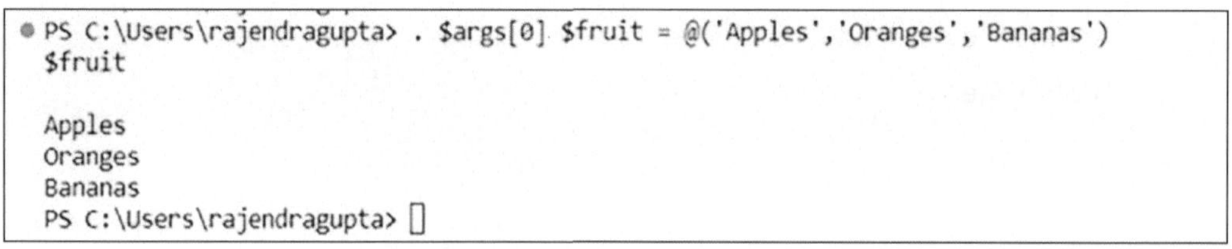

Figure 4.5: *Create an array*

You can use the **GetType()** function to check the object type of the variable. As illustrated, the object type is an array:

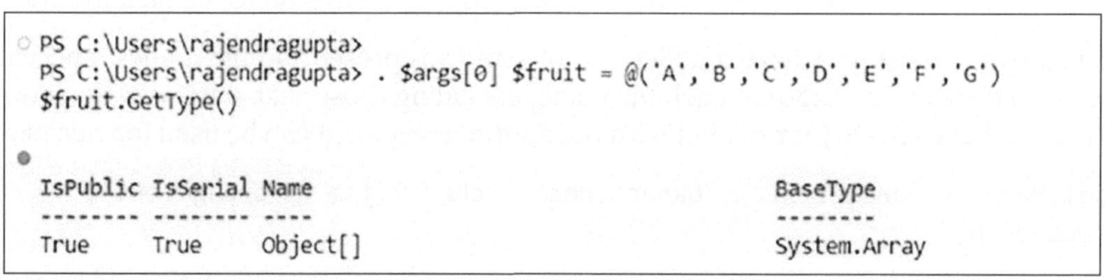

Figure 4.6: *Check object type*

To access an array's specific index position element, specify the index position as follows:

$fruit[0] for first element

$fruit[1] for second element

Suppose you have an array with the following elements:

```
$fruit = @('A','B','C','D','E','F','G')
```

You can retrieve multiple items by putting the index positions in a single command. For example, the following command retrieves elements at positions 1, 3, and 5.

```
$fruit[1,3,5]
```

```
PS C:\Users\rajendragupta> . $args[0] $fruit = @('A','B','C','D','E','F','G')
$fruit[1,3,5]

B
D
F
```

Figure 4.7: *Retrieve items from an array*

If you specify the negative number, PowerShell retrieves the records from the last records in reverse condition. For example, **`$fruit[-2] returns element F`**.

Updating Items in an Array

To update an item, specify the new value with the index position. For example, let's replace the array element at position 1 (2nd item).

```
$fruit = @('A','B','C','D','E','F','G')
$fruit[1]= 'New Item'
$fruit
```

```
PS C:\Users\rajendragupta>
PS C:\Users\rajendragupta> . $args[0] $fruit = @('A','B','C','D','E','F','G')
$fruit[1]= 'New Item'
$fruit

A
New Item
C
D
E
F
G
```

Figure 4.8: *Update items in an array*

Creating an Array of Objects

PowerShell allows the creation of an array of objects by defining a collection of custom objects or using existing objects. Here are a few ways to create an array of objects:

1. **Creating Custom Objects**: You can create custom objects with properties and then add them to an array.

```
$object1 = [PSCustomObject]@{
    Name = "John"
    Age  = 30
}

$object2 = [PSCustomObject]@{
    Name = "Alice"
    Age  = 25
}

# Creating an array of objects
$arrayOfObjects = @($object1, $object2)

# Displaying the array of objects
$arrayOfObjects
```

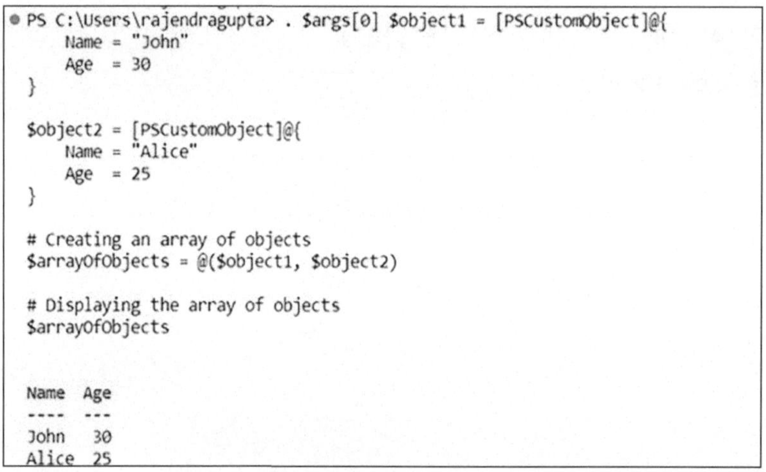

Figure 4.9: *Creating an array of objects*

2. **Using the New-Object cmdlet**: You can use the **New-Object** cmdlet to create custom objects and then add them to an array.

```
# Creating objects using New-Object
$object1 = New-Object PSObject -Property @{
    Name = "John"
    Age  = 30
}
```

```
$object2 = New-Object PSObject -Property @{
    Name = "Alice"
    Age  = 25
}

# Creating an array of objects
$arrayOfObjects = @($object1, $object2)

# Displaying the array of objects
$arrayOfObjects
```

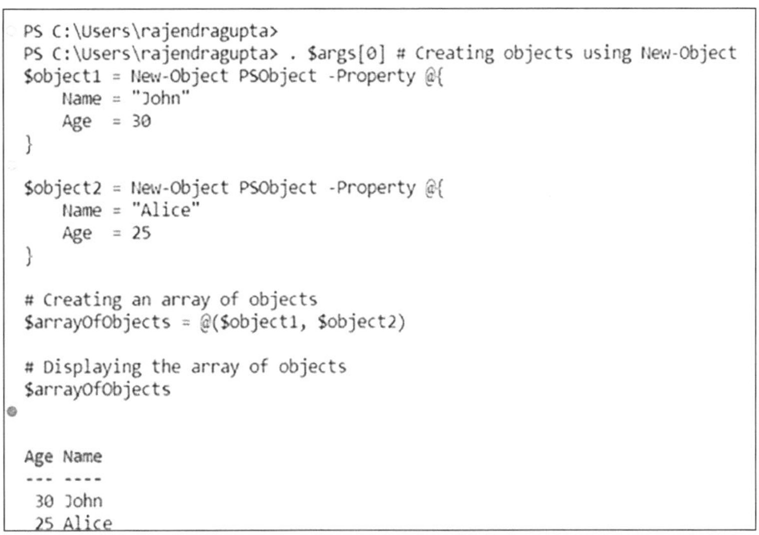

```
PS C:\Users\rajendragupta>
PS C:\Users\rajendragupta> . $args[0] # Creating objects using New-Object
$object1 = New-Object PSObject -Property @{
    Name = "John"
    Age  = 30
}

$object2 = New-Object PSObject -Property @{
    Name = "Alice"
    Age  = 25
}

# Creating an array of objects
$arrayOfObjects = @($object1, $object2)

# Displaying the array of objects
$arrayOfObjects


Age Name
--- ----
 30 John
 25 Alice
```

***Figure 4.10**: New-Object cmdlet*

3. **Using a Loop**: You can create objects in a loop and add them to an array.

```
# Creating an array of objects using a loop
$arrayOfObjects = @()

for ($i = 1; $i -le 3; $i++) {
    $newObject = [PSCustomObject]@{
        Property1 = "Value $i"
        Property2 = $i * 2
    }
```

```
    $arrayOfObjects += $newObject
}

# Displaying the array of objects
$arrayOfObjects
```

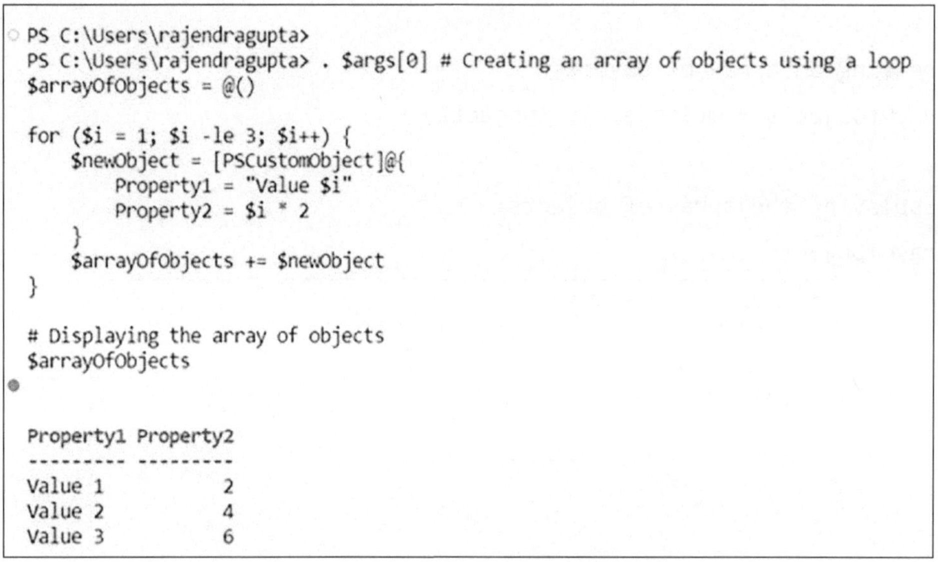

Figure 4.11: *Using a loop*

Operators for Arrays PowerShell

Here's a tabular format summarizing operators for arrays in PowerShell:

Operator	Description	Example
=	Assignment	`$myArray = 1, 2, 3, 4, 5`

+	Addition (Concatenation)	`# Concatenation`
		`$array1 = 1, 2, 3`
		`$array2 = 4, 5, 6`
		`$resultArray = $array1 + $array2`
		`# $resultArray now contains: 1, 2, 3, 4, 5, 6`
		`OR`
		`Use += operator as shown below`
		`$resultArray += $array1,$array2`

*	Multiplication (Duplicate Elements)	`# Duplication of elements`
		`$originalArray = 1, 2, 3`
		`$duplicatedArray = $originalArray * 2`
		`# $duplicatedArray now contains: 1, 2, 3, 1, 2, 3`

-eq	Equality	`$data = @('red','green','blue')`
		
		`$data -eq 'green'`

-ne	Inequality	`$data = @('red','green','blue')`
		
		`$data -ne 'green'`

-contains	Containment (Element Present)	`$data = @('red','green','blue')`
		
		`$data -contains 'green'`

-join	Joins the element	`$data = @('red','green','blue')`
		
		`$data -join '-'`

-in	Membership (Element Present)	`$data = @('red','green','blue')`
		`$data1 = ('red' -in $data)`
		`$data1`

***Table 4.3**: Operators for arrays PowerShell*

Array Types

PowerShell contains different types of arrays, and they are primarily categorized based on their indexing or structure. Here are some common types:

- Default [**`PSObject[]`**]: It is the default array type in PowerShell. It can hold any type of data value.
- Strongly Typed arrays: This array type restricts the data type or objects an array can hold. For example, you can restrict the array to have only an integer data type.

```
[int[]] $numbers = 1,2,3
$numbers
```

- **ArrayList**: An **ArrayList** is a type of collection provided by the .NET Framework. It belongs to the **System.Collections** namespace and is represented by the **System.Collections.ArrayList** class. An **ArrayList** is a dynamic array that can grow or shrink in size as needed, allowing you to add or remove elements easily.

Here's a brief explanation and examples of using ArrayList in PowerShell:

Operation	Description	Example

Create an empty **ArrayList**	Create an instance of **ArrayList**	`$arrayList = New-Object System.Collections.ArrayList`
		
		Or
		
		`$arrayList = [System. Collections. ArrayList]::new()`
		
		or
		
		`[System.Collections. ArrayList]$ ArrayList = @()`

Adding Elements	Append elements to the end of the **ArrayList**	`$ArrayList.Add("Prashanth")`
		`$ArrayList.Add("Rajendra")`
		`$ArrayList.Add(100)`

Get **ArrayList** Item Count	Counts the items from the **ArrayList**	`$ArrayList.Count`
Retrieving Elements	Access elements by index	`$elementAtIndex = $arrayList[0]`
Removing Elements by Value	Specify element value to remove from **ArrayList**	`$arrayList. Remove("Prashanth")`
Removing Elements by Index Position	Specify element index position to remove from **ArrayList**	`$arrayList.RemoveAt(0)`

Sort Elements	Sort **ArrayList** using sort-object	`$ArrayList| sort-object`
Iterate **ArrayList**	Traverse elements in the **ArrayList** using a loop	`foreach ($item in $ArrayList){ $item }`

ArrayList from an Array	Create the **ArrayList** from an existing array	`$X="A","B","C","D"`
		`[System.Collections.ArrayList]$X`
		or
		`$X="A","B","C","D"`
		`$y= New-Object System.Collections.ArrayList(,$X)`

Remove Multiple Items from an **ArrayList**	Remove more than one item from the **ArrayList**	`$y.RemoveRange(1,2)`

***Table 4.4**: ArrayType operations*

Advanced Array Functions

Beyond the fundamental operations discussed thus far, a range of advanced array functions and additional features is worth noting. As you integrate these into your scripting more frequently, you will uncover enhanced capabilities and gain a deeper understanding of array manipulation in PowerShell.

Pre-sized Arrays

In PowerShell, arrays are typically dynamically sized, meaning their size can be adjusted as elements are added or removed. However, if you need to create a pre-sized array with a specific number of elements, you can use the New-Object cmdlet and the [**Object[]**] type. Here's an example:

```
# Create a pre-sized array with 5 elements
$preSizedArray = New-Object Object[] 5


# Access and modify elements
$preSizedArray[0] = "Element 1"
$preSizedArray[1] = "Element 2"
```

```
$preSizedArray[2] = "Element 3"
$preSizedArray[3] = "Element 4"
$preSizedArray[4] = "Element 5"

# Display the pre-sized array
$preSizedArray
```

Multiplying Arrays

Multiplying arrays is not a direct operation like addition or subtraction. However, you can achieve a form of "*multiplication*" by duplicating the elements of an array. Here's an example using the multiplication operator (*):

```
# Original array
$originalArray = 1, 2, 3

# Duplicate elements using multiplication
$duplicatedArray = $originalArray * 3

# Display the duplicated array
$duplicatedArray
```

In this example, the original array's elements `[1, 2, 3]` are duplicated three times, resulting in the array `[1, 2, 3, 1, 2, 3, 1, 2, 3]`:

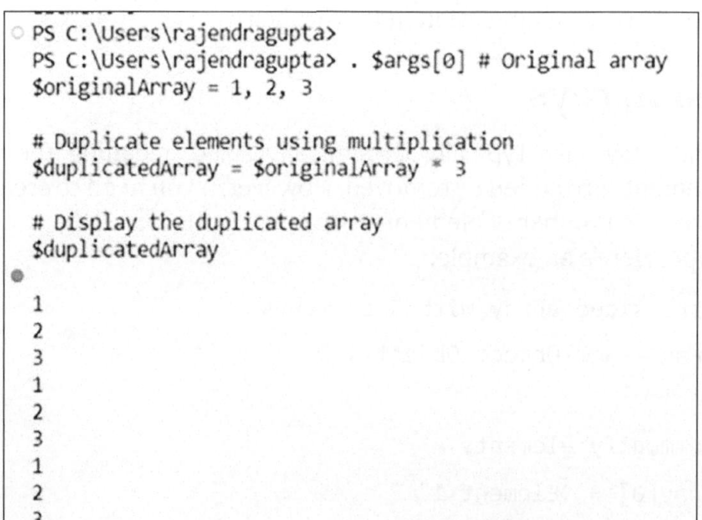

Figure 4.12: *Multiplying arrays*

Nested Arrays

You can create nested arrays, which are arrays within arrays. This allows you to represent more complex data structures, such as matrices or lists of lists. Here's an example of creating and working with nested arrays:

```
$data = @(

        @(1,2,3),

        @(4,5,6),

        @(7,8,9)

    )
```

To access a specific element, you need to specify its horizontal and vertical index position. For example, $data[1][2] returns value 6 (accesses the element at row 1, column 2).

Exploring Hashtables

A hashtable is a data structure that stores data in key-value pairs. It is a collection of key-value pairs where each key must be unique, and the associated value can be any valid PowerShell object. Hashtables are particularly useful for organizing and retrieving data in a way that is efficient and intuitive. The hashtables are defined using the @ symbol.

Here's a brief explanation and example of using hashtables in PowerShell:

Creating a Hashtable:

In this example, "**`Key1`**", "**`Key2`**", and "**`Key3`**" are the keys, and "**`Value1`**", "**`Value2`**", and "**`Value3`**" are the corresponding values:

```
$hashtable = @{
    "Key1" = "Value1"
    "Key2" = "Value2"
    "Key3" = "Value3"
}
```

Suppose you want to store information about employees in a company, associating each employee's ID with their corresponding name and department. Here's how you can use a hashtable for this purpose:

```
# Create a hashtable to store employee information
$employeeInfo = @{
    "E101" = @{
        "Name" = "John Doe"
        "Department" = "IT"
    }
    "E202" = @{
        "Name" = "Alice Smith"
        "Department" = "HR"
    }
    "E303" = @{
        "Name" = "Bob Johnson"
        "Department" = "Finance"
    }
}
```

- The keys "`E101`," "`E202`," and "`E303`" represent employee IDs.
- Each employee ID is associated with a nested hashtable containing the employee's name and department.

Accessing Values:

You can access the information for a specific employee using their ID. For instance, **`$employeeInfo["E101"]["Name"]`** retrieves the name of the employee with ID "**`E101`**."

```
$employeeName = $employeeInfo["E101"]["Name"]
$employeeDepartment = $employeeInfo["E101"]["Department"]

# Displaying information
Write-Output "Employee Name: $employeeName"
Write-Output "Employee Department: $employeeDepartment"
```

Adding and Modifying Entries:

You can add new key-value pairs or modify existing values:

```
# Add a new key-value pair
$hashtable["Key4"] = "Value4"
```

```
# Modify an existing value
$hashtable["Key1"] = "NewValue1"
```

In the existing hashtable example, let's add details of a new employee:

```
$employeeInfo["E404"] = @{
    "Name" = "Eva Rodriguez"
    "Department" = "Marketing"
}
```

Similarly, remove the entries for the employee ID E101 with the Remove function as shown in the following code:

```
# Create a hashtable to store employee information
$employeeInfo = @{
    "E101" = @{
        "Name" = "John Doe"
        "Department" = "IT"
    }
    "E202" = @{
        "Name" = "Alice Smith"
        "Department" = "HR"
    }
    "E303" = @{
        "Name" = "Bob Johnson"
        "Department" = "Finance"
    }
}

# Remove an employee entry
$removedEmployeeID = "E101"
if ($employeeInfo.ContainsKey($removedEmployeeID)) {
    $removedEmployee = $employeeInfo.Remove($removedEmployeeID)
    Write-Output "Removed employee with ID: $removedEmployeeID"
} else {
    Write-Output "Employee with ID $removedEmployeeID not found."
}
```

```
# Remove an employee entry
$removedEmployeeID = "E101"
if ($employeeInfo.ContainsKey($removedEmployeeID)) {
    $removedEmployee = $employeeInfo.Remove($removedEmployeeID)
    Write-Output "Removed employee with ID: $removedEmployeeID"
} else {
    Write-Output "Employee with ID $removedEmployeeID not found."
}

Removed employee with ID: E101
```

***Figure 4.13**: Remove an element from the Hashtable*

Updating the Values in the Hashtable:

Suppose the employee E101 department changes to Operations. You can update the existing value by using the key to select the correct key-pair.

```
# Modify the department of employee E101 to "Operations"
$employeeInfo["E101"]["Department"] = "Operations"
```

You can use the following code to display old and new values in the hashtable for employee E101:

```
# Create a hashtable to store employee information
# Display the initial employee information for E101
Write-Output "Initial Employee Information for E101:"
$initialDepartmentE101 = $employeeInfo["E101"]["Department"]
Write-Output "E101: $($employeeInfo['E101']['Name']),
$($initialDepartmentE101)"


# Modify the department of employee E101 to "Operations"
$employeeInfo["E101"]["Department"] = "Operations"


# Display the updated employee information for E101
Write-Output "Updated Employee Information for E101:"
$updatedDepartmentE101 = $employeeInfo["E101"]["Department"]
Write-Output "E101: $($employeeInfo['E101']['Name']),
$($updatedDepartmentE101)"
```

```
Initial Employee Information for E101:
E101: John Doe, IT
Updated Employee Information for E101:
E101: John Doe, Operations
```

***Figure 4.14**: Update an element in the Hashtable*

Iterating Through a Hashtable:

You can iterate through the key-value pairs in a hashtable using foreach block.

```
# Iterate through the hashtable
foreach ($key in $hashtable.Keys) {
    $value = $hashtable[$key]
    Write-Output "$key: $value"
}
```

Let's write the foreach block to show all elements in a hashtable for employee information. In this code, the foreach loop iterates through each key (**employeeId**) in the Keys collection of the hashtable **$employeeInfo**. Inside the loop, the **$employeeInfo[$employeeId]** expression retrieves the corresponding employee information (**name**, **department**) for each key.

```
# Create a hashtable to store employee information
$employeeInfo = @{
    "E101" = @{
        "Name" = "John Doe"
        "Department" = "IT"
    }
    "E202" = @{
        "Name" = "Alice Smith"
        "Department" = "HR"
    }
    "E303" = @{
        "Name" = "Bob Johnson"
        "Department" = "Finance"
    }
}
```

```
# Display employee information using a foreach loop
foreach ($employeeId in $employeeInfo.Keys) {
    $employee = $employeeInfo[$employeeId]
    Write-Host "Employee ID: $employeeId"
    Write-Host "Name: $($employee.Name)"
    Write-Host "Department: $($employee.Department)"
    Write-Host "---------------------------"
}
```

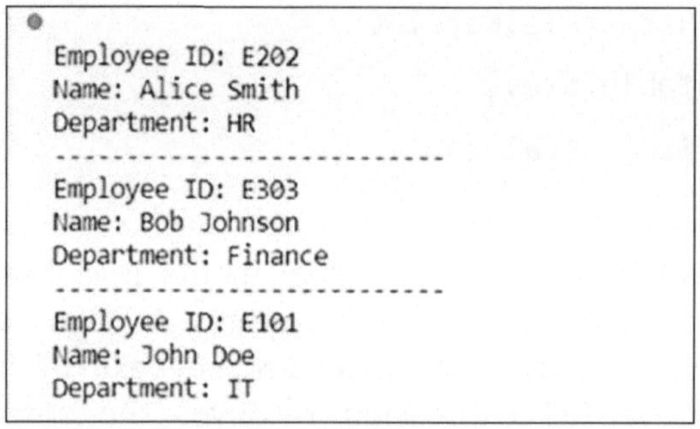

***Figure 4.15**: Foreach block to access all elements in the Hashtable*

Ordered Hashtable

The hashtables are not sorted by default. The ordered keyword can be used to create an ordered hashtable in PowerShell. An ordered hashtable maintains the order in which elements were added, making it suitable for scenarios where you want to preserve the order of keys. Here's an example using the **ordered** keyword:

```
# Create an ordered hashtable using the ordered keyword
$employeeInfo = [ordered]@{
    "E101" = @{
        "Name" = "John Doe"
        "Department" = "IT"
    }
    "E202" = @{
        "Name" = "Alice Smith"
        "Department" = "HR"
    }
    "E303" = @{
```

```
        "Name" = "Bob Johnson"
        "Department" = "Finance"
    }
}

# Iterate through the ordered hashtable and display key-value pairs
foreach ($entry in $employeeInfo.GetEnumerator()) {
    Write-Output "$($entry.Key): $($entry.Value.Name), $($entry.Value.
Department)"
}
```

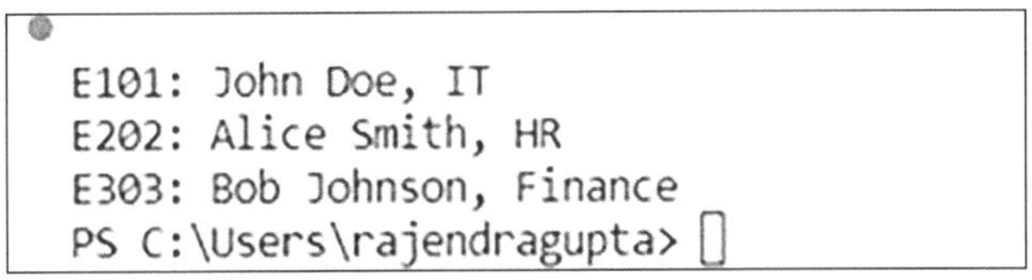

Figure 4.16: *Ordered hashtable*

Splatting Hashtables

Splatting is a technique in PowerShell that allows you to pass a set of key-value pairs as named parameters to a cmdlet or function. It's especially useful when you have a hashtable of parameters and want to apply them to a cmdlet or function clean and readable.

For example, when you want to send an email from PowerShell, you will end up with a long line of parameters:

```
Send-MailMessage -SmtpServer smtp.contoso.com -To rajendragupta@contoso.
com -From info@contoso.com -Subject 'Test message for splatting
hashtables' -Body 'Test email from PowerShell' -Priority High
```

We can use a hashtable and splat it to make this more readable. Splatting replaces all the parameters and values with a single variable. Note that we use the **@symbol** to splat the variable instead of the $:

```
# Create a hashtable with parameters for Send-MailMessage
$mailParams = @{
    SmtpServer  = "smtp.contoso.com"
    To          = " rajendragupta@contoso.com"
    From        = "info@contoso.com"
    Subject     = ' Test message for splatting hashtables'
```

```
    Body        = 'Test email from PowerShell'
    Priority    = 'High'
}

# Use splatting to send the email
Send-MailMessage @mailParams
```

Creating Objects from Hashtables

Hashtables serve well in organizing data for a singular object or for splatting purposes, but they lack the structure of true objects. A hashtable comprises only two columns: key and value. While suitable for defining specifications for an individual server, hashtables encounter limitations when managing data for multiple servers (such as the inability to reuse column names). To overcome this, it's more efficient to structure your data using objects when dealing with multiple entries. In PowerShell, the straightforward method to generate objects involves converting a hashtable into a custom PowerShell object. This is achieved by prefixing the hashtable with `` `[pscustomobject]` ``.

`[PSCustomObject]` is a type accelerator that allows you to create custom objects from hashtables. When you convert a hashtable to a custom object using **`[PSCustomObject]`**, you essentially transform the hashtable into a structured object with properties, making it easier to work with and more versatile than a simple hashtable. Here's an example to illustrate the use of **`[PSCustomObject]`** with hashtables:

```
# Create a hashtable with server specifications
$serverSpecs = @{
    Name        = "Server001"
    IP          = "192.168.1.100"
    OS          = "Windows Server 2019"
    MemoryGB    = 16
    CPU         = "Quad-Core"
}

# Convert the hashtable to a custom PowerShell object using
[PSCustomObject]
$serverObject = [PSCustomObject]$serverSpecs

# Display the custom object
$serverObject
```

```
# Convert the hashtable to a custom PowerShell object using [PSCustomObject]
$serverObject = [PSCustomObject]$serverSpecs

# Display the custom object
$serverObject


CPU       : Quad-Core
MemoryGB  : 16
IP        : 192.168.1.100
Name      : Server001
OS        : Windows Server 2019
```

***Figure 4.17**: Creating objects from hashtables*

Code Explanation:

- We create a hashtable **`$serverSpecs`** with specifications for a server, including properties like **`Name`**, **`IP`**, **`OS`**, **`MemoryGB`**, and **`CPU`**.
- We use **`[PSCustomObject]`** to convert the hashtable into a custom PowerShell object, resulting in the **`$serverObject`**.
- The **`$serverObject`** now behaves like a custom object with named properties. You can access its properties using dot notation (**`$serverObject.Name`**, **`$serverObject.MemoryGB`**, and more).

Now, we can add another server to the **`pscustomobject`** as follows:

```
function servers {
    [pscustomobject]@{
      Name         = "Server001"
      IP           = "192.168.1.100"
      OS           = "Windows Server 2019"
      MemoryGB     = 16
      CPU          = "Quad-Core"
    }
    [pscustomobject]@{
      Name         = "Server002"
      IP           = "192.168.1.102"
      OS           = "Windows Server 2019"
      MemoryGB     = 32
      CPU          = "Quad-Core"
    }
}
servers
```

```
Name     : Server001
IP       : 192.168.1.100
OS       : Windows Server 2019
MemoryGB : 16
CPU      : Quad-Core

Name     : Server002
IP       : 192.168.1.102
OS       : Windows Server 2019
MemoryGB : 32
CPU      : Quad-Core
```

***Figure 4.18**: Adding multiple items in Hashtables using objects*

Exporting Hashtable to CSV

If you have a hashtable and you want to export its key-value pairs to a CSV file, you can use the **GetEnumerator** method and then export the results to CSV.

```
# Create a hashtable with data
$employeeData = @{
    Name       = "John Doe"
    Department = "IT"
    EmployeeID = "E101"
}

# Get the enumerator for the hashtable
$enumerator = $employeeData.GetEnumerator()

# Specify the CSV file path
$csvFilePath = "C:\temp\File.csv"

# Export the key-value pairs to CSV
$enumerator | Select-Object Name, Value | Export-Csv -Path $csvFilePath
-NoTypeInformation

Write-Output "Hashtable exported to CSV: $csvFilePath"
```

In this example:

- We create a hashtable **$employeeData** with employee information.
- We obtain an enumerator using the **GetEnumerator** method.
- We specify the path where you want to save the CSV file using the variable **$csvFilePath**.
- We use **Select-Object** to extract the **Name** and **Value** properties from the enumerator.
- We use **Export-Csv** to export the key-value pairs to a CSV file. The **-NoTypeInformation** parameter is used to exclude type information from the CSV file.
- We display a message indicating that the hashtable has been exported to the CSV file.

The following code Iterate through the hashtable to convert each entry to a custom object and export the array of custom objects to CSV:

```
# Create a hashtable with employee data
$employeeData = @{
    'E101' = @{
        Name       = "John Doe"
        Department = "IT"
    }
    'E202' = @{
        Name       = "Alice Smith"
        Department = "HR"
    }
    'E303' = @{
        Name       = "Bob Johnson"
        Department = "Finance"
    }
}

# Specify the CSV file path
$csvFilePath = "C:\Path\To\Your\File.csv"

# Create an array to store custom objects
```

```
$employeeObjects = @()

# Iterate through the hashtable to convert each entry to a custom object
foreach ($entry in $employeeData.GetEnumerator()) {
    $employeeObject = [PSCustomObject]@{
        EmployeeID = $entry.Key
        Name       = $entry.Value.Name
        Department = $entry.Value.Department
    }
    $employeeObjects += $employeeObject
}

# Export the array of custom objects to CSV
$employeeObjects | Export-Csv -Path $csvFilePath -NoTypeInformation


Write-Output "Employee data exported to CSV: $csvFilePath"
```

Conclusion

This chapter equipped you with essential skills in PowerShell control flow and data structures. From implementing **if-else** conditions and utilizing **switch-case** statements to working with delays and creating diverse looping structures, you now possess the tools for dynamic script development.

Exploring arrays and hashtables helped you to enhance your ability to organize and manipulate data efficiently. As you integrate these concepts, you gain the power to create responsive scripts, automate processes, and manage data effectively. This chapter provides a solid foundation for addressing various scripting challenges in your PowerShell journey. Happy scripting!

The next chapter, *PowerShell Security*, will empower you with the knowledge and skills to fortify your PowerShell scripts, implement secure execution policies, and leverage code signing to establish trust and security in your automation processes.

Multiple Choice Questions

1. Which keyword is used for creating a loop in PowerShell?
   a. `loop`
   b. `repeat`
   c. `foreach`
   d. `continue`
2. How do you check if two values are equal in an if statement?
   a. `==`
   b. `-eq`
   c. `=`
   d. `is`
3. In a switch statement, which keyword is used to specify a default case?
   a. `default`
   b. `else`
   c. `case`
   d. `otherwise`
4. What cmdlet is commonly used to introduce delays in PowerShell scripts?
   a. `Sleep-Timeout`
   b. `Pause-Script`
   c. `Wait-Event`
   d. `Start-Sleep`
5. How do you access the first element of an array in PowerShell?
   a. `$array[0]`
   b. `$array(1)`
   c. `$array{First}`
   d. `$array.(First)`

6. Which symbol is used to define a key-value pair in a hashtable?

   a. `:`

   b. `=`

   c. `,`

   d. `->`

7. In PowerShell, what does the $_ symbol represent?

   a. Current user

   b. Current directory

   c. Current object in the pipeline

   d. Current script file

8. How do you declare a variable in PowerShell?

   a. `v MyVariable`

   b. `$MyVariable`

   c. `set MyVariable`

   d. `variable MyVariable`

9. What keyword is used to define a function in PowerShell?

   a. `method`

   b. `define`

   c. `function`

   d. `proc`

10. Which cmdlet is used for displaying the content of a text file in PowerShell?

    a. `Read-File`

    b. `Get-Content`

    c. `Read-Text`

    d. `Display-File`

Answers

1. c
2. b

3. a
4. d
5. a
6. b
7. c
8. b
9. c
10. b

Questions

- How would you use **`if-else`** conditions in PowerShell to check multiple conditions within a script? Provide an example scenario and demonstrate the implementation.
- Explain the advantages of using switch-case statements over multiple **`if-else`** conditions in certain scripting scenarios.
- Discuss the significance of introducing delays in PowerShell scripts. Can you provide a real-world scenario where incorporating delays is essential, and how would you implement it?
- Compare and contrast the various looping structures in PowerShell, such as **`foreach`**, **`for`**, **`while`**, **`do-while`**, and **`do-until`**. In what situations would you choose one looping structure over another?
- Describe the key differences between arrays and hashtables in PowerShell. When would you opt for using an array, and when would you prefer a hashtable? Provide examples illustrating their practical applications.

Key Terms

1. **Hashtable**: A hashtable is a data structure in PowerShell that allows the storage and retrieval of data using key-value pairs. It is created using the `**@{}**` syntax and provides a flexible way to organize and access structured data.
2. **Array**: An array in PowerShell is an ordered collection of elements, each identified by an index or a key. Arrays are created using the `**@()**` syntax and are useful for storing and iterating through multiple values of the same type.

3. **Loops**: Loops in PowerShell are control structures that allow the execution of a block of code repeatedly. Common types of loops include `foreach`, `for`, `while`, `do-while`, and `do-until`. Loops are instrumental for iterating through arrays, performing calculations, and automating repetitive tasks.
4. **Delay**: Delay in PowerShell refers to introducing a pause or waiting period in the execution of a script. This can be achieved using the `Start-Sleep` cmdlet, which halts script execution for a specified duration. Delays are useful for managing asynchronous operations, pacing script execution, or handling specific timing requirements.

Chapter 5
PowerShell Security

Introduction

PowerShell provides a robust set of security features to help administrators and users manage and control the execution of scripts and commands. Here is a brief description to get you started with PowerShell security.

The journey begins with an overview of PowerShell security that provides insights into the challenges and opportunities inherent in its dynamic environment. We then navigate through the intricacies of PowerShell execution policies, understanding how they govern script execution and contribute to a secure scripting environment.

Delving deeper, the chapter explores execution policy essentials to understand the various policy levels and their implications. We will learn how to tailor these policies to ensure a robust foundation for your PowerShell scripting practices.

The chapter also delves into the world of code signing and unravels the process of designing a self-signed certificate for code signing. Discover how code signing enhances the integrity and authenticity of your scripts and fosters a secure execution environment.

Security in PowerShell goes beyond scripts to encompass the handling of user credentials. Uncover best practices for securely obtaining and managing user credentials in your PowerShell scripts and safeguarding sensitive information in a dynamic and automated landscape.

Finally, the exploration extends to PowerShell constrained language, a feature designed to restrict potentially unsafe language elements.

Structure

In this chapter, we will discuss the following topics:

- PowerShell Security Overview
- PowerShell Execution Policy
- Setting Execution Policy in PowerShell Profile

- Designing a Self-Signed Certificate for Code Signing
- PowerShell for Securely Obtaining User Credentials
- PowerShell Constrained Language

PowerShell Security Overview

PowerShell, a robust cross-platform automation framework and scripting language, is equipped with built-in security features designed to protect systems and data. Understanding and implementing these security measures are crucial for maintaining a secure environment.

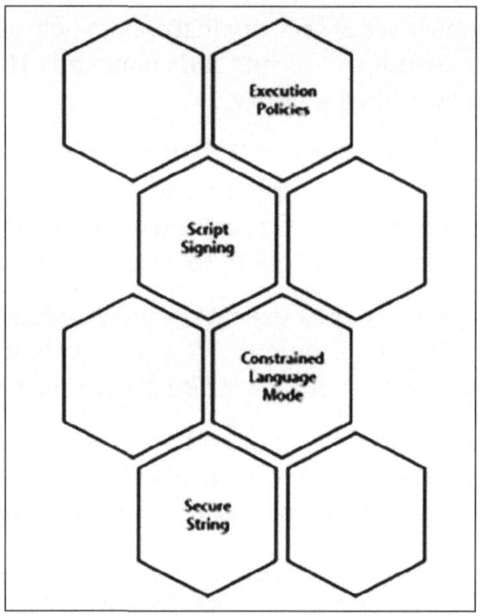

Figure 5.1: *PowerShell security*

This overview provides a solid foundation for understanding key aspects of PowerShell security.

- **Execution Policies:**

  PowerShell uses execution policies to control the running of scripts. These policies determine whether PowerShell scripts are allowed to run and, if so, under what conditions. The available execution policies include **`Restricted`**, **`AllSigned`**, **`RemoteSigned`**, **`Unrestricted`**, and **`Bypass`**. Setting and managing execution policies is fundamental for controlling script execution on a system.

- **Script Signing:**

  To enhance security, PowerShell supports script signing. By signing scripts with a digital signature, you can verify the authenticity and integrity of scripts before execution. This helps prevent the unintentional or malicious running of scripts. The **`Set-AuthenticodeSignature cmdlet`** is used for script signing.

- **Constrained Language Mode:**

  PowerShell includes a constrained language mode that restricts the use of certain language elements, providing an additional layer of security. This constrained language mode is especially useful in scenarios where untrusted scripts need to be executed.

- **Secure String:**

  PowerShell's **`SecureString`** data type allows the secure storage of sensitive information, such as passwords. This helps protect sensitive data from being easily exposed during script execution.

PowerShell Execution Policy

PowerShell execution policies are often misunderstood but they extend beyond mere user restrictions. They function as a robust defense mechanism against unauthorized script execution, positioning themselves as a crucial aspect of system-wide security. It is vital to recognize that these policies do not control user activities; this responsibility lies with the Windows account model, a foundational security boundary. PowerShell, operating as a user-mode application, aligns with the Windows security model, providing users with complete control over its functionalities. Execution policies act as safety features, akin to seatbelts – recommended but ultimately optional.

The execution policy serves as a safeguard, governing when PowerShell loads configuration files and executes scripts. It empowers users to establish basic rules, preventing inadvertent violations without imposing overly restrictive measures.

PowerShell execution policy across security layers

The PowerShell execution policy operates within a layered security framework and plays a central role in ensuring the controlled and secure execution of scripts within the Windows environment.

Here is a more detailed clarification.

Built-in Execution Policies

A palette of predefined execution policies shapes the PowerShell security landscape. "*All Signed*" mandates signed scripts from trusted publishers, while "*Bypass*" removes all barriers, suitable for scenarios where PowerShell integrates into larger applications with autonomous security implementations.

Default Execution Policies

Windows server computers default to "*Remote Signed*," necessitating digital signatures for internet-downloaded scripts, whereas Windows client computers default to "*Restricted*," allowing individual commands but disallowing script execution.

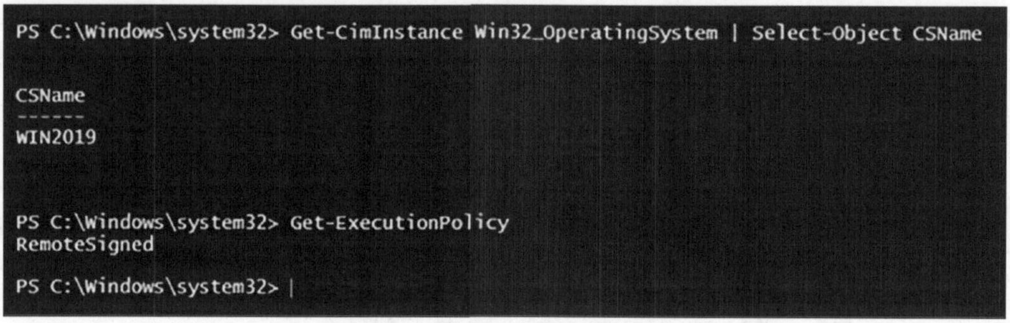

```
PS C:\Windows\system32> Get-CimInstance Win32_OperatingSystem | Select-Object CSName

CSName
------
WIN2019


PS C:\Windows\system32> Get-ExecutionPolicy
RemoteSigned
PS C:\Windows\system32> |
```

***Figure 5.2**: Default execution policy*

Scope Hierarchy and Variables

Execution policy effectiveness is influenced by a hierarchical order – **`MachinePolicy`**, **`UserPolicy`**, **`CurrentUser`**, **`Process`**, and **`LocalMachine`**. Understanding this hierarchy is crucial for tailoring security measures. The execution policy, stored as an environment variable (**`$env:PSExecutionPolicyPreference`**), is ephemeral, and clears upon the closure of a PowerShell session.

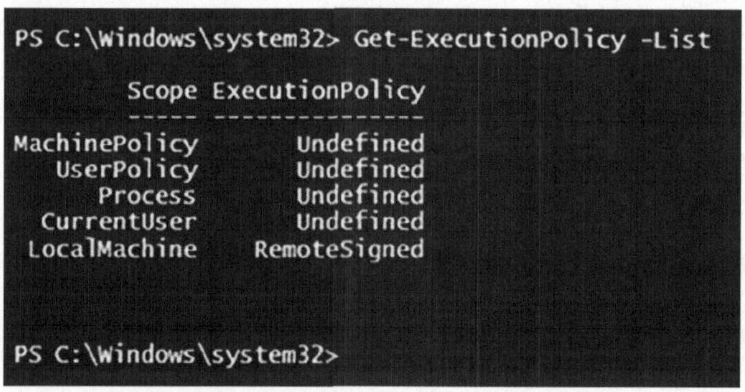

```
PS C:\Windows\system32> Get-ExecutionPolicy -List

        Scope ExecutionPolicy
        ----- ---------------
MachinePolicy       Undefined
   UserPolicy       Undefined
      Process       Undefined
  CurrentUser       Undefined
 LocalMachine    RemoteSigned


PS C:\Windows\system32>
```

***Figure 5.3**: Execution policy and scopes*

Fine-Tuning Execution Policies

Setting the execution policy through the **`Set-ExecutionPolicy`** command provides a spectrum of options. While "*Unrestricted*" might be suitable for unrestricted execution during examples, scoping to specific users in organizational settings ensures more granular control.

- **Set Execution Policy for a Specific User:**

  In this example, we set the execution policy to **`RemoteSigned`** for the current user only. This means that locally created scripts can run, but scripts from the internet must have a digital signature to run.

```
Set-ExecutionPolicy -Scope CurrentUser -ExecutionPolicy
RemoteSigned
```

Determining Effective Execution Policy

Unraveling the effective execution policy involves meticulously evaluating policies in a specific order of precedence. The hierarchy considers **`Group Policy`**, **`MachinePolicy`**, **`UserPolicy`**, **`Current Process`**, **`CurrentUser`**, and **`LocalMachine`** Policy, allowing for a nuanced approach to security configurations.

- **Set System-Wide Execution Policy**

  This command sets a more restrictive execution policy (restricted) for all users on the machine. Restricted policy only allows the execution of commands and scripts signed by a trusted publisher.

  ```
  Set-ExecutionPolicy -Scope LocalMachine -ExecutionPolicy Restricted
  ```

Launching PowerShell with Precision

Flexibility extends to launching PowerShell with a specified execution policy, adding another layer of adaptability. Whether through **`Set-ExecutionPolicy`** or launching with predefined policies, the objective is to align PowerShell's capabilities with the security needs of the environment.

Execution Policy	Description	Example Usage
`Restricted`	Default policy for Windows clients. Individual commands are allowed, but script execution is restricted.	**`# Set the execution policy to Restricted`** **`Set-ExecutionPolicy -ExecutionPolicy Restricted -Scope LocalMachine`** This is the most restrictive policy. No scripts can run, and PowerShell can only be used interactively.

AllSigned	Mandates that scripts be signed by an authorized publisher.	Suitable for environments where script integrity is crucial. **# Set the execution policy to AllSigned** **Set-ExecutionPolicy -ExecutionPolicy AllSigned -Scope CurrentUser** This policy allows scripts to run only if a trusted publisher signs them. It provides a balance between security and flexibility.
RemoteSigned	Requires scripts from the internet to be signed; local scripts are not required to be signed.	Default for Windows server computers. Digital signatures mandated for internet scripts. **# Set the execution policy to RemoteSigned** **Set-ExecutionPolicy -ExecutionPolicy RemoteSigned -Scope LocalMachine** Scripts downloaded from the internet need to be signed by a trusted publisher. Locally created scripts can run without a digital signature.
Unrestricted	No signature requirements. All scripts can run.	It is not recommended for production use due to security risks. **# Set the execution policy to Unrestricted** **Set-ExecutionPolicy -ExecutionPolicy Unrestricted -Scope CurrentUser** This policy allows the execution of all scripts without any restrictions. It is the most permissive, but also the least secure.

		Suitable for environments with strict application security implementations.
		
		`# Set the execution policy to Bypass`
		
		`Set-ExecutionPolicy -ExecutionPolicy Bypass -Scope LocalMachine`

`Bypass`	No execution policy checking. All scripts can run without any restrictions.	This policy allows the execution of all scripts and bypasses all execution policies. It is similar to Unrestricted but does not require confirmation for downloaded scripts.

Table 5.1: *Execution policies explained*

Setting Execution Policy in PowerShell Profile

To set the execution policy in your PowerShell profile, you can use the **`Set-ExecutionPolicy`** cmdlet. The profile script is a script that runs automatically when you start a PowerShell session. Each user can have their profile, with different profiles for the PowerShell console and the PowerShell Integrated Scripting Environment (ISE).

Here is how you can set the execution policy in your profile:

Check if a Profile Exists:

First, check if you have a profile by running:

```
Test-Path $Profile
```

If the outcome is $false, it signifies the non-existence of a profile. You can establish one by adhering to these steps

Create a Profile:

If you do not have a profile, you can create one. For the PowerShell console, you might use:

```
New-Item -Path $PROFILE -ItemType File -Force
```

Edit the Profile:

Open the profile file in your preferred text editor. For example:

```
notepad $PROFILE
```

Add the following line to set the execution policy. Choose the appropriate policy (for example, **"RemoteSigned"**, **"Unrestricted"**, and more):

```
Set-ExecutionPolicy -ExecutionPolicy RemoteSigned -Scope CurrentUser
```

Save the file.

Reload the Profile:

After editing the profile, you need to reload it for the changes to take effect. This can be achieved by either closing and reopening PowerShell or by executing the following command:

```
. $PROFILE
```

This command "*dots*" (sources) the profile script, which makes the changes take effect in the current session.

Designing a Self-Signed Certificate for Code Signing

Generating a self-signed certificate provides a viable solution for securing your scripts. This process involves creating a digital certificate that can be used to sign PowerShell scripts, ensuring their authenticity and integrity. Follow the steps mentioned under to craft your self-signed certificate for code signing.

Flow Diagram

A flow diagram to represent the steps to create a Self-Signed Certificate for code signing:

Generate Self-Signed Certificate

Use PowerShell and the **New-SelfSignedCertificate** cmdlet to generate a self-signed certificate.

Add Certificate to Trusted Stores

Add the generated certificate to both the root and trusted publishers certificate stores.

Verify Certificate Presence

Confirm the presence of the self-signed certificate in the personal, root, and trusted publishers certificate stores.

Retrieve Code-Signing Certificate

Fetch the code-signing certificate from the personal certificate store.

Sign PowerShell Scripts

Use the acquired code-signing certificate to sign your PowerShell scripts with the **`Set-AuthenticodeSignature cmdlet`**.

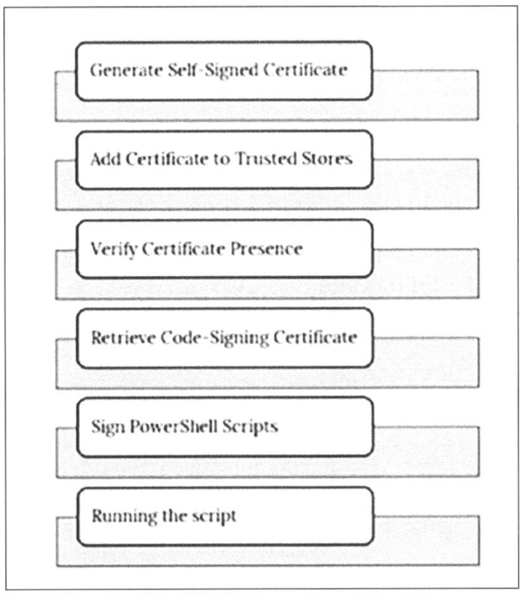

***Figure 5.4**: Steps to create a self-signed certificate for code signing*

Utilize PowerShell for Certificate Generation

Leverage PowerShell to create a self-signed certificate. The **`New-SelfSignedCertificate cmdlet`** is instrumental in this task. Specify relevant details such as the subject name, certificate store location (for example, My for the personal store), and certificate type (**`CodeSigningCert`**).

```
$certificate = New-SelfSignedCertificate -Subject "Powershell
ulitmateGuide Authenticate" -CertStoreLocation Cert:\CurrentUser\My
-Type CodeSigningCert
```

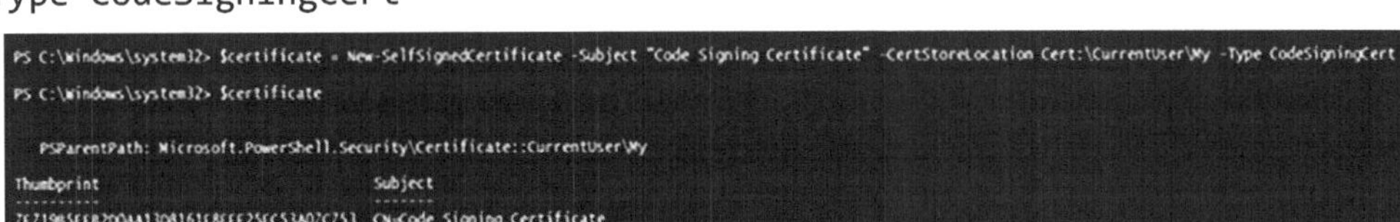

***Figure 5.5**: Create a new self-signed certificate*

Add the Certificate to Trusted Stores

For effective code signing, ensure your certificate is trusted. Add it to both the root and trusted publishers certificate stores using PowerShell. This step is crucial for establishing trust in the legitimacy of your signed scripts.

```
# Add to the root certificate store
$rootStore = [System.Security.Cryptography.X509Certificates.
X509Store]::new("Root","CurrentUser")
$rootStore.Open("ReadWrite")
$rootStore.Add($certificate)
$rootStore.Close()
# Add to the trusted publishers certificate store
$publisherStore = [System.Security.Cryptography.X509Certificates.
X509Store]::new("TrustedPublisher","CurrentUser")
$publisherStore.Open("ReadWrite")
$publisherStore.Add($certificate)
$publisherStore.Close()
```

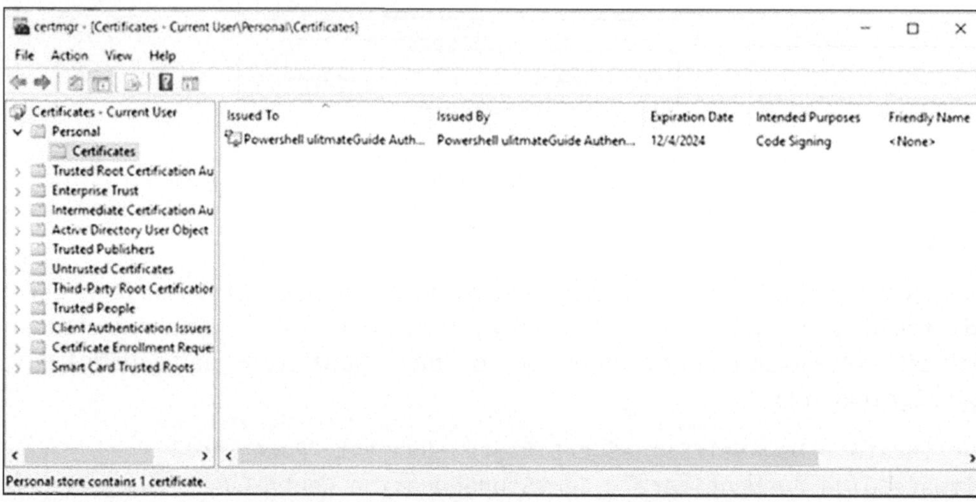

***Figure 5.6**: Add certificate to root certificate store*

Verify Certificate Presence

Confirm that your self-signed certificate is successfully added to the certificate stores by checking its existence using PowerShell commands.

```
# Check if the certificate is in the personal certificate store
Get-ChildItem Cert:\CurrentUser\My | Where-Object {$_.Subject -eq
"CN=Powershell ulitmateGuide Authenticate"}
```

```
# Verify whether the certificate is present in the root certificate store
Get-ChildItem Cert:\CurrentUser\Root | Where-Object {$_.Subject -eq
"CN=Powershell ulitmateGuide Authenticate"}
# Check if the certificate is in the trusted publishers certificate store
Get-ChildItem Cert:\CurrentUser\TrustedPublisher | Where-Object {$_.
Subject -eq "CN=Powershell ulitmateGuide Authenticate"}
```

Retrieve the Code-Signing Certificate

Find the code-signing certificate from the certificate store and prepare it to sign your PowerShell scripts.

```
# Get the code-signing certificate from the local computer's certificate
store with the name *Powershell Script Authenticate* and store it to the
$codeSigningCertificate variable.
$codeSigningCertificate = Get-ChildItem Cert:\LocalMachine\My | Where-Ob-
ject {$_.Subject -eq "CN=Powershell ulitmateGuide Authenticate"}
```

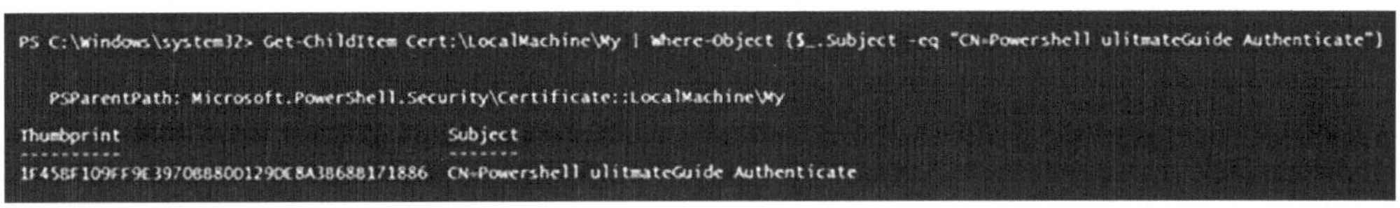

***Figure 5.7**: Retrieve the code-signing certificate*

Signing PowerShell Scripts

Finally, sign your PowerShell scripts using the acquired code-signing certificate. This step ensures that your scripts are authenticated and deemed trustworthy.

```
# Sign the PowerShell script
Set-AuthenticodeSignature -FilePath C:\temp\hello.ps1 -Certificate
$codeSigningCertificate
```

***Figure 5.8**: Signing the PowerShell scripts*

Running the script

It is important to note that changing the execution policy should be done cautiously, and the level of restriction should align with security policies and the trustworthiness of the scripts being executed. In a production environment, using "**AllSigned**" or "**RemoteSigned**" policies is often recommended for security reasons.

Get Current Execution Policy

This command checks and displays the current execution policy, which was set to "**Restricted**." In this mode, PowerShell does not allow the execution of scripts.

```
Get-ExecutionPolicy
```

Output: Restricted

Attempt to Run Script

The error occurs because the script execution is blocked due to the "**Restricted**" execution policy.

```
C:\temp\hello.ps1
```

Output: Error message stating that running scripts is disabled on the system.

Change Execution Policy to AllSigned

Executing this command modifies the execution policy to "**AllSigned**," mandating that all scripts must undergo signing by a trusted publisher before they are permitted to run.

```
Set-ExecutionPolicy AllSigned
```

Run Script Again

After changing the execution policy to "**AllSigned**," you were able to run the script successfully because it is now signed

```
C:\temp\hello.ps1
```

Output: Hello-World

Figure 5.9: *Run scripts with the signed execution policy*

View the digital signature of a signed PowerShell script using the **Get-AuthenticodeSignature** cmdlet. This cmdlet provides information about the digital signature associated with a signed script.

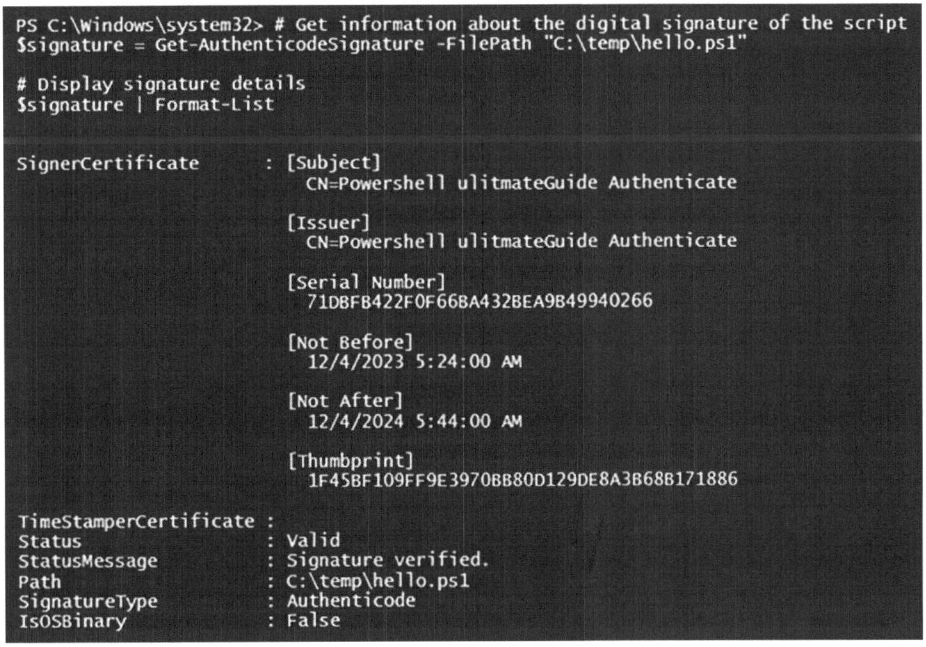

***Figure 5.10**: View the digital signature of a signed PowerShell script*

By following these steps, you will establish a secure foundation for code signing using a self-signed certificate, enhancing the integrity and authenticity of your PowerShell scripts.

Bulk Code Signing for All PowerShell Scripts

Signing PowerShell scripts is a good practice to ensure their integrity and authenticity. You can use the **`Set-AuthenticodeSignature`** cmdlet, **`Get-ChildItem`**, and the **`-Recurse`** parameter to sign all PowerShell scripts recursively in a directory and its subdirectories.

```
# Specify the path to your PowerShell scripts

$scriptDirectory = "C:\Path\To\Your\Scripts"


# Generate or obtain a code-signing certificate (replace $certificate with your actual certificate variable)

$certificate = New-SelfSignedCertificate -Subject "PowerShell Script Signing" -CertStoreLocation Cert:\CurrentUser\My -Type CodeSigningCert


# Set the Authenticode signature for all PowerShell scripts in the specified directory and its subdirectories
```

```
Get-ChildItem -Path $scriptDirectory -Recurse -Include *.ps1 |
ForEach-Object {
    Set-AuthenticodeSignature -FilePath $_.FullName -Certificate
$certificate
}
```

PowerShell for Securely Obtaining User Credentials

The script aims to request usernames and passwords from users securely. The recommended solution involves utilizing the Get-Credential cmdlet to obtain user credentials in a secure manner. The obtained credentials, stored in the $credential variable, can then be used in subsequent commands without compromising sensitive information.

Here is the provided script snippet, along with some additional explanations:

```
# To request a credential from the user securely, use the Get-Credential
cmdlet
$credential = Get-Credential
```

The Get-Credential cmdlet is employed to prompt the user for their credentials interactively. This ensures that the user's password is handled securely throughout the process. The resulting $credential variable contains the username and a **SecureString** representation of the password.

```
# Once you have the username and password, you can pass that information
securely to other commands
# that accept a PowerShell credential object
# For example, if a command supports a SecureString for its sensitive
information: #
$result = Some-Command -Credential $credential
```

The obtained credentials in the $credential variable can be easily passed to other commands that accept PowerShell credential objects. If an order supports a **SecureString** for handling sensitive information, the **PsCredential** object provides a username property for the username and a password property for a **SecureString** containing the user's password.

This approach enhances the security of handling user credentials within PowerShell scripts, maintaining the confidentiality of sensitive information.

Demonstrates the use of Invoke-Command with different variations for handling credentials.

Let us break down each section:

Using Get-Credential Prompt

In this section, the target computer is specified, user credentials are requested, and the Invoke-Command is subsequently employed to execute a script block on the remote computer using the provided credentials.

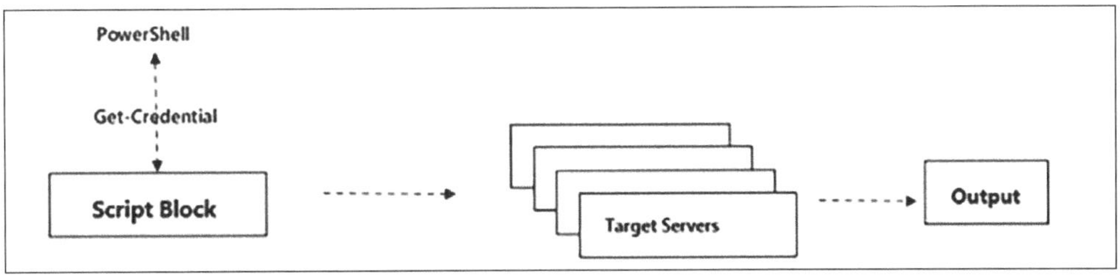

***Figure 5.11**: Demonstrates the use of Invoke-Command*

```
# Define the target computer and credentials
$remoteComputer = "Remotecomputer"
$credentials = Get-Credential -UserName "pjayaram" -Message "Enter your password"


# Define the script block or command to be executed on the remote computer
$scriptBlock = {
    # Your commands go here
    Get-Process
}


# Use Invoke-Command to run the script block on the remote computer with specified credentials
Invoke-Command -ComputerName $remoteComputer -Credential $credentials -ScriptBlock $scriptBlock
```

Using `ConvertFrom-SecureString`:

This part additionally demonstrates saving the encrypted password to a file, reading it back, and creating a **`PsCredential`** object for later use in Invoke-Command.

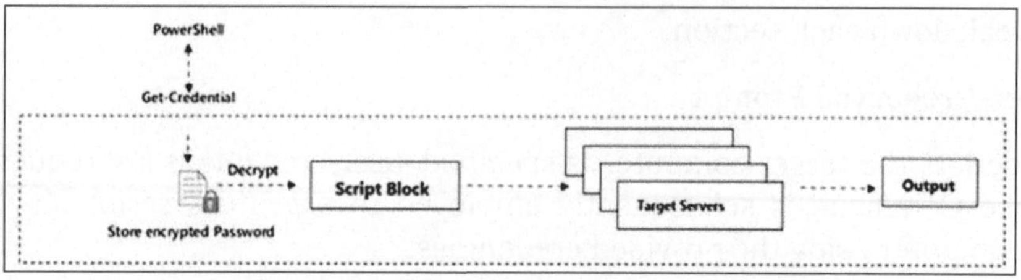

Figure 5.12: *Use the encrypted connection string*

```
# Define the target computer and credentials
$remoteComputer = "RemoteComputer"
$credentials = Get-Credential -UserName "pjayaram" -Message "Enter your
password"

# Store the password securely in a file
$credentials.Password | ConvertFrom-SecureString | Set-Content c:\temp\
password.txt

# Retrieve the password from the file
$password = Get-Content c:\temp\password.txt | ConvertTo-SecureString

# Create a PsCredential object with the stored credentials
$cred = New-Object System.Management.Automation.PsCredential "pjayaram",
$password

# Define the script block or command to be executed on the remote
computer
$scriptBlock = {
    # Your commands go here
    Get-Process
}

# Use Invoke-Command to run the script block on the remote computer with
specified credentials
Invoke-Command -ComputerName $remoteComputer -Credential $cred -Script-
Block $scriptBlock
```

Overall, these sections showcase different approaches to handling credentials with Invoke-Command, including interactive prompting and handling stored encrypted passwords. The script employs the **ConvertFrom-SecureString** and **ConvertTo-SecureString** cmdlets for secure credential persistence.

Note: *Enabling PowerShell remoting should be done cautiously, considering security implications. It allows remote execution of scripts, which can pose risks if not properly configured and secured. This will be discussed in more detail in the later chapters.*

PowerShell Constrained Language

PowerShell constrained language constitutes a language mode within the PowerShell scripting environment, strategically crafted to facilitate routine administrative tasks while concurrently imposing restrictions on access to language elements of a sensitive nature. These restricted elements could be utilized to invoke arbitrary Windows APIs, mitigating potential security risks associated with unauthorized script execution.

To activate PowerShell constrained language mode, one can effortlessly manipulate a specific property within a PowerShell session, as exemplified here:

```
$ExecutionContext.SessionState.LanguageMode

# Output: FullLanguage

$ExecutionContext.SessionState.LanguageMode = "ConstrainedLanguage"
$ExecutionContext.SessionState.LanguageMode

# Output: ConstrainedLanguage
```

In the provided example, an attempt to execute the method

```
[System.Console]::WriteLine("Hello world")
```

Within constrained language mode results in an error, exemplifying the restricted nature of this mode:

```
Cannot invoke method. Method invocation is supported only on core types in this language mode. At line:1 char:1 + [System.Console]::WriteLine ("Hello world") + ~~~~~~~~~~~~~~~~~~~~~~~~~~~~~~~~~~~~~~~~~~ + Category Info : InvalidOperation: (:) [], RuntimeException + FullyQualifiedErrorId : MethodInvocationNotSupportedInConstrainedLanguage
```

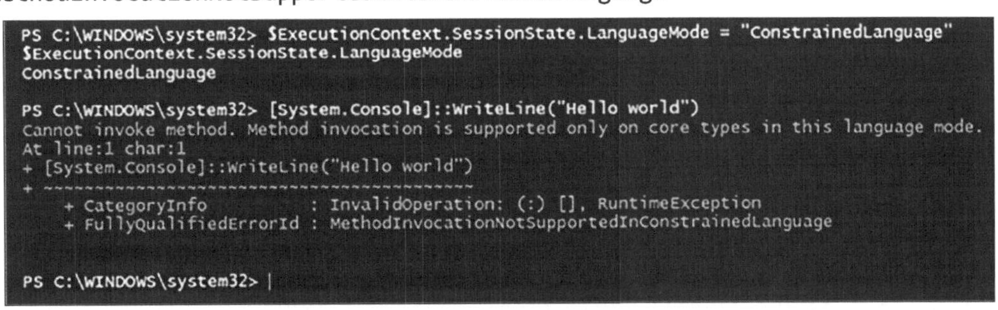

***Figure 5.13**: PowerShell constrained language*

It is important to note, however, that despite the constraints imposed by constrained language mode, its security efficacy is not absolute. A user retains the ability to initiate a new PowerShell session in full language mode, thereby circumventing the restrictions and gaining unrestricted access to the complete set of PowerShell features. Consequently, the constrained language mode serves as one layer in a comprehensive security strategy, and additional security measures and best practices should complement its effectiveness.

Conclusion

While PowerShell offers additional layers of security through features like constrained language mode, script signing, and credential management, it is crucial to recognize that relying solely on PowerShell for security is insufficient. While these features contribute significantly to mitigating risks, considering PowerShell as a standalone bastion of security is a limited perspective. Comprehensive security strategies must integrate PowerShell within a broader framework that includes robust network security, stringent access controls, regular security audits, and adherence to industry best practices. A holistic approach ensures that PowerShell is a valuable component within a fortified security architecture, enhancing its capabilities without overlooking the multifaceted nature of modern cybersecurity challenges.

In the upcoming chapter on PowerShell Advanced Functions, we will explore various topics to elevate your scripting proficiency. From understanding advanced functions and parameter attributes to leveraging the power of pipeline input and implementing robust error handling, this chapter aims to provide comprehensive insights for mastering advanced PowerShell scripting techniques.

Points to Remember

PowerShell Security Overview

PowerShell is a versatile tool for system administration and automation, but its power also poses security challenges. Understanding and implementing robust security measures are crucial.

PowerShell Execution Policy

Execution policies control script execution in PowerShell. They range from Restricted (no scripts allowed) to Unrestricted (all scripts allowed). Choosing the right policy is vital for security.

Execution Policy Essentials

Execution policies, like `Restricted` or `AllSigned`, dictate how PowerShell scripts run. They serve as a fundamental security control, preventing unauthorized or malicious script execution.

Setting Execution Policy in PowerShell Profile

Setting execution policies in PowerShell profiles ensures consistent policy enforcement. It is a best practice to tailor policies to specific environments and security requirements.

Designing a Self-Signed Certificate for Code Signing

Code signing using self-signed certificates enhances script security. This process involves creating and using certificates to verify script integrity and authenticity.

PowerShell for Securely Obtaining User Credentials

PowerShell offers secure methods for obtaining and handling user credentials. Emphasizing encryption and adherence to secure protocols is essential to protect sensitive information.

PowerShell Constrained Language

Constrained language mode in PowerShell restricts potentially unsafe language elements, enhancing security by minimizing attack vectors. It is beneficial in scenarios where a more restrictive script environment is needed.

Multiple Choice Questions

1. What does a PowerShell Execution Policy control?
   a. Network access
   b. Script execution
   c. User authentication
   d. System updates
2. Which execution policy allows scripts signed by a trusted publisher to run?
   a. `Restricted`
   b. `RemoteSigned`
   c. `AllSigned`
   d. `Unrestricted`
3. What is the primary purpose of code signing with a self-signed certificate in PowerShell?
   a. Encrypting scripts
   b. Enhancing script readability

c. Verifying script integrity and authenticity

d. Allowing unrestricted script execution

4. In PowerShell, what does constrained language mode aim to restrict?

    a. Script execution on weekends

    b. Access to network resources

    c. Potentially unsafe language elements

    d. User authentication processes

5. What is a best practice for securely handling user credentials in PowerShell scripts?

    a. Storing credentials in plaintext

    b. Using unencrypted HTTP for credential transmission

    c. Implementing encryption and secure protocols

    d. Sharing credentials openly within the script

Answers

1. b
2. c
3. c
4. c
5. c

Questions

- Describe the role of a PowerShell execution policy in script management.
- Explain the significance of code signing with a self-signed certificate in PowerShell script development.
- In what scenarios might constrained language mode in PowerShell be particularly beneficial?
- Discuss the importance of secure credential handling in PowerShell scripting and automation.
- How can PowerShell Execution Policies be adjusted to balance security and operational requirements in different environments?

Key Terms

- **PowerShell Execution Policy:** Rules that determine the conditions for running PowerShell scripts.
- **Code Signing:** Code Signing involves digitally signing scripts or code to confirm their source and guarantee their integrity.
- **Self-Signed Certificate:** A digital certificate generated and signed by the entity to which it is issued, providing a way to verify the authenticity of scripts.
- **Constrained Language Mode:** A security feature in PowerShell that restricts access to potentially unsafe language elements.
- **Credential Management:** Secure handling and storage of user credentials to prevent unauthorized access.
- **Script Authentication:** Verifying the authenticity of scripts to ensure they come from trusted sources.
- **Execution Policy Level:** The specific setting within the PowerShell Execution Policy, such as `Restricted`, `AllSigned`, `RemoteSigned`, `Unrestricted`, or `Bypass`.
- **Security Profile:** Custom configurations and settings applied to PowerShell sessions, often stored in profiles to enforce security measures.
- **Best Practices:** Recommended guidelines and methods recognized as effective and secure for specific tasks or operations.

CHAPTER 6

PowerShell Advanced Functions

Introduction

Welcome to the chapter on PowerShell advanced functions and scripting techniques. This chapter explores the intricacies of crafting advanced functions in PowerShell. The topics covered include parameter validation, pipeline support, utilizing script blocks, switch parameters, navigating through function parameters, and leveraging common parameters. You will learn how to create functions that are not only powerful but also adaptable to various scenarios. Additionally, we touch upon the significance of adequate documentation, providing a comprehensive guide to mastering PowerShell scripting.

Structure

In this chapter, we will cover the following topics:

- PowerShell Advanced Functions
    - Parameter Validation
    - Pipeline Support
    - Using Script Blocks
    - Switch Parameter
    - Navigating Parameters
- Common Parameters
- Harnessing the Magic of Parameter Splatting
- Running Scripts
- Debugging and Error Handling

PowerShell Advanced Functions

PowerShell functions are named blocks of code that can perform a specific task or set of tasks. Functions are essential for creating reusable and modular code, and promote better script organization and maintainability. They allow you to encapsulate logic, parameters, and output within a defined scope.

Here is a basic structure of a PowerShell function:

```
function MyFunction {
[CmdletBinding()]
    param (
        [parameter type] $Parameter1,
        [parameter type] $Parameter2
    )
    # Function logic here
    return $result
}
```

Let us break down the key elements:

- **`Function`**: This keyword is used to declare the beginning of a function.
- **`MyFunction`**: This is the name of the function.
- **`param`**: This keyword is used to declare the function parameters. These parameters allow you to pass values to the function when it is called.
- **`$Parameter1`**, **`$Parameter2`**: These are examples of parameters. You can specify the expected parameters with their types.
- **`Function Logic`**: This is where you write the actual code that the function will execute.
- **`return $result`**: If you want your function to produce output, use the **`return`** keyword. The **`$result`** variable can be replaced with the result you wish to return.

You can then call your function by typing its name and providing any required arguments:

```
$result = MyFunction -Parameter1 "Value1" -Parameter2 "Value2"
```

Basic Parameter Syntax:

Here is a basic example of a function with parameters and default values:

```
function Get-Message {
[CmdletBinding()]
    param (
        [string]$Text = "Hello",
        [int]$Repeat = 1
    )

    1..$Repeat | ForEach-Object {
        Write-Output $Text
    }
}

# Example usage:
Get-Message                          # Uses default values "Hello" and 1
Get-Message -Text "Hi"               # Uses "Hi" for Text and default value 1 for Repeat
Get-Message -Text "Greetings" -Repeat 3  # Uses "Greetings" for Text and 3 for Repeat
```

PowerShell functions can use the following parameter in its definition:

Parameter	Description
`Position`	Specifies the position of the parameter in the parameter list. Parameters with lower positions are supplied first.
`Mandatory`	Indicates whether the parameter is required. If set to **`$true`**, the user must provide a value for the parameter.
`ValueFromPipeline`	Allows the parameter to accept input from the pipeline. When this is set to $true, the parameter can receive pipeline input directly.
`ValueFromPipelineByPropertyName`	Enables the parameter to accept input from the pipeline by property name. The parameter value is matched with the property name of the incoming pipeline object. If there is a match, the parameter is populated with the corresponding property value.

***Table 6.1**: Parameters and their descriptions*

Let us look at a few examples of using functions in PowerShell.

- **A basic PowerShell function that adds two numbers:**

```
function Add-Numbers {
[CmdletBinding()]
    param (
        [Parameter(Position=0, Mandatory=$true)]
        [int]$Number1,

        [Parameter(Position=1, Mandatory=$true)]
        [int]$Number2
    )

    $result = $Number1 + $Number2
    Write-Output "The sum of $Number1 and $Number2 is: $result"
}

# Usage example:
Add-Numbers -Number1 5 -Number2 10
```

- **Function to calculate the area of a rectangle:**

```
function Get-RectangleArea {
[CmdletBinding()]
    param (
        [Parameter(Position=0, Mandatory=$true)]
        [double]$Length,
        [Parameter(Position=1, Mandatory=$true)]
        [double]$Width
    )

    $area = $Length * $Width
    Write-Output "The area of the rectangle with length $Length and
width $Width is: $area square units"
}

# Usage example:
Get-RectangleArea -Length 5.5 -Width 3.2
```

Let us delve into parameter validation, pipeline support, and advanced scripting techniques in PowerShell:

- **Parameter Validation:**

Parameter validation is a way to ensure that the values provided for the parameters meet specific criteria before the function or script proceeds. PowerShell provides several validation attributes that you can use to define parameter constraints.

Here are some common validation attributes:

- **`[ValidateNotNull()]`**: Ensures that the parameter is not null.
- **`[ValidateNotNullOrEmpty()]`**: Ensures that the parameter is not null or an empty string.
- **`[ValidateRange()]`**: It specifies a range of valid values for numerical parameters.
- **`[ValidateSet()]`**: Restricts the parameter to a predefined set of values.
- **`[ValidateScript({})]`**: Allows you to provide a script block that defines custom validation logic.

For example, the following code uses **`[ValidateRange(1, 100)]`** to ensure that the **`SideLength`** parameter must be between 1 and 100.

```
function Get-Square {
[CmdletBinding()]
    param (
        [Parameter(Position=0, Mandatory=$true)]
        [ValidateRange(1, 100)]
        [int]$SideLength
    )

    $area = $SideLength * $SideLength
    Write-Output "The area of the square with side length $SideLength
is: $area square units"
}
```

PowerShell code gives an error if a user inputs a value other than a defined parameter value (refer to *Figure* 6.1).

```
Get-Square: C:\temp\SampleNumbers.Ps1:11:12
Line |
  11 |  Get-Square 1222
     |             ~~~~
     | Cannot validate argument on parameter 'SideLength'. The 1222 argument is greater than the maximum allowed range of 100. Supply an
     | argument that is less than or equal to 100 and then try the command again.
```

Figure 6.1: *Parameter validation error*

- **Pipeline Support:** PowerShell supports pipeline input that can pass the output of one command as input to another. To enable a function to accept pipeline input, you use the **`ValueFromPipeline`** or **`ValueFromPipelineByPropertyName`** parameter attribute.
    - **`ValueFromPipeline`**: Allows the function to accept input directly from the pipeline.
    - **`ValueFromPipelineByPropertyName`** enables the function to accept input by property name from the pipeline.

The following function, **`Get-CubeVolume`**, accepts input from the pipeline and calculates the volume for each side length.

```
function Get-CubeVolume {
    [CmdletBinding()]
    param (
        [Parameter(Position=0, Mandatory=$true, ValueFromPipeline=$true, 
ValueFromPipelineByPropertyName=$true)]
        [int]$SideLength
    )

    process {
        $volume = $SideLength * $SideLength * $SideLength
        Write-Output "The volume of the cube with side length 
$SideLength is: $volume cubic units"
    }
}

# Usage example:
1..3 | Get-CubeVolume
```

```
PS C:\temp> . 'C:\temp\SampleNumbers.Ps1'
The volume of the cube with side length 1 is: 1 cubic units
The volume of the cube with side length 2 is: 8 cubic units
The volume of the cube with side length 3 is: 27 cubic units
PS C:\temp>
```

***Figure 6.2**: Pipeline support*

- **Using Script Blocks**: We can also leverage script blocks **`({})`** for advanced logic or for creating dynamic pieces of code.

Consider a real-world scenario where you might want to use a script block for advanced logic. In this example, we will create a function that retrieves information about a file or folder and allows the user to specify custom properties to display. We will use a script block to select and display properties dynamically.

```
function Execute-ScriptBlock {
[CmdletBinding()]

    param (
        [scriptblock]$CodeBlock
    )

    Write-Host "Executing the provided script block..."
    & $CodeBlock
    Write-Host "Script block execution complete."
}
```

The following example demonstrates passing a simple script block that writes a message to the console.

```
# Using a simple script block
$SimpleBlock = { Write-Host "Hello from the script block!" }
Execute-ScriptBlock -CodeBlock $SimpleBlock
```

The following example shows passing a script block that includes a parameter. The function then provides a value for that parameter during execution.

```
# Using a script block with parameters
$ParamsBlock = {
    param ($Name)
    Write-Host "Hello, $Name!"
}
Execute-ScriptBlock -CodeBlock $ParamsBlock -Name "John"
```

- **Switch Parameters**: Switch parameters are boolean parameters that do not require a value. They are used when you want to include or exclude a certain behavior without specifying a value.

The following example utilizes a switch statement for handling different cases based on the value of **`$Fruit`**. Depending on the fruit, it includes additional information about **`color`** and **`taste`**.

```
function Get-FruitInfo {
[CmdletBinding()]
```

```
    param (
        [string]$Fruit,
        [switch]$IncludeColor,
        [switch]$IncludeTaste
    )

    $fruitInfo = "Information for $Fruit"

    switch ($Fruit) {
        "Apple" {
            $fruitInfo += "`nType: Tree Fruit"
            if ($IncludeColor) { $fruitInfo += "`nColor: Red or Green"
}
            if ($IncludeTaste) { $fruitInfo += "`nTaste: Sweet" }
        }
        "Banana" {
            $fruitInfo += "`nType: Tropical Fruit"
            if ($IncludeColor) { $fruitInfo += "`nColor: Yellow" }
            if ($IncludeTaste) { $fruitInfo += "`nTaste: Sweet and
Creamy" }
        }
        "Orange" {
            $fruitInfo += "`nType: Citrus Fruit"
            if ($IncludeColor) { $fruitInfo += "`nColor: Orange" }
            if ($IncludeTaste) { $fruitInfo += "`nTaste: Citrusy" }
        }
        default {
            $fruitInfo += "`nSorry, information not available for
$Fruit."
        }
    }

    Write-Host $fruitInfo
```

```
}

# Example 1: Get information for an Apple with color and taste details
Get-FruitInfo -Fruit "Apple" -IncludeColor -IncludeTaste
Output:
```

```
Information for Apple
Type: Tree Fruit
Color: Red or Green
Taste: Sweet
```

Figure 6.3: *Code example 1 output*

```
# Example 2: Get information for a Banana with color details
Get-FruitInfo -Fruit "Banana" -IncludeColor
Output:
```

```
Information for Banana
Type: Tropical Fruit
Color: Yellow
```

Figure 6.4: *Code example 2 output*

```
# Example 3: Get information for an Orange with taste details
Get-FruitInfo -Fruit "Orange" -IncludeTaste
Output:
```

```
Information for Orange
Type: Citrus Fruit
Taste: Citrusy
```

Figure 6.5: *Code example 3 output*

```
# Example 4: Try to get information for an unknown fruit
Get-FruitInfo -Fruit "Grape"
Output:
```

```
Information for Grape
Sorry, information not available for Grape.
```

Figure 6.6: *Code example 4 output*

- **Navigating Parameters:**

Providing arguments in the correct order is crucial when dealing with positional parameters. Switch parameters, however, are optional and can be included or excluded as needed. If a function or cmdlet has both positional and switch parameters, positional parameters should be provided before switch parameters. For example:

```
# Correct
Show-Details "John" 25 -City "New York"
```

```
# Incorrect (will result in an error)
Show-Details -City "New York" "John" 25
```

Common Parameters

Common parameters are a set of parameters available in all cmdlets and advanced functions. They provide consistent behavior across PowerShell commands.
Some common parameters include:

- **-Verbose:** Provides detailed information about the operation.

  Example: **Get-Process -Name "notepad" -Verbose**
- **-Debug**: Enables the debug mode.

  Example: **Get-Service -Name "wuauserv" -Debug**
- **-ErrorAction**: Specifies the action to take for non-terminating errors.

  Example: **Remove-Item -Path "C:\Nonexistent\File.txt" -ErrorAction Stop**
- **-ErrorVariable**: Stores error information in a variable.

  Example: **Get-ChildItem -Path "C:\Nonexistent" -ErrorVariable MyErrors**

$MyErrors

- **-OutVariable:** Stores output in a variable.

  Example: **Get-Process -Name "explorer" -OutVariable MyProcess**

$MyProcess

- **-OutBuffer:** Sets the number of objects to buffer before sending the output.

Example: **Get-Process -OutBuffer 5**

Let us create a function that uses several common parameters, including **Verbose**, **Debug**, **ErrorAction**, **ErrorVariable**, **OutVariable**, and **OutBuffer**.

```
function Get-ModifiedFiles {
    [CmdletBinding()]
    param (
        [Parameter(Position=0, Mandatory=$true,
ValueFromPipeline=$true)]
        [string]$Path,

        [Parameter(Position=1)]
```

```
        [string]$Extension = "*"
    )

    process {
        try {
            # Enable Verbose and Debug modes
            Write-Verbose "Searching for files in $Path with extension
$Extension"
            Write-Debug "Debug mode enabled: Performing detailed
operations"

            # Get files with the specified extension
            $files = Get-ChildItem -Path $Path -Filter "*.$Extension"
-File -ErrorAction Stop

            # Simulate a non-terminating error for demonstration
            if ($files.Count -eq 0) {
                throw "No files found with extension $Extension in $Path"
            }

            # Simulate output buffering
            $files | ForEach-Object {
                $_
                Start-Sleep -Seconds 1
            }

        } catch {
            # Handle errors and store in the error variable
            Write-Error "Error: $_"
            $script:MyErrors += $_
        }
    }
}
```

```
# Example Usage:
$script:MyErrors = @()  # Initialize the error variable
$modifiedFiles = Get-ModifiedFiles -Path "C:\Example" -Extension "txt"
-Verbose -Debug -ErrorAction Stop -ErrorVariable MyErrors -OutVariable
ModifiedFiles -OutBuffer 3
```

Documenting Your PowerShell

Documenting your PowerShell scripts and functions is crucial to maintaining and sharing code. PowerShell uses comment-based help to provide documentation for functions and scripts. Comment-based help lets you include information about the purpose, usage, parameters, examples, and more within your script. This documentation becomes accessible through the Get-Help cmdlet.

Here is a guide on how to document your PowerShell scripts and functions effectively:

1. **Comment-Based Help Structure**

Use comment blocks (`<# ... #>`) at your script's or function's beginning to structure your comment-based help. This type of documentation allows users to understand how to use the function, its purpose, and the parameters it accepts and provides examples.

The function Get-Factorial calculates the factorial of a given number using recursion. Comment-Based Help provides information about the function's purpose, parameters, and examples.

```
<#
.SYNOPSIS
Brief description of the script or function.


.DESCRIPTION
Detailed explanation of the functionality.


.PARAMETER ParameterName
Description of each parameter with details like type, purpose, and
constraints.


.EXAMPLE
Examples demonstrating how to use the script or function.
```

```
.NOTES
Additional notes, such as author, version, or updates.
#>
```

Let us look at an example of using a command-based help structure in a function or script.

```
<#
.SYNOPSIS
This function adds two numbers.

.DESCRIPTION
The Add-Numbers function takes two numbers as input and returns their
sum.


.PARAMETER Number1
The first number to be added. (Type: int, Mandatory: $true)


.PARAMETER Number2
The second number to be added. (Type: int, Mandatory: $true)


.EXAMPLE
Add-Numbers -Number1 5 -Number2 10
Calculates the sum of 5 and 10.


.NOTES
Author: Your Name
Version: 1.0
#>
function Add-Numbers {
[CmdletBinding()]

    param (
        [Parameter(Position=0, Mandatory=$true)]
        [int]$Number1,
```

```
        [Parameter(Position=1, Mandatory=$true)]
        [int]$Number2
    )

    $result = $Number1 + $Number2
    Write-Output "The sum of $Number1 and $Number2 is: $result"
}
Usage:
Get-Help Add-Numbers
```

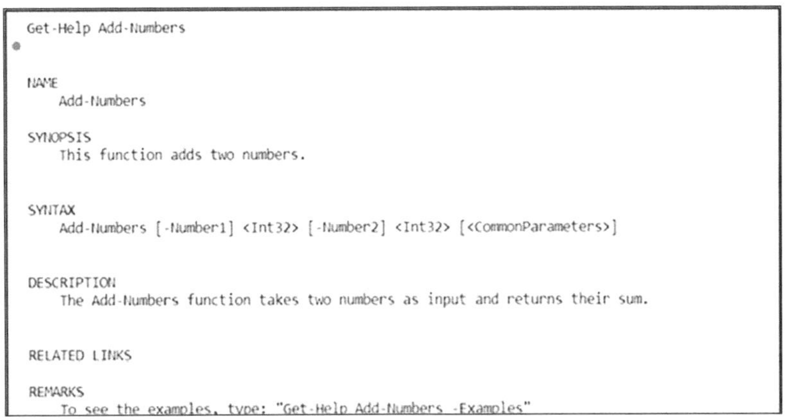

```
Get-Help Add-Numbers

NAME
    Add-Numbers

SYNOPSIS
    This function adds two numbers.


SYNTAX
    Add-Numbers [-Number1] <Int32> [-Number2] <Int32> [<CommonParameters>]


DESCRIPTION
    The Add-Numbers function takes two numbers as input and returns their sum.


RELATED LINKS

REMARKS
    To see the examples, type: "Get-Help Add-Numbers -Examples"
```

Figure 6.7: *Command-based help structure*

2. **Function Comment-based Help**

You can leverage comment-based help to document functions within your PowerShell scripts. This approach is akin to the previously demonstrated example but is explicitly tailored to document a function's parameters, inputs, outputs, and examples.

The following example serves as an illustration of utilizing comment-based help for documenting a function.

```
<#
.SYNOPSIS
    This function demonstrates the usage of comment-based help in
PowerShell functions.

.DESCRIPTION
    The Get-Info function retrieves information based on the provided
parameters.
```

```
.PARAMETER Name
    Specifies the name for which information is to be retrieved.

.PARAMETER Age
    Specifies the age for filtering information.

.EXAMPLE
    Get-Info -Name "John"
    Retrieves information for the person with the name "John".

.EXAMPLE
    Get-Info -Age 25
    Retrieves information for all persons with the age of 25.

.NOTES
    File Name      : Get-Info.ps1
    Author         : Your Name
    Version History:
        1.0 - Initial release
#>

function Get-Info {
    [CmdletBinding()]
    param (
        [Parameter(Position=0, Mandatory=$true, ValueFromPipeline=$true,
ValueFromPipelineByPropertyName=$true)]
        [string]$Name,

        [Parameter(Position=1, ValueFromPipeline=$true,
ValueFromPipelineByPropertyName=$true)]
        [int]$Age
    )
```

```
    process {
        # Actual logic to retrieve information would go here
        $result = "Information for $Name"
        if ($Age) {
            $result += " with age $Age"
        }
        Write-Output $result
    }
}

# Usage example:
# Get-Info -Name "John"
# Get-Info -Age 25
```

In this example:

- The `<# ... #>` block initially comment-based help with a synopsis, description, parameter details, examples, and notes.
- The **Get-Info** function retrieves information based on the provided parameters (name and age).
- Inline comments are used for additional explanations within the function.
- Examples of how to use the function are provided in the comment-based help.

When you run **Get-Help Get-Info**, PowerShell will display the information provided in the comment-based help, giving users a clear understanding of the function's purpose and usage.

```
NAME
    Get-Info

SYNOPSIS
    This function demonstrates the usage of comment-based help in PowerShell functions.


SYNTAX
    Get-Info [-Name] <String> [[-Age] <Int32>] [<CommonParameters>]


DESCRIPTION
    The Get-Info function retrieves information based on the provided parameters.


RELATED LINKS

REMARKS
    To see the examples, type: "Get-Help Get-Info -Examples"
    For more information, type: "Get-Help Get-Info -Detailed"
    For technical information, type: "Get-Help Get-Info -Full"
```

Figure 6.8: *Get-help cmdlet*

Harnessing the Magic of Parameter Splatting

Parameter splatting in PowerShell is a powerful technique, and it allows you to pass a collection of key-value pairs (a hashtable) as parameters to a cmdlet or function. This can make your code more readable, flexible, and easier to maintain. Let us explore the magic of parameter splatting in PowerShell.

Basics of Parameter Splatting

- **Hashtable Creation**

Create a hashtable (**@{}**) where keys represent parameter names and values represent the corresponding values.

```
$params = @{
    Parameter1 = "Value1"
    Parameter2 = "Value2"
}
```

- **Splatting Syntax**

Use the splatting syntax (**@**) to pass the hashtable as a parameter to a cmdlet or function.

```
Invoke-Command @params
```

We can write the code again with the PowerShell Splatting as follows:

```
$Params = @{
    "Path"        = "C:\Temp\TestFile.txt"
    "Destination" = "C:\Temp\SQL\CopiedFile.txt"
 }

  Copy-Item @Params
```

Similarly, the example that follows uses Splatting to specify parameters in the function.

```
# Function that uses parameters
function Get-User {
[CmdletBinding()]

    param (
        [string]$FirstName,
        [string]$LastName,
```

```
        [int]$Age
    )

    Write-Output "User Information:"
    Write-Output "First Name: $FirstName"
    Write-Output "Last Name: $LastName"
    Write-Output "Age: $Age"
}

# Using parameter splatting
$userParams = @{
    FirstName = "John"
    LastName = "Doe"
    Age = 30
}
Get-User @userParams
```

- The **`Get-User`** function accepts individual parameters.
- We create a hashtable (**`$userParams`**) with keys corresponding to the parameter names.
- By using splatting (**`@userParams`**), we pass the parameters to the function in a clean and readable way.

Understanding `$Args` and `$PSBoundParameters` in PowerShell Splatting

`$Args` and **`$PSBoundParameters`** are variables that help manage and access command-line arguments passed to a script or function.

- **$Args**: **`$Args`** is an automatic variable representing an array of values passed to a script or function.

It holds all the values provided as arguments without explicitly naming the parameters.

```
function Display-Arguments {
    foreach ($arg in $Args) {
        Write-Output "Argument: $arg"
    }
```

```
}
Display-Arguments 1 "Hello" -Flag $true
```

In this example, **`$Args`** will contain 1, "**`Hello`**", and **`-Flag $true`**. It captures all values passed, including positional arguments and named parameters.

- **`$PSBoundParameters`**: It is an automatic variable with a dictionary of named parameters explicitly declared in a function or script. It includes only the parameters defined within the function or script.

```
function Display-BoundParameters {
[CmdletBinding()]

    param (
        [string]$Name,
        [int]$Age,
        [switch]$IsStudent
    )

    Write-Output "Name: $Name"
    Write-Output "Age: $Age"
    # Check if the -IsStudent switch is present
    if ($PSBoundParameters.ContainsKey('IsStudent')) {
        Write-Output "Is Student: $($IsStudent.ToBool())"
    }
}

# Example usage
$parameters = @{
    Name = "John"
    Age = 25
    IsStudent = $true
}

Display-BoundParameters @parameters
Display-BoundParameters -Name "John" -Age 30 -Flag $true
```

The **Display-BoundParameters** function has explicit parameters **$Name**, **$Age**, and a switch parameter **$IsStudent**.

Inside the function, it outputs the values of the explicitly named parameters (**$Name** and **$Age**).

It then checks if the **-IsStudent** switch is present in **$PSBoundParameters** using **$PSBoundParameters.ContainsKey('IsStudent')**. If it is present, it outputs the value of the switch.

When working with splatting (@) in PowerShell, you can leverage **$Args** and **$PSBoundParameters** by including them as part of the splatted parameter set. It lets you dynamically pass all or specific arguments, making your scripts and functions more flexible.

Suppose, we have a function that performs various operations on a given set of values, and we want to allow flexibility in how users can provide inputs.

```
function Process-Values {
[CmdletBinding()]

    param (
        [string]$Operation,
        [int]$Multiplier,
        [switch]$Verbose
    )

    # Display explicitly named parameters
    Write-Output "Operation: $Operation"
    Write-Output "Multiplier: $Multiplier"

    # Check if the -Verbose switch is present
    if ($PSBoundParameters.ContainsKey('Verbose')) {
        Write-Output "Verbose mode is enabled."
    }

    # Use $Args to perform the operation on provided values
    foreach ($value in $Args) {
        $result = switch ($Operation) {
```

```
            "Multiply" { $value * $Multiplier }
            "Add" { $value + $Multiplier }
            default { $value }
        }

        # Output results
        if ($Verbose) {
            Write-Output "Result of $Operation with $value and
Multiplier $Multiplier is: $result"
        } else {
            Write-Output "Result: $result"
        }
    }
}

# Example usage with both positional and named parameters
Process-Values -Operation "Multiply" -Multiplier 2 -Verbose 3 5 7
```

In this example:

- The **Process-Values** function has explicit parameters such as **$Operation**, **$Multiplier**, and the **-Verbose** switch.
- Inside the function, it first outputs the values of explicitly named parameters.
- It then checks if the **-Verbose** switch is present using **$PSBoundParameters.ContainsKey('Verbose')**.
- The function utilizes **$Args** to perform the specified operation on values passed as positional arguments.

When you run this function with the provided parameters, you will see the following output:

```
# Example usage with both positional and named parameters
Process-Values -Operation "Multiply" -Multiplier 2 -Verbose 3 5 7

Operation: Multiply
Multiplier: 2
Verbose mode is enabled.
Result of Multiply with 3 and Multiplier 2 is: 6
Result of Multiply with 5 and Multiplier 2 is: 10
Result of Multiply with 7 and Multiplier 2 is: 14
PS C:\Users\rajendragupta>
```

Figure 6.9: *Example of positional and named parameter*

This example showcases how you can combine **$Args** and **$PSBoundParameters** to create a function that provides flexibility in accepting various inputs, whether explicitly named parameters or positional arguments.

Running Scripts

Running scripts in PowerShell can be done using several methods. Here are some common ways to run scripts:

1. **Executing a script**: You can specify its path in the PowerShell console. For example:

```
.\YourScript.ps1
```

This assumes the script is located in the current directory. Provide the full or relative path if it is in a different directory.

Note:

By default, PowerShell only allows scripts to be run if a trusted publisher signs them. To run your scripts, you must set the execution policy to "**RemoteSigned**" or "**Unrestricted.**"

```
Set-ExecutionPolicy RemoteSigned
```

```
Set-ExecutionPolicy Unrestricted
```

In case the script has parameters, type the parameters and parameter values after the script filename for running it.

```
.\YourScript.ps1 -Parameter parametername
```

Script Scope and Dot Sourcing

Script scope refers to the scope in which a script or function is executed. PowerShell uses a hierarchical scope system, and understanding the scope is crucial for managing variables and their lifetimes. Dot sourcing is a technique used to run a script in the current scope instead of launching a new one.

- **Local Scope**: Variables defined within a script or function have local scope by default. They are accessible only within the script or function.
- **Script Scope**: Variables defined in the script without a specific scope modifier have script scope. They are accessible throughout the entire script, including functions.
- **Global scope**: Global variables are accessible across all scopes, including scripts, functions, and the PowerShell session. They are defined with the **$global: scope** modifier.
- **Dot Sourcing**: Dot sourcing is running a script in the current scope rather than launching a new PowerShell session. This allows the script to share

variables with the calling script or session. To dot source a script, use the dot (`.`) operator followed by the script's path.

Example: `C:\scripts\UtilityFunctions.ps1 or. .\UtilityFunctions.ps1`

Let us save a PowerShell script in `C:\Temp\ UtilityFunctions.ps1`

```
function New-Profile
[CmdletBinding()]


{
  Write-Host "Running New-Profile function"
  $profileName = split-path $profile -leaf


  if (test-path $profile)
    {write-error "Profile $profileName already exists on this computer."}
  else
    {new-item -type file -path $profile -force }
}
```

When you execute the UtilityFunctions.ps1 script within its distinct script scope, the New-Profile function and the **`$ProfileName`** variable are only present for the duration of the script's execution. Once the script concludes, both the function and variable cease to exist, as demonstrated in the following illustration:

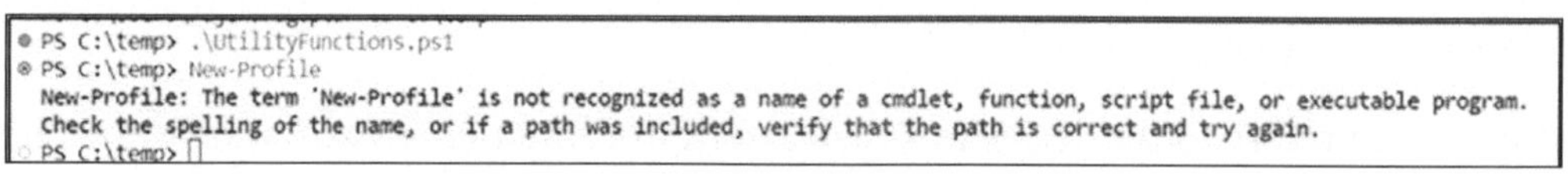

***Figure 6.10** : Error demonstration*

Upon dot-sourcing and executing the script, it introduces the **`New-Profile`** function and the **`$ProfileName`** variable into your session within your current scope. After the script's execution, you can employ the **`New-Profile`** function in your ongoing session, exemplified in the following scenario:

```
C:\PS> . .\UtilityFunctions.ps1


C:\PS> New-Profile
```

Debugging and Error Handling

Debugging and error handling are crucial aspects of scripting and programming in any language, including PowerShell. Here is why they are essential:

Debugging

- **Identifying issues**: Debugging helps identify and locate issues in your code. It lets you understand how your script executes and where it might go wrong.
- **Variable inspection**: Debugging enables you to inspect the values of variables at different points in your script. This is essential for understanding the state of your script during execution.
- **Logic verification**: It helps you verify the logic of your code. By stepping through the script, you can confirm that each part of your code is doing what you expect.
- **Error isolation**: Debugging helps isolate errors to specific lines or blocks of code, making pinpointing and fixing issues easier.
- **Breakpoints**: Placing breakpoints allows you to pause script execution at specific points and inspect the environment, making identifying the cause of problems easier.
- **Interactive debugging**: Tools like Visual Studio Code with the PowerShell extension offer interactive debugging features, making it easier to set breakpoints, step through code, and visualize variables.

Error Handling

- **Graceful Failure**: Proper error handling ensures that your script can fail gracefully. Instead of crashing, it can provide meaningful error messages and exit gracefully.
- **User Feedback**: Error handling lets you provide users with clear and informative error messages. It can help users understand what went wrong and how to resolve it.
- **Preventing Silent Failures**: Errors might go unnoticed without error handling, leading to silent failures. Proper error handling ensures that errors are detected and addressed.
- **Logging**: Error handling facilitates logging, allowing you to record details about errors for later analysis. This is especially important for scripts running in production environments.
- **Security**: Effective error handling helps prevent security vulnerabilities. You can avoid exposing sensitive information or potential security risks by handling errors properly.
- **Maintainability**: Code with proper error handling is more maintainable. It makes it easier for you or others to understand and modify the code in the future.

PowerShell provides different mechanisms to handle errors effectively.

`ErrorAction` Parameter: The **`-ErrorAction`** parameter is used to specify what action should be taken when an error occurs during the execution of a command or script. It allows you to control how PowerShell responds to errors. It accepts different values, each representing an additional action to be taken when an error occurs. Here are some common values:

Value	Description

`Stop`	Stops the command or script immediately upon encountering an error. It is similar to throwing an exception.
	
	`Get-Item -Path "NonExistentPath" -ErrorAction Stop`
	
	`Write-Host "This line will not be executed."`

`Continue`	Ignores the current error and continues with the next command in the script. Allows the script to continue execution despite errors.
	
	`Get-Item -Path "NonExistentPath" -ErrorAction Continue`
	`Write-Host "This line will be executed even if an error occurs."`

`SilentlyContinue`	This is useful for suppressing the error message and continuing with the next command. No error messages are displayed, and the script continues running.
	
	`Get-Item -Path "NonExistentPath" -ErrorAction SilentlyContinue`
	`Write-Host "This line will be executed even if an error occurs, and no error message will be displayed."`

`Ignore`	Ignores the error and continues with the following command. No error message is displayed.
	
	`Get-Item -Path "NonExistentPath" -ErrorAction Ignore`
	`Write-Host "This line will be executed even if an error occurs, and no error message will be displayed."`

***Table 6.2**: ErrorAction parameters*

`$ErrorActionPreference` variable: The **`$ErrorActionPreference`** variable in PowerShell is a global variable that determines the default behavior for how cmdlets respond to non-terminating errors. It is a preference variable that allows you to set a default error action for the entire session or script.

- `SilentlyContinue: $ErrorActionPreference = "SilentlyContinue"`
- `Continue: $ErrorActionPreference = "Continue"`
- `Stop: $ErrorActionPreference = "Stop"`
- `$ErrorActionPreference = "Ignore"`

Example:

```
# Set the default error action preference for the session
$ErrorActionPreference = "Stop"
# Now, any subsequent cmdlet in this session will stop on errors unless overridden
Get-Item -Path "NonExistentPath"
```

`$Error` variable

The **`$Error`** variable is an automatic variable that contains an array of error objects that occurred during the current session. It stores information about the most recent error at index 0, the second most recent at index 1, and so on. Each error object contains **`Exception`**, **`CategoryInfo`**, **`FullyQualifiedErrorId`** properties, and more.

- Accessing the most recent error: **`$Error[0]`**
- Displaying error message: **`Write-Host "Error Message: $($Error[0].Exception.Message)"`**
- Checking if an error occurred:

  ```
  if ($Error) {
      Write-Host "An error occurred."
  }
  Looping through recent errors:

  foreach ($err in $Error) {
      Write-Host "Error: $($err.Exception.Message)"
  }
  ```
- Clearing the error array: **`$Error.Clear()`**

The **`$Error`** variable is particularly useful for examining and handling errors, especially when you want to provide custom error handling or logging. Note that **`$Error`** is a limited-size stack, and new errors push older ones out. The default size is 256, but you can modify it using **$MaximumErrorCount**.

```
# Access the most recent error
$errorDetails = $Error[0]

# Display error details
Write-Host "Error Message: $($errorDetails.Exception.Message)"
Write-Host "Error Category: $($errorDetails.CategoryInfo.Category)"
Write-Host "Error ID: $($errorDetails.FullyQualifiedErrorId)"
```

Try-Catch-Finally

The **try-catch-finally** construct in PowerShell allows you to handle errors in a structured way. It consists of three blocks:

- **Try** Block: The code that might generate an error is placed within the try block.
- **Catch** Block: The catch block code will be executed if an error occurs within the try block. It specifies the type of exception to catch.
- **Finally** Block: The finally block will be executed regardless of whether an error occurred or not. It is useful for cleanup tasks.

Here is an example of using **try-catch-finally**:

```
try {
    # Code that might cause an error
    $result = Get-Item -Path "NonExistentPath"
    Write-Host "Success! Item found: $result"
}
catch {
    # Code to handle the error
    Write-Host "An error occurred: $($_.Exception.Message)"
}
finally {
    # Code that always runs, whether there was an error or not
    Write-Host "Finally block executed."
}
```

Here is a more detailed example using **try-catch-finally** in a script that attempts to read and display the content of a file. If the file does not exist or an error occurs during the process, it will handle the error and display a message.

```
try {
    # Code that might cause an error
    $filePath = "C:\NonExistentFile.txt"
    $fileContent = Get-Content -Path $filePath
    Write-Host "File content: $fileContent"
}
catch [System.IO.FileNotFoundException] {
    # Code to handle the specific error of file not found
    Write-Host "File not found: $($_.Exception.Message)"
}
catch {
    # Code to handle any other type of error
    Write-Host "An error occurred: $($_.Exception.Message)"
}
finally {
    # Code that always runs, whether there was an error or not
    Write-Host "Finally block executed."
}
```

TRAP

The **trap** statement is used for error handling and allows you to define actions to take when specific errors occur. It can catch and handle exceptions within a script or function.

Here is a basic example of how the trap statement works:

```
try {
    # Code that may throw an exception
    $result = 10 / 0
}
catch {
    # Handle the exception
    Write-Host "An error occurred: $($_.Exception.Message)"
}
finally {
    # Code to run regardless of whether an exception occurred or not
    Write-Host "Finally block executed."
```

```
}
```

Now, let us incorporate the trap statement into the example:

```
trap {
    # Handle the exception
    Write-Host "An error occurred: $($_.Exception.Message)"
}
try {
    # Code that may throw an exception
    $result = 10 / 0
}
finally {
    # Code to run regardless of whether an exception occurred or not
    Write-Host "Finally block executed."
}
```

In this case, the trap statement is an alternative to the catch block. Both serve similar purposes, but the trap statement is a bit older in PowerShell and is often considered less flexible than the more modern **try/catch/finally** approach. However, you may still encounter scripts that use trap for error handling.

Here are tabular differences between **try/catch/finally** and **trap** in PowerShell:

Aspect	**try/catch/finally**	**trap**
Purpose	Used for structured exception handling.	Used for catching and handling exceptions.
Syntax	**try {<code>}** **catch {<code>}** **finally {<code>}**	**trap {<code>}**
Blocks	- **try**: It contains the code that might throw an exception. - **catch**: Handles the exception. - **finally**: Contains code that always runs, regardless of an exception.	- **trap**: Contains code to handle exceptions.
Flexibility	More flexible and versatile. Allows handling specific exception types.	Less flexible. Generally catches all exceptions.

Nested Handling	Supports nesting **`try/catch`** blocks for different levels of exception handling.	Can be more challenging for nested error handling scenarios.
Multiple `catch` Blocks	Supports multiple **`catch`** blocks for different exception types.	Handles all exceptions in a single `trap` block.
Scoping	Variables defined in the **`try`** block are scoped to the entire **`try/catch/finally`** construct.	Variables defined in the `trap` block have local scope only within the `trap` block.
Usage in Modern PowerShell	Preferred for modern PowerShell scripting.	Considered less modern and less flexible. It is still used in some scripts.

***Table 6.3**: Try/catch/finally*

Write-Host, Write-Verbose, and Write-Debug:

Write-Host, Write-Verbose, and Write-Debug are different cmdlets in PowerShell that output information, messages, and debugging details to the console. Each cmdlet serves a specific purpose and is helpful in different scenarios.

Cmdlet	**Purpose**	**Controlled by**
`Write-Host`	Display output directly to the console.	N/A
`Write-Verbose`	Display detailed, verbose messages.	**`$VerbosePreference`**
`Write-Debug`	Display messages intended for debugging purposes.	**`$DebugPreference`**

***Table 6.4**: Cmdlets for output*

Let us create a simple script with a function that utilizes **`Write-Host`**, **`Write-Verbose`**, and **`Write-Debug`** for different types of messaging:

```
function Process-Data {
[CmdletBinding()]

    param (
        [string]$InputData
    )
```

```
    # Regular message using Write-Host
    Write-Host "Processing data: $InputData"

    # Verbose message using Write-Verbose
    Write-Verbose "Executing detailed processing steps for data:
$InputData"

    # Debugging information using Write-Debug
    Write-Debug "Debugging info: Input data length is $($InputData.
Length)"

    # Simulating some processing
    $ProcessedData = $InputData.ToUpper()

    # Output the processed data
    $ProcessedData
}

# Set preferences for verbose and debug
$VerbosePreference = 'Continue'
$DebugPreference = 'Continue'

# Call the function with different input data
$result = Process-Data -InputData "example"

# Display the result
Write-Host "Processed result: $result"
```

In this script:

- **`Write-Host`** is used for regular messages to inform about the processing of data.
- **`Write-Verbose`** provides detailed steps about the processing (visible with -Verbose).
- **`Write-Debug`** gives additional debugging information about the length of the input data (visible with -Debug).

- The processed data is returned and displayed using **Write-Host**.

To see the verbose and debug messages, you can run the script with the **-Verbose** and **-Debug** switches:

```
.\YourScript.ps1 -Verbose -Debug
```

This way, you can control the level of detail displayed based on the script's execution context and requirements. Regular messages using **Write-Host** are always visible. The verbose and debug messages are conditionally displayed based on the preferences set and the switches used when invoking the script.

BreakPoints

Breakpoints in PowerShell are markers set in the PowerShell script or function that pause script execution at a specific line or condition, allowing you to inspect variables, step through code, and troubleshoot issues. There are several ways to set breakpoints in PowerShell.

Here is a tabular summary of the cmdlets related to breakpoints in PowerShell:

Cmdlet	Description	Syntax	Example
Set-PSBreakpoint	Set breakpoints in scripts or functions.	Set-PSBreakpoint [-Script] <String> [-Line <Int32>] [-Column <Int32>] ...	Set-PSBreakpoint -Script .\YourScript.ps1 -Line 5
Get-PSBreakpoint	Retrieve information about breakpoints.	Get-PSBreakpoint [[-Script] <String>] [-Line <Int32>] ...	Get-PSBreakpoint
Disable-PSBreakpoint	Disable one or more breakpoints.	Disable-PSBreakpoint [-Id] <Int32[]> ...	Disable-PSBreakpoint -Id 1
Enable-PSBreakpoint	Enable one or more disabled breakpoints.	Enable-PSBreakpoint [-Id] <Int32[]> ...	Enable-PSBreakpoint -Id 1
Remove-PSBreakpoint	Remove one or more breakpoints.	Remove-PSBreakpoint [-Id] <Int32[]> ...	Remove-PSBreakpoint -Id 1

***Table 6.5**: Breakpoints*

Suppose a PowerShell script "**SampleNumbers.PS1**" prints the numbers.

```
# Specify the range for the numbers
$lowerLimit = 1
$upperLimit = 10

# Initialize an empty array to store the generated numbers
$numbers = @()

# Use a for loop to generate numbers and add them to the array
for ($i = $lowerLimit; $i -le $upperLimit; $i++) {
    $numbers += $i
}

# Display the generated numbers
Write-Host "Generated Numbers: $numbers"
```

Use the **Set-PSBreakpoint** to set the breakpoint at line 9, as shown in *Figure 6.11*.

```
Set-PSBreakpoint "SampleNumbers.Ps1" -Line 9
```

```
PS C:\temp> Set-PSBreakpoint "SampleNumbers.Ps1" -Line 9

  ID Script                      Line Command                    Variable
  -- ------                      ---- -------                    --------
   5 SampleNumbers.Ps1              9
```

***Figure 6.11**: Set-breakpoint example*

If you run the **Get-PSBreakPoint** cmdlet, it lists the applied breakpoints.

```
PS C:\temp> Get-PSBreakpoint

  ID Script                      Line Command                    Variable
  -- ------                      ---- -------                    --------
   5 SampleNumbers.Ps1              9
```

***Figure 6.12:** Get-PSBreakpoint example*

Now, run the script and it enters into the debug mode.

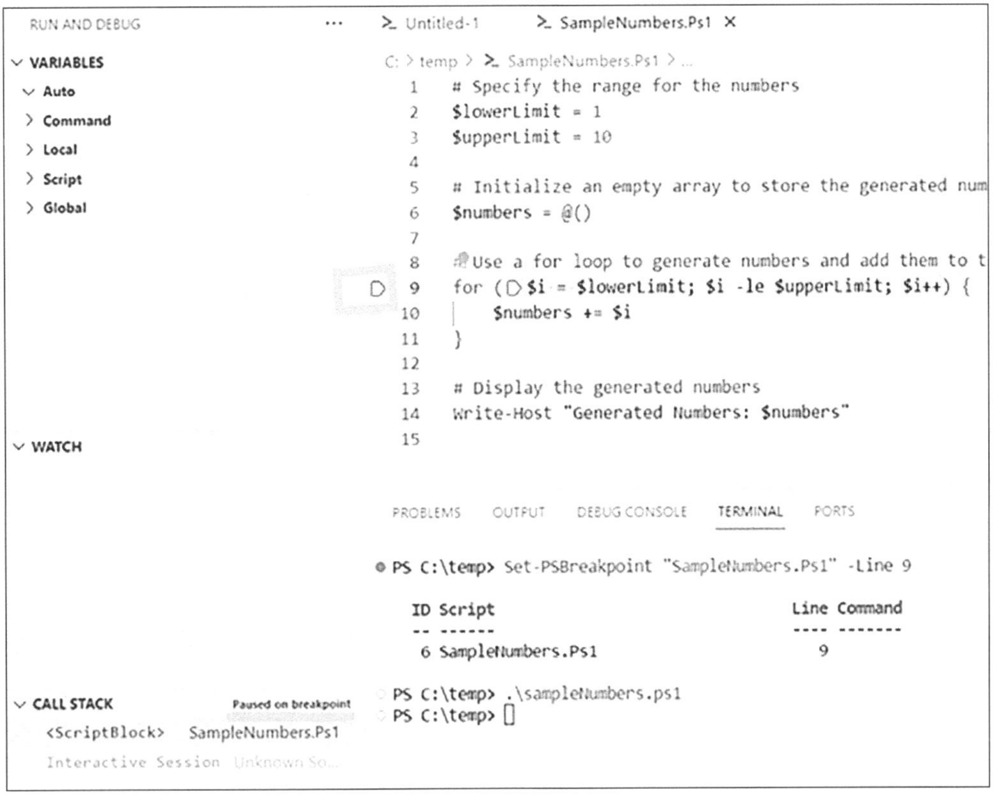

Figure 6.13: *Debugging in PowerShell*

If you type question mark(**?**) or **h**, it lists the options as follows:

```
PS C:\temp> ?

 s, stepInto         Single step (step into functions, scripts, etc.)
 v, stepOver         Step to next statement (step over functions, scripts, etc.)
 o, stepOut          Step out of the current function, script, etc.

 c, continue         Continue operation
 q, quit             Stop operation and exit the debugger
 d, detach           Continue operation and detach the debugger.

 k, Get-PSCallStack Display call stack

 l, list             List source code for the current script.
                     Use "list" to start from the current line, "list <m>"
                     to start from line <m>, and "list <m> <n>" to list <n>
                     lines starting from line <m>

 <enter>             Repeat last command if it was stepInto, stepOver or list

 ?, h                displays this help message.
```

Figure 6.14: *Debugging help*

You can check the code conditions or line at the breakpoint. To continue executing the code, enter c and press enter.

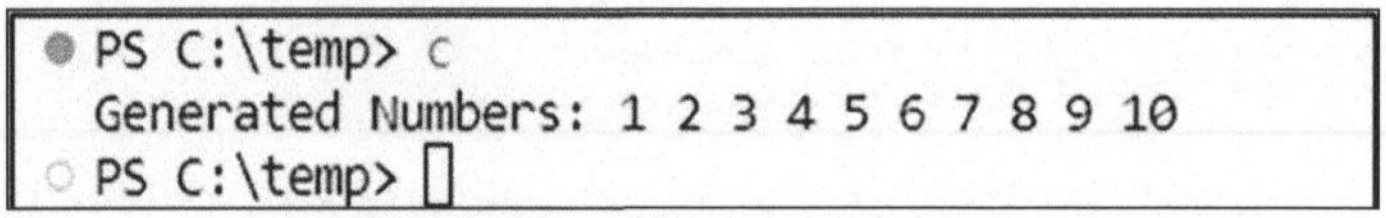

Figure 6.15: *Breakpoint example*

Variable Breakpoint

A variable breakpoint allows you to pause script execution when a specific variable is read, written, or has its value changed. This can be useful for debugging to understand how a variable's value is being manipulated during script execution.

```
# Define a variable
$myVariable = 42

# Set a variable breakpoint on the variable $myVariable
Set-PSBreakpoint -Variable myVariable -Mode ReadWrite -Action {
    Write-Host "Variable breakpoint triggered for myVariable. Value: $($myVariable)"
}

# Perform some operations that involve the variable
$myVariable = $myVariable * 2
$myVariable++

# Remove the variable breakpoint when done debugging
Remove-PSBreakpoint -Id 1  # Replace 1 with the actual breakpoint ID displayed when the breakpoint was set
```

Wait-Debugger

The Wait-Debugger cmdlet is used to pause script execution and wait for a debugger to attach. This can be helpful when you want to debug a PowerShell script or function.

```
# Some code before the debugger pause
Write-Host "Executing code before Wait-Debugger"

# Script to Pause and wait for a debugger to attach
Wait-Debugger
```

```
# Code after the debugger has attached
Write-Host "Executing code after Wait-Debugger"
```

When the Wait-Debugger cmdlet is encountered in the script, it will pause execution, and you will see a message prompting you to attach a debugger. You can then attach a debugger, such as Visual Studio Code with the PowerShell extension, to inspect variables, step through code, and troubleshoot issues.

Remember to remove or comment out the Wait-Debugger line when you are done debugging, as it will prevent the script from running continuously if a debugger is not attached.

Conclusion

This chapter equipped you with essential knowledge and techniques for harnessing the full power of PowerShell in advanced scripting scenarios. From mastering parameter validation to embracing the flexibility of script blocks, switch parameters, and pipeline support, you explored the intricacies of building robust and adaptable functions.

Understanding the nuances of navigating parameters and incorporating common parameters enhances the efficiency and consistency of your scripts. Additionally, we emphasized the importance of thorough documentation, recognizing it as a key element in maintaining, sharing, and scaling your PowerShell scripts effectively.

Armed with these advanced functions and scripting techniques, you are well-prepared to confidently elevate your PowerShell skills and tackle real-world automation challenges. As you continue your journey in PowerShell scripting, remember that constant exploration and practice will further refine your abilities and open doors to even more sophisticated automation solutions.

The upcoming chapter "*Windows Administration using PowerShell*" broadens the scope of Windows administration by leveraging PowerShell to manage and automate various tasks performed by Windows administrators.

CHAPTER 7
Windows Administration Using PowerShell

Introduction

In this chapter, we embark on a journey through the essential tools and techniques that empower Windows administrators to manage and automate tasks in diverse system environments efficiently. As PowerShell has become the *de facto* scripting language for Windows, mastering its capabilities is crucial for administrators looking to streamline administrative workflows and enhance productivity.

We will begin by exploring the fundamental commands every Windows administrator should have in their toolkit. These commands and practical examples form the cornerstone of day-to-day system management. From querying system information to executing remote administration tasks, we will cover the top 10 commands that will empower users to navigate the complexities of Windows environments easily.

We will delve deeper into the powerful realm of Windows Management Instrumentation (WMI) and then shift focus to Common Information Model (CIM) cmdlets, providing an in-depth exploration of their usage in managing system resources. These cmdlets extend the capabilities of PowerShell by leveraging industry standards, offering a standardized way to interact with diverse systems.

We will guide you through reading and writing text files, CSV, XML, and JSON files. As modern systems increasingly rely on these formats for configuration and data exchange, administrators must be adept at seamlessly integrating them into their PowerShell workflows.

Finally, we will conclude our exploration by tackling the challenges of remote administration. PowerShell's robust capabilities in efficiently executing tasks on remote machines make it an indispensable tool for managing distributed environments. We will cover best practices and security considerations and demonstrate how to perform various remote administration tasks.

Structure

In this chapter, we will cover the following topics:

- Windows Administration using PowerShell
- Top 10 Commands for Windows Administrators with Examples
- Querying Windows Management Instrumentation
- Common Information Model (CIM) Cmdlets
- Reading and Writing Text Files
- Working with CSV, XML, and JSON Files
- Performing Remote Administration Tasks

Windows Administration using PowerShell

PowerShell, a robust scripting language and command-line shell built on the .NET Framework, is a powerful tool for automating administrative tasks on the Windows system.

Here are fundamental concepts and commands to help you get started with PowerShell for Windows administration:

- **Cmdlets**: These are the building blocks of PowerShell, like commands in other shells. They are typically written in verb-noun pairs (for example, `Get-Process`, `Stop-Service`).
- **Pipelines**: You can connect cmdlets using the pipe symbol (|) to chain commands and process data sequentially.
- **Objects**: PowerShell handles data as objects with properties and methods, allowing for rich interaction and manipulation.
- **Providers**: They enable PowerShell to access different data stores, including the file system, registry, or Windows Management Instrumentation (WMI).

Common Administration Tasks with PowerShell

The following table lists common administration PowerShell cmdlets and their description.

Task	Cmdlet(s)	Description
Process Management	`Get-Process`, `Stop-Process`	View and stop running processes.
Service Management	`Get-Service`, `Start-Service`, `Stop-Service`	View, start, and stop services.
File and Folder Management	`Get-Item`, `New-Item`, `Remove-Item`	Get information, create, and delete files and folders.
User and Group Management	`Get-ADUser`, `New-ADUser`, `Remove-ADUser`, `Get-ADGroup`, `Add-ADGroupMember`	Manage Active Directory users and groups.
Network Configuration	`Get-NetIPAddress`, `Set-NetIPAddress`, `Test-NetConnection`	View, configure, and test network connectivity.
Registry Management	`Get-ItemProperty`, `Set-ItemProperty`	Read and modify registry values.

***Table 7.1**: Common administration task with PowerShell*

Top 10 Commands for Windows Administrators with Examples

In this section, we will discuss the 10 useful PowerShell commands for Windows administrators, with examples for each:

1. **`Get-Process`**: The **`Get-Process`** cmdlet in PowerShell fetches the active processes on the local or remote system(s). These processes encompass both applications and system-level processes, mirroring the entries visible in the Task Manager's Process tab.

The cmdlet **`Get-Process`** without any parameter returns all active processes, as follows:

```
PS C:\Users\rajendragupta> . $args[0] Get-Process

 NPM(K)    PM(M)      WS(M)     CPU(s)      Id  SI ProcessName
 ------    -----      -----     ------      --  -- -----------
     15    12.25      10.73       0.00   34308   5 Acrobat
     85   312.81     303.38      10.86   35356   5 Acrobat
     28    40.91      44.06       0.14   38780   5 Acrobat
     13     3.26      10.01       0.33   64736   5 Acrobat
     21     9.32      22.35       0.03   13844   5 AcroCEF
     21    33.30      50.32       0.31   18448   5 AcroCEF
     33    17.35      44.70       0.14   22908   5 AcroCEF
     18     7.90      18.37       0.00   26244   5 AcroCEF
     24     9.33      26.25       0.05   28516   5 AcroCEF
```

***Figure 7.1**: Get-Process cmdlet*

To filter records for a specific application or process, filter it using the **-Name** parameter. For example, the following command filters **Chrome** processes.

```
Get-Process -Name chrome
```

```
PS C:\Users\rajendragupta> . $args[0] Get-Process -Name chrome

 NPM(K)    PM(M)      WS(M)     CPU(s)      Id  SI ProcessName
 ------    -----      -----     ------      --  -- -----------
     45   289.63     329.41      24.66    2792   5 chrome
     36   217.01     245.17      13.94   16028   5 chrome
     27   107.74     161.40      11.14   17240   5 chrome
     25    48.43      66.56       0.19   17268   5 chrome
     18    18.34      22.09       0.08   21000   5 chrome
     22    26.34      48.93       0.02   25156   5 chrome
     26   116.23     148.14       2.47   25184   5 chrome
```

Figure 7.2: *Get-Process cmdlet example with filter records*

To filter multiple processes, separate process names with commas as follows:

```
Get-Process -Name chrome , WINWORD
```

Filter records for the process IDs (PIDs) with the parameter PID.

```
Get-Process -PID 17656,15698,1269
```

With the following command, you can filter the Get-Process results by Window Title, such as Notepad.

```
Get-Process | Where-Object {$_.MainWindowTitle -match "Untitled -
Notepad"}
```

```
PS C:\Users\rajendragupta> . $args[0] Get-Process | Where-Object {$_.MainWindowTitle -match "Untitled - Notepad"}

 NPM(K)    PM(M)      WS(M)     CPU(s)      Id  SI ProcessName
 ------    -----      -----     ------      --  -- -----------
     41    82.45      77.98       0.22   29268   5 Notepad
```

Figure 7.3: *Get-Process cmdlet to filter application*

You can run the PowerShell with administrative privileges and use the

-IncludeUserName to see all the processes running with the different users.

```
Get-Process -IncludeUserName
```

However, you can use the following command to look for a specific user process, like a system user.

```
Get-Process -IncludeUserName | where {$_.Username -like "*System*"}
```

Note: *You may get this error if PowerShell is not running under administrative privileges. In this case, close the PowerShell and relaunch with administrative rights.*

```
PS C:\Users\rajendragupta>
PS C:\Users\rajendragupta> . $args[0] Get-Process -IncludeUserName | where {$_.Username -like "*System*"}
Get-Process: untitled:Untitled-1:1:1
Line |
   1 |  Get-Process -IncludeUserName | where {$_.Username -like "*System*"}
     |  ~~~~~~~~~~~~~~~~~~~~~~~~~~~~
     | The 'IncludeUserName' parameter requires elevated user rights. Try running the command again in a session that has been opened with elevated user
     | rights (that is, Run as Administrator).
```

Figure 7.4: *Error with IncludeUserName parameter in Get-Process*

2. **`Get-Service`**: The PowerShell cmdlet **`Get-Service`** helps acquire information about services on local and remote computers, including operating system and application services. It furnishes details such as the services' start type, **`Status`**, **`Name`**, and **`DisplayName`**. The output in the PowerShell console mirrors the services listed in the Services.msc Microsoft Management Console (MMC).

By default, it gives the service name, display name, and status as **`Stopped`**, **`Running`**.

```
PS C:\Users\rajendragupta> . $args[0] Get-Service

Status   Name               DisplayName
------   ----               -----------
Stopped  AarSvc_f7db7d7     Agent Activation Runtime_f7db7d7
Running  AdobeARMservice    Adobe Acrobat Update Service
Stopped  AdtAgent           Microsoft Monitoring Agent Audit Forw…
Stopped  AJRouter           AllJoyn Router Service
Stopped  ALG                Application Layer Gateway Service
Running  aoservice          Citrix Gateway AlwaysOn Service
Stopped  AppIDSvc           Application Identity
Running  Appinfo            Application Information
```

Figure 7.5: *Get-Service cmdlet output*

Filter a specific service, such as **`Winmgmt`**, using the following code.

```
Get-Service -Name Winmgmt
```

```
PS C:\Users\rajendragupta> . $args[0] Get-Service -Name Winmgmt

Status   Name               DisplayName
------   ----               -----------
Running  Winmgmt            Windows Management Instrumentation
```

Figure 7.6: *Get-Service cmdlet with its parameter*

You can also use the wildcard to search the service information.

```
Get-Service -Name Win*
```

```
PS C:\Users\rajendragupta> . $args[0] Get-Service -Name Win*

Status   Name               DisplayName
------   ----               -----------
Stopped  WinDefend          Microsoft Defender Antivirus Service
Running  WinHttpAutoProxyS… WinHTTP Web Proxy Auto-Discovery Serv…
Running  Winmgmt            Windows Management Instrumentation
Stopped  WinRM              Windows Remote Management (WS-Managem…
```

Figure 7.7: *Get-Service with wildcard parameter*

You can provide the **-Displayname** parameter to the **Get-Service** cmdlet to retrieve service information.

```
Get-Service -DisplayName "Print Spooler"
```

```
PS C:\Users\rajendragupta> . $args[0] Get-Service -DisplayName "Print Spooler"

Status   Name               DisplayName
------   ----               -----------
Running  Spooler            Print Spooler
```

***Figure 7.8**: Filter records with a service display name in Get-Service*

To get the dependent services information of the service, use the following PowerShell command.

```
Get-Service MSSQLSERVER -DependentServices
```

```
PS C:\Users\rajendragupta> . $args[0] Get-Service MSSQLSERVER -DependentServices

Status   Name               DisplayName
------   ----               -----------
Stopped  SQLSERVERAGENT     SQL Server Agent (MSSQLSERVER)
```

***Figure 7.9**: Get dependent service information with Get-Service*

If you right-click the **MSSQLSERVER** service in services.msc and go to the **Dependencies** tab, it lists the dependent services list as shown here:

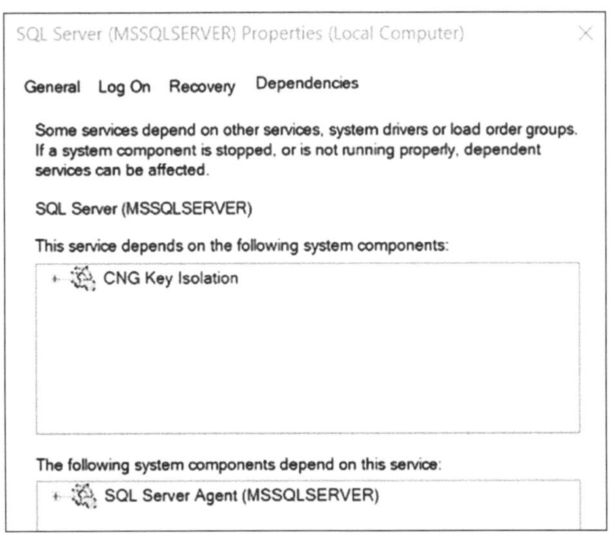

***Figure 7.10**: Service status in services.msc*

Similarly, use the parameter **RequiredServices** to get information on required services.

```
Get-Service MSSQLSERVER -RequiredServices
```

```
PS C:\Users\rajendragupta> . $args[0] Get-Service MSSQLSERVER -RequiredServices

Status   Name               DisplayName
------   ----               -----------
Running  KEYISO             CNG Key Isolation
```

***Figure 7.11**: Fetch required services in the Get-Service cmdlet*

`Get-Service` cmdlet default output contains only a few table items like **`DisplayName`**, **`Name`**, and **`Status`**, but to display all the properties, use the **`Format-List`** keyword as follows.

```
PS C:\Users\rajendragupta> . $args[0] Get-Service Spooler | Format-List *

UserName            : LocalSystem
Description         : This service spools print jobs and handles interaction with the printer.  If you
                      be able to print or see your printers.
DelayedAutoStart    : False
BinaryPathName      : C:\WINDOWS\System32\spoolsv.exe
StartupType         : Automatic
Name                : Spooler
RequiredServices    : {RPCSS, http}
CanPauseAndContinue : False
CanShutdown         : False
CanStop             : True
DisplayName         : Print Spooler
DependentServices   : {Fax}
MachineName         : .
ServiceName         : Spooler
```

***Figure 7.12**: Select the required columns in the Get-Service cmdlet output*

You can have the selected properties with the **`Select-Object`** (alias: **`Select`**) parameter.

```
Get-Service winmgmt | Select Name, DisplayName, Starttype, Status
```

```
PS C:\Users\rajendragupta> . $args[0] Get-Service winmgmt | Select Name, DisplayName, Starttype, Status

Name    DisplayName                        StartType Status
----    -----------                        --------- ------
winmgmt Windows Management Instrumentation Automatic Running
```

***Figure 7.13**: Select-Object cmdlet*

3. **`Start-Service`**: The PowerShell cmdlet `Start-Service` initiates halted services. When applied to a service already in an active state, the command is disregarded without generating an error message. The service can be identified for initiation by specifying its name, display name, or by presenting the service itself as an input object.

For example, the following command starts the **`Spooler`** service if it is not running.

```
Start-Service -Name Spooler
```

If we use the **`Start-Service`** cmdlet and start a service, it does not return the service status. We can explicitly use the **`Get-Service`** cmdlet to check it. However, if we use the parameter **`-Passthru`** with the Start-Service cmdlet, it displays the output in the console, and you do not need to write the **Get-Service** command to get the service information.

```
Start-Service -Name Spooler -PassThru
```

```
PS C:\Users\rajendragupta> . $args[0] Start-Service -Name Spooler -PassThru

Status   Name               DisplayName
------   ----               -----------
Running  Spooler            Print Spooler
```

***Figure 7.14**: Start-Service cmdlet*

If we want user confirmation before starting the service, use the **-confirm** parameter. In this case, the PowerShell console confirms with the user before starting the service.

```
Start-Service -Name Spooler -confirm
```

```
PS C:\Users\rajendragupta> . $args[0] Start-Service -Name Spooler -Confirm

Confirm
Are you sure you want to perform this action?
Performing the operation "Start-Service" on target "Print Spooler (Spooler)".
[Y] Yes  [A] Yes to All  [N] No  [L] No to All  [S] Suspend  [?] Help (default is "Y"): y
PS C:\Users\rajendragupta>
```

***Figure 7.15**: Confirmation prompt before starting a service*

4. **Stop-Service**: The **Stop-Service** is employed to stop a currently running service on local or remote computers. This cmdlet allows the stopping of one or multiple services simultaneously. Services can be identified for cessation by specifying their Name, DisplayName, or providing the service as an Input Object.

The following command stops the **Spooler** service on the local computer.

```
Stop-Service -Name Spooler
```

Like the Get-Service cmdlet, you can use the **-PassThru** parameter to show the service status after running the **Stop-Service** cmdlet.

```
Stop-Service -Name Spooler -PassThru
```

```
PS C:\Users\rajendragupta> . $args[0] Stop-Service -Name Spooler -PassThru

Status   Name               DisplayName
------   ----               -----------
Stopped  Spooler            Print Spooler
```

***Figure 7.16**: Stop service using Stop-Service*

Certain services have dependencies, meaning they rely on other services, and attempting to stop them directly might be problematic without stopping their dependent services first. The **-Force** parameter allows you to forcefully stop a service, even if the service is currently in use or has dependent services. When you use **-Force**,

PowerShell will attempt to stop the service without prompting for confirmation and stop any dependent services.

```
Stop-Service -Name "ExampleService" -Force
```

The **NoWait** parameter initiates the stop service operation without waiting for the service to stop completely. Without **-NoWait**, PowerShell waits for the service to stop before returning control to the console.

```
Stop-Service -Name "ExampleService" -NoWait
```

5. **Get-EventLog**: Examining Windows event logs is often the initial step for administrators in dissecting issues and identifying their origins. However, the purpose of logging events extends beyond troubleshooting alone. We can use the PowerShell **Get-EventLog** cmdlet to retrieve certain event log operations.

The following command retrieves the event logs on a computer.

```
Get-EventLog -List
```

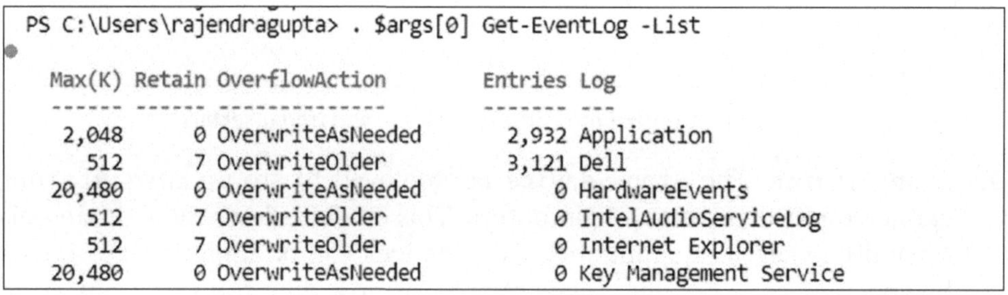

Figure 7.17: *Get-EventLog cmdlet*

The following command is used to get the top 10 most recent entries from a specific event log, such as an **Application** log.

```
Get-EventLog -Newest 10 -LogName "Application"
```

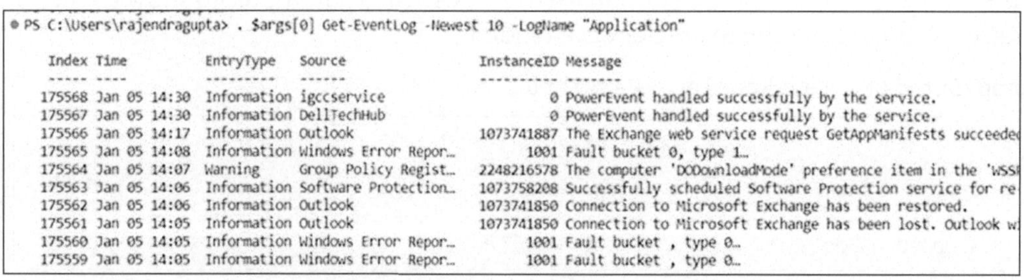

Figure 7.18: *Fetch the newest logs from the application log*

You can use the following code to filter a specific event ID from the **System** log.

```
Get-EventLog -LogName System | Where-Object {$_.InstanceID -eq '10010'}
```

`Get-WinEvent` vs `Get-EventLog`

PowerShell includes two cmdlets, **`Get-WinEvent`** and **`Get-EventLog`**, for capturing Windows event logs.

- **`Get-WinEvent`**: Works with classic event logs (introduced in Windows Vista) and newer log formats.
- **`Get-EventLog`**: Works with classic event logs only.

The following table describes the difference between **`Get-WinEvent`** and **`Get-EventLog`**.

Feature	**`Get-WinEvent`**	**`Get-EventLog`**
Compatibility	Classic and newer logs for Windows Vista and later	Classic logs only for Windows XP and later
Data Access	Direct access	Windows API
Ease of Use	More powerful and flexible for advanced scenarios. Allows for more complex queries and filtering.	Simpler syntax, suitable for basic tasks.
Underlying Technology	Utilizes the Windows Event Log infrastructure introduced in Windows Vista and later.	Uses the .NET framework's **`EventLog`** class.
Features	Advanced filtering, sorting, event handling	Limited feature set
Performance	It can be slower for large datasets	Faster in small datasets
Specific use cases	If you need to filter events by date and time efficiently, **`Get-EventLog`**'s **`-After`** and **`-Before`** parameters might be more convenient.	For complex filtering and analysis, **`Get-WinEvent`**'s advanced features are often preferred.
Example	**`Get-WinEvent -LogName Security -FilterXPath "*[System[(EventID=4625)]]" -MaxEvents 10`**	**`Get-EventLog -LogName Security -EntryType FailureAudit -After (Get-Date).AddDays(-1)`**

***Table 7.2**: Difference between Get-WinEvent and Get-EventLog*

6. **`Get-ChildItem`**: **`Get-ChildItem`** is a cmdlet in PowerShell used to retrieve a list of items in a specified location. The location can be a local, remote directory, shared path, certificate store, or registry hive.

To list all items in a directory, specify the path in **`Get-ChildItem`** as follows:

```
Get-ChildItem C:\temp\PowerShell
```

```
PS C:\Users\rajendragupta>
PS C:\Users\rajendragupta> . $args[0] Get-ChildItem C:\temp\PowerShell

    Directory: C:\temp\PowerShell

Mode                 LastWriteTime         Length Name
----                 -------------         ------ ----
d----          05-01-2024     16:53                New folder
-a---          28-12-2023     09:46            103 MyData.csv
-a---          19-12-2023     09:27              0 New Text Document.txt
-a---          06-12-2023     18:02              0 Script1.ps1
-a---          06-12-2023     18:02              0 Script2.ps1
```

***Figure 7.19**: Get-ChildItem cmdlet*

The mode column can have the following values:

- **l** – link
- **d** – directory
- **a** – archive
- **r** – read-only
- **h** – hidden
- **s** – system

By default, **Get-ChildItem** returns all files and directories in the specified path. We can filter to list only files or directories.

- List only directories in a directory: `Get-ChildItem C:\temp\PowerShell -Directory`

```
PS C:\Users\rajendragupta> . $args[0] Get-ChildItem C:\temp\PowerShell -Directory

    Directory: C:\temp\PowerShell

Mode                 LastWriteTime         Length Name
----                 -------------         ------ ----
d----          05-01-2024     16:53                New folder
```

***Figure 7.20**: List only directories with Get-ChildItem*

- List only files in a directory: `Get-ChildItem C:\temp\PowerShell -File`

```
PS C:\Users\rajendragupta> . $args[0] Get-ChildItem C:\temp\PowerShell -File

    Directory: C:\temp\PowerShell

Mode                 LastWriteTime         Length Name
----                 -------------         ------ ----
-a---          28-12-2023     09:46            103 MyData.csv
-a---          19-12-2023     09:27              0 New Text Document.txt
-a---          06-12-2023     18:02              0 Script1.ps1
-a---          06-12-2023     18:02              0 Script2.ps1
```

***Figure 7.21**: List only files in a directory with Get-ChildItem*

The following table explores a few practical examples of the cmdlet **`Get-ChildItem`**.

Description	**Command**
List all items, including hidden ones.	`Get-ChildItem C:\Path\To\Directory -Force`
Lists files in a directory and its subdirectories	`Get-ChildItem C:\Path\To\Directory -Recurse -File`
Filter items based on a specific file extension	`Get-ChildItem C:\Path\To\Directory -Filter *.txt`
List only items modified in the last 7 days.	`Get-ChildItem C:\Path\To\Directory | Where-Object { $\_.LastWriteTime -gt (Get-Date).AddDays(-7) }`
List only items that match a specific pattern using wildcard characters	`Get-ChildItem C:\Path\To\Directory -Filter *pattern*`
List all items in a registry key	`Get-ChildItem -Path 'HKLM:\Software\YourRegistryKey'`
List items in a specific subkey	`Get-ChildItem -Path 'HKLM:\Software\YourRegistryKey\Subkey'`
Display values within a registry key	`Get-Item -Path 'HKLM:\Software\YourRegistryKey' | Get-ItemProperty`

***Table 7.3**: Examples of Get-ChildItem cmdlet*

7. **`New-Item`**: The **`New-Item`** cmdlet in PowerShell creates a new item, such as a file, directory, registry key, or other items in various PowerShell providers. Here are some examples:

Description	**Command**
Create a new directory	`New-Item -ItemType Directory -Path C:\NewDirectory`
Create a new text file	`New-Item -ItemType File -Path C:\NewDirectory\NewFile.txt`
Create a new registry key	`New-Item -Path 'HKLM:\Software\NewRegistryKey'`
Create a new registry entry with a specific value	`New-ItemProperty -Path 'HKLM:\Software\NewRegistryKey' -Name 'RegistryValueName' -Value 'NewValue'`

Create a new environment variable	`New-Item -Path Env: -Name 'NewVariable' -Value 'VariableValue'`
Create a new alias	`New-Item -Path Alias: -Name 'NewAlias' -Value 'Get-Command'`

Table 7.4: *Examples of New-Item cmdlet*

8. **`Join-Path`**: The **`Join-Path`** cmdlet in PowerShell is used to concatenate and join two or more parts of a path to create a new path. It helps ensure the resulting path is formatted correctly with the correct path separator.

Here are some examples of using **`Join-Path`**:

Description	**Command**

Join two path components	`$basePath = "C:\Users"`
	
	`$newPath = Join-Path -Path $basePath -ChildPath "JohnDoe"`
	
	`Result: C:\Users\JohnDoe`

Join multiple path components	`$basePath = "C:\Users"`
	
	`$username = "JohnDoe"`
	
	`$documentsFolder = "Documents"`
	
	`$fullPath = Join-Path -Path $basePath -ChildPath $username -ChildPath $documentsFolder`
	
	`Result: C:\Users\JohnDoe\Documents`

Join paths using variables	`$basePath = "C:\Users"`
	
	`$username = "JohnDoe"`
	
	`$documentsFolder = "Documents"`
	
	`$fullPath = Join-Path -Path $basePath -ChildPath ($username + "\" + $documentsFolder)`
	
	`Result: C:\Users\JohnDoe\Documents`

Join paths using the pipeline	`$basePath = "C:\Users"`
	
	`$username = "JohnDoe"`
	
	`$fullPath = $username | Join-Path -Parent $basePath`
	
	`Result: C:\Users\JohnDoe`

Table 7.5: *Examples of Join-Path cmdlet*

9. **`Move-Item`**: The **`Move-Item`** cmdlet in PowerShell is used to move (or rename) an item, such as a file or directory, from one location to another. It can change the location, rename the item, or both.

Here are some examples of using **`Move-Item`**:

- Move a file to a different directory: **`Move-Item -Path C:\Source\Example.txt -Destination C:\Destination\`**

This command moves the file "**`Example.txt`**" from the "**`C:\Source`**" directory to the "**`C:\Destination`**" directory.

- Move and rename a file:

```
Move-Item -Path C:\Source\Example.txt -Destination C:\Destination\NewName.txt
```

This command moves the file "**`Example.txt`**" from the "**`C:\Source`**" directory to the "**`C:\Destination`**" directory and renames it to "**`NewName.txt`**" in the process.

- Move multiple files to a directory:

```
Move-Item -Path C:\Source\*.txt -Destination C:\Destination\
```

This command moves all files with the "**`.txt`**" extension from the "**`C:\Source`**" directory to the "**`C:\Destination`**" directory.

- Move a directory and its contents to another location:

```
Move-Item -Path C:\Source\ExampleDirectory -Destination D:\Backup\
```

This command moves the entire "**`ExampleDirectory`**" and its contents from "**`C:\Source`**" to "**`D:\Backup`**".

10. **`Test-Path`**: The **`Test-Path`** cmdlet in PowerShell checks whether a file, directory, or registry key exists at a given path. It returns a boolean value (**`True`** or **`False`**) based on whether the specified path exists.

Here are some examples of using **`Test-Path`**:

- Check if a file exists: **`Test-Path C:\Example\File.txt`**

This command returns **`True`** if the file "**`File.txt`**" exists in the "**`C:\Example`**" directory and **`False`** otherwise.

- Check if a directory exists:

```
Test-Path C:\Example\Directory
```

This command returns **`True`** if the directory "**`Directory`**" exists in the "**`C:\Example`**" path and **`False`** otherwise.

- Check if a registry key exists

```
Test-Path HKLM:\Software\ExampleKey
```

This command returns **True** if the registry key "**ExampleKey**" exists under "**HKLM:\Software**" and **False** otherwise.

- Use the **-PathType** parameter to specify the type of path:

```
Test-Path -Path C:\Example\File.txt -PathType Leaf
```

This command checks if the specified path is a file using the -PathType parameter with the value Leaf. It returns **True** if the path points to a file and **False** otherwise.

- Check if multiple paths exist:

```
Test-Path C:\Example\File1.txt, C:\Example\File2.txt
```

This command checks if either "**File1.txt**" or "**File2.txt**" exists in the "**C:\Example**" directory and returns an array of boolean values.

Querying Windows Management Instrumentation

Windows Management Instrumentation or WMI, is a technology in Microsoft Windows that provides a way for systems and devices to communicate with each other. WMI exposes a consistent and unified interface for gathering information about the system, configuring components, and managing system resources. PowerShell leverages WMI through its **Get-WmiObject** cmdlet, allowing you to interact with WMI data using PowerShell scripts and commands.

You can use **Get-Command** to get the cmdlets related to the WMI.

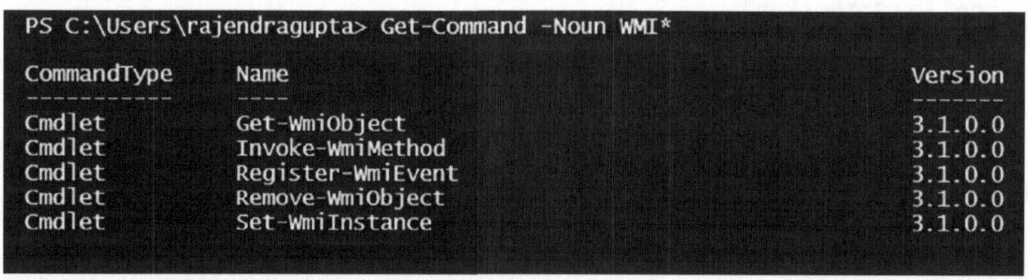

Figure 7.22: *Querying Windows Management Instrumentation*

Note: *The WMI cmdlets have been deprecated and are inaccessible in PowerShell 6 and later versions. However, they are discussed here for reference, as you might come across them in older scripts designed for Windows PowerShell. For contemporary development, it is recommended to utilize the CIM cmdlets instead.*

Common Information Model (CIM) cmdlets

Common Information Model (CIM) cmdlets in PowerShell provide a modern and standardized way to interact with CIM classes and instances. CIM is an industry standard that ensures consistent management information and operations across different systems.

The CIM cmdlets were introduced in PowerShell version 3.0 and are designed to be helpful in both Windows and non-Windows machines. The following **`Get-Command`** lists all cmdlets related to the CIM module.

```
Get-Command -Module CimCmdlets
```

```
PS C:\Users\rajendragupta> . $args[0] Get-Command -Module CimCmdlets

CommandType     Name                                Version    Source
-----------     ----                                -------    ------
Cmdlet          Get-CimAssociatedInstance           7.0.0.0    CimCmdlets
Cmdlet          Get-CimClass                        7.0.0.0    CimCmdlets
Cmdlet          Get-CimInstance                     7.0.0.0    CimCmdlets
Cmdlet          Get-CimSession                      7.0.0.0    CimCmdlets
Cmdlet          Invoke-CimMethod                    7.0.0.0    CimCmdlets
Cmdlet          New-CimInstance                     7.0.0.0    CimCmdlets
Cmdlet          New-CimSession                      7.0.0.0    CimCmdlets
Cmdlet          New-CimSessionOption                7.0.0.0    CimCmdlets
Cmdlet          Register-CimIndicationEvent         7.0.0.0    CimCmdlets
Cmdlet          Remove-CimInstance                  7.0.0.0    CimCmdlets
Cmdlet          Remove-CimSession                   7.0.0.0    CimCmdlets
Cmdlet          Set-CimInstance                     7.0.0.0    CimCmdlets
```

***Figure 7.23**: Get CIM cmdlets*

The following table lists the CIM cmdlets, their description, and usage commands.

Cmdlet	Description	Example Usage
`Get-CimInstance`	Retrieves instances of CIM classes	`Get-CimInstance -ClassName Win32_OperatingSystem`
`Get-CimClass`	Retrieves CIM class definitions	`Get-CimClass -ClassName Win32_Process`
`Invoke-CimMethod`	Invokes methods of CIM classes	`Invoke-CimMethod -ClassName Win32_Process -MethodName Create -Arguments @{CommandLine = "notepad.exe"}`

New-CimInstance	Creates a new instance of a CIM class	`New-CimInstance -ClassName Win32_UserAccount -Property @{Name = "NewUser"; Password = "Password123"}`
Remove-CimInstance	Deletes an instance of a CIM class	`Remove-CimInstance -Query "SELECT * FROM Win32_UserAccount WHERE Name='OldUser'"`
Set-CimInstance	Modifies properties of an existing CIM instance	`Set-CimInstance -CimInstance $existingInstance -Property @{Status = "Active"}`

***Table 7.6**: CIM cmdlets examples*

Let us look at a few examples of using CIM cmdlet.

The following command retrieves information about the processors using the **`Win32_Processor`** CIM class and then formats the output as a list using **`Format-List`**. The output will include various details about each processor on the system,

```
Get-CimInstance win32_processor | Format-List
```

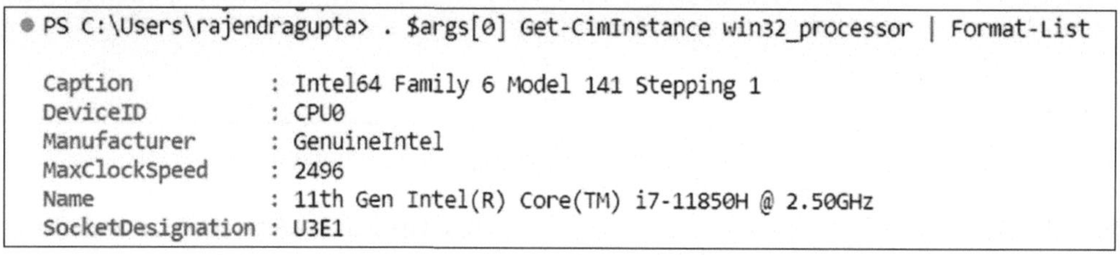

```
PS C:\Users\rajendragupta> . $args[0] Get-CimInstance win32_processor | Format-List

Caption           : Intel64 Family 6 Model 141 Stepping 1
DeviceID          : CPU0
Manufacturer      : GenuineIntel
MaxClockSpeed     : 2496
Name              : 11th Gen Intel(R) Core(TM) i7-11850H @ 2.50GHz
SocketDesignation : U3E1
```

***Figure 7.24**: Get CIM cmdlets*

The following command uses the **`Get-CimClass`** cmdlet to retrieve information about the CIM class named **`Win32_Process`** and format the output as a list.

```
Get-CimClass -ClassName Win32_Process | Format-List
```

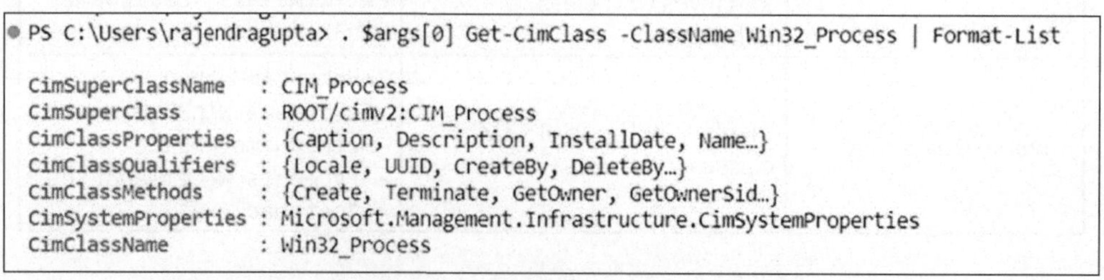

```
PS C:\Users\rajendragupta> . $args[0] Get-CimClass -ClassName Win32_Process | Format-List

CimSuperClassName   : CIM_Process
CimSuperClass       : ROOT/cimv2:CIM_Process
CimClassProperties  : {Caption, Description, InstallDate, Name…}
CimClassQualifiers  : {Locale, UUID, CreateBy, DeleteBy…}
CimClassMethods     : {Create, Terminate, GetOwner, GetOwnerSid…}
CimSystemProperties : Microsoft.Management.Infrastructure.CimSystemProperties
CimClassName        : Win32_Process
```

***Figure 7.25**: Get-CimClass cmdlet output*

Similarly, we can use **`Get-CimInstance`** to check the device-related information shown here:

```
Get-CimInstance -Class Win32_Processor | Format-List
```

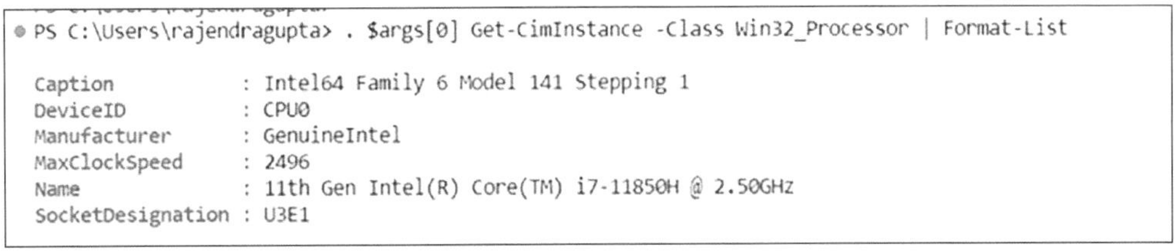

Figure 7.26: *Get-CimInstance cmdlet output*

The PowerShell command retrieves information about local user accounts on a Windows system and formats the output as a table.

```
Get-CimInstance -Class Win32_UserAccount -Filter "LocalAccount=True"  |
Format-Table PSComputerName, Name, PasswordExpires
```

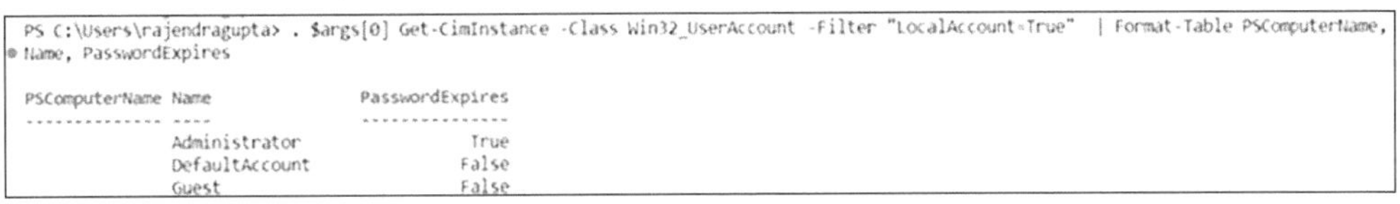

Figure 7.27: *Get-CimClass cmdlet output*

The PowerShell script you provided retrieves the last boot time of a remote computer, calculates the system uptime, and then outputs the result.

```
$bootTime = Get-CimInstance -ClassName Win32_OperatingSystem -Computer-
Name $machine.computer | Select-Object -ExpandProperty LastBootupTime

$upTime = New-TimeSpan -Start $bootTime

$days = [int]$upTime.TotalDays

Write-Output "System has been up for $days days."
```

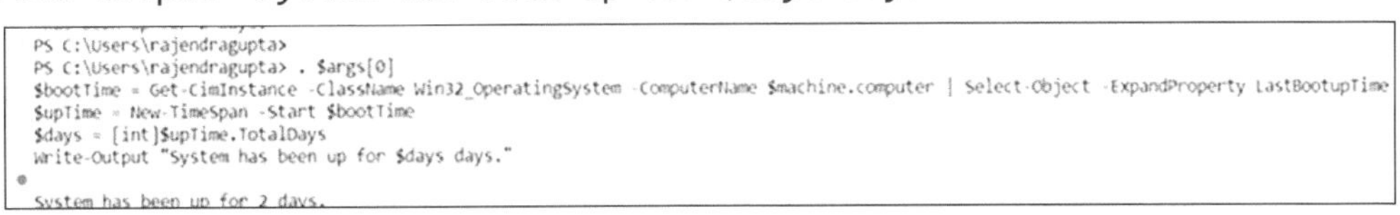

Figure 7.28: *Check the last boot time using the CIM cmdlet*

Reading and Writing text files

Get-Content for reading text file: The **`Get-Content`** command is the primary method for reading a text file in PowerShell. To utilize this command within your PowerShell script, provide the path to the file as an argument and either assign the output to a variable or display it directly in the PowerShell console.

```
Get-Content -Path "C:\Temp\Sample3.txt"
```

```
PS C:\Users\rajendragupta> . $args[0] Get-Content -Path "C:\Temp\Sample3.txt"

 01
03/22 08:51:01 INFO   :.main: *************** RSVP Agent started ***************
 02
03/22 08:51:01 INFO   :...locate_configFile: Specified configuration file: /u/user10/rsvpd1.conf
03/22 08:51:01 INFO   :.main: Using log level 511
03/22 08:51:01 INFO   :..settcpimage: Get TCP images rc - EDC8112I Operation not supported on socket.
 03
03/22 08:51:01 INFO   :..settcpimage: Associate with TCP/IP image name = TCPCS
03/22 08:51:02 INFO   :..reg_process: registering process with the system
03/22 08:51:02 INFO   :..reg_process: attempt OS/390 registration
03/22 08:51:02 INFO   :..reg_process: return from registration rc=0
 04
```

***Figure 7.29**: Read text file using PowerShell*

- Reading a Text File into a Variable:

```
$content : Get-Content -Path "C:\Temp\Sample3.txt"
```

Reading a Text File Line by Line:

```
$FilePath = "C:\Temp\Sample3.txt"
$FileContents = Get-Content -Path $FilePath

$i = 1
# Read the file line by line
ForEach ($Line in $FileContents) {
    # Process each line here
    Write-Host "Line# $i :" $Line
    $i++
}
```

```
PS C:\Users\rajendragupta>
PS C:\Users\rajendragupta> . $args[0] $FilePath = "C:\Temp\Sample3.txt"
$FileContents = Get-Content -Path $FilePath

$i = 1
# Read the file line by line
ForEach ($Line in $FileContents) {
    # Process each line here
    Write-Host "Line# $i :" $Line
    $i++
}


Line# 1 :
Line# 2 :  01
Line# 3 : 03/22 08:51:01 INFO   :.main: *************** RSVP Agent started ***************
Line# 4 :  02
Line# 5 : 03/22 08:51:01 INFO   :...locate_configFile: Specified configuration file: /u/user10/rsvpd1.conf
Line# 6 : 03/22 08:51:01 INFO   :.main: Using log level 511
Line# 7 : 03/22 08:51:01 INFO   :..settcpimage: Get TCP images rc - EDC8112I Operation not supported on socket.
```

***Figure 7.30**: Read text file line by line using PowerShell*

Alternatively, you can use the **StreamReader** class to read the file one line at a time. Here is an example using **StreamReader**:

```
$Reader = New-Object System.IO.StreamReader("C:\Temp\Sample3.txt")


while($Line = $Reader.ReadLine()) {
    # do something with each line
    Write-host $Line
}
$Reader.Close()
```

- Get the first two lines from the text file using **-TotalCount** parameter:

```
$FilePath = "C:\Temp\Sample3.txt"
Get-Content -Path $FilePath -TotalCount 2
```

- Get the last N lines from the text file using **-Tail** parameter:

```
$FilePath = "C:\Temp\Sample3.txt"
Get-Content -Path $FilePath -Tail 2
```

- Reading Large Text Files using **-ReadCount** parameter: The **-ReadCount** parameter of the `**Get-Content**` cmdlet enables reading a designated number of lines per iteration, thereby minimizing memory usage when dealing with extensive text files. By setting a higher value for `**-ReadCount**`, multiple lines are processed in each iteration, enhancing overall performance.

```
# Define the path to the file
$filePath = "C:\Path\To\Your\File.txt"
# Use Get-Content with -ReadCount to read the file in chunks of 3 lines
Get-Content -Path $filePath -ReadCount 3 | ForEach-Object {
    # Process each chunk of lines
    foreach ($line in $_) {
        # Perform your desired operations on each line
        Write-Output "Processing line: $line"
    }
    # Add a separator between chunks for clarity
    Write-Output "------------------"
}
```

Out-File and Set-Content for Writing in a Text File

The **`Out-File`** cmdlet in PowerShell is used to send output to a file. It allows you to write content to a file or create a new file with the specified content. In this example, we will retrieve a list of processes and filter those that have a specific status, then write the results to a text file:

```
# Get a list of processes where the Working Set (WS) is greater than
100 MB
$Processes = Get-Process | Where-Object { $_.WorkingSet -gt 100MB }
# Write the list of processes to a text file
$Processes | Out-File -FilePath 'C:\Temp\Processes.txt'
```

- Append PowerShell Output to an existing Text File using the **-Append** parameter in the Out-File:

```
This will be appended text in the text file" | Out-File -FilePath C:\
Temp\Processes.txt -Append
```

`Set-Content`: The **`Set-Content`** cmdlet in PowerShell is used to write content to a file, similar to Out-File. However, set content is more commonly used when you want to create or overwrite a file with new content.

Here are a few examples:

- Writing a Single Line to a New File

```
# Specify the path to the output file
$outputFilePath = 'C:\Temp\Example1_SetContent.txt'

# Specify the content to be written to the file
$content = 'This is a single line of content.'

# Write content to the new file
Set-Content -Path $outputFilePath -Value $content -Encoding UTF8
```

- Overwriting an Existing File

```
# Specify the path to the existing file
$existingFilePath = 'C:\Temp\Example1_SetContent.txt'

# Specify new content
$newContent = @"
This is the new content that will overwrite the existing file.
```

```
"@

# Overwrite content in the existing file
Set-Content -Path $existingFilePath -Value $newContent -Encoding UTF8
```

- Writing an Array of Lines to a New File:

```
# Specify the path to the output file
$outputFilePath = 'C:\Temp\Example3_SetContent.txt'

# Create an array of lines
$contentArray = @(
    'First line of content.',
    'Second line of content.',
    'Third line of content.'
)

# Write content to the new file
Set-Content -Path $outputFilePath -Value $contentArray -Encoding UTF8
```

- Write cmdlet output to a text file:

```
# Get a list of running services
$services = Get-Service | Where-Object {$_.Status -eq 'Running' & -ne }

# Specify the path to the output file
$outputFilePath = 'C:\Temp\ServicesSetContent.txt'

# Use Set-Content to write the list of running services to a file
$services | Set-Content -Path $outputFilePath -Encoding UTF8
```

Here is a tabular representation of the key differences between Out-File and Set-Content:

Feature	**Out-File**	**Set-Content**
Primary Use	Writing output to a file	Creating or overwriting files with specific content
Overwriting	Can overwrite files by default or append (**-Append**)	Can create or overwrite files

Use Case	Commonly used for writing script or cmdlet output	Used when explicit control over file content is needed
Additional Options	Offers more formatting options when using the pipeline	More straightforward and more direct when setting specific content
Example	`` `'Content from Out-File' ``	`` Out-File -FilePath 'C:\Temp\OutFileExample.txt' -Encoding UTF8` ``

Table 7.7: *Key differences between Out-File and Set-Content*

Working with CSV, XML, and JSON Profiles

Working with CSV, XML, and JSON files in PowerShell allows you to read and manipulate structured data easily. Here are examples for each file type:

Working with CSV Files

- Reading CSV using Import-CSV cmdlet:

```
# Specify the path to the CSV file
$csvFilePath = 'C:\Path\To\Your\File.csv'
# Read the CSV file into a variable
$csvData = Import-Csv -Path $csvFilePath
# Display the content
$csvData
```

- Writing CSV using Export-Csv cmdlet:

```
# Specify the path for the new CSV file
$newCsvFilePath = 'C:\Path\To\Your\NewFile.csv'
# Create some sample data
$newCsvData = @"
Name, Age, City
John, 25, New York
Jane, 30, Los Angeles
"@
# Convert the string to CSV and write to a new file
$newCsvData | ConvertFrom-Csv | Export-Csv -Path $newCsvFilePath
-NoTypeInformation
```

Working with XML Files

- Reading XML using the Get-Content cmdlet:

```
# Specify the path to the XML file
$xmlFilePath = 'C:\Path\To\Your\File.xml'

# Read the XML file into a variable
$xmlData = [xml](Get-Content -Path $xmlFilePath)
# Display the content
$xmlData
```

- Writing XML using out-file:

```
# Specify the path for the new XML file
$newXmlFilePath = 'C:\Path\To\Your\NewFile.xml'
# Create some sample XML data
$newXmlData = @"
<Root>
    <Person>
        <Name>John</Name>
        <Age>25</Age>
        <City>New York</City>
    </Person>
    <Person>
        <Name>Jane</Name>
        <Age>30</Age>
        <City>Los Angeles</City>
    </Person>
</Root>
"@
# Save the XML string to a new file
$newXmlData | Out-File -FilePath $newXmlFilePath -Encoding UTF8
```

Working with JSON Files

- Reading JSON using Get-Content cmdlet:

```
# Specify the path to the JSON file
$jsonFilePath = 'C:\Path\To\Your\File.json'

# Read the JSON file into a variable
$jsonData = Get-Content -Path $jsonFilePath | ConvertFrom-Json

# Display the content
$jsonData
```

- Writing JSON using Out-file:

```
# Specify the path for the new JSON file
$newJsonFilePath = 'C:\Path\To\Your\NewFile.json'

# Create some sample JSON data
$newJsonData = @"
{
    "People": [
        {"Name": "John", "Age": 25, "City": "New York"},
        {"Name": "Jane", "Age": 30, "City": "Los Angeles"}
    ]
}
“@

# Save the JSON string to a new file
$newJsonData | Out-File -FilePath $newJsonFilePath -Encoding UTF8
```

Performing Remote Administration Tasks

The **ComputerName** parameter in Windows PowerShell cmdlets allows you to perform operations on remote computers. These cmdlets leverage various communication protocols and work across different Windows operating systems without requiring special configuration.

Here is a tabular format with examples for the mentioned PowerShell cmdlets that have the ComputerName parameter:

Cmdlet	Description	Example
`Restart-Computer`	Restarts a remote computer.	`Restart-Computer -ComputerName "RemoteComputer"`
`Test-Connection`	Tests the connectivity to a remote computer.	`Test-Connection -ComputerName "RemoteComputer"`
`Clear-EventLog`	Clears the specified event log on a remote computer.	`Clear-EventLog -ComputerName "RemoteComputer" -LogName "Application"`
`Get-EventLog`	Retrieves events from the specified event log on a remote computer.	`Get-EventLog -ComputerName "RemoteComputer" -LogName "Application"`
`Get-HotFix`	Retrieves information about installed hotfixes on a remote computer.	`Get-HotFix -ComputerName "RemoteComputer"`
`Get-Process`	Retrieves information about processes running on a remote computer.	`Get-Process -ComputerName "RemoteComputer"`
`Get-Service`	Retrieves information about services on a remote computer.	`Get-Service -ComputerName "RemoteComputer"`
`Set-Service`	Sets the status of a service on a remote computer.	`Set-Service -ComputerName "RemoteComputer" -Name "ServiceName" -Status Running`
`Get-WinEvent`	Retrieves events from the specified log on a remote computer.	`Get-WinEvent -ComputerName "RemoteComputer" -LogName "Security"`
`Get-WmiObject`	Retrieves management information from WMI on a remote computer.	`Get-WmiObject -ComputerName "RemoteComputer" -Class Win32_BIOS`

***Table 7.8**: PowerShell cmdlets for remote administration*

For example, the following code uninstalls the Microsoft OLE DB driver for the SQL Server package on the computer.

```
$packages = @("Microsoft OLE DB Driver for SQL Server")
foreach($package in $packages){
  $app = Get-WmiObject -Class Win32_Product | Where-Object {
    $_.Name -match "$package."
```

```
    }
    $app.Uninstall()
}
```

PowerShell Modules

Microsoft has fully embraced PowerShell and integrated it into its entire software portfolio, making it possible to install and manage the entire Microsoft software environment dynamically. Third-party manufacturers have also embraced PowerShell by integrating the modules, which provide complete management capabilities for various products, including network devices, storage subsystems, virtualization guests and hosts, security appliances, and other third-party devices.

PowerShell modules organize and package PowerShell code, making it easier to reuse and share functionality across different scripts and sessions. Cmdlets are the building blocks of PowerShell commands that perform specific tasks. Functions are user-defined blocks of code that encapsulate a particular set of tasks and can be included in modules to provide additional functionality. Modules can contain variables that store information and settings for use within the module.

We are reviewing the value of the **$ENV:PSModulePath** variable, a list of directories that PowerShell searches for modules. This variable is an environment variable that specifies where PowerShell looks for modules to load automatically. The standard locations for saving PowerShell modules include:

```
PS:\>$ENV:PSModulePath
```

For example, a common path to save a module on a system would be

```
%SystemRoot%\users\<user>\Documents\WindowsPowerShell\Modules\<modName>
%windir%\System32\WindowsPowerShell\v1.0\Modules
%UserProfile%\Documents\WindowsPowerShell\Modules
```

User-Specific Module Path

This directory stores user-specific modules, with each user having their own modules.

```
%UserProfile%\Documents\WindowsPowerShell\Modules\<ModuleName>
```

System-Wide Module Path

This path is used for system-wide modules accessible to all users on the system.

```
%windir%\System32\WindowsPowerShell\v1.0\Modules\<ModuleName>
```

When you either create or download a PowerShell module, you can store it in one of two locations for accessibility. For instance, if you have a module named "**MyModule**," you might save it in **%UserProfile%\Documents\WindowsPowerShell\Modules**

MyModule for user-specific or **%windir%\System32\WindowsPowerShell\v1.0\Modules\MyModule** for system-wide modules.

Note: *You can customize $ENV:PSModulePath by adding additional paths for PowerShell to search for modules. However, it is generally recommended to use the default module paths.*

Installing a Published Module

You can install a published module using the PowerShell Gallery or another registered repository. The **PowerShellGet** and **Microsoft.PowerShell.PSResourceGet** modules offer cmdlets that help you find, install, and publish PowerShell modules to these repositories.

```
# Install the SQlServer module from the PowerShell Gallery

Install-Module -Name SQLServer -Scope CurrentUser
```

Note: *You must have an internet connection to download modules from the PowerShell Gallery. Additionally, ensure you have the appropriate permissions to install modules on your system. You might need to run PowerShell as an administrator if you encounter any issues.*

Autoloading PowerShell Module

PowerShell automatically imports the module when you run a command from an installed module for the first time. The module should be stored in the locations specified in the **$env:PSModulePath** environment variable. If you have modules elsewhere, import them using the Import-Module cmdlet.

Module autoloading enables you to use the commands in a module without any set up or profile configuration. You do not need to manage modules after installing them on your computer.

Note: *Automatic module importing can be convenient, but controlling module loading explicitly may be necessary for better predictability and performance. Please refer to the official documentation* `about_Preference_Variables` *for more information.*

Automatic loading is another significant benefit of modules. PowerShell automatically loads modules when needed, reducing the need to import scripts manually.

```
# Get the first directory in $env: PSModulePath

$modulePath = $env:PSModulePath -split ';' | Select-Object -Index 2


# Specify the name of the folder you want to create

$newFolderName = "MathModule"
```

```
# Create the full path for the new folder
$newFolderPath = Join-Path $modulePath $newFolderName

# Check if the folder already exists
if (-not (Test-Path $newFolderPath -PathType Container)) {
    # If not, create the folder
    New-Item -Path $newFolderPath -ItemType Directory -Force
    Write-Output "Folder '$newFolderName' created in $modulePath."
} else {
    Write-Output "Folder '$newFolderName' already exists in
$modulePath."
}
```

This script does the following:

- Retrieves the first directory in **`$env:PSModulePath`**.
- Specifies the name of the new folder (**`MathModule`** in this example).
- Creates the full path for the new folder.
- Checks if the folder already exists.
- If not, it creates the folder and outputs a success message. If the folder already exists, it outputs a message indicating that.

After running this script, you should see the new folder created in the first directory of **`$env:PSModulePath`**. Adjust the folder name (**`$newFolderName`**) if needed.

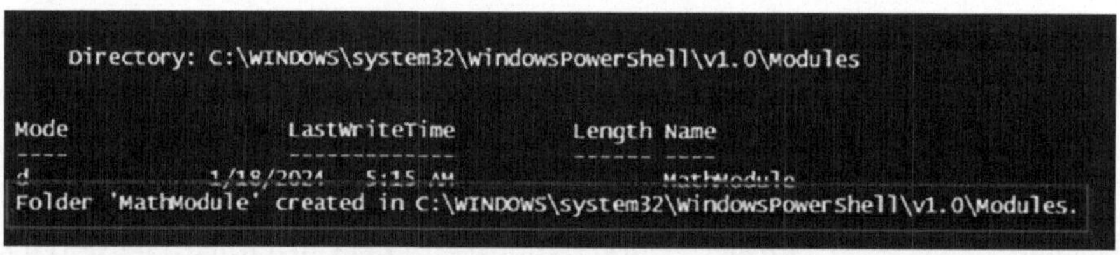

***Figure 7.31**: PowerShell modules*

Copy or type the contents of **`MathModule.psm1`**. This file contains a PowerShell function named **`Get-Square`** that calculates the square of a given number. The function takes a single parameter, which is a double data type representing the number to be squared.

```
# MathModule.psm1


function Get-Square {
    param (
```

```
        [double]$Number
    )

    Write-Output "Calculating the square of $Number"
    $result = $Number * $Number
    $result
}
```

Open the new PowerShell console and call **`Get-Square`** to ensure module autoloading is successful.

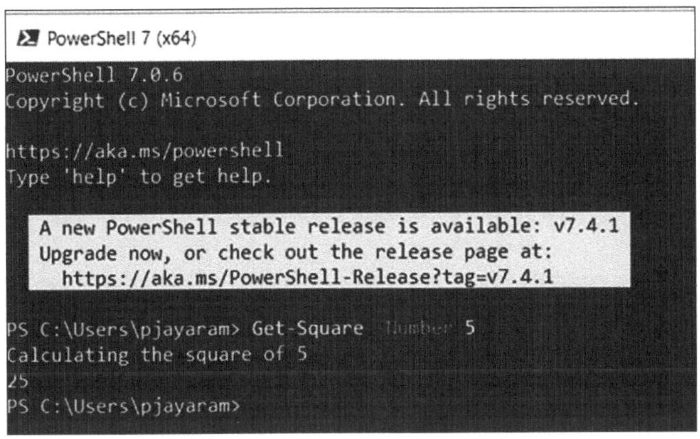

Figure 7.32: *PowerShellModule example*

Manually import a module.

When a module cannot be found in the specified locations by the **`$env:PSModulePath`** environment variable or is provided as a standalone file, it must be manually imported.

To manually import a PowerShell module, you can use the **`Import-Module`** cmdlet. Here is an example:

```
# Manually import a module from a specific path
Import-Module -Name "C:\Path\To\Your\Module\ModuleName" -Force
```

Replace "**`C:\Path\To\Your\Module\ModuleName`**" with the actual path to your module directory. Ensure the module directory contains a valid module file (**`.psm1`**) or a module manifest (**`.psd1`**).

If your module is in the PowerShell module path or the current directory, you can simply specify the module name:

```
# Manually import a module from the module path or current directory
Import-Module -Name "ModuleName" -Force
```

Module Namespace Isolation

Namespace isolation is another significant benefit of modules. They provide a namespace for your code, helping to prevent naming conflicts with other scripts or modules. For example, if you have a function named **Get-Info** in multiple modules, using modules helps to avoid conflicts by accessing functions through module prefixes (for example, **ModuleA\Get-Info, ModuleB\Get-Info**).

Step 1: Create ModuleA

Create a folder named **ModuleA** and save the following content in a file named **ModuleA.psm1** inside that folder:

```
# ModuleA.psm1

Function Get-Info { Write-Output "This is Get-Info from ModuleA" }
```

Step 2: Create ModuleB

Create a folder named **ModuleB** and save the following content in a file named **ModuleB.** psm1 inside that folder:

```
# ModuleB.psm1

function Get-Info { Write-Output "This is Get-Info from ModuleB" }
```

Step 3: Create the Main Script

Create a script file (for example, **MainScript.ps1**) with the following content:

Code Link: https://github.com/ava-orange-education/Ultimate-PowerShell-Automation-Guide/blob/main/Ch%207%20/MainScript.ps1

Step 4: Run the Script

Run the **MainScript.ps1** script. The output should demonstrate that you can access each module's version of Get-Info without conflicts:

This example illustrates namespace isolation. Even though both modules have a function named Get-Info, they are accessed using module prefixes (**ModuleA\Get-Info and ModuleB\Get-Info**), preventing naming conflicts in the script.

```
# Call Get-Info from ModuleB
Write-Output "Calling Get-Info from ModuleB:"
ModuleB\Get-Info

Information about ModuleA:


Name              : ModuleA
Path              : C:\Ultimate PowerShell Automation\ModuleA.psm1
Description       :
ModuleType        : Script
Version           : 0.0
NestedModules     : {}
ExportedFunctions : Get-Info
ExportedCmdlets   :
ExportedVariables :
ExportedAliases   :



Information about ModuleB:


Name              : ModuleB
Path              : C:\Ultimate PowerShell Automation\ModuleB.psm1
Description       :
ModuleType        : Script
Version           : 0.0
NestedModules     : {}
ExportedFunctions : Get-Info
ExportedCmdlets   :
ExportedVariables :
ExportedAliases   :



Calling Get-Info from ModuleA:
This is Get-Info from ModuleA
Calling Get-Info from ModuleB:
This is Get-Info from ModuleB

PS C:\WINDOWS\system32>
```

***Figure 7.33**: Run the script using the PowerShell module*

Understanding the Four Main Types of PowerShell Modules

The four module types cater to different use cases and scenarios, allowing PowerShell users to choose the most appropriate type based on their specific requirements.

A concise description of the four main types of PowerShell modules:

Script Modules

Script modules are collections of PowerShell functions and cmdlets saved in a `.psm1` file. They are written in the PowerShell script language.

Usage: Script modules are ideal for encapsulating and organizing reusable PowerShell functions. Script developers and administrators commonly use them.

To organize the provided code into a script module, "`administration`", follow these steps:

1. First, create a folder named "**administration**" in your PowerShell module path. You can choose any of the directories specified in **$env:PSModulePath** (for example, **C:\WINDOWS\system32\WindowsPowerShell\v1.0\Modules\administration**).
2. Next, create an "**administration.psm1**" file inside the **administration** folder. This file will contain the functions, cmdlets, or other script code.

Code Link: https://github.com/ava-orange-education/Ultimate-PowerShell-Automation-Guide/blob/main/Ch%207%20/administration.psm1

- Optionally, you can create a module manifest file (**administration.psd1**) to provide metadata about your module.

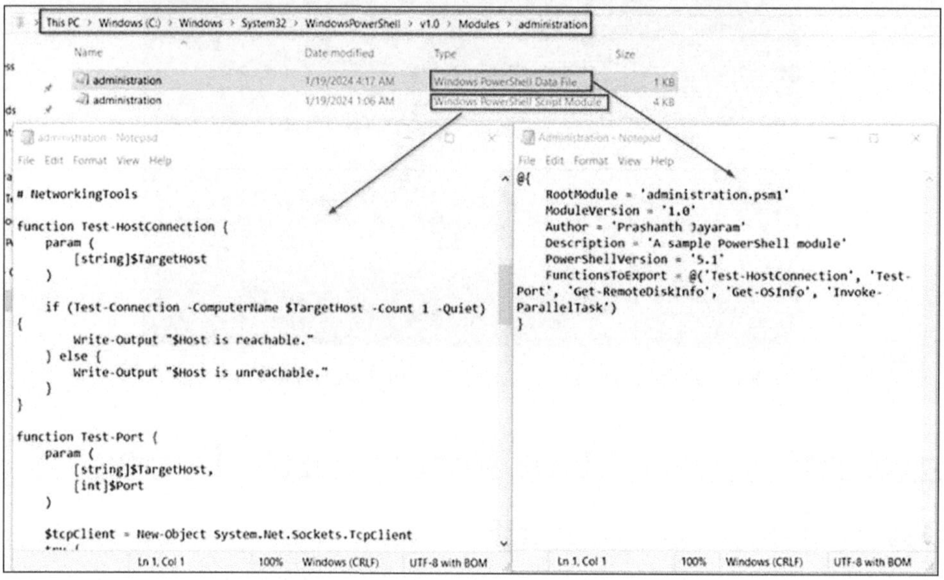

***Figure 7.34**: Create a module manifest file*

We must provide metadata about the module to create a module manifest file. Here's a basic example for your "**administration**" module:

```
# Administration.psd1


@{

    ModuleVersion = '1.0.0'

    Author = 'Your Name'

    Description = 'A collection of tools for PowerShell.'

    PowerShellVersion = '5.1.0'
```

```
    FunctionsToExport = @('Test-HostConnection', 'Test-Port',
'Get-RemoteDiskInfo', 'Get-OSInfo', 'Invoke-ParallelTask')
            PSData = @{
             Tags = @('Administration', 'Networking', 'Tools')
              ReleaseNotes = 'Initial release.'
        }
    }
}
```

We have successfully imported the "**administration**" module and retrieved information about it. We confirmed that it is a script module with a **ModuleType** of Script. We also demonstrated how to run the help documentation for the **Get-OSInfo** function and executed the **Get-OSInfo** function to display information about the operating system on the local computer.

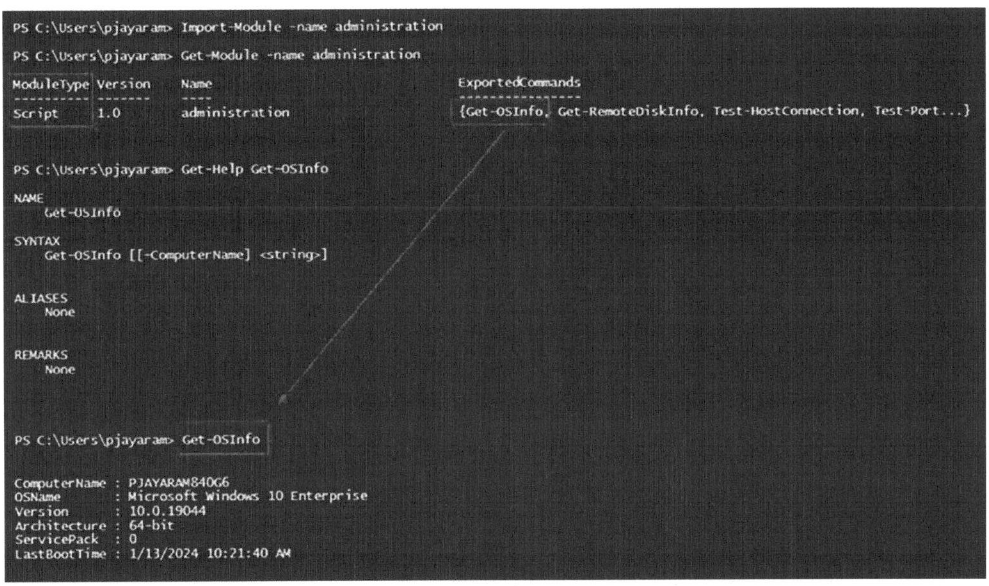

***Figure 7.35**: Get-OSInfo function to display information about the operating system*

Binary Modules

Binary modules are compiled modules written in languages such as C# and compiled into DLLs. They typically have better performance than script modules.

Usage: Binary modules are suitable for high-performing scenarios or when integration with existing .NET code is necessary. These modules may contain compiled cmdlets or functions.

C# code creates a custom PowerShell cmdlet named **`Get-FileDetails`** to retrieve file details of a specified directory and output them as custom objects.

Code Link: https://github.com/ava-orange-education/Ultimate-PowerShell-Automation-Guide/tree/main/Ch%207%20

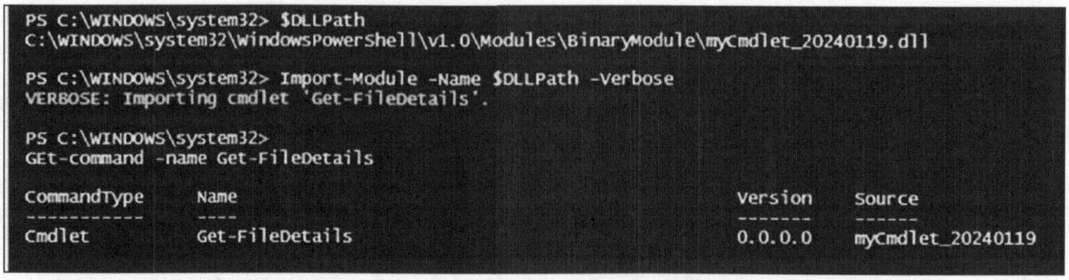

```
PS C:\WINDOWS\system32> $DLLPath
C:\WINDOWS\system32\WindowsPowerShell\v1.0\Modules\BinaryModule\myCmdlet_20240119.dll

PS C:\WINDOWS\system32> Import-Module -Name $DLLPath -Verbose
VERBOSE: Importing cmdlet 'Get-FileDetails'.

PS C:\WINDOWS\system32>
GEt-command -name Get-FileDetails

CommandType     Name                                               Version    Source
-----------     ----                                               -------    ------
Cmdlet          Get-FileDetails                                    0.0.0.0    myCmdlet_20240119
```

Figure 7.36: *Use the custom cmdlet*

```
# Use the custom cmdlet
Get-FileDetails -Path "C:\Ultimate PowerShell Automation\ExportedTem-
plate-MyPowerShellRG\"
```

This cmdlet can be compiled into a DLL and then loaded into a PowerShell session, allowing users to run **`Get-FileDetails`** to retrieve file details from a specified directory.

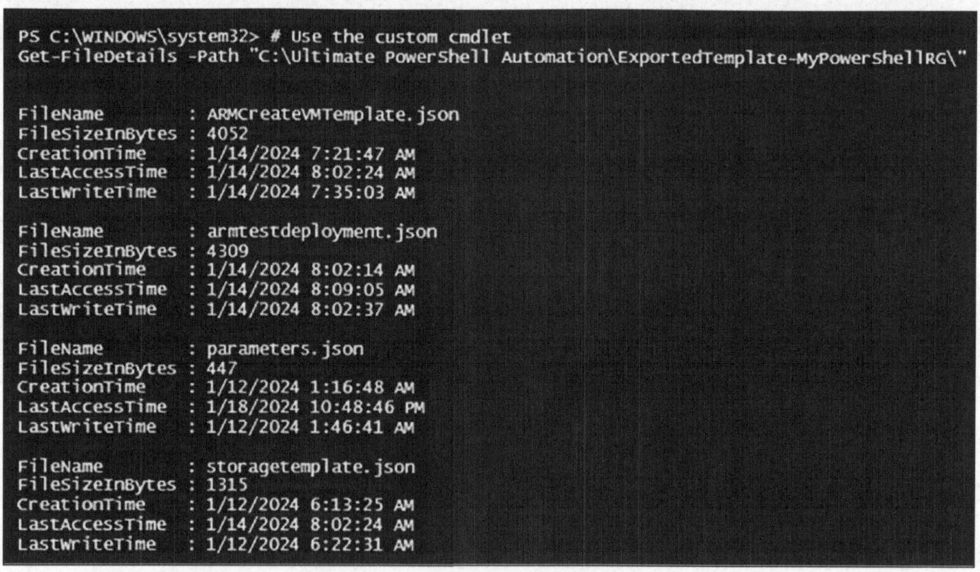

```
PS C:\WINDOWS\system32> # Use the custom cmdlet
Get-FileDetails -Path "C:\Ultimate PowerShell Automation\ExportedTemplate-MyPowerShellRG\"


FileName        : ARMCreateVMTemplate.json
FileSizeInBytes : 4052
CreationTime    : 1/14/2024 7:21:47 AM
LastAccessTime  : 1/14/2024 8:02:24 AM
LastWriteTime   : 1/14/2024 7:35:03 AM

FileName        : armtestdeployment.json
FileSizeInBytes : 4309
CreationTime    : 1/14/2024 8:02:14 AM
LastAccessTime  : 1/14/2024 8:09:05 AM
LastWriteTime   : 1/14/2024 8:02:37 AM

FileName        : parameters.json
FileSizeInBytes : 447
CreationTime    : 1/12/2024 1:16:48 AM
LastAccessTime  : 1/18/2024 10:48:46 PM
LastWriteTime   : 1/12/2024 1:46:41 AM

FileName        : storagetemplate.json
FileSizeInBytes : 1315
CreationTime    : 1/12/2024 6:13:25 AM
LastAccessTime  : 1/14/2024 8:02:24 AM
LastWriteTime   : 1/12/2024 6:22:31 AM
```

Figure 7.37: *Get-FileDetails to retrieve file details from a specified directory*

Manifest Modules

Manifest modules have a module manifest file (**`.psd1`**) that contains metadata about the module, such as version, author, and dependencies. The manifest can also define aliases and variables.

Usage: Manifest modules and additional metadata package and distribute modules. They provide a structured way to manage module information.

A manifest module is a file that provides information about a module and controls certain aspects of its usage. Although a module can exist without a manifest, if it has one, the manifest file has the same name as the module it describes but with a `.psd1` file extension. The manifest file contains a limited subset of the PowerShell script, which returns a hashtable consisting of a set of keys. These keys and their values specify the manifest elements for that module. Essentially, they describe the contents and attributes of the module, define any prerequisites, and determine how the components are processed.

You can view a simple module manifest file in the scripting module section.

Dynamic Modules

Dynamic modules are created dynamically during runtime using the **`New-Module`** cmdlet. They can be used to create ad-hoc modules with specific functions and variables.

Usage: Dynamic modules are helpful when creating temporary modules on the fly. They offer flexibility and can be customized based on runtime conditions or user inputs.

The following code is written in PowerShell and defines two functions, namely **`Get-DiskSpace`** and **`Get-OSInfo`**, within a script block. The **`Get-DiskSpace`** function uses the WMI to obtain disk space information, while the **`Get-OSInfo`** function retrieves operating system information with the help of CIM. Additionally, a separate function with the same name as the function within the script block named **`Get-OSInfo`** is created as a placeholder to write a test message to the console.

Find the code at: https://github.com/ava-orange-education/Ultimate-PowerShell-Automation-Guide/blob/main/Ch%207%20/Get-OSInfo.ps1

A dynamic module is created using the script block, called **`'dynamic'`**, and designed as a script module (**`-ModuleType`** ScriptModule). This module encapsulates the defined functions, providing modularity and encapsulation for functions.

To call functions from the dynamic module, use the syntax **`$module.'FunctionName'("localhost")`**. The placeholder function can also be called directly, demonstrating that functions outside the dynamic module can also be accessed.

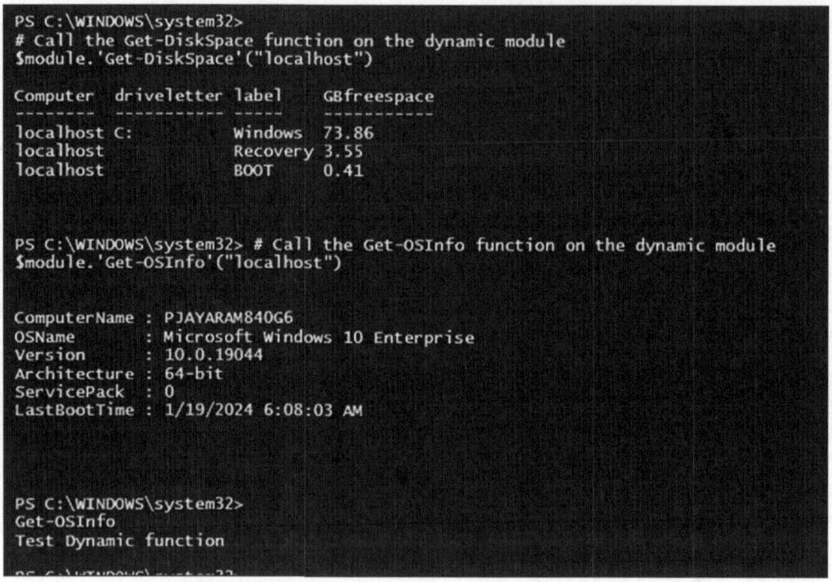

Figure 7.38: *Using dynamic module*

When we create a dynamic function with the same name as an existing cmdlet, we are essentially overwriting the original definition of that cmdlet. As a result, any calls to the cmdlet will invoke the dynamic version we created rather than the original cmdlet. It can be helpful in customizing the behavior of existing cmdlets or creating entirely new functionality.

Conclusion

In wrapping up our exploration of Windows administration using PowerShell, we have covered fundamental commands, delved into querying WMI and leveraging CIM cmdlets, mastered text file operations, and expanded our reach to working with structured data formats. The chapter concluded with a focus on remote administration tasks. This comprehensive journey equips administrators with the essential skills to efficiently manage and automate Windows environments. As you continue your PowerShell journey, these foundational skills will be invaluable in navigating the complexities of the modern IT landscape.

We will explore the power of concurrent execution and task scheduling in our next chapter, "*PowerShell Tasks and Jobs*." We will learn to optimize workflows, manage background tasks, and enhance productivity. We will also uncover the secrets of parallel execution for efficient automation. The next chapter details PowerShell tasks and jobs for automating the execution of the script. Get ready to elevate your PowerShell skills to the next level.

Multiple Choice Questions

1. Which cmdlet is commonly used to retrieve information about the operating system on a Windows machine?
   a. `Get-Service`
   b. `Get-Process`
   c. `Get-OSInfo`
   d. `Get-CimInstance -ClassName Win32_OperatingSystem`
2. What is the primary purpose of the `-ReadCount` parameter in the `Get-Content` cmdlet?
   a. To specify the file encoding
   b. To filter content based on a condition
   c. To limit the number of lines read at a time
   d. To display the content in a tabular format
3. Which CIM class is commonly used for querying information about user accounts on a Windows system?
   a. `Win32_Service`
   b. `Win32_UserAccount`
   c. `Win32_Process`
   d. `Win32_ComputerSystem`
4. What does the `Select-Object -ExpandProperty` cmdlet do in PowerShell?
   a. Sorts the output based on a specified property
   b. Filters the output based on a condition
   c. Expands the specified property and displays its value
   d. Groups the output based on a specified property
5. Which data format is commonly used to represent structured data in PowerShell and suitable for configuration files?
   a. JSON
   b. CSV

    c. XML

    d. TXT

6. Which cmdlet creates a new time span object in PowerShell for calculating system uptime?

    a. `New-Object`

    b. `New-TimeSpan`

    c. `New-Variable`

    d. `New-Item`

7. Which PowerShell cmdlet is specifically designed for working with remote systems?

    a. `Invoke-Command`

    b. `Get-Service`

    c. `Start-Job`

    d. `Export-CSV`

8. Which WMI class provides information about the physical processors on a Windows machine?

    a. `Win32_OperatingSystem`

    b. `Win32_ComputerSystem`

    c. `Win32_Process`

    d. `Win32_Processor`

Answers

1. d
2. c
3. b
4. c
5. c
6. b
7. a
8. d

Questions

- Write a PowerShell script that you would use to read and analyze log files on a Windows server. Explain the key components of the script and how they contribute to effective log file management.
- Imagine you need to perform a series of administrative tasks on multiple remote Windows servers. Describe your approach using PowerShell to automate these tasks efficiently and securely.
- Imagine you are tasked with analyzing and extracting specific information from a large CSV file using PowerShell. Develop a script that accomplishes this task and explains the steps in efficiently processing the CSV data.
- Describe a situation where you would use CIM (Common Information Model) cmdlets in PowerShell to manage system resources. How do these cmdlets enhance the capabilities of PowerShell in comparison to other approaches?

Key Terms

Certainly! Here are some key terms related to Windows Administration using PowerShell:

- **Common Information Model (CIM)**: A standard for representing and organizing management information about devices and services in a computing environment, often used with PowerShell for system management.
- **Windows Management Instrumentation (WMI)**: It is a set of extensions to the Windows Driver Model providing an operating system interface through which instrumented components provide information and notification.
- **Cmdlet**: A lightweight command used in PowerShell, typically designed to perform a specific function. Cmdlets follow a verb-noun naming convention (for example, `Get-Process`, `Set-ExecutionPolicy`).
- **Remote Administration**: The process of managing and administering a computer or system from a remote location using tools like PowerShell for tasks such as configuration, troubleshooting, and maintenance.
- **Structured Data Formats**: Formats like CSV, XML, and JSON (JavaScript Object Notation) are used to organize and store data in a structured way.

Part 3
PowerShell Advanced Topics

CHAPTER 8
PowerShell Tasks and Jobs

Introduction

At an advanced level, it is crucial to delve deep into PowerShell background jobs to master the implementation. Background jobs refer to discreetly executed tasks in the background of an application or system, allowing users to focus on other tasks. They are especially useful for resource-intensive or time-consuming operations, such as extensive data processing or automated email dispatches.

PowerShell background jobs offer several advantages that significantly enhance workflow and operational efficiency. They empower users to delegate prolonged or resource-intensive tasks to the background, freeing up time for concurrent work. Additionally, these jobs provide robust error handling and logging functionalities, ensuring job reliability and simplifying troubleshooting in case of issues. Furthermore, they streamline task management and automate repetitive processes.

One notable feature of PowerShell background jobs is their ability to execute tasks remotely, eliminating the need for direct access to a remote computer and simplifying remote task execution. Depending on the nature of the task, various types of background jobs can be employed. Asynchronous jobs enable multiple tasks to run concurrently without blocking the primary PowerShell session. Scheduled jobs are executed at specified intervals or times, suitable for tasks like backups or routine system updates.

Structure

In this chapter, we will discuss the following topics:

- PowerShell Tasks and Jobs
- Understanding PowerShell Background Jobs
- Creating and Managing Background Jobs

- Creating and Scheduling Tasks and Jobs
- Monitoring and Retrieving Results of Background Jobs
- Automating Administrative Tasks with Scheduled Jobs
- Creating Scheduled Tasks

PowerShell Tasks and Jobs

PowerShell tasks and jobs enhance your scripting capabilities by introducing parallel processing and background execution. These features are invaluable for handling resource-intensive operations, such as data processing or automated tasks. Whether you are managing job lifecycles or leveraging the **`-AsJob`** parameter, mastering PowerShell tasks empowers you to optimize workflow efficiency.

Utilizing the **`-AsJob`** parameter in these scenarios enables asynchronous execution, enhancing the efficiency of PowerShell scripts and commands by running them in the background. This capability is particularly advantageous for tasks involving remote systems or complex WMI operations where background execution can significantly improve overall script performance and responsiveness.

```
PS C:\Users\pjayaram> Get-Help * -Parameter AsJob | Sort-Object name |
Format-Table name, synopsis -AutoSize -Wrap
```

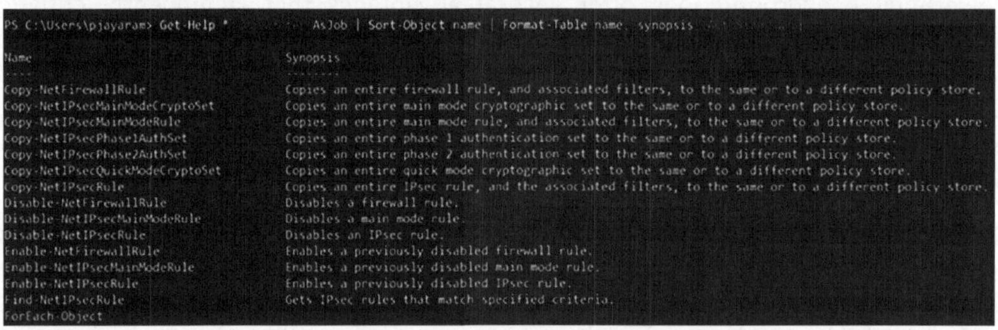

Figure 8.1: *Get a list of cmdlets related to Jobs*

PowerShell jobs offer a robust framework for enhancing productivity and managing complex operations efficiently. Understanding their usage and integration can significantly elevate your scripting capabilities.

The comprehensive set of cmdlets and techniques empowers users to effectively manage and leverage the power of background jobs in PowerShell.

Starting a Job on the Local Computer:

To start a background job locally, use the Start-Job cmdlet. Enclose the command in curly braces and use the **`ScriptBlock`** parameter.

```
Start-Job -ScriptBlock {Get-Process}
```

The command returns immediately, allowing continued work in the session while the job runs.

Getting Job Objects

Use **`Get-Job`** to retrieve background job objects, containing information about their state, location, and command.

```
Get-Job
```

Getting Job Results

To obtain job results, use **`Receive-Job`**. Results may not appear immediately, and running the command again gets additional results.

```
Receive-Job -Job $job
```

Waiting for Results:

The **`Wait-Job`** cmdlet suppresses the prompt until the job completes, ensuring all results are available.

```
Wait-Job -ID 10
```

Stopping and Removing Jobs

`Stop-Job` halts a job, and **`Remove-Job`** deletes it.

```
$job | Stop-Job Remove-Job -Job $job
```

Investigating Failed Jobs

Inspect the reason property of a failed job to determine the cause.

```
$job.ChildJobs[0].JobStateInfo.Reason
```

Listing Job-related Cmdlets

Depending on the modules and cmdlets available in your PowerShell environment, the list may include various job-related cmdlets.

The output of this command will be a list of command names related to jobs in PowerShell. These command names typically include verbs such as "**`Start`**," "**`Stop`**," "**`Get`**," and others, indicating actions you can perform with PowerShell jobs:

```
PS C:\Users\pjayaram> Get-Command -Noun Job | Select-Object -Property
Name
```

```
PS C:\Users\pjayaram> Get-Command -Noun Job | Select-Object -Property Name

Name
----
Debug-Job
Get-Job
Receive-Job
Remove-Job
Start-Job
Stop-Job
Wait-Job
```

***Figure 8.2**: Listing job-related cmdlets*

Understanding PowerShell Background Jobs

PowerShell background jobs are a powerful feature that allows you to run commands or scripts asynchronously in the background, enabling you to perform other tasks in the foreground without waiting for the background job to complete. This can significantly improve efficiency and parallelize tasks. Let us delve into understanding PowerShell background jobs.

This table provides a concise overview of each cmdlet, its purpose, and a brief description of its functionality.

Cmdlet	**Purpose**	**Description**
`Debug-Job`	Enables debugging of a background job by entering a debugging session for the specified job.	Useful for troubleshooting and identifying issues in executing a background job.
`Get-Job`	Retrieves background job information, including status, output, and properties.	Allows monitoring and management of background jobs in the current PowerShell session.
`Receive-Job`	Retrieves the results of a background job, collecting any output generated by the job since the last call to Receive-Job.	Useful for retrieving job output and processing results in the current session.
`Remove-Job`	Removes a background job from the list of active jobs, allowing cleanup and removal of completed or unnecessary jobs.	Helps in managing system resources by removing completed or unnecessary jobs.

`Start-Job`	Initiates the execution of a script block or command as a background job, allowing for asynchronous execution.	Enables parallel processing and background execution of tasks, freeing up the main session.
`Stop-Job`	Halts the execution of a background job, forcefully stopping a running job.	Useful for terminating a job if it is not completing as expected or needs immediate cessation.
`Wait-Job`	Pauses the script execution until a background job has completed, allowing synchronization with the job's completion.	Enables the script to wait for the completion of a specific job before proceeding.

Table 8.1: *Overview of cmdlet for PowerShell background jobs*

Overview of Key Job cmdlets

Once a job has been initiated in PowerShell, various job cmdlets become invaluable for effectively interacting with and managing these background tasks. Here is an overview of some key Job cmdlets:

`Get-Job`

Retrieves information about all jobs associated with the current session.

Parameters:

- **`-Before`**, **`-After`**: Filters jobs based on their completion time.
- **`-Newest`**: Specifies the number of newest jobs to retrieve.
- **`-State`**: Filters jobs based on their current state.

```
Get-Job -State Completed
```

`Wait-Job`

Pauses script execution until a job has output ready to be retrieved.

```
Wait-Job -Id 1
```

`Receive-Job`

Retrieves any output generated by the job since the last call to Receive-Job.

```
Receive-Job -Id 1
```

`Stop-Job`

Halts the execution of a job.

```
Stop-Job -Id 1
```

`Remove-Job`

Removes a job from the list of active jobs.

```
Remove-Job -Id 1
```

Additionally, PowerShell provides a convenient way to execute cmdlets in the background using the **`-AsJob`** parameter. This feature can be particularly useful with cmdlets like **`Invoke-Command`** (especially when operating against remote computers) and a set of WMI-related cmdlets.

`Invoke-Command` with `-AsJob`

Executes a script block on a remote computer as a background job.

```
Invoke-Command -ComputerName Server01 -ScriptBlock { Get-Process }
-AsJob
```

WMI-Related Cmdlets with `-AsJob`

Allows WMI-related tasks to be performed in the background.

```
Get-WmiObject -Class Win32_Bios -AsJob
```

Knowing More About PowerShell Jobs

PowerShell jobs provide a way to manage and monitor the execution of commands or scripts in the background, allowing users to parallelize tasks, improve efficiency, and maintain better control over concurrent operations. Here are a few key points:

Background Execution

PowerShell jobs allow you to run commands or scripts in the background, freeing up the console for additional tasks. This is especially useful for time-consuming operations that you do not want to tie up the main PowerShell session.

```
$job = Start-Job -ScriptBlock { Start-Sleep -Seconds 10;
"Job Completed!" }
```

Parallel Processing

You can use jobs to execute multiple tasks concurrently, using multicore systems to improve overall performance. This is particularly beneficial for tasks such as processing multiple files or performing independent calculations or inventory generation.

```
1..5 | ForEach-Object -Parallel { Write-Output $_ } -AsJob
```

Monitoring and Control

PowerShell provides cmdlets like **`Get-Job`**, **`Receive-Job`**, and **`Wait-Job`** that allow you to monitor the status of jobs, retrieve their output, and wait for their completion. This gives you control over the execution flow and enables you to take action based on the results.

Utilize cmdlets like **`Get-Job`**, **`Receive-Job`**, and **`Wait-Job`** for monitoring job status, retrieving output, and waiting for completion.

```
Get-Job Wait-Job $job Receive-Job $job
```

Asynchronous Operation

Jobs in PowerShell operate asynchronously, meaning you can initiate a job and continue working in the console without waiting for the job to complete. This asynchronous behavior enhances productivity and allows for a more responsive user experience.

```
$job = Start-Job -ScriptBlock { Start-Sleep -Seconds 10;
"Job Completed!" }
```

Task Manager Analogy

Comparing PowerShell jobs to a task manager is apt. It reflects the ability to initiate, monitor, and manage multiple tasks independently, similar to how a task manager allows you to observe and control running processes on a computer.

Here is a simple example to illustrate the concept:

```
# Start a background job

$job = Start-Job -ScriptBlock { Start-Sleep -Seconds 10 "Job Completed!"
}

# Monitor job status

Get-Job

# Wait for the job to complete

Wait-Job $job

# Retrieve job output

Receive-Job $job
```

In this example, a job is started to sleep for 10 seconds, and you can use the various job cmdlets to check its status, wait for completion, and retrieve the output.

Security Considerations

Proper security measures are crucial to prevent vulnerabilities. This includes access control, secure credential storage, encryption of sensitive data, digital signing, and adhering to the principle of least privilege.

To learn more about security considerations, please refer to the *Remote Job Example* section in this chapter.

Performance Considerations

Thread jobs are faster and lighter but may have overhead. Consider performance factors based on the nature of tasks.

For more information on this topic, please refer to the *Optimizing* WMI *Operations Use-Case* section in this chapter.

Creating and Managing Background Jobs

Exploring the landscape of PowerShell jobs introduces us to a spectrum of types, each tailored for specific scenarios. From one-time jobs and remote jobs to thread jobs, background jobs, event-based jobs, and workflow jobs, we navigate through the versatile capabilities of PowerShell to address many automation needs.

One-Time Jobs

In contrast, one-time jobs are designed for singular execution and automatically deleted upon completion. They are ideal for tasks that do not necessitate persistence or do not contribute to ongoing background processing.

```
# Start a one-time job to perform a specific task

Start-Job -ScriptBlock { Send-MailMessage -To "user@example.com"
-Subject "Job Completed" -Body "Task executed successfully." }
```

Remote Jobs

Remote jobs facilitate the initiation of tasks on remote computers or servers, streamlining remote task execution. This capability is particularly advantageous when managing distributed systems or orchestrating operations across multiple machines.

```
# Start a job on a remote server to retrieve system information

Invoke-Command -ComputerName RemoteServer -ScriptBlock { Get-WmiObject
Win32_ComputerSystem } -AsJob
```

Thread Jobs

Thread jobs harness the multi-threading capabilities of PowerShell, enhancing performance and execution speed. This is especially beneficial for computationally intensive tasks that can be parallelized.

```
# Start a thread job to process items concurrently

1..10 | ForEach-Object -Parallel { $_ * 2 } -ThrottleLimit 5 -AsJob
```

There are two ways to start thread-based jobs:

- **`Start-ThreadJob`** : from the **`ThreadJob`** module

- **ForEach-Object -Parallel -AsJob** : the parallel feature was added in PowerShell 7.0

  Using **Start-ThreadJob**

The **ThreadJob** module first shipped with PowerShell 6. It can also be installed from the PowerShell Gallery for Windows PowerShell 5.1.

Indeed, PowerShell 7 introduced the **-Parallel** parameter for the **ForEach-Object** cmdlet, allowing parallel execution of script blocks. The **-ThrottleLimit** parameter controls the number of script blocks running concurrently.

Here is a basic example:

```
# Using ForEach-Object -Parallel

Measure-Command { 1..5 | ForEach-Object -Parallel { param($item) Start-
Sleep -Seconds 1 Write-Output "Processed item: $item" } -ThrottleLimit 5
} | Select-Object TotalSeconds
```

In this example:

1..5 represents the input range.

ForEach-Object -Parallel processes each item in parallel.

The **-ThrottleLimit** 5 allows up to 5 parallel executions.

The script block inside **-Parallel** can include any commands or logic you want to execute in parallel.

Remember to adjust the **-ThrottleLimit** based on your machine's capabilities. If you're working with CPU-bound tasks, setting it close to the number of available cores might be beneficial.

This approach is particularly useful for tasks that involve waiting for external resources, like file operations or remote calls, as it allows other threads to continue processing while one is waiting.

Event-Based Jobs

Event-based jobs respond to specific events or conditions, such as changes in the file system or breaches of performance thresholds. They provide a dynamic approach to task execution based on real-time triggers.

```
# Register an event-based job to execute when a file is created

Register-ObjectEvent -InputObject (Get-Item "C:\Path\to\File.txt")
-EventName Created -Action { Write-Host "File Created!" } -AsJob
```

Register-ObjectEvent in PowerShell provides a powerful mechanism for responding to diverse events, including those within the Windows Event logs. This discussion focuses on its application specifically for Windows Event logs monitoring.

Constructing a Query

To formulate a query for **`Register-ObjectEvent`**, the **`xPath`** notation is utilized. Despite its initial complexity, a practical approach involves using the Event Viewer to filter logs in the GUI and examining the XML tab for results.

For example, when monitoring failed login attempts with Event ID 4625 in the Security logs, the GUI filter looks like this:

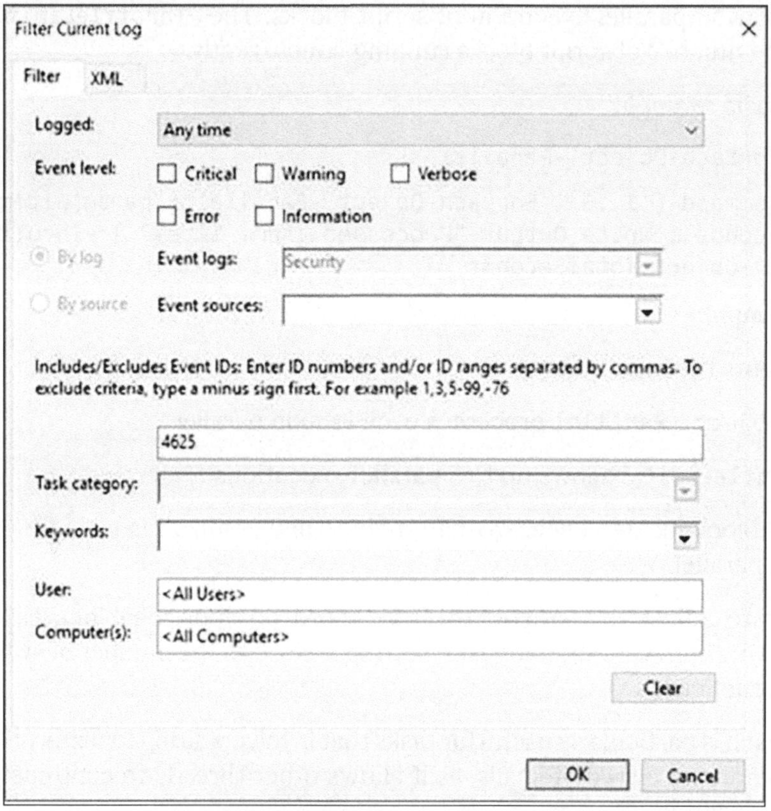

***Figure 8.3**: Filter current logs*

And the corresponding xPath query extracted from the XML tab:

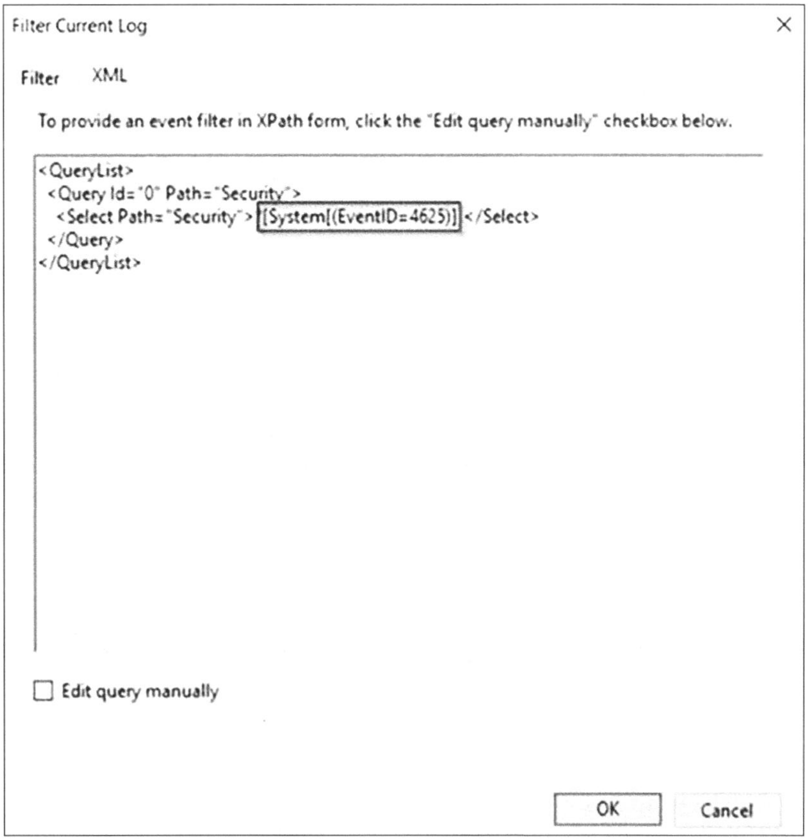

Figure 8.4*: View XPath Query from XML tab*

Code

The xPath query is translated into a query object using .NET:

```
$eventId = 4625

$logName = 'Security'

$select = "*[System[(EventID=$eventId)]]"

$query = [System.Diagnostics.Eventing.Reader.EventLogQuery]::new($lo-
gName, [System.Diagnostics.Eventing.Reader.PathType]::LogName, $select)
```

Creating a Watcher

Building the watcher involves creating it with .NET and ensuring its activation:

```
$watcher = [System.Diagnostics.Eventing.Reader.EventLogWatcher]::new
($query)

$watcher.Enabled = $true
```

Action

When using the **Register-ObjectEvent** cmdlet, an action in the form of a script block must be specified. This script block executes when the event is triggered. In the following example, a simple script is demonstrated:

```
$action = {
    $string = @»
- Attempted logon from: $($eventArgs.EventRecord.properties[19].value)
- Targeting account: $($eventArgs.EventRecord.properties[5].value)
- on domain: $($eventArgs.EventRecord.properties[6].value)
"@
    Write-Host $string
    $string | Out-File C:\tmp\security.log -Append
}
```

Integration

The complete script integrates the preceding components:

```
$eventId = 4625
$logName = 'Security'
$select = "*[System[(EventID=$eventId)]]"
$query = [System.Diagnostics.Eventing.Reader.EventLogQuery]::new($logName,
[System.Diagnostics.Eventing.Reader.PathType]::LogName, $select)
$watcher = [System.Diagnostics.Eventing.Reader.EventLogWatcher]::new
($query)
$watcher.Enabled = $true
$action = {
    $string = @"
$(Get-Date -Format yyyyMMddTHHmmssfff) - Attempted logon from: $($eventArgs.
EventRecord.properties[19].value)
  - Targeting account: $($eventArgs.EventRecord.properties[5].value)
  - on domain: $($eventArgs.EventRecord.properties[6].value)
"@
    Write-Host $string
    $string | Out-File C:\temp\badlogins.log -Append
```

```
}
$job = Register-ObjectEvent -InputObject $watcher -EventName
'EventRecordWritten' -Action $action
Receive-Job $job
```

Workflow Jobs

Workflow jobs execute a predetermined sequence of steps in a structured order, facilitating complex and multi-step task automation. This is advantageous for orchestrating intricate processes with dependencies.

Windows PowerShell workflow offers powerful capabilities, often overlooked due to perceived complexity.

```
# This example demonstrates a workflow simulating a long-running operation.

workflow Simulate-LongRunningWorkflow {

    # Simulate a time-consuming operation
    Start-Sleep -Seconds 10

    # Suspend the workflow, allowing for manual intervention or later
resumption
    Suspend-Workflow

    # Attempt to retrieve information about logical disks (executed upon
workflow resumption)
    Get-WmiObject -Class Win32_LogicalDisk |
        Where-Object { $_.DriveType -eq 3 } |
        Select-Object DeviceID, @{Name='Size(GB)'; Expression={ $_.Size
/ 1GB }},
            @{Name='FreeSpace(GB)'; Expression={ $_.FreeSpace / 1GB }}
}

# Start the workflow as a background job
Simulate-LongRunningWorkflow
```

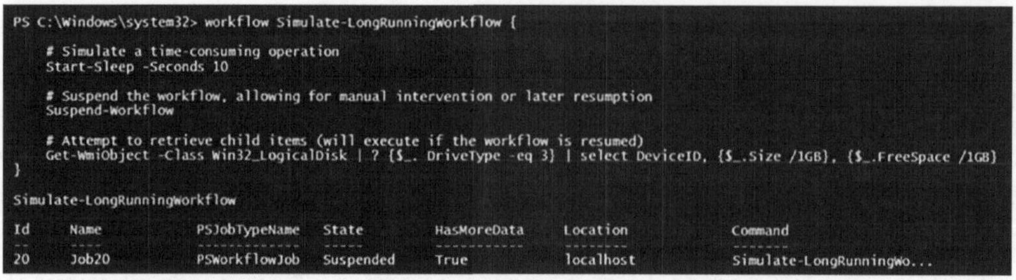

***Figure 8.5**: Demonstrating a workflow simulating a long-running operation*

The **Suspend-Workflow** cmdlet suspends the workflow, allowing for manual intervention or later resumption.

The workflow attempts to retrieve information about logical disks upon resumption.

```
# Retrieve the output of the resumed workflow
Receive-Job -Id 20


# Retrieve information about the background job
Get-Job -Id 20


# Resume the suspended workflow
Resume-Job -Id 20
```

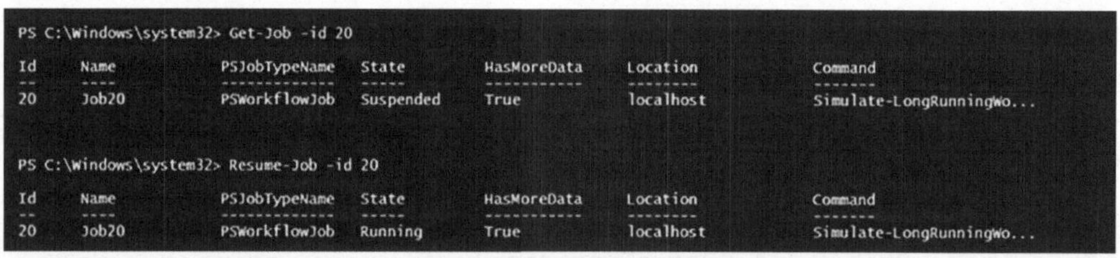

***Figure 8.6**: Retrieve information about logical disks*

Now, we can check the status of the job (**Get-Job**), resume the suspended workflow (**Resume-Job**), and retrieve the output (**Receive-Job**) after the resumption.

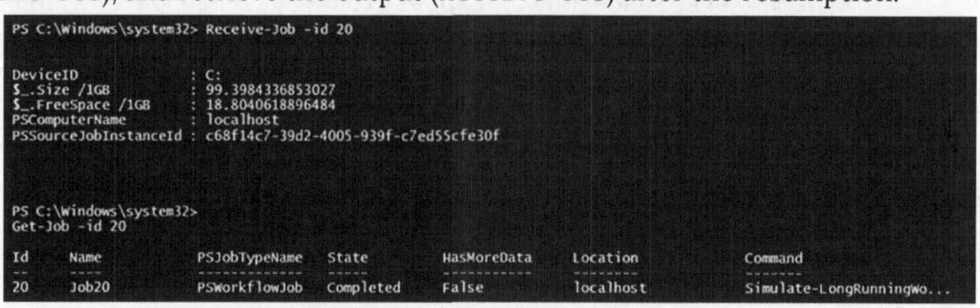

***Figure 8.7**: Check the status of the job*

Optimizing WMI Operations Use-Case

When conducting expansive WMI operations across numerous computers, managing the rate at which these operations are executed is essential to avoid network congestion and improve overall efficiency.

Solution

Employ the **-ThrottleLimit** parameter in conjunction with the **Get-WmiObject** cmdlet and execute it as a background job:

```
# Retrieve the list of computer names from a file
$computers = Get-Content computers.txt
# Initiate WMI query with throttle control and background execution
Get-WmiObject Win32_OperatingSystem -Computer $computers -ThrottleLimit
```

The solution addresses a common issue encountered in large-scale WMI operations where sequential processing can lead to significant wait times due to network latency. By using the -**ThrottleLimit** parameter, the script limits the number of concurrent WMI operations, preventing network congestion and enhancing overall performance.

In this example, a throttle limit of 10 is set, meaning that the script will concurrently process WMI queries for up to 10 computers at a time. This approach is beneficial when dealing with many remote systems, as it optimizes resource utilization and reduces the time required to complete the operation.

Remember to adjust the throttle limit based on your network capacity, system resources, and the specific requirements of your WMI operation.

Real-Time Examples

PowerShell background jobs allow for executing commands or expressions in the background, enabling concurrent operations without affecting the current session.

PowerShell facilitates concurrent execution of commands and scripts through background jobs. There are three main types of jobs that enable this concurrency:

Remote Job Example

RemoteJobs enable the execution of commands and scripts on a remote session. This provides a high isolation level, ensuring that errors or issues within the job do not impact other running jobs or the parent session. However, the remote execution introduces additional overhead, primarily due to the serialization and deserialization of objects passed between the local and remote sessions.

We can save the **SecureString** to a file and then read it later. However, remember that storing credentials in a file poses security risks, and you should ensure that the file is adequately protected.

Saving the SecureString to a File

PowerShell users can use the **ConvertFrom-SecureString** cmdlet to encrypt the input and store it in a file when prompted for a password. This encrypted representation can later be retrieved for reuse without exposing the actual password.

```
# Prompt user for password
$decryptedPassword = Read-Host -Prompt "Enter your password"
-AsSecureString
# Save the SecureString to a file
$decryptedPassword | ConvertFrom-SecureString | Set-Content -Path "C:\
Path\To\SecureString.txt"
```

This code snippet guides users through entering a password securely and then encrypts and stores it in the specified file location. Keep in mind that securing this file is crucial to prevent unauthorized access to sensitive information.

Note: *Always exercise caution when handling passwords and consider additional security measures, such as restricting file permissions and employing encryption, to safeguard stored credentials.*

Reading the SecureString from File

When there is a need to reuse an encrypted password stored in a file, PowerShell provides a method to read the **SecureString** representation safely. This process involves retrieving the encrypted string from the file and converting it back into a **SecureString** for secure use in scripts.

```
# Read the SecureString from the file
$encryptedPassword = Get-Content -Path "C:\Path\To\SecureString.txt" |
ConvertTo-SecureString


# Use the SecureString to create PSCredential
$User = "SaasCloud\pjayaram"
$Cred = New-Object System.Management.Automation.PSCredential($User,
$encryptedPassword)
```

```
# Create a background job with the saved credentials
$job = Invoke-Command -ComputerName opssaas -ScriptBlock { Get-Process }
-AsJob -Credential $Cred


# Wait for the job to complete and then receive the job output
Wait-Job $job
Receive-Job $job
```

Please note that while this approach can save you from entering the password each time, it is crucial to protect the file containing the **`SecureString`** to prevent unauthorized access. Additionally, be aware of the inherent security considerations associated with storing credentials, and consider alternative solutions, such as using managed service accounts or key vaults, depending on your environment and requirements.

```
PS C:\Windows\system32> $job=Invoke-Command -computername opssaas -scriptblock { Get-process} -AsJob -Credential $Cred

Id     Name            PSJobTypeName   State         HasMoreData     Location             Command
--     ----            -------------   -----         -----------     --------             -------
6      Job6            RemoteJob       Running       True            opssaas               Get-process


PS C:\Windows\system32> get-job -Id 6

Id     Name            PSJobTypeName   State         HasMoreData     Location             Command
--     ----            -------------   -----         -----------     --------             -------
6      Job6            RemoteJob       Completed     True            opssaas               Get-process


PS C:\Windows\system32> Receive-Job $job

Handles  NPM(K)    PM(K)      WS(K)     CPU(s)     Id  SI ProcessName                    PSComputerName
-------  ------    -----      -----     ------     --  -- -----------                    --------------
   1615     125    67880     139304     231.89   5268   0 App                            opssaas
    442      28     5196      16476       3.88   1908   0 svc                            opssaas
    230      15     4872      15716       0.08   3668   5 backgroundTaskHost             opssaas
    174       9     6876      10156       0.78  16584   2 bash                           opssaas
```

Figure 8.8: *Reading the SecureString from file*

Note: *In a real-world scenario, it is crucial to handle sensitive information securely and avoid storing or displaying passwords in plain text, even in demonstration code.*

BackgroundJob Example

`BackgroundJobs` run commands and scripts in a separate process on the local machine. This maintains a degree of isolation similar to **`RemoteJobs`** but with less overhead. This is beneficial for tasks that require concurrency without the complexities associated with remote execution.

```
Start-Job -ScriptBlock { Get-Service }
```

PSTaskJob or ThreadJob Example

`PSTaskJobs` or **`ThreadJobs`** execute commands and scripts in a separate thread within the same process on the local machine. This offers a compromise between isolation and overhead. While these jobs have reduced overhead compared to remote and background jobs, they are less robust as they share the same process. If one thread-based job encounters a critical error, it may affect other jobs in the same process.

```
Start-ThreadJob -ScriptBlock { Get-EventLog -LogName System }
```

Running scripts remotely or in separate processes provides isolation, preventing errors in one job from affecting others or the parent session. However, remoting introduces overhead due to object serialization.

Thread-based jobs, while less robust, have lower overhead as they run in the same process. Errors in one thread-based job can affect others in the same process.

It is important to note that the parent session monitors job status and terminates child jobs and processes if they are terminated. There are two ways to avoid this: using Invoke-Command for jobs in disconnected sessions or Start-Process for creating a new process instead of a job.

Performance Measurement

Performance measurement is a critical aspect of PowerShell scripting, especially when dealing with various types of jobs. Understanding and optimizing performance is critical to efficient automation, whether it is background jobs, remote tasks, or scheduled operations. This section delves into the tools and techniques available for measuring and enhancing performance across different job types.

```
# Using ForEach-Object

Measure-Command {1..5 | ForEach-Object {Start-Sleep 1} } | Select-Object
TotalSeconds


# Using Start-Job

Measure-Command {1..5 | ForEach-Object {Start-Job {Start-Sleep 1}} |
Wait-Job} | Select-Object TotalSeconds


# Using Start-ThreadJob

Measure-Command {1..5 | ForEach-Object {Start-ThreadJob -ThrottleLimit 5
{Start-Sleep 1}} | Wait-Job} | Select-Object TotalSeconds


# Using ForEach-Object -Parallel

Measure-Command {1..5 | ForEach-Object -Parallel {Start-Sleep 1}
-ThrottleLimit 5} | Select-Object TotalSeconds
```

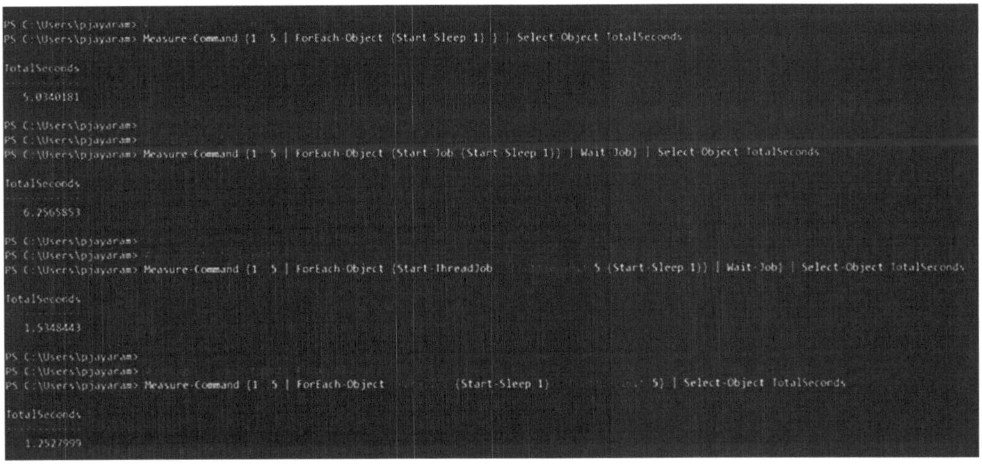

Figure 8.9: *Performance measurement of PowerShell scripting*

Notes:

- For simple and sequential tasks, **`ForEach-Object`** may suffice.
- **`Start-Job`** could be a suitable choice when job management overhead is acceptable.
- For improved performance with a higher degree of parallelism, especially in resource-intensive tasks, **`Start-ThreadJob`** is beneficial.
- **`ForEach-Object -Parallel`** is recommended for scenarios where efficient parallel processing is essential and careful throttle limit tuning is required.

Benchmarking and testing each approach in the context of the specific tasks and system requirements is crucial to determine the most effective solution. Consider factors such as task complexity, resource utilization, and system responsiveness when deciding.

Parallel processing is an excellent solution when you have tasks or jobs that can be executed independently of each other. It allows you to divide the workload among multiple threads or processes, taking advantage of the available resources and potentially reducing the overall execution time.

PowerShell Job Security

Considering security in the creation and management of background jobs is paramount. Failure to secure background jobs properly can pose vulnerabilities in the system. It's essential to ensure that only authorized users have the privilege to run or manage jobs and implement security measures to prevent injection attacks. Key security considerations include access control, restricting access to PowerShell background jobs exclusively to authorized users, secure credential storage using methods like PowerShell Secure String or Credential Manager, encryption of sensitive data transmitted between machines or stored in files during job execution, digital signing of PowerShell code to prevent malicious code execution, and adhering to the principle of least privilege, running jobs with the minimum level of privilege to mitigate potential security risks.

To illustrate, let us consider a scenario where a PowerShell background job involves transferring confidential data between two servers. In this context, robust security measures should encompass user access controls, encryption of the transmitted data, secure storage of credentials, and the application of least privilege principles to minimize potential security risks.

Encryption Code

This code snippet illustrates the fundamental steps involved in encrypting a password using PowerShell:

```
# Original password
$plainPassword = "Prashanth@123"

# Convert the password to a secure string
$securePassword = ConvertTo-SecureString -String $plainPassword
-AsPlainText -Force

# Convert the secure string to an encrypted string
$encryptedPassword = ConvertFrom-SecureString $securePassword

# Display the encrypted password
Write-Host "Encrypted Password: $encryptedPassword"
```

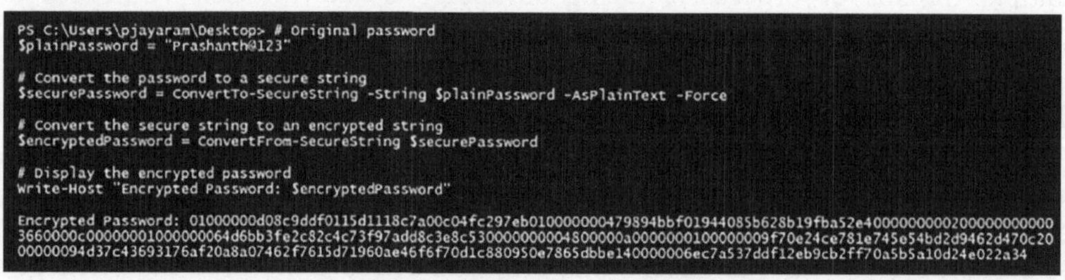

Figure 8.10: *Encryption code*

Decryption Code

This code snippet illustrates the fundamental steps involved in decrypting a password using PowerShell. It demonstrates how to use the Marshal class to decrypt an already encrypted password.

```
# Display the encrypted password (for demonstration purposes)
Write-Host "Encrypted Password: $encryptedPassword"

# Convert the encrypted string back to a secure string
$decryptedSecurePassword = ConvertTo-SecureString -String $encrypted-
Password

# Use Marshal class for decryption
$marshal = [System.Runtime.InteropServices.Marshal]

# Convert secure string to binary string (BSTR)
$binaryString = $marshal::SecureStringToBSTR($decryptedSecurePassword)

# Convert BSTR to plain text string (password)
$decryptedPassword = $marshal::PtrToStringAuto($binaryString)

# Display the decrypted password
Write-Host "Decrypted Password: $decryptedPassword"

# Clear unmanaged memory
$marshal::ZeroFreeBSTR($binaryString)
```

The output demonstrates decrypting an encrypted password using the **Marshal** class in PowerShell.

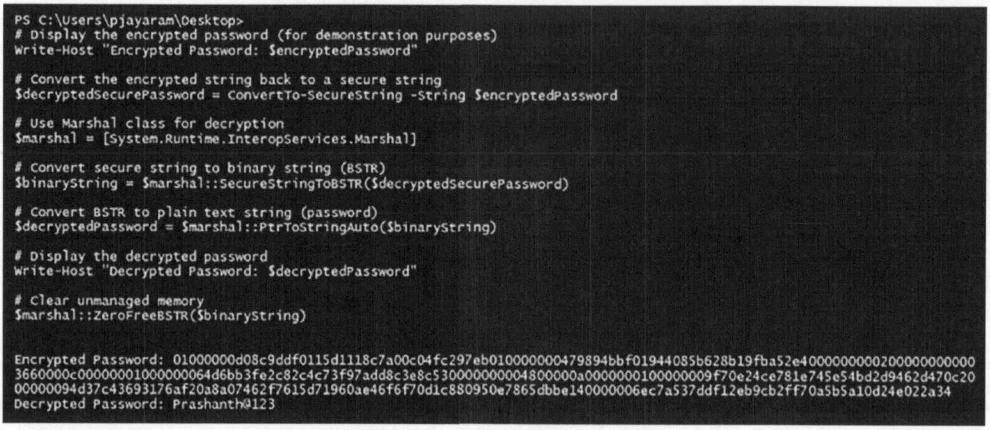

Figure 8.11: *Decryption code*

Creating a Scheduled Task on Target Machine

In this example, we will explore using PowerShell to create a scheduled task on a remote machine, providing a seamless way to automate tasks on user logon. Let us walk through the process step-by-step.

PowerShell script demonstrates how to create a scheduled task that runs a PowerShell script every Monday at 5 am.

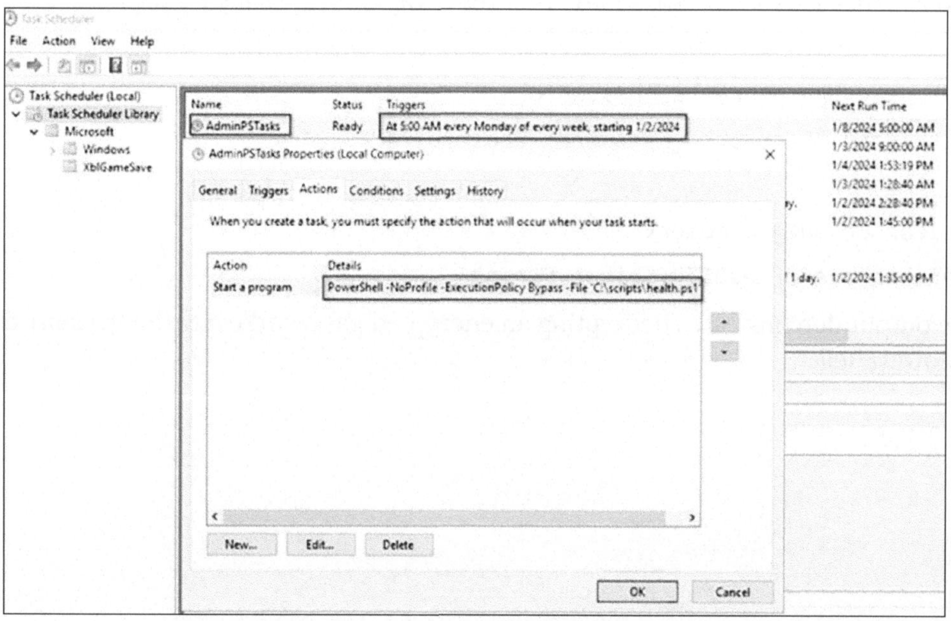

Figure 8.12: *Creating a scheduled task on target machine*

```
# Define the scheduled task trigger for a weekly execution on Monday at 5
am
$taskTrigger = New-ScheduledTaskTrigger -Weekly -DaysOfWeek Monday -At
5am


# Define the action to be performed by the scheduled task using
PowerShell
$taskAction = New-ScheduledTaskAction -Execute "PowerShell" -Argument
"-NoProfile -ExecutionPolicy Bypass -File 'C:\scripts\health.ps1' -Output
'HTML'" -WorkingDirectory 'C:\scripts'


# Register the scheduled task with advanced configurations
Register-ScheduledTask -Action $taskAction -Trigger $taskTrigger -Task-
Name 'AdminPSTasks' -User 'NT AUTHORITY\SYSTEM' -Force


# Configure additional settings for the scheduled task (optional)
$taskSettings = Get-ScheduledTask -TaskName 'AdminPSTasks'
```

Let us break down the script:

A trigger (**$taskTrigger**) is configured to run the task weekly on Monday at 5 am using the **New-ScheduledTaskTrigger** cmdlet.

The action (**$taskAction**) is defined to execute a PowerShell script (**Health.ps1**) with specific execution options and output settings using the **New-ScheduledTaskAction** cmdlet. You can replace the **Health.ps1** script with any other related script to test the functionality.

The **Register-ScheduledTask** cmdlet is used to register the scheduled task with the specified action and trigger. The task is named **'AdminPSTasks'** and runs with elevated system privileges (**NT AUTHORITY\SYSTEM**). The **-Force** parameter ensures that the task is registered even if it already exists.

Conclusion

Exploring the advanced capabilities of PowerShell, including background jobs and workflows, unveils a powerful arsenal for efficient task execution and automation. Background jobs excel in parallel processing, allowing users to run scripts or commands asynchronously, enhancing productivity by freeing up the console for concurrent tasks. The job monitoring cmdlets, such as **Get-Job**, **Receive-Job**, and **Wait-Job**, provide precise control over execution flow, making it akin to managing processes through a task manager.

Remote execution stands out as a distinctive feature, enabling the initiation of tasks on remote computers without direct access. This capability simplifies remote task execution, making it an invaluable asset for managing distributed environments and facilitating seamless automation across a network.

Integrating Windows Management Instrumentation (WMI) further extends PowerShell's reach into system management and monitoring. WMI enables querying and interacting with system information, services, and events, providing a comprehensive toolkit for system administrators and automation enthusiasts.

Security considerations are paramount, emphasizing access control, secure credential storage, encryption, and adherence to the principle of least privilege. The diverse set of cmdlets for job management, including **`Start-Job`**, **`Stop-Job`**, and **`Remove-Job`**, empowers users with precise control over background jobs.

Although perceived as complex, workflows offer a structured approach to handling time-consuming operations. Their ability to suspend and resume allows for manual intervention and seamless continuation, contributing to a robust framework for managing complex automation scenarios.

In the realm of performance, PowerShell's multi-threading capabilities, exemplified by thread jobs, harness the full potential of multi-core systems, significantly improving overall execution speed.

By delving into these advanced PowerShell features, users streamline task management and address security concerns, and unlock the potential for comprehensive system management, remote automation, and performance optimization in diverse computing environments. The journey into PowerShell's advanced functionalities opens doors to a new level of scripting efficiency and automation control.

The next chapter will introduce you to PowerShell remoting, which is a feature in Windows PowerShell that lets you run commands or scripts on a remote machine. This feature is especially useful for system administrators and IT professionals, as it enables them to manage and automate tasks on remote computers.

Multiple Choice Questions

1. What is the purpose of the `Start-Job` cmdlet in PowerShell?
    a. Stop a running job
    b. Start a new background job
    c. Retrieve information about jobs
    d. Remove a completed job

2. Which cmdlet is used to retrieve the results of a background job in PowerShell?
   a. `Get-Job`
   b. `Receive-Job`
   c. `Wait-Job`
   d. `Start-Job`
3. In PowerShell, what does the `Suspend-Workflow` cmdlet do?
   a. Starts a workflow
   b. Suspends a running workflow
   c. Resumes a suspended workflow
   d. Stops a workflow
4. What is the purpose of the `Register-ObjectEvent` cmdlet in PowerShell?
   a. Register a new PowerShell event
   b. Register an event on an object
   c. Register a scheduled event
   d. Register an event log entry
5. How can you run a PowerShell script block as a background job?
   a. Using the `Invoke-Command` cmdlet
   b. Using the `Start-Job` cmdlet
   c. Using the `Wait-Job` cmdlet
   d. Using the `Receive-Job` cmdlet
6. What does the `Get-WmiObject` cmdlet in PowerShell allow you to do?
   a. Retrieve information from a remote computer
   b. Create a new WMI object
   c. Stop a Windows service
   d. Remove a WMI namespace

7. What is the purpose of the `SecureStringToBSTR` method in PowerShell?
    a. Encrypt a secure string
    b. Convert a secure string to a binary string
    c. Convert a secure string to plain text
    d. Free unmanaged memory
8. Which PowerShell feature allows you to execute tasks on remote computers?
    a. Background jobs
    b. Workflows
    c. Remote execution
    d. Event-based jobs
9. What cmdlet is used to debug a background job in PowerShell?
    a. `Debug-Job`
    b. `Start-Job`
    c. `Stop-Job`
    d. `Get-Job`
10. How does the Wait-Job cmdlet in PowerShell differ from the `Receive-Job` cmdlet?
    a. `Wait-Job` pauses script execution until job completion
    b. `Receive-Job` retrieves job output
    c. `Wait-Job` retrieves job output
    d. `Receive-Job` pauses script execution until job completion

Answers

1. b
2. b
3. b
4. b
5. b
6. a

7. b
8. c
9. a
10. a

Questions

- Which cmdlet is used to monitor the status of background jobs in PowerShell?
- What security measure is recommended to prevent injection attacks in PowerShell background jobs?
- What is the purpose of the `ConvertFrom-SecureString` cmdlet in PowerShell encryption?
- Which cmdlet is used to remove a background job from the list of active jobs?
- How can you execute tasks on remote computers in PowerShell without direct access?

Key Terms

- **PowerShell Background Jobs:** PowerShell background jobs allow the asynchronous execution of commands or scripts, freeing up the console for additional tasks, enabling parallel processing, and providing monitoring and control mechanisms.
- **Security:** In the context of PowerShell, security involves implementing measures such as access control, prevention of injection attacks, least privilege principles, secure credential storage, encryption of sensitive data, and digital signing of code to protect systems from vulnerabilities.
- **PowerShell Cmdlets:** Cmdlets, or command-lets, are lightweight PowerShell commands that perform specific tasks. Examples include `Start-Job`, `Stop-Job`, `Wait-Job`, `Get-Job`, Receive-Job, Remove-Job, and Debug-Job, which are essential for managing background jobs.
- **Encryption:** Encryption in PowerShell involves converting sensitive data into a secure format. `ConvertTo-SecureString` transforms a plain text string into a secure string, while `ConvertFrom-SecureString` reverses the process.
- **Remote Execution:** Remote execution in PowerShell is facilitated by cmdlets like `Invoke-Command` and `New-PSSession`, allowing the initiation and execution of scripts or commands on remote computers.
- **PowerShell Workflows:** PowerShell workflows are sequences of PowerShell commands designed to perform long-running and parallelizable tasks. They

can be suspended and resumed, providing flexibility in managing complex operations.

- **WMI (Windows Management Instrumentation):** WMI is a set of specifications from Microsoft that provides a standardized way to manage network devices and systems. In PowerShell, `Get-WmiObject` is used to interact with WMI.
- **Performance:** In the context of PowerShell, performance refers to optimizing the execution of tasks. Multicore systems are leveraged for parallel processing, enhancing overall performance in tasks that can be divided into independent components.

Chapter 9
PowerShell Remoting

Introduction

PowerShell Remoting is a feature that empowers administrators to execute commands on remote systems, enabling seamless management of machines without physically accessing them. This functionality allows the administrator's local PowerShell session to connect to a remote session on a different machine. Commands entered in the local system are transmitted to the remote computer and executed as if the administrator were physically present. The results are then sent back to the local system. PowerShell Remoting relies on the Windows Remote Management (WinRM) framework and Windows Management Instrumentation (WMI) within the WinRM framework. PowerShell Remoting occurs over TCP, HTTP, and HTTPS protocols.

In PowerShell version 7, there are three main approaches to using PowerShell Remoting. The first involves using the computer name parameter in various cmdlets. The second method employs the **`Invoke-Command`** cmdlet, which runs PowerShell locally and pushes the values to the remote computer, utilizing a PowerShell session. The third option is to initiate an interactive PowerShell session, akin to SSH, where the local terminal can be used to execute commands on a remote machine, with the input and output directed straight to the console.

PowerShell introduces the concept of sessions as a means to manage connections to remote computers, serving as the foundation for executing commands in a remote environment. These sessions encapsulate the remote execution context, handling authentication and code execution. In practical terms, PowerShell remoting parallels the interactivity of Telnet, enabling interactive command execution on a remote system or unattended script execution seamlessly.

Structure

In this chapter, we will discuss the following topics:

- Understanding PowerShell Remoting
- Enabling PowerShell Remoting
- Identifying cmdlets that Support own Remoting

- Powershell Remoting Technologies
- Learning Open SSH and Remoting
- Key difference between OpenSSH and PowerShell Remoting
- Installing OpenSSH on Windows and Linux
- Configuring OpenSSH using `sshd_config` on Windows and Linux
- Testing PowerShell Remoting
- Validating OpenSSH Server Configurations on Windows and Linux
- Real-Time PowerShell Remoting Examples

Remoting in PowerShell is a powerful feature that allows you to manage remote servers from your local workstation without physically being on the console of each machine. This capability streamlines administrative tasks and provides a more efficient way to handle tasks across multiple servers. Let us delve into the key concepts and methods of PowerShell remoting.

Understanding PowerShell Remoting

PowerShell remoting relies on the ability to execute commands on remote machines. Here are the fundamental aspects.

Session Concept

PowerShell uses the concept of sessions to establish and maintain connections to remote computers. A session is created when you connect to a remote computer, and it acts as a channel for command execution.

Establishing a Remote Session

Use **`Enter-PSSession`** to connect to a remote machine interactively. Alternatively, **`Invoke-Command`** is used for executing commands on remote computers non-interactively.

The cmdlets **`New-PSSession`**, **`Enter-PSSession`**, and **`Invoke-Command`** have been enhanced with a new parameter set to accommodate this remoting connection. This includes parameters such as **`HostName`**, **`UserName`**, and **`KeyFilePath`**, allowing users to specify the target computer, provide a user name, and employ SSH key authentication with a private key file. For interactive executions, users are prompted for a password, while SSH key authentication streamlines the process, although the key creation method varies by platform.

These technologies allow administrators to perform a wide range of tasks on remote systems, including querying system information, executing commands, managing processes, and configuring system settings. PowerShell's flexibility and extensibility make it a powerful tool for remote administration in Windows environments.

Enabling PowerShell Remoting

Before remoting, you need to ensure that remoting is enabled on the target machines.

```
# Enable remoting on a remote machine

Enable-PSRemoting -Force
```

This command configures the necessary settings for PowerShell Remoting.

Identifying cmdlets that Support Remoting

PowerShell, a robust and versatile automation framework, comes into play, providing administrators with powerful tools for remote communication.

This topic delves into the various methods of connecting to remote machines using PowerShell, exploring techniques like the computer **`name`** parameter, **`Invoke-Command`**, and interactive PowerShell sessions.

Interactive Remoting

Interactive remoting in PowerShell allows you to establish a session on a remote computer and interact with it in real-time, similar to using a local terminal. This method enables you to run commands on the remote machine and receive the output directly in your local console. Interactive remoting provides a seamless and direct way to manage and control a remote system.

To connect to a remote machine interactively:

```
Enter-PSSession -ComputerName RemoteServer
```

This command establishes an interactive session on the specified server.

Non-Interactive Remoting

To run commands on a remote computer without any manual interaction, we can use the **`Invoke-Command`** command. This command has a **`"computername"`** parameter that lets us specify the computer on which we want to run the command. We also have a **`ScriptBlock`** parameter where we can encapsulate the commands to be executed on the remote computer.

The command you provided, **`Get-Help * -Parameter computername | Sort-Object name | Format-Table name, synopsis -AutoSize -Wrap`**, retrieves help information for cmdlets that have a "**computername**" parameter, which is commonly associated with remoting in PowerShell.

```
Get-Help * -Parameter computername | Sort-Object name | Format-Table
name, synopsis -AutoSize -Wrap
```

```
Get-Command -ParameterName computer* | Format-Table -AutoSize -Wrap
```

In the context of remoting, cmdlets with a "**computername**" parameter are often used to perform operations on remote machines. This command helps you quickly identify and understand the available cmdlets related to remoting, making it easier to leverage remoting capabilities in PowerShell.

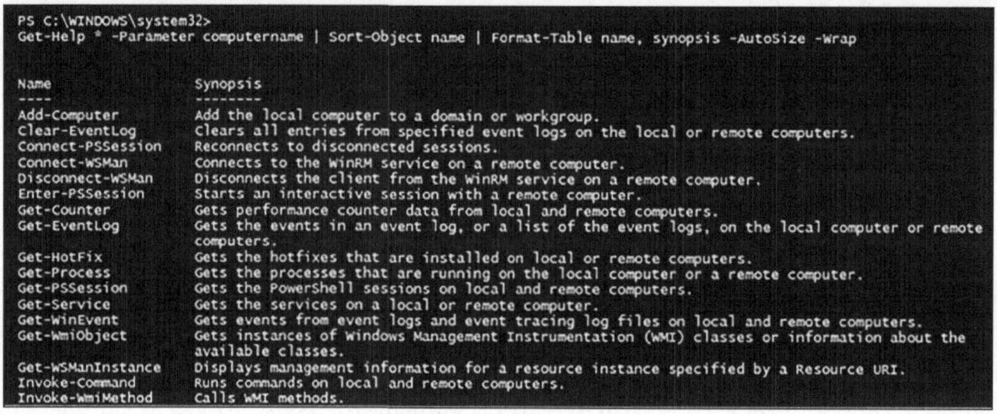

```
PS C:\WINDOWS\system32>
Get-Help * -Parameter computername | Sort-Object name | Format-Table name, synopsis -AutoSize -Wrap

Name                 Synopsis
----                 --------
Add-Computer         Add the local computer to a domain or workgroup.
Clear-EventLog       Clears all entries from specified event logs on the local or remote computers.
Connect-PSSession    Reconnects to disconnected sessions.
Connect-WSMan        Connects to the WinRM service on a remote computer.
Disconnect-WSMan     Disconnects the client from the WinRM service on a remote computer.
Enter-PSSession      Starts an interactive session with a remote computer.
Get-Counter          Gets performance counter data from local and remote computers.
Get-EventLog         Gets the events in an event log, or a list of the event logs, on the local computer or remote
                     computers.
Get-HotFix           Gets the hotfixes that are installed on local or remote computers.
Get-Process          Gets the processes that are running on the local computer or a remote computer.
Get-PSSession        Gets the PowerShell sessions on local and remote computers.
Get-Service          Gets the services on a local or remote computer.
Get-WinEvent         Gets events from event logs and event tracing log files on local and remote computers.
Get-WmiObject        Gets instances of Windows Management Instrumentation (WMI) classes or information about the
                     available classes.
Get-WSManInstance    Displays management information for a resource instance specified by a Resource URI.
Invoke-Command       Runs commands on local and remote computers.
Invoke-WmiMethod     Calls WMI methods.
```

***Figure 9.1**: Cmdlets related to remoting*

For non-interactive tasks across multiple servers:

```
Invoke-Command -ComputerName Server1, Server2, Server3 -ScriptBlock {
'YourCommandHere' }
```

This command executes the specified command on the listed servers.

Credential Handling

Credential handling in **Invoke-Command** is a crucial aspect of PowerShell remoting, especially when dealing with remote machines that require authentication. The **Invoke-Command** cmdlet allows you to execute commands on remote computers, and providing the appropriate credentials is essential for secure and authorized access.

When connecting to remote machines, you might need to provide credentials:

```
$credential = Get-Credential
Enter-PSSession -ComputerName RemoteServer -Credential $credential
```

Scripting and Automation

PowerShell remoting is often used in scripts for automation. For example, deploying a script to multiple servers:

```
Invoke-Command -ComputerName Server1, Server2, Server3 -FilePath "C:\
Scripts\YourScript.ps1"
```

This command runs a script on multiple remote servers simultaneously.

Security Considerations

PowerShell Remoting uses WS-Man (Windows Remote Management) or SSH protocols. Ensure proper firewall configurations and trusted hosts settings for secure communication.

PowerShell Remoting Technologies

PowerShell provides diverse remote management options beyond its core remoting support. The flexibility of PowerShell is evident in the fact that various commands, as revealed by the output of **Get-Command**, offer a **-ComputerName** parameter, each employing its unique built-in remoting technology. For instance, the WMI cmdlets utilize a WMI-specific form of DCOM-based remoting, the WSMan cmdlets use SOAP-based remoting, and several others employ RPC-based remoting. This diversity allows administrators to choose the most suitable remoting method for different scenarios, ensuring adaptability to various remote management needs. Whether interacting with Windows Management Instrumentation (WMI), utilizing Web Services for Management (WSMan), or relying on Remote Procedure Call (RPC), PowerShell accommodates a range of technologies to facilitate efficient remote management of systems.

Here is a brief overview of the mentioned remote computing technologies.

Windows Management Instrumentation (WMI)

WMI is a management framework that allows system administrators to access and interact with management data in an enterprise environment. PowerShell can leverage WMI to perform administrative tasks on remote systems.

```
# Querying remote system information using WMI
Get-WmiObject -Class Win32_OperatingSystem -ComputerName RemoteComputer
```

Remote Procedure Call (RPC)

RPC is a communication protocol that one program can use to request services from a program located on another computer in a network. PowerShell can utilize RPC for remote communication and management tasks.

```
# Running a command on a remote computer using RPC
Invoke-Command -ComputerName RemoteComputer -ScriptBlock { Get-Process }
```

Web Services for Management (WS-Management)

WS-Management is a standardized web services protocol used for remote management of systems. PowerShell Remoting uses WS-Management as one of its underlying technologies to facilitate secure communication between machines.

```
# Enabling PowerShell Remoting on a remote computer
Enable-PSRemoting -Force
# Running a command on a remote computer using PowerShell Remoting
Enter-PSSession -ComputerName RemoteComputer
```

The **Enable-PSRemoting** cmdlet plays a crucial role in configuring a computer to accept remote PowerShell commands through the WS-Management technology. It is important to note that WS-Management-based PowerShell remoting is exclusively supported on the Windows platform. While Windows server platforms inherently have PowerShell remoting enabled by default, the **Enable-PSRemoting** cmdlet serves as a means to enable remoting on other compatible versions of Windows. Additionally, it proves useful in scenarios where remoting becomes disabled, allowing for the re-enabling of this essential functionality. This capability enhances the reach and manageability of PowerShell commands across diverse Windows environments.

These operations include:

1. Utilizes the **Set-WSManQuickConfig** cmdlet to carry out the following tasks.
2. Initiates the WinRM (Windows Remote Management) service.
3. Configures the startup type for the WinRM service, setting it to automatic.
4. Establishes a listener capable of accepting requests on any IP address.
5. Facilitates a firewall exception to accommodate WS-Management communications.
6. If necessary, generates both simple and long name session endpoint configurations.
7. Activates all session configurations for enhanced remoting capabilities.
8. Adjusts the security descriptor of all session configurations to permit remote access.
9. Executes a restart of the WinRM service to implement the aforementioned changes effectively.

Learning OpenSSH Remoting

PowerShell remoting typically relies on WinRM for connection negotiation and data transport. However, introducing OpenSSH has expanded remoting capabilities to both Linux and Windows platforms, enabling genuine cross-platform PowerShell remoting.

SSH remoting facilitates basic PowerShell session remoting between Windows and Linux machines. In this approach, an SSH subsystem establishes a PowerShell host process on the target computer.

OpenSSH Configuration Files

The OpenSSH utility includes configuration files for both server and client settings. Detailed information regarding OpenSSH configuration files, including client settings, can be found in the **`ssh_config`** manual page. For OpenSSH server configuration files, consult the **`sshd_config`** manual page.

In the default configuration, the OpenSSH server (sshd) reads configuration data from the file located at **`%programdata%\ssh\sshd_config`** on Windows systems. This file serves as the primary source for configuring various aspects of the OpenSSH server's behavior on the Windows platform.

Note:

ssh_config manual page - https://man.openbsd.org/ssh_config

sshd_config manual page - https://man.openbsd.org/sshd_config

To establish the default command shell, start by verifying that the OpenSSH installation folder is included in the system path. In Windows, the standard installation directory is **`%systemdrive%\Windows\System32\openssh.`**

OpenSSH and Remoting PowerShell

This table summarizes the key differences between OpenSSH and Remoting PowerShell, highlighting their platform compatibility, primary functionalities, underlying protocols, and authentication methods.

Feature	OpenSSH	Remoting PowerShell
Platform	Cross-platform (Linux, macOS, Windows)	Windows-specific
Functionality	Secure remote login, file transfer	Remotely execute PowerShell commands, Windows automation

Protocol	Secure Shell (SSH)	Windows Remote Management (WinRM)
Authentication	Public-key cryptography	Windows authentication (Active Directory, Kerberos)

Table 9.1: *Comparison between OpenSSH and Remoting PowerShell*

Setting Up OpenSSH

To set up remote PowerShell remoting using SSH, ensure that the following prerequisites are met:

- **PowerShell 6 or Higher:** Ensure that PowerShell version 6 or a higher version is installed on all computers involved in the remoting set up.
- **SSH Installation:** Install both the SSH client (ssh.exe) and server (sshd.exe) components on all computers. This is essential for establishing remote connections using SSH.
- **Windows 10 Build 1809 or Windows Server 2019:** For Windows systems, OpenSSH for Windows is required. It is available in Windows 10 build 1809 and Windows server 2019. Make sure to have OpenSSH installed on these systems. Refer to the "*Manage Windows with OpenSSH*" documentation for additional details.
- **SSH Installation on Linux:** For Linux systems, ensure that SSH is installed, including the **sshd** server component. Choose the appropriate SSH package based on your Linux distribution.

Note: *The default location of the PowerShell executable on a Windows system is typically C:\Program Files\PowerShell\7\pwsh.exe. However, this location can vary based on the installation method. If you installed PowerShell through different means or in a customized location, the executable path may differ.*

Installing OpenSSH on Windows

The command checks the availability of OpenSSH capabilities on the system. If OpenSSH-Server is not installed, you can proceed with the installation.

Here is a summary of the steps:

1. Open an administrative PowerShell session.
2. Run the following command to check the availability of OpenSSH capabilities:

   ```
   Get-WindowsCapability -Online | Where-Object Name -like 'OpenSSH*'
   ```

   This command lists the OpenSSH capabilities available on your system.

3. If OpenSSH-Server is not installed, install it using the **`Add-WindowsCapability`** cmdlet. Here is an example:

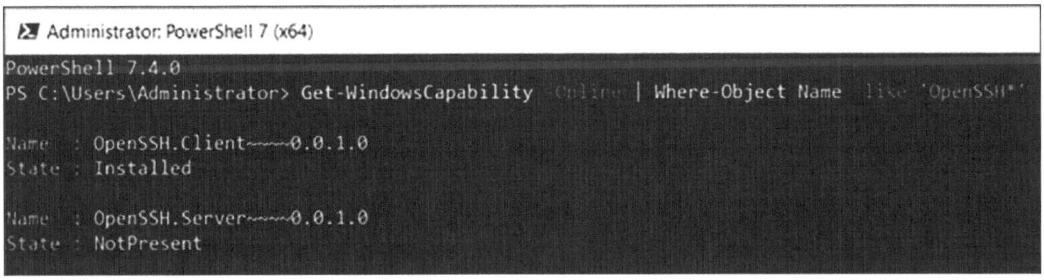

***Figure 9.2**: Install OpenSSH*

4. Install the OpenSSH server.

```
# Install the OpenSSH Server
Add-WindowsCapability -Online -Name OpenSSH.Server~~~~0.0.1.0
```

This command installs the OpenSSH server capability on your Windows system.

5. After running these commands, the OpenSSH client and server components should be installed on your Windows machine.

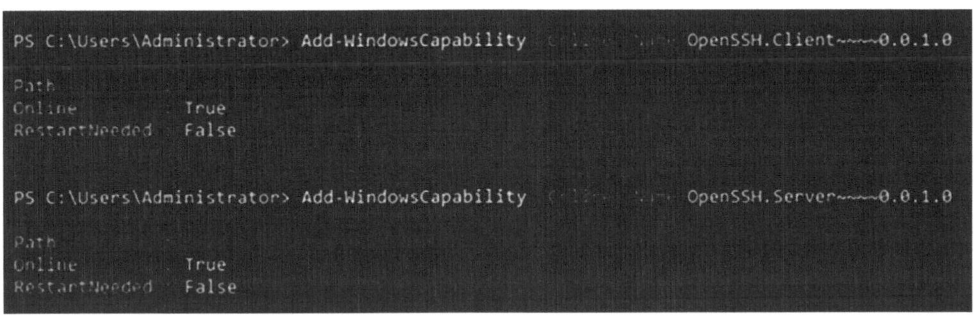

***Figure 9.3**: Check OpenSSH client and server components*

Troubleshooting Error `0x8024401c` During `Add-WindowsCapability`

Encountering the **`0x8024401c`** error code during attempts to install or enable Windows features using **`Add-WindowsCapability`** often points to an underlying issue with Windows update.

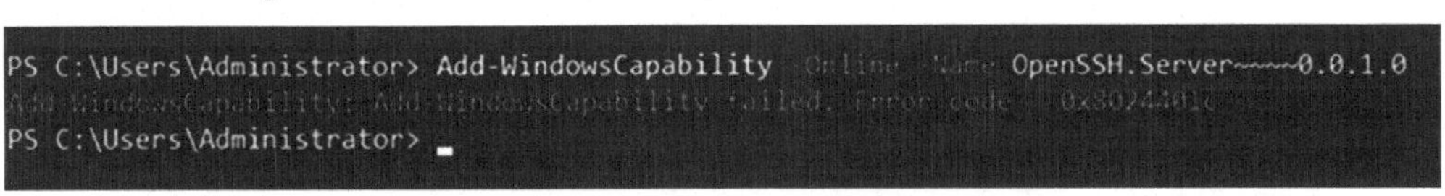

Figure 9.4**: Troubleshoot error **0x8024401c

The error code **0x8024401c** typically indicates a problem with Windows update. This error may occur when installing or enabling Windows features using **Add-WindowsCapability**.

Here are a few steps you can take to troubleshoot and resolve this issue.

Access the **Group Policy Editor** (gpedit.msc) and navigate to a specific setting related to Windows Update. By setting **"Specify intranet Microsoft update service location"** to **"Disabled,"** you are likely configuring the system to use the default Windows Update servers rather than an intranet-based update service.

Here are the steps:

1. Open the Group Policy Editor by running gpedit.msc.
2. Navigate to **Computer Configuration** -> **Administrative Templates** -> **Windows Components** -> **Windows Update**.
3. Locate the policy named **Specify intranet Microsoft update service location**.
4. Set the policy to **Disabled**.

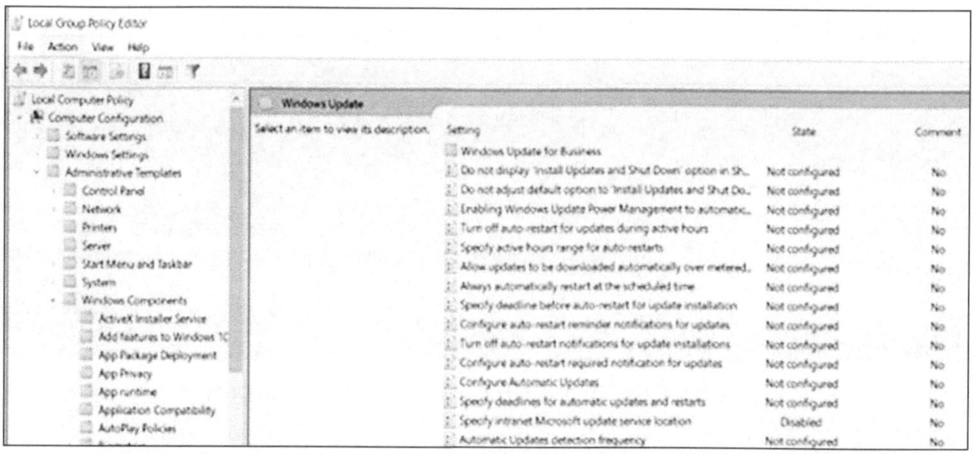

Figure 9.5: *Disable policy specify intranet Microsoft update service location*

Command Output:

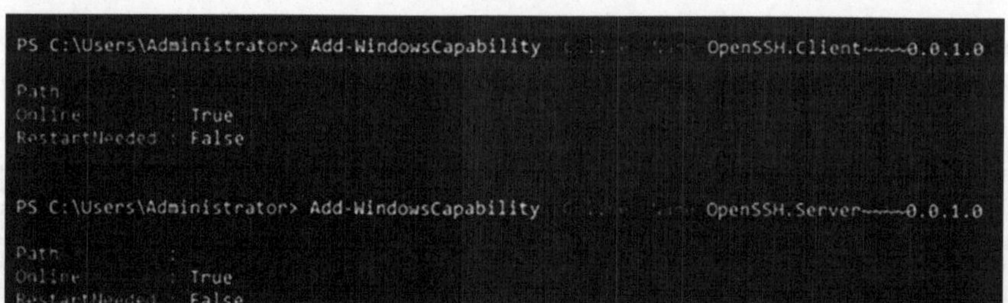

Figure 9.6: *Check OpenSSH server and client status*

5. To configure the default SSH shell in Windows, modify the Windows registry by appending the complete path to the shell executable to **HKEY_LOCAL_MACHINE\SOFTWARE\OpenSSH** in the string value **DefaultShell**.

Illustratively, the subsequent elevated PowerShell command designates **powershell.exe** as the default shell:

```
New-ItemProperty -Path "HKLM:\SOFTWARE\OpenSSH" -Name DefaultShell
-Value "C:\Windows\System32\WindowsPowerShell\v1.0\powershell.exe"
-PropertyType String -Force
```

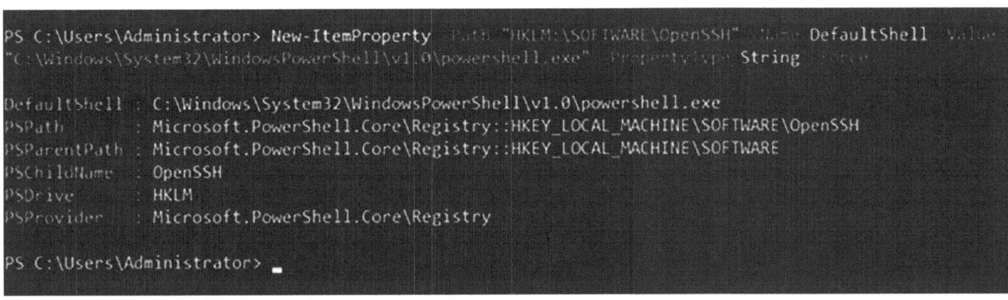

***Figure 9.7**: Configure the default shell in Windows*

The PowerShell command sets **powershell**.exe as the default shell, indicating that PowerShell should be invoked when connecting via SSH. This customization enables users to work with their preferred command-line environment when utilizing SSH on Windows.

6. Start the SSH service.

This command initiates the **SSH service**, allowing it to accept incoming SSH connections.

```
# Start the SSH service
Start-Service sshd
```

Updating sshd_config File on Windows

Let us elevate a PowerShell session and run commands with administrator privileges to update **sshd_config** file.

```
# Define the path to the sshd_config file
$sshdConfigPath = "$env:ProgramData\ssh\sshd_config"

# Check if the file exists before attempting to edit it
if (Test-Path $sshdConfigPath) {
    # Open the sshd_config file in Notepad for editing
```

```
    notepad $sshdConfigPath
} else {
    Write-Host "The sshd_config file does not exist at $sshdConfigPath."
}
```

After running this script, you can make the necessary changes to the **sshd_config** file using Notepad. The essential parameters that need to be configured in the **sshd_config** file are as follows:

1. **Port:** Sets the port number on which the SSH server listens for incoming connections. Using a non-standard port is recommended for security reasons.

   ```
   Port 22
   ```

2. **PermitRootLogin:** Controls whether the root user can log in directly to the SSH server. Setting this parameter to "**no**" is recommended to prevent remote attackers from attempting to brute-force the root password.

   ```
   PermitRootLogin no
   ```

3. **PubkeyAuthentication:** Controls whether public key authentication is allowed for SSH sessions. Public key authentication is considered more secure than password-based authentication.

   ```
   PubkeyAuthentication yes
   ```

4. **PasswordAuthentication:** Controls whether password authentication is allowed for SSH sessions. Setting this parameter to "**no**" is recommended to prevent brute-force attacks on user passwords.

   ```
   PasswordAuthentication no
   ```

5. **Subsystem:** Specifies a service executed on the server side and can be accessed remotely by clients using the SSH protocol.

   The following code configures the PowerShell Subsystem for SSH on a Windows system using PowerShell 7 (pwsh.exe), allowing you to use PowerShell over SSH.

   To create an SSH subsystem that hosts a PowerShell process on the remote computer, you can add the following entry to the **sshd_config** file:

   ```
   Subsystem powershell c:/progra~1/powershell/7/pwsh.exe -sshs
   -nologo
   ```

You will see the **sshd_config** file as shown in *Figure* 9.8:

```
sshd_config - Notepad
File  Edit  Format  View  Help
#LoginGraceTime 2m
#PermitRootLogin prohibit-password
#StrictModes yes
#MaxAuthTries 6
#MaxSessions 10

PubkeyAuthentication yes

# The default is to check both .ssh/authorized_keys and .ssh/authorized_keys2
# but this is overridden so installations will only check .ssh/authorized_keys
AuthorizedKeysFile      .ssh/authorized_keys

#AuthorizedPrincipalsFile none

# For this to work you will also need host keys in %programData%/ssh/ssh_known_hosts
#HostbasedAuthentication no
# Change to yes if you don't trust ~/.ssh/known_hosts for
# HostbasedAuthentication
#IgnoreUserKnownHosts no
# Don't read the user's ~/.rhosts and ~/.shosts files
#IgnoreRhosts yes

# To disable tunneled clear text passwords, change to no here!
PasswordAuthentication yes
#PermitEmptyPasswords no

#AllowAgentForwarding yes
#AllowTcpForwarding yes
#GatewayPorts no
#PermitTTY yes
#PrintMotd yes
#PrintLastLog yes
#TCPKeepAlive yes
#UseLogin no
#PermitUserEnvironment no
#ClientAliveInterval 0
#ClientAliveCountMax 3
#UseDNS no
#PidFile /var/run/sshd.pid
#MaxStartups 10:30:100
#PermitTunnel no
#ChrootDirectory none
#VersionAddendum none

# no default banner path
#Banner none

# override default of no subsystems
Subsystem       sftp    sftp-server.exe
Subsystem powershell c:/progra~1/powershell/7/pwsh.exe -sshs -nologo
```

Figure 9.8: *Edit the sshd config*

1. Adding the OpenSSH remoting path to the PATH environment variable is crucial for making the ssh.exe executable easily accessible from any location in the command prompt or PowerShell.

```
# Define the OpenSSH installation path
$opensshPath = "C:\Program Files\OpenSSH"

# Get the current PATH variable
$currentPath = [System.Environment]::GetEnvironmentVari-
able('PATH', [System.EnvironmentVariableTarget]::Machine)

# Check if the OpenSSH path is already in the PATH variable
if ($currentPath -notlike "*$opensshPath*") {
    # Add the OpenSSH path to the PATH variable
    [System.Environment]::SetEnvironmentVariable('PATH',
"$currentPath;$opensshPath", [System.EnvironmentVariable
Target]::Machine)

    Write-Host "OpenSSH path added to the PATH variable."
} else {
    Write-Host "OpenSSH path is already in the PATH variable."
}
```

2. Executing these PowerShell commands ensures that the sshd service starts automatically upon system boot.

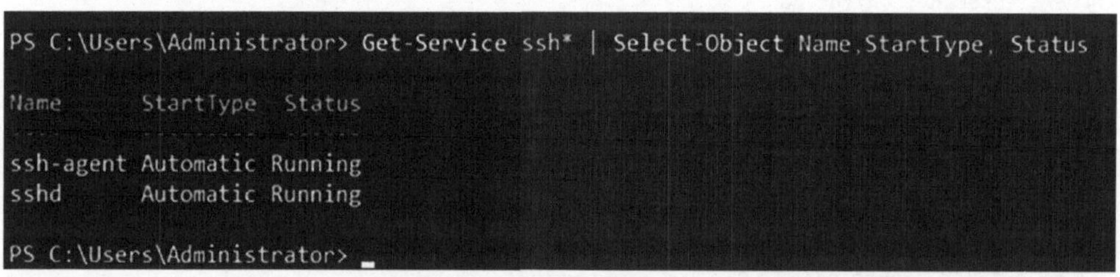

Figure 9.9: *Check sshd service status*

3. Use the netstat command to check if the SSH server is running and listening on TCP **port 22**, you can execute the following in a terminal or command prompt:

```
netstat -an | findstr "22"
```

***Figure 9.10**: NetStat command to check SSH service port*

This indicates that the SSH server is actively listening on TCP **`port 22`**

4. Check the existing firewall rules related to SSH

The **`Get-NetFirewallRule`** cmdlet in PowerShell is used to retrieve information about Windows firewall rules. The following command is used to get information about firewall rules with a display name containing “**`SSH`**.”

```
Get-NetFirewallRule -DisplayName "*SSH*"
```

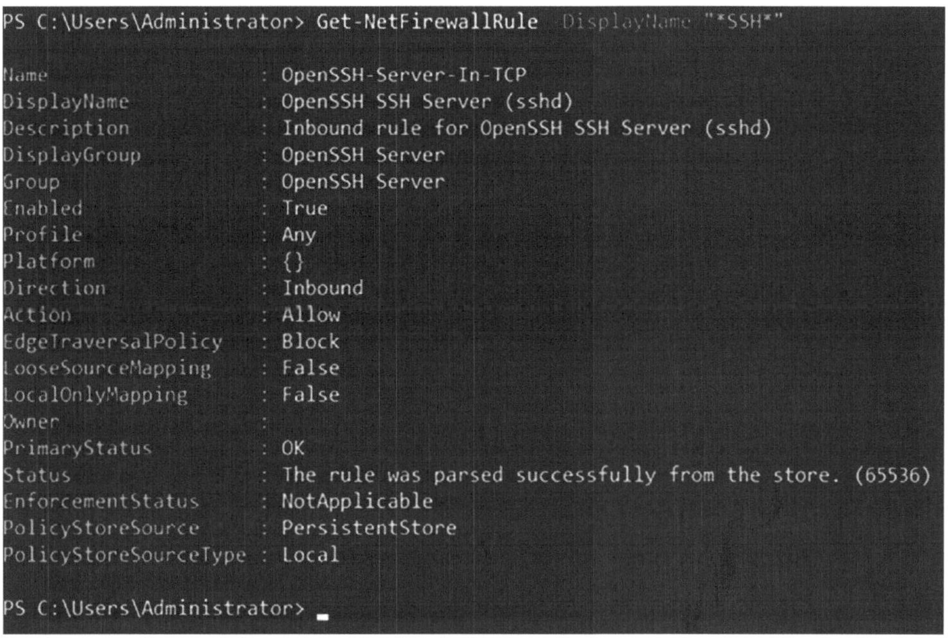

***Figure 9.11**: Check the firewall rule related to SSH*

This command lists existing firewall rules with **`"SSH"`** in their display name. Confirm that there is a rule allowing inbound traffic on **`TCP port 22`**.

Note: *If the SSH rule is disabled or missing, you can use the New-NetFirewallRule cmdlet to create a new inbound rule for SSH. Here is an example PowerShell command.*

```
# Create a new inbound rule for SSH on TCP port 22 if it's missing or disabled

New-NetFirewallRule -DisplayName "Allow SSH Inbound" -Direction Inbound -Protocol TCP -LocalPort 22 -Action Allow -Enabled True
```

5. After making changes to the **sshd_config** file, remember to restart the SSH service for the changes to take effect:

```
# Change the startup type of the sshd service to Automatic
Set-Service -Name sshd -StartupType 'Automatic'

# Start the sshd service
Start-Service sshd
```

PowerShell Remoting Testing on Windows Machine

Testing remoting on a single computer is a great way to understand the basics of PowerShell remoting. Here is an example of how you can create a remote session back to the same Windows computer:

```
# Get the current computer name
$computerName = $env:COMPUTERNAME

# Create a PSSession (PowerShell remote session) to the local computer
$remoteSession = New-PSSession -hostname $computerName -username
administrator

# Enter the remote session
Enter-PSSession -Session $remoteSession

# Now you are in a remote PowerShell session on the same computer
# You can run commands as if you are on a remote computer
Get-Service ssh*

# Exit the remote session
Exit-PSSession

# Remove the PSSession (optional)
Remove-PSSession -Session $remoteSession
```

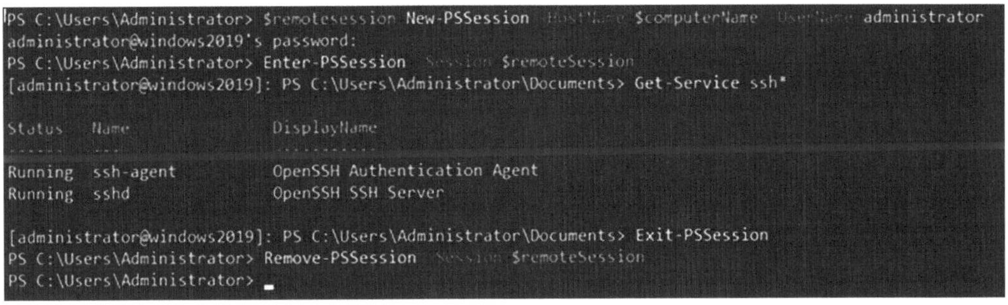

Figure 9.12: *PowerShell remoting testing on Windows machine*

Installing OpenSSH on Linux

The instructions guide you through the process of installing the latest version of PowerShell and setting up the Ubuntu OpenSSH Server on a Linux system.

Install the Latest Version of PowerShell

Follow the instructions for installing the latest version of PowerShell on Ubuntu. Refer to *Chapter 2, Introduction to PowerShell Core.*

Install Ubuntu OpenSSH Server

Use the following commands to install your Ubuntu system's OpenSSH client and server:

```
sudo apt install openssh-client
sudo apt install openssh-server
```

Edit the `sshd_config` File

Navigate to the location **`/etc/ssh`** and edit the **`sshd_config`** file. Ensure that password authentication is enabled by adding the following line:

```
PasswordAuthentication yes
```

The preceding line specifies whether password authentication is allowed when connecting to the SSH server. The value "**`yes`**" means that password authentication is enabled.

Optionally, enable key authentication by adding:

```
PubkeyAuthentication yes
```

Add a PowerShell Subsystem Entry

Enhance the SSH server capabilities by adding a PowerShell subsystem entry to the sshd_config file.

```
Subsystem powershell /usr/bin/pwsh -sshs -nologo
```

Note: *The default location of the PowerShell executable is /usr/bin/pwsh, but it may vary based on your installation method.*

Restarting the OpenSSH Service

To apply configuration changes or refresh the OpenSSH service on a Linux system, use the following command:

```
sudo systemctl restart sshd.service
```

Testing PowerShell Remoting

Explore the functionality of PowerShell remoting by conducting tests between various systems.

Testing PowerShell remoting across various systems is crucial to ensure seamless communication.

Here is how you can test PowerShell remoting between different systems:

Within Windows Environment

Evaluate PowerShell remoting from one Windows machine to another.

```
PS C:\Users\Administrator> Enter-PSSession -hostname 172.16.237.252
-UserName administrator

administrator@172.16.237.252's password:

[administrator@172.16.237.252]: PS C:\Users\Administrator\Documents>
systeminfo | findstr /B /C:"OS Name" /C:"OS Version"

OS Name:                   Microsoft Windows Server 2019 Standard

OS Version:                10.0.17763 N/A Build 17763
```

We have successfully entered a PowerShell session on a remote Windows Server (**172.16.237.252**) using the **Enter-PSSession** cmdlet. The provided output indicates that the remote system is running Microsoft Windows Server 2019 Standard with version information.

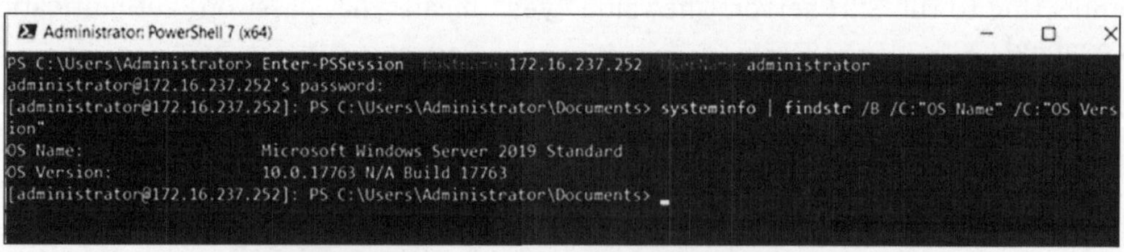

Figure 9.13: *Enter a remote server PowerShell session*

Bridging Windows and Linux

Investigate the interoperability of PowerShell remoting from Linux to Windows.

```
[root@linuxcsvmct ~]# pwsh

PowerShell 7.4.0

PS /root> Enter-psSession -HostName 172.16.237.146 -UserName administrator

The authenticity of host '172.16.237.146 (172.16.237.146)' can't be established.

ECDSA key fingerprint is SHA256:dvzKuh5hUoAPOd8fRS4vTm4mzWl/hXGYTnL1b-0badxY.

Are you sure you want to continue connecting (yes/no/[fingerprint])?

Warning: Permanently added '172.16.237.146' (ECDSA) to the list of known hosts.

administrator@172.16.237.146's password:

[administrator@172.16.237.146]: PS C:\Users\Administrator\Documents>
```

The first time you connect to a remote server using SSH, a standard SSH (secure shell) prompt will appear to establish the connection and verify the authenticity of the host.

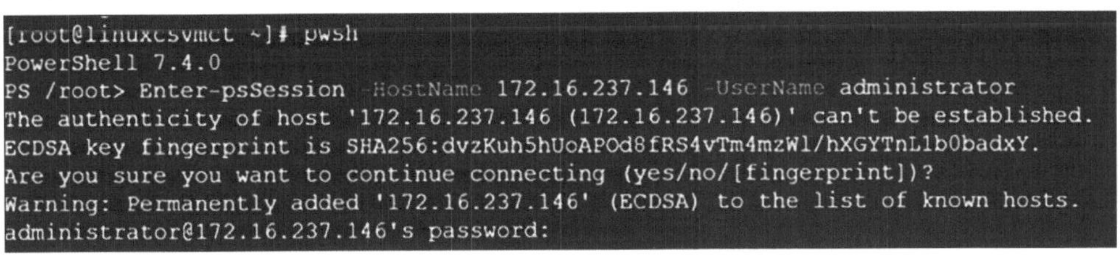

Figure 9.14: *Bridging Windows and Linux*

```
[administrator@172.16.237.146]: PS C:\Users\Administrator\Documents> systeminfo | findstr /B /C:"OS Name" /C:"OS Version"

OS Name:                   Microsoft Windows Server 2019 Standard

OS Version:                10.0.17763 N/A Build 17763
```

The prompt ensures a successful connection to the remote server using OpenSSH in PowerShell. Now, run the following command to retrieve system information details to verify we are connected to the correct server.

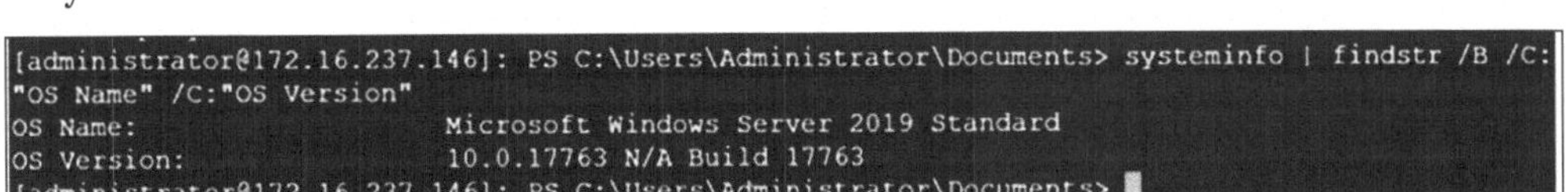

Figure 9.15: *Establish a session from a Linux to a remote Windows server*

We successfully entered a PowerShell session from a Linux machine to a remote Windows server (172.16.237.146) using PowerShell 7.4.0. The output confirms that the remote Windows server is running Microsoft Windows server 2019 standard with version information.

Validating OpenSSH Configurations on Windows and Linux

To inspect the **sshd_config** file and verify whether the desired changes are applied, you can use a text editor or commands to display the file content. Here is how you can do it.

We are attempting to use the **`sshd -T`** command on a system with OpenSSH and then filtering the output to find lines containing "**`subsystem`**" to ensure server configuration is correct and available.

```
sshd -T | Select-String "subsystem"
```

`sshd -T` tests the sshd server configuration and shows the effective configuration"**|**". Pipe operator passes the command output on the left as input to the command on the right. Select-String "**`subsystem`**" selects lines from the input that contain the specified string ("**`subsystem`**").

If the configuration is absent or there is an issue, you should review and adjust your OpenSSH server configuration file (**sshd_config**). Ensure that the subsystems are correctly defined in the configuration file.

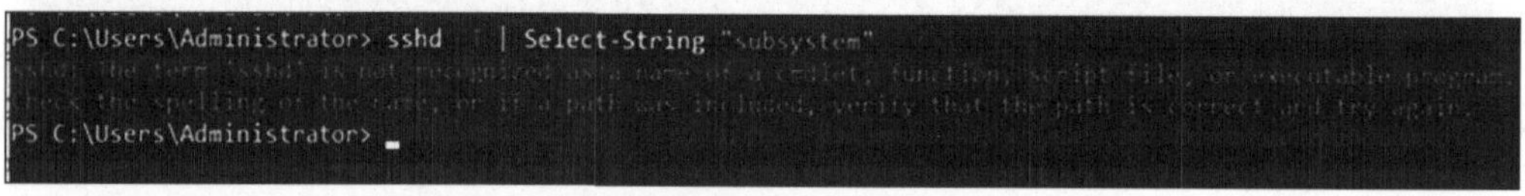

***Figure 9.16**: Validating the OpenSSH configuration*

On Windows, run the following command.

***Figure 9.17**: Validating OpenSSH configurations on Windows*

On Linux, run the following command.

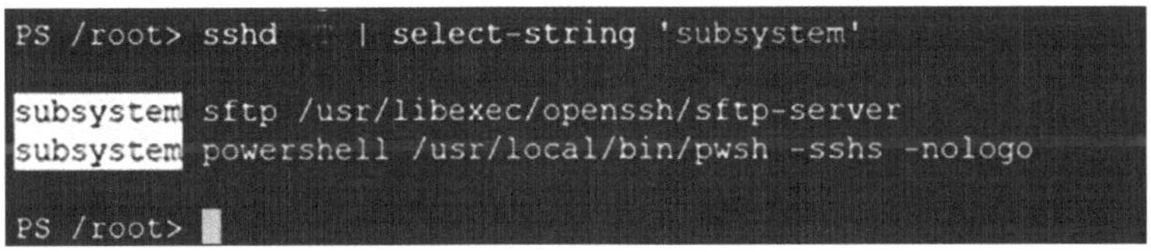

***Figure 9.18**: Validating OpenSSH configurations on Linux*

```
# Display the line containing PasswordAuthentication
grep "PasswordAuthentication" /etc/ssh/sshd_config

# Display the line containing PubkeyAuthentication
grep "PubkeyAuthentication" /etc/ssh/sshd_config

# Display the line containing Subsystem powershell
grep "Subsystem powershell" /etc/ssh/sshd_config
```

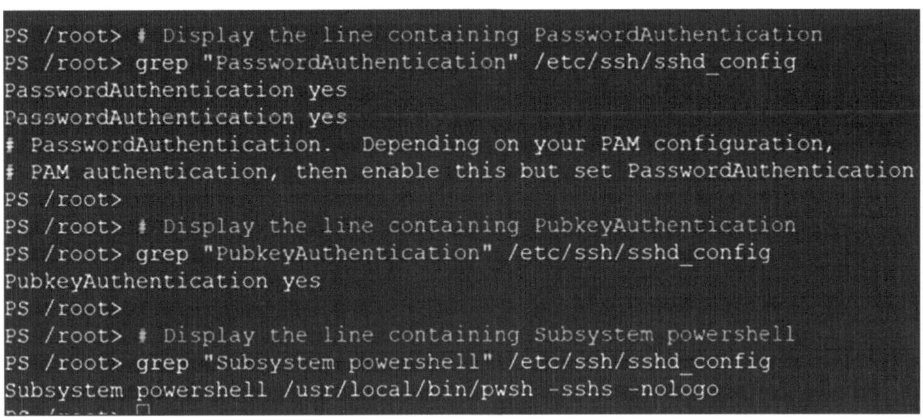

***Figure 9.19**: Verify sshd configs*

Importing a Remote Session

The **Import-PSSession** cmdlet in PowerShell is used to import commands from a remote session into the current session. This is particularly useful in PowerShell Remoting scenarios where you want to use commands from a remote session locally.

PowerShell remoting from Linux to Windows allows you to execute commands on Windows machines, but it does not inherently provide access to Windows-specific modules like Active Directory. Active Directory cmdlets are part of the Active Directory module, which is primarily designed to work in a Windows environment.

However, the goal is to manage Active Directory from a Linux machine; by now, we all know that PowerShell 7 is cross-platform and can be installed on Linux. While not all Windows-specific modules are available, some basic Active Directory functionality might be possible.

Note: *The landscape of PowerShell and its capabilities can evolve, so it is a good idea to check the latest documentation or community discussions for any updates or advancements in PowerShell compatibility on Linux or Active Directory module support.*

PowerShell remoting allows seamless management of remote machines, leveraging the flexibility to import modules, execute commands, and efficiently handle sessions without the need for direct interaction on the remote machine:

```
PS /root> $import_session=New-PSSession -HostName 172.16.237.146
-UserName administrator     administrator@172.16.237.146's password:

PS /root> import-pssession -session $import_session -Module
ActiveDirectory


ModuleType Version    PreRelease Name                               Ex-
portedCommands

---------- -------    ---------- ----                               ---
-------------

Script     1.0                   tmp_syyrae2e.nra
{Add-ADCentralAccessPo…
```

Now, we have successfully created a new PowerShell session (**`$import_session`**) to a remote machine with the IP address **`172.16.237.146`** and the username "**`administrator`**." Subsequently, we have imported the Active Directory module from that remote session.

The output indicates that the Active Directory module has been successfully imported from the remote session, and it provides information about the module, including its **`ModuleType`**, Version, **`PreRelease`** status, **`Name`**, and the **`ExportedCommands`** it contains.

Now, you should be able to use **`ActiveDirectory`** cmdlets locally on your machine, even though the module is running on the remote machine.

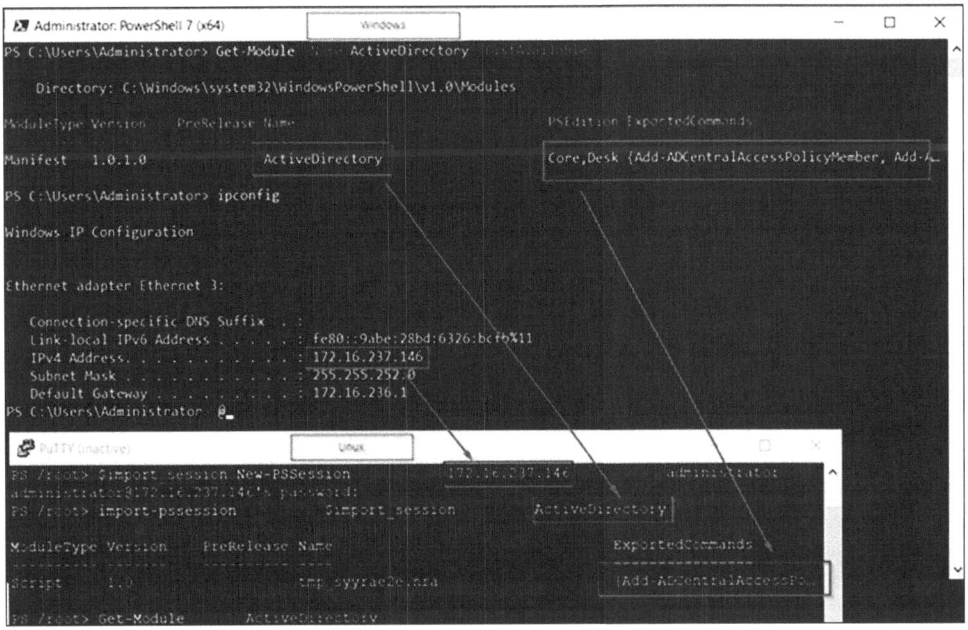

***Figure 9.20**: Importing a remote session in Linux*

Enabling PowerShell Remoting in an Enterprise Setting

To enable PowerShell Remoting in an enterprise setting, leveraging group policy is the recommended approach for its flexibility and scalability. Group Policy settings allow for the automatic configuration of WinRM endpoints and firewall rules, streamlining the process of implementing and managing PowerShell Remoting across multiple systems. For detailed information and guidance on troubleshooting and optimizing remote configurations, you can refer to the documentation by typing **`Get-Help about_remote_troubleshooting`** in the PowerShell environment. This method ensures consistent and centralized control over PowerShell Remoting settings, making it well-suited for enterprise-level deployments.

Let us delve into the steps involved in editing group policy to enable PowerShell Remoting.

Edit group policy: **`Computer Configuration`** -> **`Administrative Templates`** -> **`Windows Components`** -> **`Windows PowerShell`** -> **`Enable PowerShell Remoting`**

Real-Time PowerShell Remoting Examples

Upon successfully configuring remoting, a process slightly different from Linux on Windows Server or client, managing connections becomes crucial.

Next, the **New-PSSession** cmdlet is employed. Unlike **Enter-PSSession**, which creates an interactive session directly connected to the machine, **New-PSSession** instantiates and retains the session for future use. This flexibility allows multiple sessions to different machines simultaneously. The resulting session is stored in a variable, making it accessible later.

To enter the session, **Enter-PSSession** is used, specifying the session variable. This facilitates executing commands directly within the created session, validating the connection by checking the host name. Exiting the session does not eliminate the session; it persists until explicitly deleted.

To manage sessions, the **Get-PSSession** cmdlet lists available sessions, while **Remove-PSSession** selectively removes sessions by ID. Additionally, the ability to import modules from remote sessions is showcased using **Import-PSSession**.

Creating a Scheduled Task on Remote Computers

We have successfully executed a PowerShell remoting command to create a scheduled task on a remote machine named "**TestMachine.cloud.com**." The task, named "**RunOnLogon**," is set to run a PowerShell script (**C:\temp\hello-world.ps1**) upon user logon.

```
PS C:\WINDOWS\system32> Invoke-Command -ComputerName "TestMachine.cloud.
com" -ScriptBlock {
 $action = New-ScheduledTaskAction -Execute "C:\temp\hello-world.ps1"
 $trigger = New-ScheduledTaskTrigger -AtLogOn
 Register-ScheduledTask -Action $action -Trigger $trigger -TaskName
"RunOnLogon" }


TaskPath                                       TaskName
State      PSComputerName
--------                                       --------
-----      --------------
\                                              RunOnLogon
Ready      Testmachine.cloud.com
```

The output indicates that the task has been registered successfully, and it is in a "**Ready**" state, meaning it is prepared to execute when the specified trigger condition (in this case, logon) occurs.

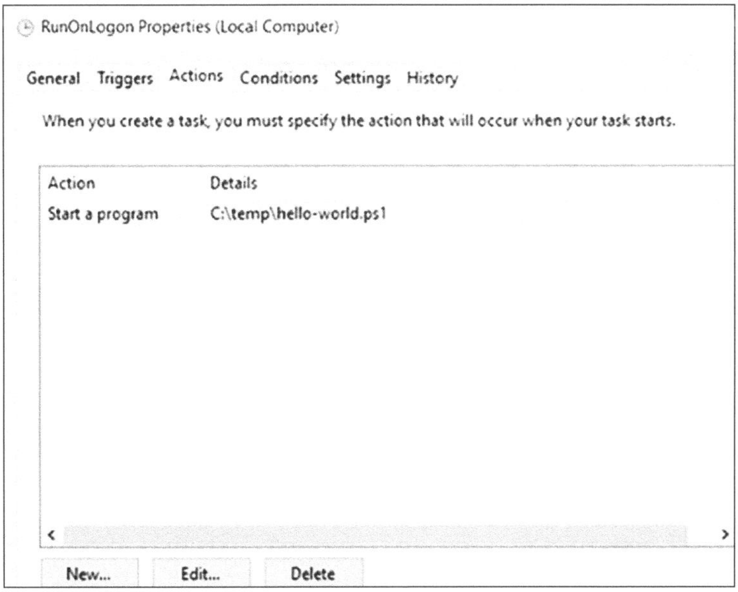

***Figure 9.21**: Create a scheduled task using PowerShell remoting*

Checking Disk Space on Remote Computers:

```
Invoke-Command -ComputerName "RemoteComputer1", "RemoteComputer2"
-ScriptBlock { Get-WmiObject Win32_LogicalDisk | Select-Object DeviceID,
FreeSpace, Size }
```

Querying System Information on Remote Computers:

```
Invoke-Command -ComputerName "RemoteComputer1", "RemoteComputer2"
-ScriptBlock { Get-CimInstance Win32_ComputerSystem | Select-Object
Name, Manufacturer, Model }
```

Restarting Remote Computers:

```
Invoke-Command -ComputerName "RemoteComputer1", "RemoteComputer2"
-ScriptBlock { Restart-Computer -Force }
```

Creating a New Folder on Remote Computers:

```
Invoke-Command -ComputerName "RemoteComputer1", "RemoteComputer2"
-ScriptBlock { New-Item -ItemType Directory -Path "C:\NewFolder" }
```

Checking for Pending Updates on Remote Computers:

```
Invoke-Command -ComputerName "RemoteComputer1", "RemoteComputer2"
-ScriptBlock { Get-HotFix -Description "Update" }
```

Collecting Network Configuration Information:

```
Invoke-Command -ComputerName "RemoteComputer1", "RemoteComputer2"
-ScriptBlock { Get-NetIPAddress | Select-Object IPAddress,
InterfaceAlias }
```

Stopping a Specific Process on Remote Computers:

```
Invoke-Command -ComputerName "RemoteComputer1", "RemoteComputer2"
-ScriptBlock { Stop-Process -Name "ProcessName" -Force }
```

Installing Windows Updates on Remote Computers:

```
Invoke-Command -ComputerName "RemoteComputer1", "RemoteComputer2"
-ScriptBlock { Install-WindowsUpdate -Force }
```

Querying Installed Software on Remote Computers:

```
Invoke-Command -ComputerName "RemoteComputer1", "RemoteComputer2"
-ScriptBlock { Get-ItemProperty -Path "HKLM:\Software\Microsoft\Windows\
CurrentVersion\Uninstall\*" | Select-Object DisplayName, DisplayVersion
}
```

Conclusion

PowerShell Remoting is a powerful tool for system administrators, offering efficient ways to manage and execute commands on remote machines. Through technologies like Windows Remote Management (WinRM), PowerShell facilitates seamless communication between local and remote sessions, enabling administrators to execute tasks, gather information, and automate processes across multiple machines.

The ability to connect, disconnect, and reconnect PowerShell sessions enhances the flexibility and adaptability of remote management. Administrators can tailor their approach to meet the specific demands of their tasks and environments by using the straightforward computer name parameter, the Invoke-Command cmdlet, or engaging in interactive PowerShell sessions.

Moreover, security considerations are crucial in implementing PowerShell Remoting, emphasizing the need for secure communication protocols and proper credential handling. Group Policy settings offer a scalable solution for enterprise-wide remoting configuration, ensuring consistent and secure remoting across organizational systems.

As PowerShell evolves, its remote management capabilities continue to empower administrators to navigate and administer diverse computing environments efficiently. Whether leveraging RPC-based remoting, DCOM-based remoting for WMI cmdlets, or the SOAP-based remoting of WSMan cmdlets, PowerShell remains a versatile and indispensable tool for remote administration. In summary, PowerShell Remoting stands at the forefront of remote management solutions, contributing to the agility, security, and efficiency of administrative tasks in local and enterprise contexts.

Multiple Choice Questions

1. What technology does PowerShell Remoting primarily utilize for remote access?

   a. SSH

   b. RPC

   c. WinRM

   d. DCOM

2. Which cmdlet is commonly used to enable PowerShell Remoting on a machine?

   a. `Set-RemoteConfiguration`

   b. `Enable-PSRemoting`

   c. `Start-RemoteService`

   d. `Configure-WinRM`

3. Which of the following protocols is used by PowerShell Remoting?

   a. FTP

   b. HTTP

   c. WSMan

   d. SMTP

4. How can you initiate an interactive PowerShell session on a remote machine?

   a. `Invoke-Command`

   b. `Enter-PSSession`

   c. `Start-RemoteSession`

   d. `Begin-PSRemoting`

5. What is the primary purpose of PowerShell Remoting?

   a. File transfer

   b. Secure remote Login

   c. Running PowerShell commands remotely

   d. Database management

6. Which parameter is commonly used to specify the remote computer when using PowerShell Remoting?
    a. `-RemoteHost`
    b. `-ComputerName`
    c. `-TargetMachine`
    d. `-RemoteSystem`
7. What technology is NOT directly associated with PowerShell Remoting?
    a. SSH
    b. WMI
    c. WinRM
    d. DNS
8. How can you enable PowerShell Remoting through group policy?
    a. Set-GPO PowerShellRemoting -Enable
    b. `Configure-GroupPolicy -RemotingEnabled $true`
    c. Edit Group Policy: `Computer Configuration` -> `Administrative Templates` -> `Windows Components` -> `Windows PowerShell` -> `Enable PowerShell Remoting`
    d. `Enable-RemotingPolicy -GroupPolicy`

Answers:

1. c
2. b
3. c
4. b
5. c
6. b
7. d
8. c

Questions

- What is the purpose of PowerShell Remoting?
- How can you enable PowerShell Remoting on Windows machines?
- Which protocol does PowerShell Remoting use for communication?
- What cmdlet is used to create an interactive PowerShell session for remoting?
- What security considerations should be taken into account when using PowerShell Remoting?

Key Terms

- **PowerShell Remoting:** The feature that allows administrators to run PowerShell commands on remote systems.
- **WinRM (Windows Remote Management):** The framework used by PowerShell Remoting for communication between local and remote systems.
- **Remote Session:** An interactive or non-interactive connection established between the local and remote PowerShell environments.
- **`Invoke-Command`:** A cmdlet used for executing PowerShell commands on one or more remote computers.
- **`Enable-PSRemoting`:** Cmdlet used to configure a computer to receive PowerShell remote commands.
- **`Enter-PSSession`:** Cmdlet used to start an interactive session with a remote computer.
- **Session:** A persistent connection between the local and remote systems, often created with **`New-PSSession`**.
- **Remoting Endpoints:** Configurations that allow PowerShell Remoting to function, including firewall rules and WinRM settings.
- **Group Policy:** A feature in Windows that enables centralized management and configuration of settings, including PowerShell Remoting.
- **Security:** Practices and configurations to ensure secure communication and data exchange during PowerShell Remoting.

Chapter 10

Managing Cloud Operations Using PowerShell

Introduction

The term "*cloud*" is ubiquitous in today's tech-centric world. This technology has become an integral part of our daily lives, with virtually everyone, from seasoned computer experts to young tablet and game console enthusiasts, leveraging its capabilities.

In this era, the cloud is not just a buzzword; it encapsulates services catering to end users and information workers worldwide. Many individuals may unknowingly engage with cloud services, using them for activities such as email communication, online gaming, or file storage through platforms like iCloud or OneDrive.

Despite its widespread usage, some individuals resist embracing the cloud, perhaps unaware that they are already incorporating it into their daily routines. Paradoxically, the cloud stands out as one of the fastest-growing technologies in the history of the computer industry. Each day brings forth new vendors offering diverse cloud services, and every login to a cloud service portal reveals innovative features.

To navigate this explosion of features effectively and maintain control, it is crucial to equip ourselves with the right tools. In this context, this book emphasizes PowerShell as an indispensable tool in the technology toolbox. Beyond being a scripting language, PowerShell serves as a powerful automation engine, simplifying complex tasks and saving time and effort. Additionally, PowerShell plays a pivotal role as a platform supporting various features in Microsoft Azure, such as the Azure automation engine built upon PowerShell's workflow feature. Further details on these aspects will be explored in depth in the upcoming chapters.

Structure

In this chapter, we will discuss the following topics:

- Managing Cloud Operations Using PowerShell
- Getting Practice with PowerShell and Cloud
- PowerShell Adoption
- Loading Azure PowerShell Modules
- Choosing the Right Azure Command-line Tool
- Connecting to Azure Environment
- Getting Started with Azure Automation
- Using PowerShell in Azure Automation
- Creating Runbook using Azure Automation
- Azure Automation Assets
- Why ARM
- Install Azure Resource Manager Tools Extension
- Understanding ARM Template Structure
- Getting Started with ARM Tcmplate
- Using parameters to fine-tune ARM Templates
- Deploying Azure Virtual Machine with ARM Template
- ARM Templates for Infrastructure as Code
- Azure Inventory
- Learning AWS PowerShell Modules
- Learning Google PowerShell Modules

PowerShell Adoption

Azure stands as Microsoft's comprehensive solution for cloud computing, offering a dual framework encompassing both Infrastructure-as-a-Service (IaaS) and Platform-as-a-Service (PaaS). Serving as a versatile platform, Azure facilitates the creation, deployment, delivery, and management of resilient, secure, and scalable applications and services. Importantly, it extends its compatibility beyond Microsoft's technologies, allowing seamless integration with tools, operating systems, and programming languages from various vendors. This adaptability ensures that users can leverage diverse resources within the Azure ecosystem to meet their specific needs.

PowerShell has emerged as an exceptional automation tool over the years. Its ability to automate and simplify complex and repetitive tasks has made it a go-to tool. Therefore, it is highly recommended that you master it to make the most of its potential. What sets PowerShell apart and rapidly makes it a top choice is its user-friendly language and its role as a comprehensive automation platform. Besides being a scripting language, it encompasses an automation framework, remoting, WMI, workflow engine, Desired State Configuration (DSC), and many other features. Remarkably, PowerShell extends its reach beyond the Microsoft realm and finds applications in both Microsoft and non-Microsoft products. Take VMware, a major Microsoft competitor, for instance – they employ PowerShell, specifically PowerCLI, to automate and manage VMware vSphere.

Azure PowerShell stands out as a module integrated into the Azure SDK in the Microsoft ecosystem. This module has a set of cmdlets empowering users to effortlessly manage, deploy, and automate diverse aspects and workloads within Azure. However, Azure PowerShell is not confined just to Azure's services. In the upcoming topics, you will discover that Azure Automation services are intricately built on top of PowerShell's robust workflow engine, showcasing the tool's versatility and integration across various platforms.

The Az PowerShell module, being built on the .NET Standard, offers versatile compatibility. It functions seamlessly with PowerShell 10.0.6 LTS and PowerShell 10.1.3 or any higher versions. Importantly, it provides consistent support across diverse platforms, including Windows, Linux, and MacOS.

Furthermore, users can also leverage the Az PowerShell module with Windows PowerShell 5.1, ensuring backward compatibility for those working with earlier versions of the PowerShell environment. This adaptability across different PowerShell versions and platforms enhances the module's usability and accessibility for many users.

Note: *In the Az PowerShell module, the cmdlets generate output as .NET objects. Like any PowerShell command that yields output, users can employ the pipeline functionality to direct the Az PowerShell module cmdlet output to the Get-Member cmdlet.*

The Az PowerShell module is consistent with the general behaviour of PowerShell cmdlets. PowerShell cmdlets typically output objects, and you can use the **`Get-Member`** cmdlet to inspect the properties and methods of those objects. This consistency is intentional and aligns with the design principles of PowerShell, promoting a unified and predictable experience for users across various modules and cmdlets. Therefore, users can leverage their existing knowledge of PowerShell conventions when working with the Az PowerShell module.

Note: *The transition from AzureRM PowerShell modules to Az PowerShell modules marks a significant advancement, offering enhanced capabilities and features. In order to streamline and ensure continued support, Microsoft has decided to retire the AzureRM PowerShell modules on 29 February 2024.*

Loading Azure PowerShell Modules

As you are more familiar with the structure of PowerShell modules, you will find that navigating and discovering cmdlets becomes more intuitive. Locating in-house cmdlets within a module involves understanding the use of nouns and verbs to narrow down your search.

This command installs the Azure PowerShell module "**Az**" in PowerShell, which allows direct management of Azure resources from the command line.

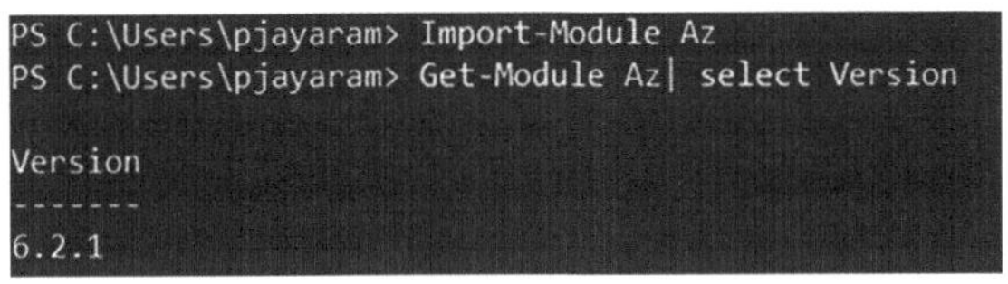

```
PS C:\Users\pjayaram> Import-Module Az
PS C:\Users\pjayaram> Get-Module Az| select Version

Version
-------
6.2.1
```

***Figure 10.1**: Get Azure module version*

The **Get-Module** command with the parameter **-ListAvailable -Name Az*** is used to list all available modules whose names match the pattern "**Az***".

```
PS C:\Users\pjayaram> Get-Module -ListAvailable -Name Az*
```

***Figure 10.2**: List all Azure modules*

This is a helpful command to check which versions of the Azure PowerShell module ("**Az**") are available on your system, or to find modules with names starting with "**Az**".

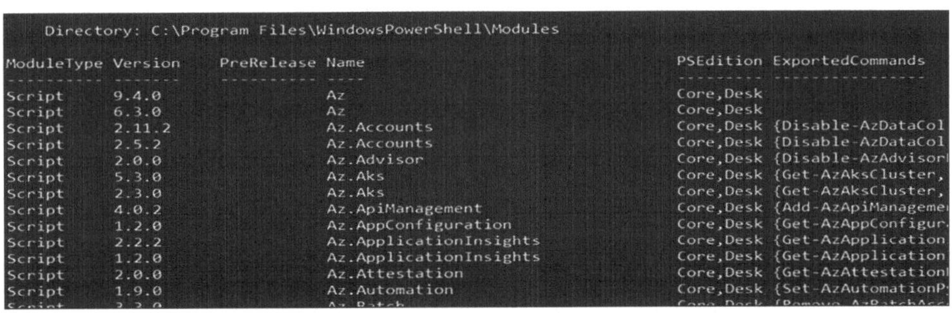

```
    Directory: C:\Program Files\WindowsPowerShell\Modules

ModuleType Version    PreRelease Name                     PSEdition ExportedCommands
---------- -------    ---------- ----                     --------- ----------------
Script     9.4.0                 Az                       Core,Desk
Script     6.3.0                 Az                       Core,Desk
Script     2.11.2                Az.Accounts              Core,Desk {Disable-AzDataCol
Script     2.5.2                 Az.Accounts              Core,Desk {Disable-AzDataCol
Script     2.0.0                 Az.Advisor               Core,Desk {Disable-AzAdvisor
Script     5.3.0                 Az.Aks                   Core,Desk {Get-AzAksCluster,
Script     2.3.0                 Az.Aks                   Core,Desk {Get-AzAksCluster,
Script     4.0.2                 Az.ApiManagement         Core,Desk {Add-AzApiManageme
Script     1.2.0                 Az.AppConfiguration      Core,Desk {Get-AzAppConfigur
Script     2.2.2                 Az.ApplicationInsights   Core,Desk {Get-AzApplication
Script     1.2.0                 Az.ApplicationInsights   Core,Desk {Get-AzApplication
Script     2.0.0                 Az.Attestation           Core,Desk {Get-AzAttestation
Script     1.9.0                 Az.Automation            Core,Desk {Set-AzAutomationP
```

***Figure 10.3**: Check module, commands, and supported PS edition*

The Az PowerShell module is strategically crafted as a wrapper module, consolidating various Azure service-specific PowerShell modules. Each distinct Azure service, such as **Az.Compute** for Azure computing services or **Az.AKS** for Azure Kubernetes Service, is encapsulated within its dedicated module.

```
PS C:\Users\pjayaram> Get-Command -Module Az.compute -Type Cmdlet
```

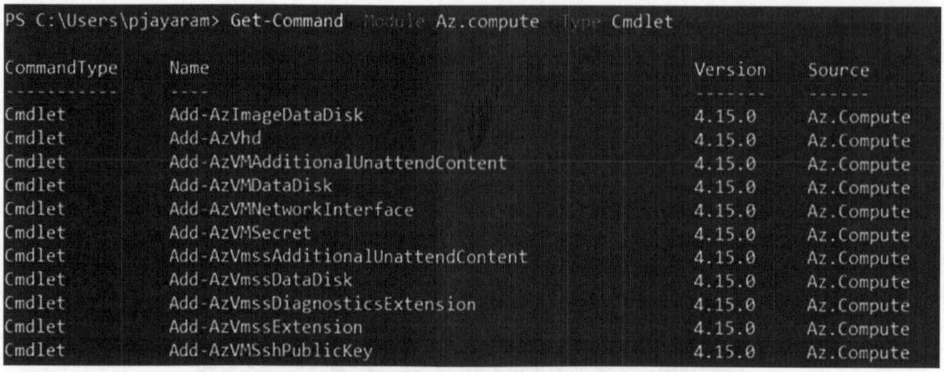

Figure 10.4: *Get Azure cmdlets information*

The number of cmdlets in the Azure PowerShell module may change with updates. To get the most accurate and up-to-date information, check directly in your PowerShell environment using this command.

This command counts the number of cmdlets available in the "**`Az.compute`**" module with Azure PowerShell.

Figure 10.5: *Count the cmdlets*

As you are more familiar with the structure of PowerShell modules, you will find that navigating and discovering cmdlets becomes more intuitive. Locating in-house cmdlets within a module involves understanding the use of nouns and verbs to narrow down your search.

```
Get-Command -Verb Get -Noun *VM* -Module Az.Compute
```

The **`Get-Command`** statement is aimed at retrieving cmdlets within the "**`Az.Compute`**" module that has the verb "**`Get`**" and a noun starting with "**`AzVM`**."

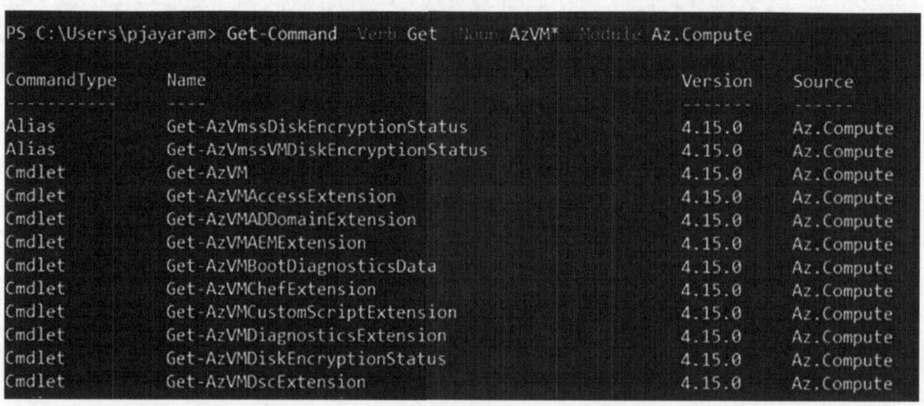

Figure 10.6: *Retrieving cmdlets within the "Az.Compute" module*

The **`Get-Command`** statement is aimed at retrieving cmdlets within the "**`Az.Compute`**" module that has the verb "**`Get`**" and a noun starting with "**`AzVM`**."

The functionality of the Az PowerShell module extends to both control plane and data plane operations in Azure. The control plane is employed for resource management within your subscription, while the data plane empowers users to leverage capabilities exposed by specific instances of resource types. This dual-plane approach enables comprehensive control and utilization of Azure resources through a unified and versatile PowerShell module.

Choosing the Right Azure Command-Line Tool

Azure command-line tools are an excellent way to automate routine operations, standardize database failovers, and extract powerful insights from data. Command-line tools allow you to scale your tasks in Azure and make it much easier to share your work with others. Sharing a script is much simpler than creating a lengthy Wiki page with time-consuming screenshots.

Note: *It is worth noting that in all the use-cases covered so far, we used a combination of Azure Portal and Azure commands. Knowing how to use an Azure command-line tool can be very helpful. There are two main tools for managing Azure resources: Azure CLI and Azure PowerShell. Both of these tools work on Windows, MacOS, and Linux. While you do not need to use these tools all the time, having this skill can be beneficial. In this lesson, we will not be covering `Az-Cli` in detail, but we did provide a brief comparison with Azure PowerShell.*

It is worth noting that both tools operate in different shell environments. For instance, Azure CLI supports Cmd and Bash, while Azure PowerShell supports Windows PowerShell and PowerShell.

Shell Environment	**Azure PowerShell**	**Azure CLI**
Cmd	-	Supported
Bash	Supported	Supported
Windows PowerShell	Supported	Supported
PowerShell	Supported	Supported

Table 10.1: *Comparison between Shell, Azure PowerShell, and Azure CLI*

This table compares the commands used in Azure CLI and Azure PowerShell for different functionalities.

Criteria	Azure PowerShell	Azure CLI
Cross-platform availability	Available on Windows, MacOS, Linux	Available on Windows, MacOS, Linux
Language used	Operates within PowerShell scripting language	Uses a command-line interface with Bash and other Unix-like shells
Installation method	Installed as a PowerShell module (Az)	Includes Azure CLI executable
Community support	Support from Azure community	Large and active community
Shell environments	Operates in Windows PowerShell and PowerShell	Works in various shell environments
Integration with Azure services	Offers deeper integration with Azure services	Supports Azure but may lack some integration

***Table 10.2**: Comparison between Azure CLI and Azure PowerShell*

The following commands showcase how to perform identical actions in Azure CLI and Azure PowerShell. These include tasks such as finding the version, getting help, signing in, managing subscriptions, and listing Azure locations. This list can go on and cover a broad range of Azure CLI and Azure PowerShell commands for multiple tasks related to Azure resource management.

Command	Azure PowerShell	Azure CLI
Find version	`Get-InstalledModule -Name Az`	`az --version`
Get help	`Get-Help`	`az --help`
View command help	`Get-Help -Name New-AzVM`	`az vm --help`
Sign in with web browser	`Connect-AzAccount`	`az login`
Get available subscriptions	`Get-AzSubscription`	`az account list`
Set subscription	`Set-AzContext -Subscription <SubscriptionID>`	`az account set --subscription <SubscriptionId>`
List Azure locations	`Get-AzLocation`	`az account list-locations`

***Table 10.3**: Commands in Azure PowerShell and Azure CLI*

Azure Cloud Shell

Azure Cloud Shell is an excellent tool for managing resources in the Azure cloud environment. It simplifies Azure resource management and is a preferred choice among users. One of the best features of Cloud Shell is that it is accessible through a web browser, which allows you to access it from anywhere and on any device. It is also highly versatile and can be integrated with other tools like Windows Terminal and Visual Studio Code. This makes it even more efficient and convenient to use. Overall, Azure Cloud Shell is a powerful and efficient tool for managing Azure resources, thanks to its web-based accessibility, pre-installed Azure tools, and integration with other tools.

Connecting to the Azure Environment

Azure PowerShell offers different authentication methods that allow users to sign in to Azure from Azure PowerShell. The method you choose will depend on your specific use case. For instance, if you need to manage Azure resources on an ad hoc basis, you can sign in using an interactive login. However, if you are writing a script for automation, you can sign in with a service principal. And if you are running Azure PowerShell within an Azure resource, you can sign in with a managed identity.

Interactive Login

Interactive logins in Azure PowerShell offer a flexible and user-friendly experience. Users can directly authenticate themselves for quick management tasks without pre-configuration of non-interactive authentication methods.

Use Case: Ad hoc Management of Azure Resources

If you are working with Azure PowerShell for occasional, manual management of resources, you can sign in interactively. This method involves prompting you for credentials through an interactive login process.

A step-by-step guide for interactive login in Azure PowerShell is as follows:

1. Open PowerShell and run the following command:

   ```
   Connect-AzAccount
   ```

If Azure PowerShell can open your default browser, it initiates the authorization code flow and opens the default browser to load the Azure sign-in page.

OR

If Azure PowerShell cannot open your default browser, it initiates the device code flow. In this case, you will see a message instructing you to open a browser page at **`aka.ms/devicelogin`** and enter the code displayed in your PowerShell session.

2. Sign in with your Azure account credentials in the browser.

Once successfully authenticated, you will see the details of your Azure account in the PowerShell session.

Note: *If you have access to multiple subscriptions, you are signed in to the first subscription Azure returns. Commands will run against this subscription by default. To change your active subscription for the current session, you can use the Set-AzContext cmdlet. To change your active subscription and have it persist between sessions on the same system, use the `Select-AzContext` cmdlet.*

If you encounter issues with opening a web browser during the interactive login process, you can force the device code flow instead. Here is how you can do it in Azure PowerShell.

Device Code Authentication

Open PowerShell and run the following command with the **`-UseDeviceAuthentication`** parameter:

1. **`Connect-AzAccount -UseDeviceAuthentication`**
2. A message will be displayed in the PowerShell session, instructing you to open a browser page at **`aka.ms/devicelogin`** and enter the displayed code.
3. Open a web browser and navigate to **`aka.ms/devicelogin`**.
4. Enter the displayed code in the web page.
5. Sign in with your Azure account credentials in the browser.

Once successfully authenticated, you will see the details of your Azure account in the PowerShell session.

Service Principal

You can sign in using a service principal for automation tasks like writing scripts. A service principal is a non-interactive account that can be used for unattended scripting and automation scenarios. This approach enhances security by avoiding the need for manual intervention during script execution.

Use Case: Scripting for Automation

To automate scripting, we need to create an Azure AD service principal, retrieve its secret, get the Azure AD tenant ID from the current context, and assign the '*contributor*' or '*reader*' role to the service principal. We take care to securely store sensitive information using the **`ConvertTo-SecureString`** cmdlet to define the client secret as a secure string. Then, we create a **`PSCredential`** object using the service principal ID and client secret. This step is crucial for storing credentials. Finally, we establish a connection to Azure using the **`Connect-AzAccount`** cmdlet. This provides detailed output of the authenticated account, including the service **`principal ID`**,

subscription name, **tenant ID**, and **Azure environment**. As a result, we have successfully authenticated Azure using a service principal.

```
# Create a new Azure AD service principal with the given display name
$sp = New-AzADServicePrincipal -DisplayName AutomationTest

# Retrieve the secret (password) of the service principal
$spPassword = $sp.PasswordCredentials.SecretText

# Display the secret (password)
Write-Host "Service Principal Secret (Password): $spPassword"

Service Principal Secret (Password): E-R8Q~m4OhXhuPtwsNfsIa9MOWzwflzeuy-fBVc3u



# Retrieve the Azure AD tenant ID from the current context
$tenantId = (Get-AzContext).Tenant.Id

# Display the Azure AD tenant ID
Write-Host "Azure AD Tenant ID: $tenantId"

Azure AD Tenant ID: da9d7617-d9fc-461d-80ec-72cc0de2fddb



# Assign the 'Contributor' role to the service principal
New-AzRoleAssignment -ApplicationId $sp.ApplicationId -RoleDefinitionName 'Contributor'

RoleAssignmentName : 1ecd6676-dfef-4491-8e8e-6761d946b614
RoleAssignmentId   : /subscriptions/002762c5-25ad-47ea-815d-71bba2cee58d/providers/Microsoft.Authorization/roleAssignments/1ecd6676-dfef-4491-8e8e-6761d946b614
Scope              : /subscriptions/002762c5-25ad-47ea-815d-71bba2cee58d
DisplayName        : AutomationTest
```

```
SignInName         :
RoleDefinitionName : 'Contributor'
RoleDefinitionId   : acdd72a7-3385-48ef-bd42-f606fba81ae7
ObjectId           : 8ab63153-9641-4948-b79f-8379c60ecabe
ObjectType         : ServicePrincipal
CanDelegate        : False
Description        :
ConditionVersion   :
Condition          :

# Define the client secret as a secure string
$clientSecret = 'E-R8Q~m4OhXhuPtwsNfsIa9MOWzwflzeuyfBVc3u' | Convert-
To-SecureString -AsPlainText -Force

# Create a PSCredential object using the service principal ID and client
secret
$connectCreds = New-Object -TypeName System.Management.Automation.PSCre-
dential -ArgumentList 'd27561a7-ecc1-49f9-a97e-ea4c0469c6ba', $clientSe-
cret

# Connect to Azure using the service principal
Connect-AzAccount -ServicePrincipal -Credential $connectCreds -Tenant
'da9d7617-d9fc-461d-80ec-72cc0de2fddb'
```

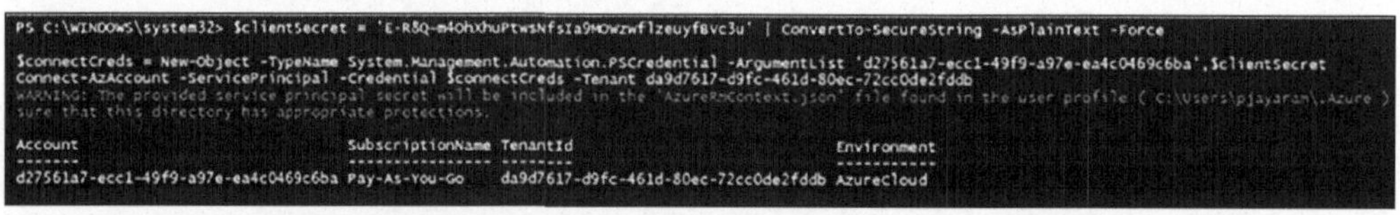

Figure 10.7: *Connect to Azure using the service principal*

```
Get-AzSubscription -SubscriptionId '002762c5-25ad-47ea-815d-71bba-
2cee58d' | Set-AzContext
```

If multiple subscriptions exist under the same tenant ID, it is important to identify the one that allows us to access the resources needed to carry out our business operations effectively. To retrieve information about a specific subscription, use the command "**Get-AzSubscription -SubscriptionId '002762c5-25ad-47ea-815d-71bba2cee58d'**". Then use the "**Set-AzContext**" cmdlet to set the current context to the subscription context obtained from the previous command.

Figure 10.8: *Set the current context using Set-AzContent cmdlet*

However, the warning indicates that the provided service principal secret will be included in the **`'AzureRmContext.json'`** file found in the user profile directory. Therefore, ensuring that this directory has appropriate protections to secure sensitive information is highly recommended. The successful authentication to Azure will enable us to access the necessary resources to carry out our business operations effectively.

Managed Identity:

- Managed identities are a useful feature in Azure that simplifies managing identities for your resources. There are two types of managed identities:
  - System-assigned managed identity
  - User-assigned managed identity

Creating an automation account is the first step to creating a managed identity.

To create a new automation account on Azure:

1. Sign in to the **`Azure`** portal.
2. Select **`+ Create`** a resource from the top menu.
3. Under categories, select IT and management tools, and then select **`automation`**.
4. Fill in the subscription, resource group, automation account name, and region fields.

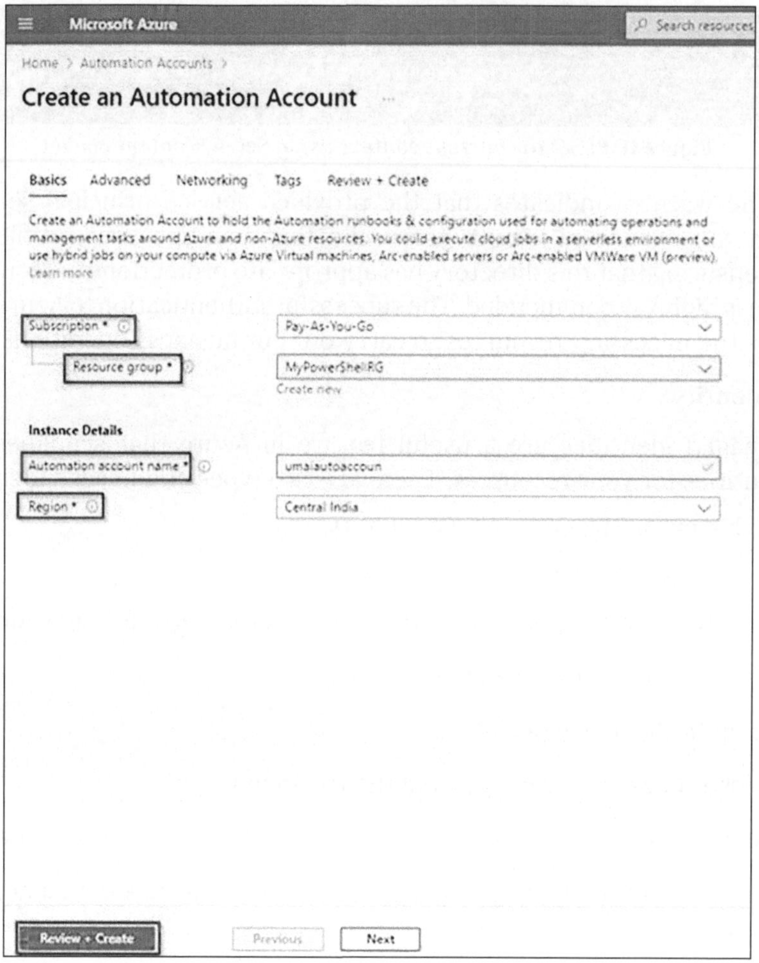

***Figure 10.9**: Create a new automation account*

Note: *By default, a system-assigned managed identity is enabled for the automation account. If you want to enable both options in the advanced settings of your automation account, you need to select the "Add user-assigned identities" option for the user-assigned identity. Next, you will be taken to the "Select user assigned managed identity" page where you can choose a subscription and add one or more user-assigned identities created within that subscription to assign to the automation account.*

However, in this case, we choose to enable managed identities later, the automation account will be created without a managed identity.

System-Assigned Managed Identity

System-assigned managed identity is tied to a specific Azure resource, like a virtual machine or automation account. When enabled, it creates a unique identity in your Azure AD that can be used to set specific permissions for that resource.

To assign roles to system-assigned managed identity, go to the automation account and select **"Identity"** from the left menu. Enable the system-assigned identity and click **"Save"**. Next, select **"Permissions"** and then click **"Azure role assignments"**. Choose **"Add"** and select the scope as **"subscription"**. Choose the **"Contributor"** role and click **"Save"**.

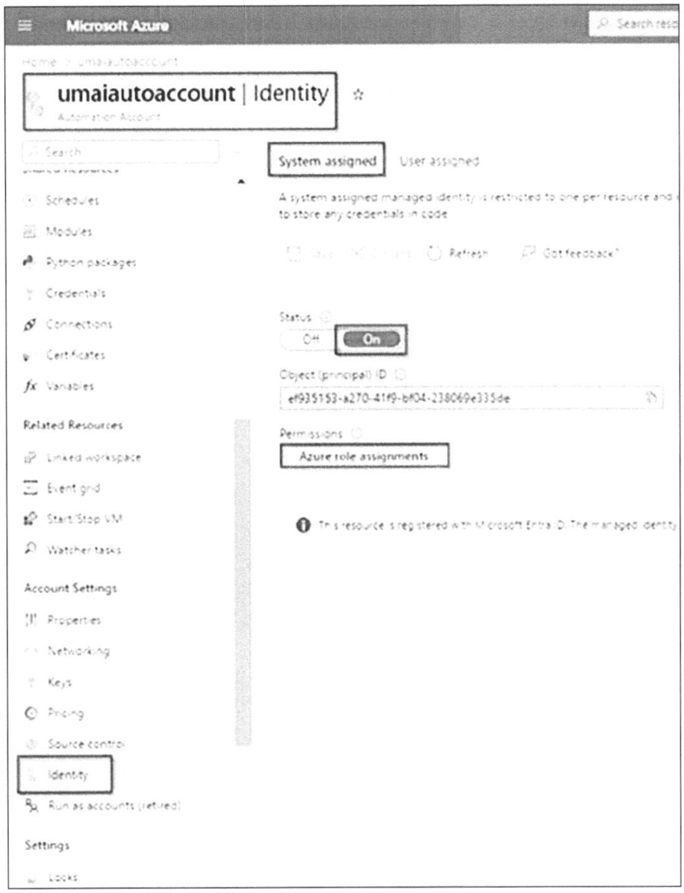

***Figure 10.10**: Set permissions for automation account*

User-Assigned Managed Identity

User-assigned managed identity, as a standalone Azure resource can associate with one or more Azure services. This provides greater flexibility and control over managing identities. It allows you to create, manage your own identities, and use them for multiple resources.

You can sign in using a managed identity if you are executing Azure PowerShell within an Azure resource (such as virtual machine or an Azure function) . Managed identities eliminate the need for explicit credentials in your code. The identity is associated with the Azure resource itself, offering a secure and seamless authentication method.

Note: *Managed Identities are considered more secure as their credentials are only accessible to the assigned resource and are never exposed in any code. Unlike other account types that require an administrator to manage the credentials at some point, managed identities credentials are never handled by any system administrator or any other individual.*

Creating User-Assigned Managed Identity

To create a managed identity, let us navigate to the managed identities Azure portal. If you cannot find it, use the search bar to locate it. Next, click "**`Create`**" to go to the "**`Create User Assigned Managed Identity`**" page. From there, select "**`PowerShellRG`**" as the resource group from the dropdown and choose "**`Central India`**" as the region by scrolling up. For the name, enter "**`demouami`**" and click the appropriate button to proceed.

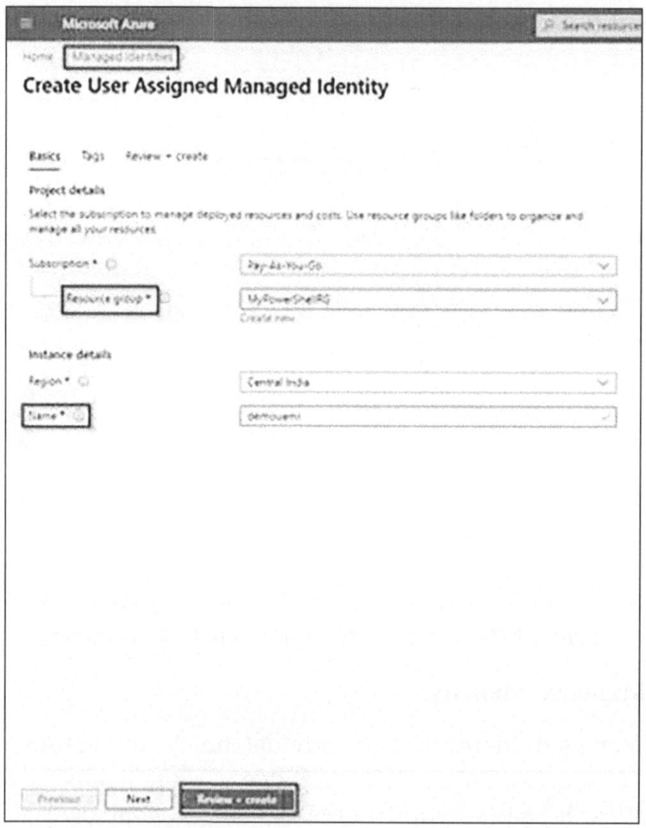

Figure 10.11: *Create user assigned managed identity*

Let us search for "**`Subscription`**" in the search bar and click the first link that appears. This will take us to the subscriptions page. Once we are there, we need to click the subscription name and then click the **`Access Control (IAM)`** option. On the right side of the page, click "**`Role Assignments`**" and "**`Add Role Assignment`**." From the list of roles, select "**Contributor**" and then click "**Members.**" On the members page, choose "**Managed Identity,**" then click "**Select Members.**" Select the only user-assigned managed identity from the dropdown and click it. This will show the **uamidemoaccount**, the managed identity we just created. Click it, and then click "**Select.**" Finally, click "**Review + Assign**" twice to assign the **uamidemo** account the contributor access to this subscription. To confirm that the managed identity has been assigned the correct role, scroll down to the "**Role Assignments**" section of the page.

***Figure 10.12**: Add role assignment*

Click "**Add role assignment**", and then click "**Add role assignment**", select Privileged administrator roles, from the list of roles, select "**Contributor,**" and then click "**Members.**" On the members page, choose "**Managed Identity,**" then click "**Select Members.**" Select the only user-assigned managed identity from the dropdown and click on it. This will show the **uamidemoaccount**, the managed identity we just created. Click on it, and then click on "**Select.**" Finally, click "**Review + Assign**" twice to assign the **uamidemoaccount** the contributor access to this subscription.

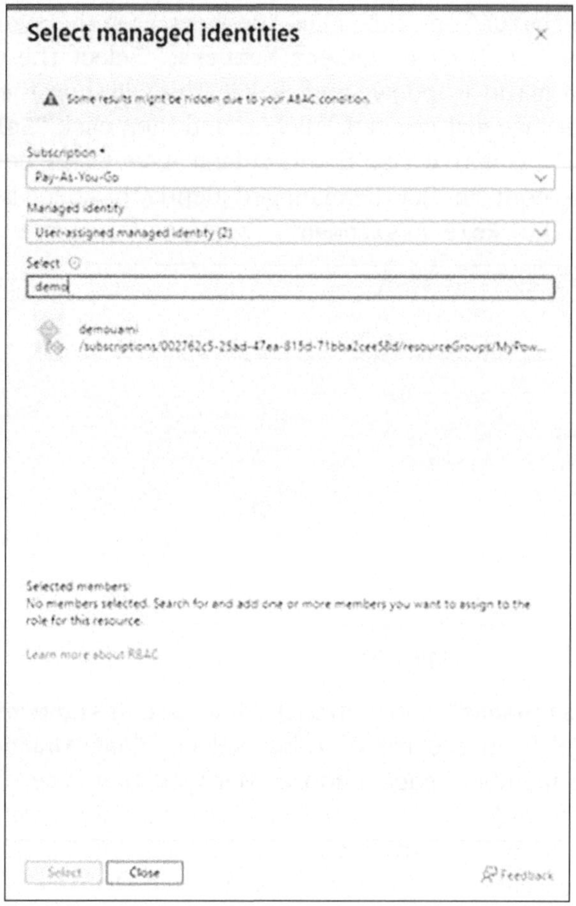

Figure 10.13: *Select managed identities*

To confirm that the managed identity has been assigned the correct role, scroll down to the "**Role Assignments**" section of the page.

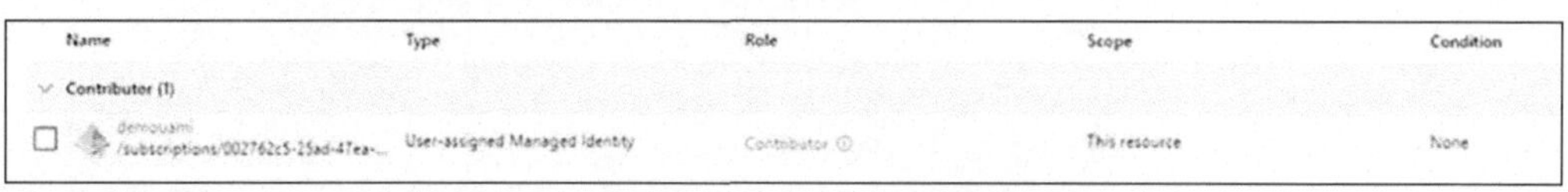

Figure 10.14: *Validate the role assignments*

Here are the steps to manage your user-assigned managed identities in the Azure portal:

1. In the Azure portal, browse the automation account named "**umaiautoaccount**".
2. Click "**Identity**" and select "**User assigned**".
3. Click "**Add**" and then select "**Add user managed identity**".

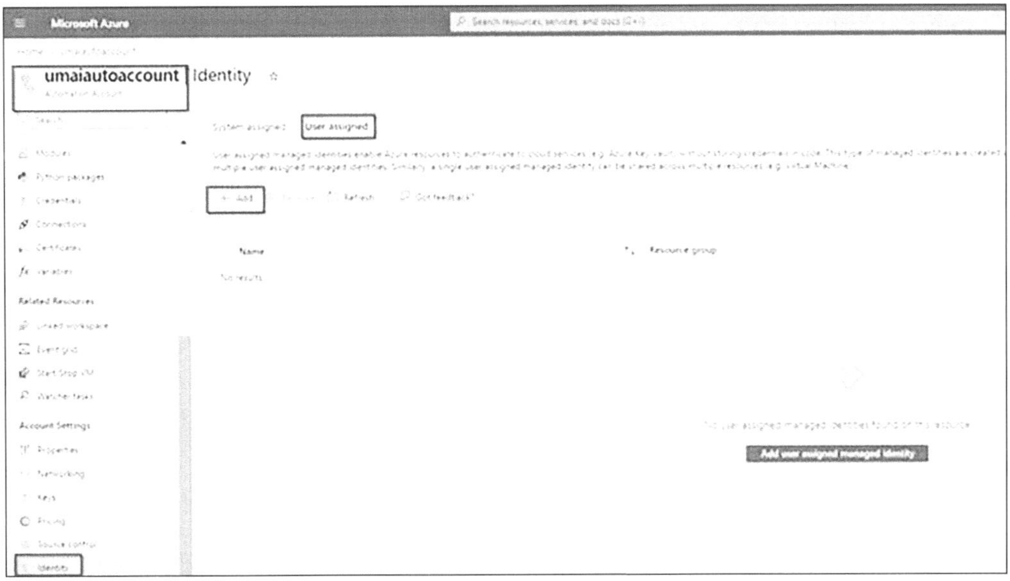

Figure 10.15: *User-assigned managed identities*

4. Next, select the user managed identity account named "**`demoumia`**" and click "**`Add`**".

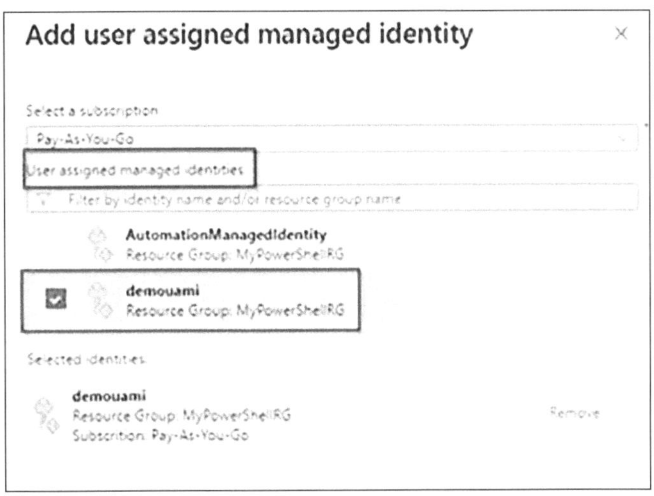

Figure 10.16: *Add user-assigned managed identity*

That is it! You are all set to test the managed identity feature.

Note: *You need to have the Azure PowerShell module installed (Az module) before you can use any of these authentication methods. You can install it by running the following command:*

Install-Module -Name *`Az.ManagedServiceIdentity -AllowPrerelease`*

By understanding these authentication methods, users can pick the most suitable approach based on their specific requirements, whether it is for interactive management, scripting, or running within Azure resources.

Getting Started with Azure Automation

Automating operational tasks is crucial for streamlining infrastructure management on-premises and in the cloud. Microsoft Azure Automation provides capabilities to help administrators automate their cloud-based, operational, and repetitive tasks. Being built on top of the reliable PowerShell, it is a useful tool for any Azure cloud administrator. Azure runbooks are easy to create, edit, and execute, and they can integrate well with almost all resources in the Microsoft Azure ecosystem.

Azure Automation has significantly changed since its inception as a small feature in the Azure classic portal. Azure resource manager (ARM) model and the new Azure portal, Azure automation has significantly ramped up with many new features. As more and more organizations move towards the cloud, automation is in high demand to maximize return on investment (ROI).

This chapter introduces you to the ARM deployment model in Azure, and the various components of Azure Automation in the ARM model. These include, but are not limited to, the Azure Automation overview dashboard, PowerShell, runbooks, jobs, Runbook Gallery, and Azure Automation security. We will focus on establishing a basic understanding of the key concepts of Azure Automation.

Microsoft Azure is a leader in the cloud market, and developing skill sets in Azure Automation is a valuable tool for a cloud administrator.

To create a new Azure Automation account, use the **`New-AzAutomationAccount`** cmdlet in PowerShell. The command breakdown is:

```
New-AzAutomationAccount -Name "myazureautomationacct" -Location "central India" -ResourceGroupName "MyPowerShellRG"
```

Figure 10.17: *Create a new Azure Automation account*

1. **`-Name`**: Specifies the account name.
2. **`-Location`**: Specifies the Azure region where the account will be created.

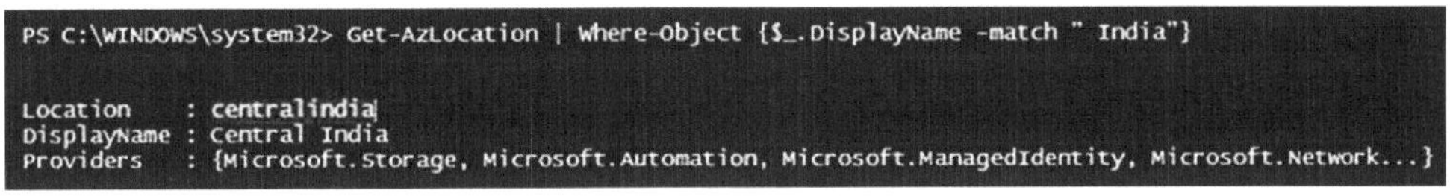

Figure 10.18: *Specify the Azure region*

3. **`-ResourceGroupName`**: It specifies the Azure resource group in which to create the account.

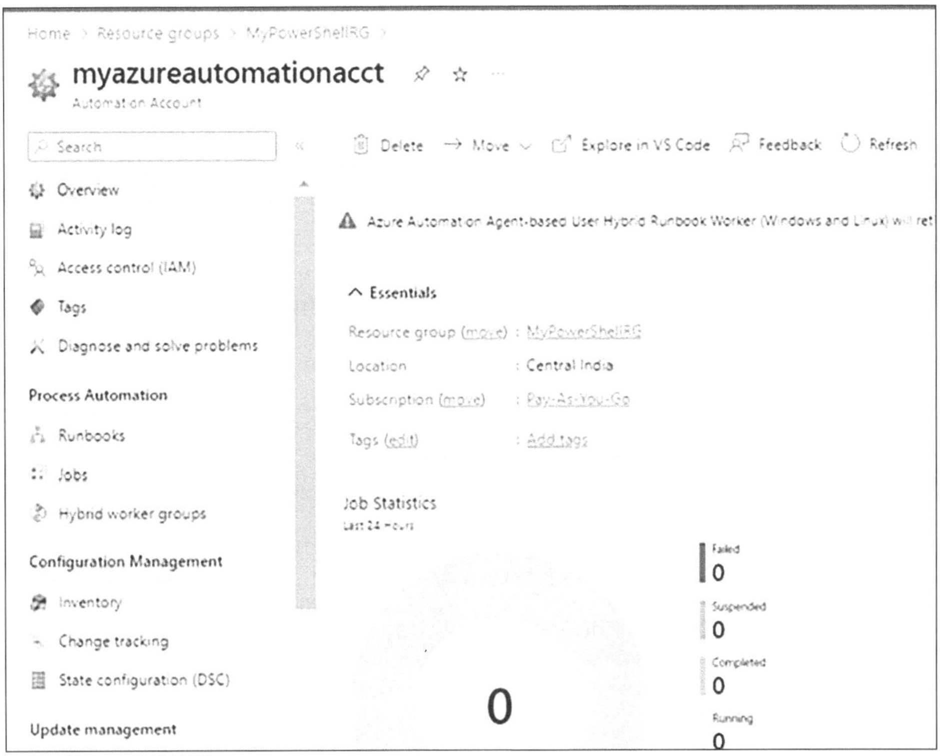

Figure 10.19: *Specify the Azure resource group*

Using PowerShell in Azure Automation

Azure Automation runbooks are based entirely on PowerShell. There are four types of runbooks available: PowerShell, PowerShell Workflow, Graphical, and Graphical PowerShell Workflow. Each type has its own unique features and limitations.

The basic PowerShell-based runbooks in Azure Automation work similarly to executing Azure PowerShell module-based commands from the Azure portal. To use advanced features such as parallel processing of tasks and runbook checkpoints, you will need to switch to PowerShell workflow-based runbooks. However, you can still create runbooks using simple Azure PowerShell-based scripts and schedule them.

PowerShell workflow runbooks are designed for complex tasks that involve executing steps in parallel, calling other child runbooks, and more. They use PowerShell workflows that leverage Windows workflow foundation, allowing you to set checkpoints in your script to restart the script if an exception occurs during execution.

Graphical runbooks can be created from the Azure portal and represent data flow visually in an easy-to-understand format. Unlike PowerShell and PowerShell workflow runbooks, they cannot be edited or created outside the portal. However, there is an option to convert graphical runbooks to graphical PowerShell workflow and vice versa.

Graphical PowerShell workflow runbooks are based on PowerShell workflows and can be edited and managed only from within the Azure portal.

Creating Runbook using Azure Automation

To create a new runbook in your Azure portal Automation account, follow these steps:

1. Use the credentials to sign in to the Azure portal.
2. Navigate to your automation account.
3. Choose runbooks under process automation.
4. Click the "`Create a Runbook`" button.
5. Name your runbook "`StartOrStopVM`".
6. Select PowerShell workflow from the runbook type drop-down.
7. Choose either 10.1 (preview) or 5.1 from the runtime version drop-down.
8. Enter an appropriate description.
9. Create the runbook by clicking the "`Create`" button.
10. In the runbook editor, copy and paste the following code.
11. Test the code.
12. Save, then publish, and then yes when prompted.
13. From the overview page, select start.
14. Populate the parameters and then select `OK`.

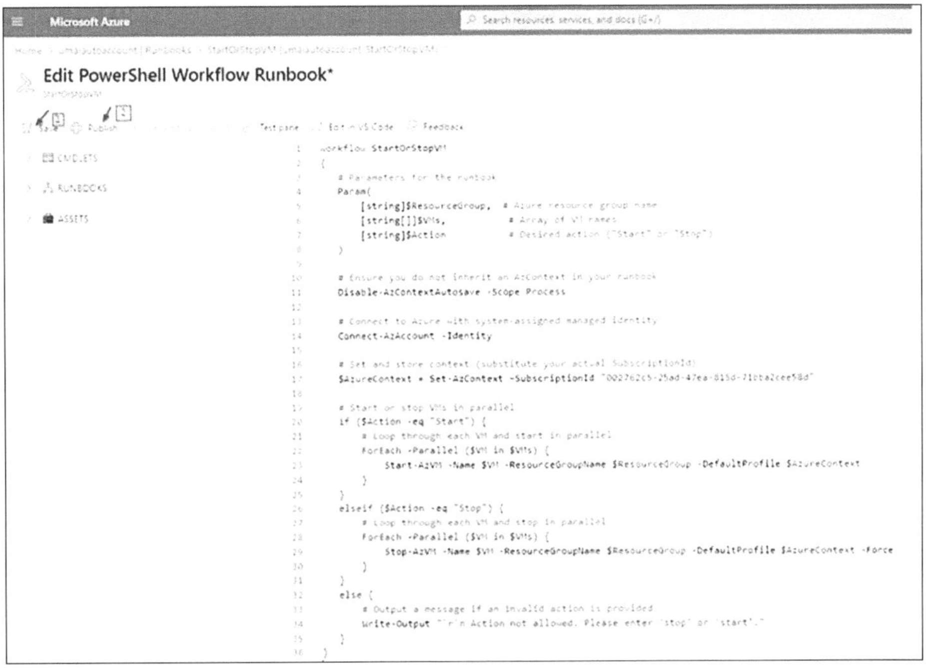

Figure 10.20: *Edit the PowerShell workflow runbook*

That is it! You have successfully created a new runbook in your Azure portal automation account.

The code will enable you to start a stopped virtual machine or stop a running virtual machine.

```
workflow StartOrStopVM
{
   <#
   .SYNOPSIS
   This runbook starts or stops virtual machines in parallel within a specified Azure resource group.


   .DESCRIPTION
   The runbook requires the following parameters:
   - ResourceGroup: Enter the name of the resource group of the VMs.
   - VMs: Enter the names of the virtual machines using the following syntax: ["VM1","VM2","VM3"]
   - Action: Enter "stop" or "start".
   #>
```

```
# Parameters for the runbook
Param(
    [string]$ResourceGroup,  # Azure resource group name
    [string[]]$VMs,          # Array of VM names
    [string]$Action          # Desired action ("Start" or "Stop")
)

# Ensure you do not inherit an AzContext in your runbook
Disable-AzContextAutosave -Scope Process

# Connect to Azure with system-assigned managed identity
Connect-AzAccount -Identity

# Set and store context (substitute your actual SubscriptionId)
$AzureContext = Set-AzContext -SubscriptionId "002762c5-25ad-47ea-
815d-71bba2cee58d"

# Start or stop VMs in parallel
if ($Action -eq "Start") {
    # Loop through each VM and start in parallel
    ForEach -Parallel ($VM in $VMs) {
        Start-AzVM -Name $VM -ResourceGroupName $ResourceGroup
-DefaultProfile $AzureContext
    }
}
elseif ($Action -eq "Stop") {
    # Loop through each VM and stop in parallel
    ForEach -Parallel ($VM in $VMs) {
        Stop-AzVM -Name $VM -ResourceGroupName $ResourceGroup
-DefaultProfile $AzureContext -Force
    }
}
else {
```

```
        # Output a message if an invalid action is provided
        Write-Output "`r`n Action not allowed. Please enter 'stop' or
'start'."
    }
}
```

The PowerShell script that creates an Azure Automation runbook workflow named **StartOrStopVM**. This workflow takes in three parameters: the name of the Azure resource group, an array of VM names, and the desired action to perform on those VMs ("**Start**" or "**Stop**").

The script begins by disabling the Azure context autosave feature to prevent inheriting an existing context. It then connects to Azure using the system-assigned managed identity and sets and stores the context.

The workflow uses the **ForEach-Parallel** loop to start or stop VMs in parallel based on the specified action. If the action parameter is set to "**Start**", the script iterates through each VM in the array and uses the **Start-AzVM** cmdlet to start the VM with the specified name and resource group. Similarly, if the action parameter is set to "**Stop**", the script iterates through each VM in the array and uses the **Stop-AzVM** cmdlet to stop the VM with the specified name and resource group.

If an invalid action is provided, the script outputs a message stating that only "**stop**" or "**start**" are allowed. This ensures that the script only performs explicitly defined actions and avoids unintended consequences.

Thoroughly testing runbooks before deploying in a production environment is crucial. Azure Automation provides multiple testing options to ensure automation processes are reliable and efficient.

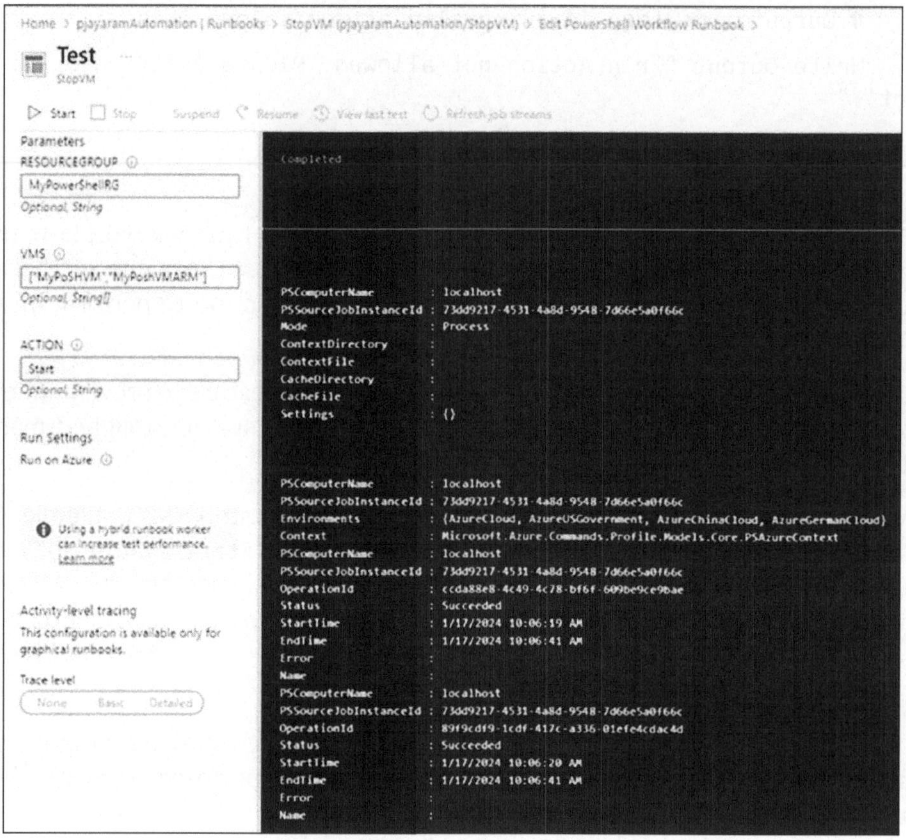

Figure 10.21: *Azure Automation testing options*

If you prefer to use a user-managed identity instead of a system-assigned identity in your runbook, you can modify the code to do so. All you need to do is replace the **'Connect-AzAccount -Identity'** line with the following code:

```
# Connect using a user-managed identity
$clientId = "<YourClientId>"
# Replace <YourClientId> with the actual client ID
try {
$AzureContext = (Connect-AzAccount -Identity -AccountId $clientId).
context
}
catch {
Write-Output "There is no user-assigned managed identity. Aborting."
exit
}
```

In this code, you must replace '<code><YourClientId></code>' with the client ID you obtained from the managed identity overview page. This modification ensures that the runbook connects to Azure using the specified user-managed identity. The rest of the runbook logic remains the same, leveraging the Azure context and managing the VM state based on the provided action.

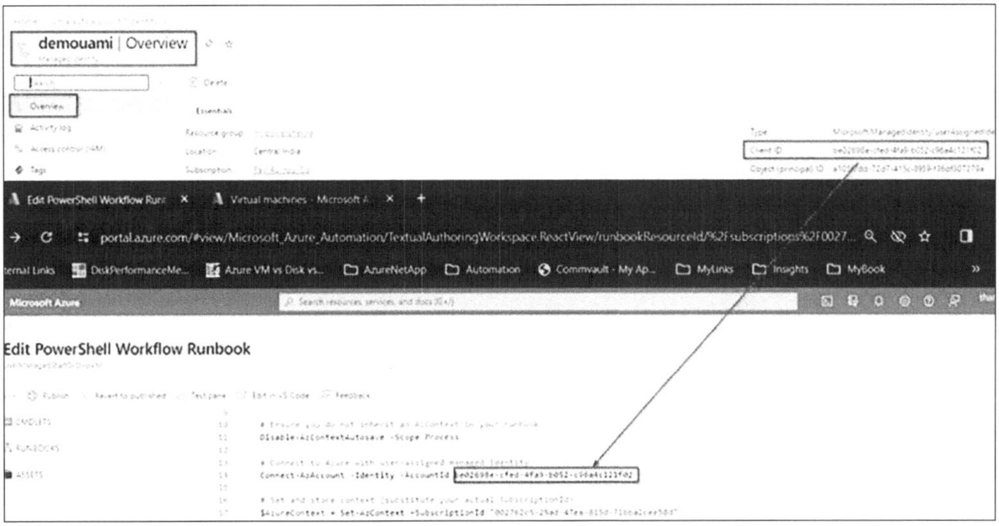

Figure 10.22: *Connect Runboo to Azure with specified user-managed identity*

To publish a runbook on the Azure portal, follow these steps:

1. Go to your Azure Automation account on the portal.
2. From the menu, select "**`Runbooks`**" and choose the runbook you wish to publish.
3. On the runbook's details page, click "**`Edit`**" to access the code editor.
4. You may need to replace the **`client_id`** in the code with the appropriate value. This is necessary when using user-managed identity.
5. Once you have made any necessary changes, click "**`Save`**" to save the code.
6. To publish the changes, click "**`Publish`**".

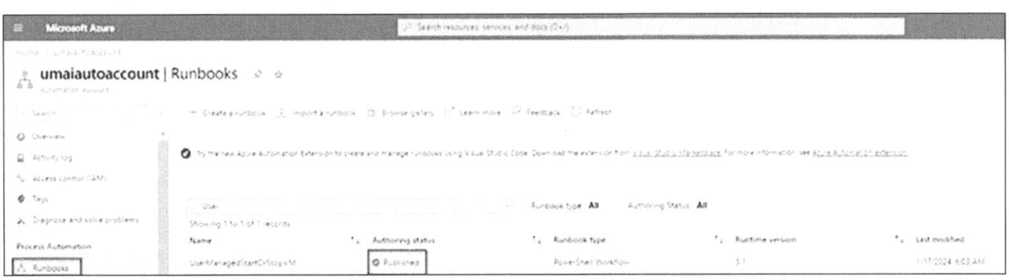

Figure 10.23: *Publish the runbook changes*

To start a job, follow these steps:

1. After publishing, go back to the runbook's details page.
2. Click "**Start**" to initiate a new job for the runbook.
3. Configure any required parameters for the job.
4. Optionally, schedule the job to run at specific intervals or trigger it manually.
5. Confirm the job settings and click "**OK**" to start the job.

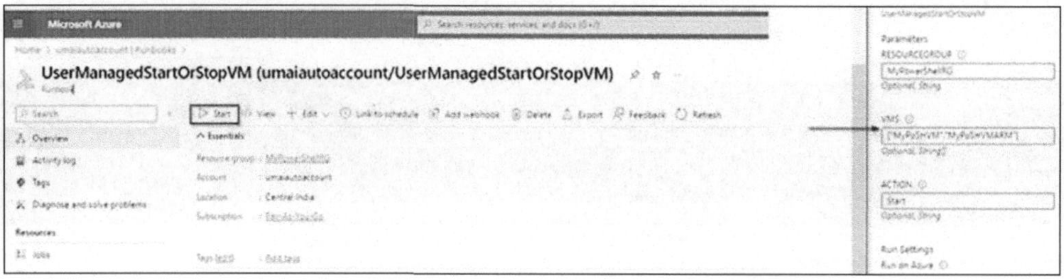

***Figure 10.24**: Click Start to initiate a new job*

Validating the success and correctness of your workflow execution in Azure Automation can be achieved by thoroughly reviewing the job output, input parameters, and error messages.

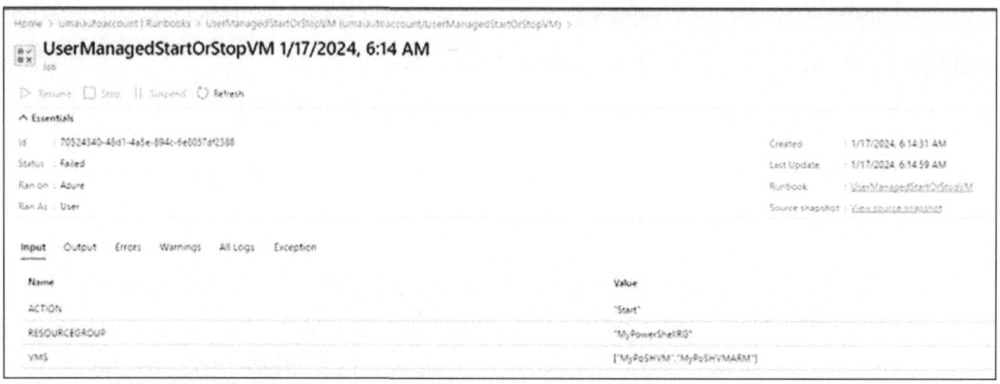

***Figure 10.25:** Validate the success and correctness of workflow execution*

Azure Automation Assets

Azure Automation assets are significant elements that allow you to centrally administer and utilize various settings across the runbooks in your Automation account. There are five main categories of assets in Azure Automation, including schedules, modules, variables, connections, certificates, and credentials.

Schedules define the timing and recurrence pattern for executing the associated runbook, which is useful for orchestrating runbooks at specific intervals or on a recurring basis.

Modules refer to packages of code that can be imported into runbooks, containing PowerShell cmdlets, DSC resources, or other types of automation content. This feature facilitates the organization and reuse of code snippets or functions across multiple runbooks.

Variables can store and retrieve data within an Automation account and act as placeholders for values that may change over time. They are ideal for storing configuration data or dynamic values used by runbooks.

Connections represent named connections to external systems and store details such as connection strings, API keys, or other credentials required for connecting to external services. This feature is useful for securely storing and managing authentication details for external services.

Certificates provide a way to store X.509 certificates within the automation account securely. These certificates can be used for authentication or securing communications, making them suitable for scenarios requiring secure communication or authentication using certificates.

Credentials store usernames and passwords securely, which can be referenced in runbooks for authentication purposes without exposing sensitive information directly in the runbook code. This feature is important for securely handling authentication details in runbooks.

The Need of ARM

The cloud has evolved significantly since its inception, bringing forth several years of advancements and innovations in how we consume and utilize it for building systems. The challenge lies in making the cloud more user-friendly, simpler, and efficient, particularly in creating models that align well with enterprise needs. Initially, when cloud services were novel, the approach involved setting up a service model, defining the front end and back end, and possibly including a database. However, the focus shifted towards enhancing usability and simplifying the process of designing and implementing cloud-based systems for better alignment with enterprise requirements.

In the early days of cloud services, designing a system involved creating various endpoints, front-end, and back-end networks, and configuring different zones before converting it all into a cloud service. The process was somewhat manual and required scripting or clicking through interfaces to create each element in a specific order. There were limitations regarding access control, tagging, and networking, making it challenging to manage subscriptions effectively.

Microsoft introduced the Azure Resource Model (ARM) to address these issues. This model, based on JSON templates, allows for declarative descriptions of the desired end state of a system. Unlike imperative scripting, ARM templates focus on defining the outcome, ensuring consistency and reproducibility. These templates are idempotent, meaning they yield the same state each time they are executed, making them reliable.

The latest Resource Manager, version two, is versatile, supporting various services across multiple regions and providing extensibility.

This approach offers a more efficient and structured way to create complex services in Azure, offering a template-driven, declarative method that ensures consistency and scalability across multi-service, multi-region environments.

Unlocking the potential of Azure Resource Manager (ARM) templates is all about embracing simplicity. Let me show you how using ARM templates can simplify your life compared to traditional on-premises deployments. Here are three compelling reasons.

- **Declarative Ease**

ARM templates work on a declarative model, which makes them easy to understand and write. Even if you are new to deployment, you will find them straightforward.

- **Repeatable Efficiency**

The beauty of ARM templates is that they are repeatable. Once created, you can reuse them to replicate deployments quickly. You can run them many times and get consistent, reliable results.

- **Orchestrated Seamlessness**

With ARM templates, you do not have to worry about sequencing concerns. They are orchestrated, so you do not need to micromanage the order of functions. This coordination ensures that the deployment process runs smoothly, freeing you from manual interventions.

Setting Up An Environment

Get ready to explore the most essential tool for Azure Resource Manager – the Azure Resource Manager Tools! With this incredible tool, you can easily identify problems within your template and receive a lot of feedback with intellisense just by typing in a few terms.

Install Azure Resource Manager Tools Extension

To install "**Azure Resource Manager Tools**" extension in Visual Studio Code, follow these steps:

1. Click the extensions icon in the activity bar or press *Ctrl+Shift*+X (Windows/Linux) or *Cmd+Shift*+X (MacOS) to open the extensions view.

2. In the search box of the extensions view, type "**Azure Resource Manager Tools**".
3. Look for the extension provided by Microsoft.
4. Click the "**Install**" button in VS code to install the extension.

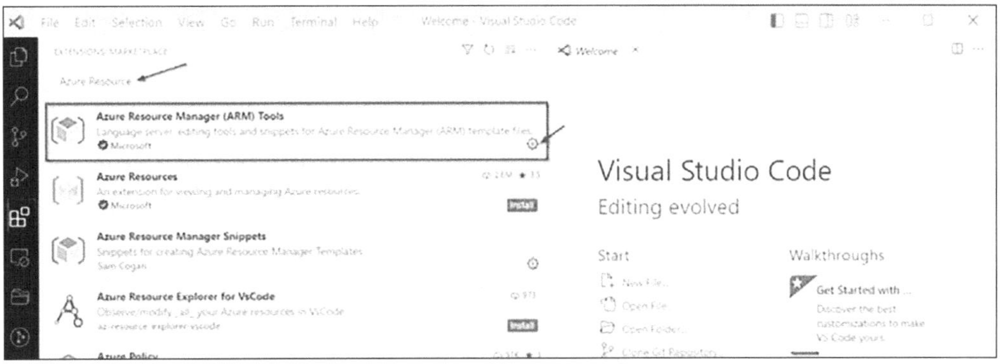

Figure 10.26: *Install Azure Resource Manager Tool extension*

It is an absolute game-changer that will make your work so much more exciting and efficient! Let us scroll down the screen and see how amazing it is.

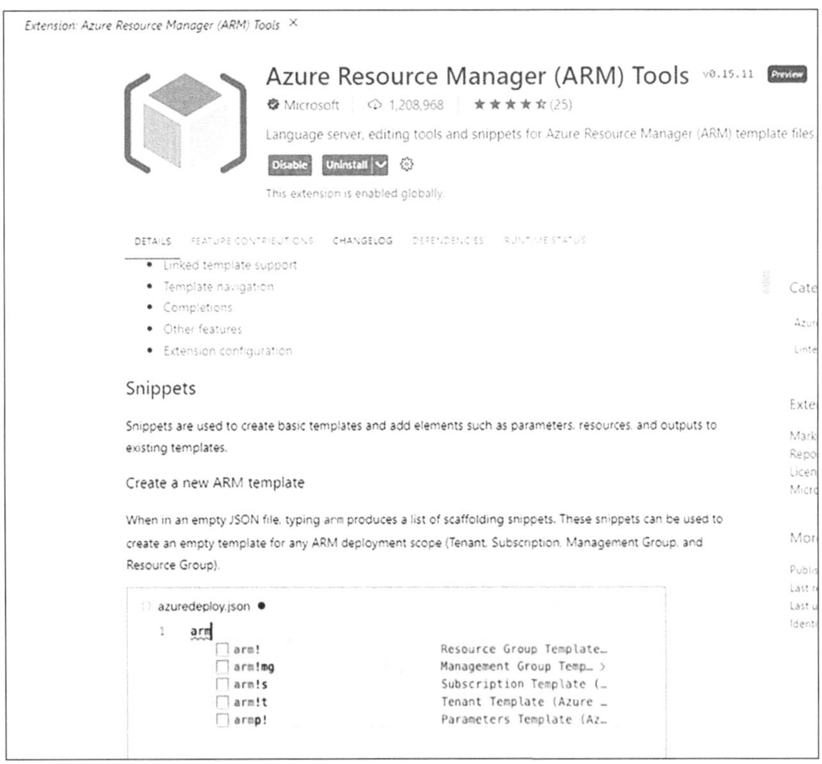

Figure 10.27: *Azure Resource Manager (ARM) tools*

Creating ARM templates using Visual Studio Code is now easier, specifically for simple templates.

Understanding ARM Template Structure

In the past, setting up a business infrastructure took a long time, often several days, weeks, or even months. But with the introduction of ARM templates and cloud computing, whole environments can now be set up in just a few minutes. This chapter will show you how to use ARM templates to deploy on Azure quickly and easily. ARM templates offer speed, security, reusability, and reliability, making them a vital tool for modern cloud computing. Our approach is to simplify the complexities and take you back to the basics, ensuring you understand ARM templates' fundamental concepts. Whether you are new to this or looking to improve your skills, this section will give you all the essential information you need to get started with **`ARM template`** deployments.

The Azure Resource Manager (ARM) template is a file written in JSON format that has a specific structure. It consists of various elements and properties that you can include in the file.

Here is a breakdown of the main elements that you need to know:

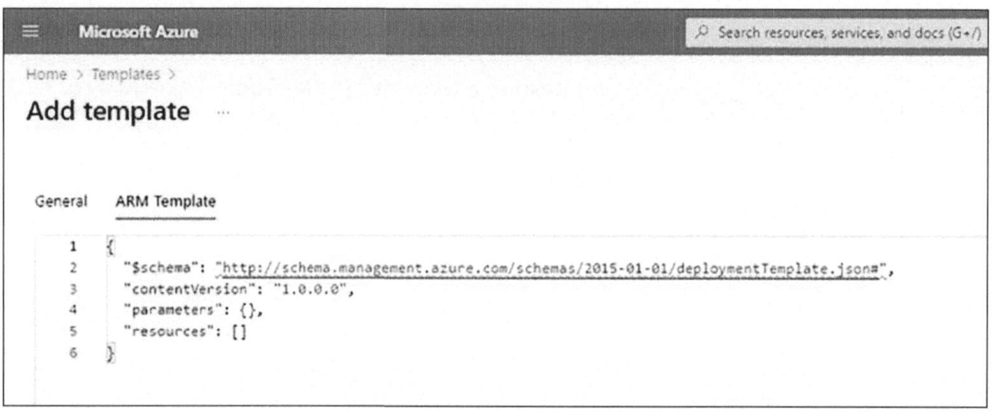

***Figure 10.28**: Add ARM template*

```
{
  "$schema": "https://schema.management.azure.com/schemas/2019-04-01/
deploymentTemplate.json#",
  "languageVersion": "",
  "contentVersion": "",
  "apiProfile": "",
  "definitions": { },
  "parameters": { },
```

```
  "variables": { },
  "functions": [ ],
  "resources": [ ], /* or "resources": { } with languageVersion 2.0 */
  "outputs": { }
}
```

- **$schema** (required): Specifies the location of the JSON schema file describing the version of the template language. You must use the latest version for resource group deployments in Visual Studio Code.
- **contentVersion** (required): Indicates the version of the template. You should document significant changes in your template using this value.
- **apiProfile** (optional): An API version that serves as a collection of API versions for resource types. This can be useful to avoid specifying API versions for each resource, especially when deploying to different environments.
- **languageVersion** (optional): Indicates the version of the template language used. You can use 2.0 for enhancements. For more details, refer to languageVersion 2.0.
- **definitions** (optional): Schemas used to validate array and object values. This element is only supported in languageVersion 2.0.
- **parameters** (optional): Values provided when deployment is executed to customize resource deployment. Parameters make your template flexible and reusable.
- **variables** (optional): Values used as JSON fragments in the template to simplify template language expressions. This can be helpful for reducing redundancy in your template.
- **functions** (optional): User-defined functions available within the template. You can define custom functions to reuse logic in your template.
- **resources** (required): Resource types that are deployed or updated in a resource group or subscription. This is the core section where you define the infrastructure components.
- **outputs** (optional): Values returned after deployment. This can be useful for capturing and displaying information about the deployed resources.

Getting Started with ARM Template

Are you ready to deploy some templates to make your work easier? All you need to do is open up Visual Studio Code and type in or copy the content provided below. Check out the image that follows for complete code of the template file. It is all set and ready for deployment. Let us dive in and see just how easy it is to get started!

We are planning to use an ARM template to accomplish a task. In this demo, we will be creating an ARM template that will be used to deploy a storage account. We will explore some of the elements that are included in the template. It is important to note that we have kept the template simple, as there are many components to a storage account. The goal is to demonstrate how an ARM template can be utilized simply.

Now that we have the necessary plug-ins installed, we can simply type in "*arm*" and hit return to set up the JSON template. Open the Visual Studio Code, type or copy the content provided below, and start the deployment process.

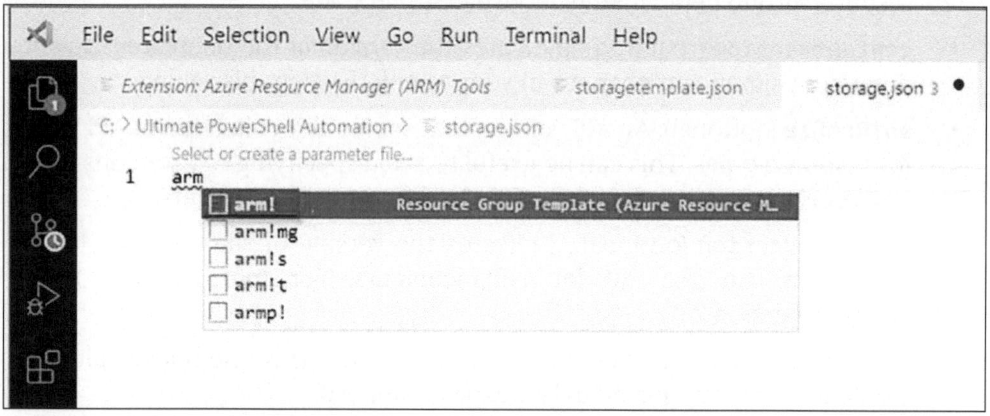

Figure 10.29: *Type code in Visual Studio Code*

This template includes the schema, content version, parameters, functions, variables, resources, and outputs. To proceed, we need to add something inside the currently empty brackets.

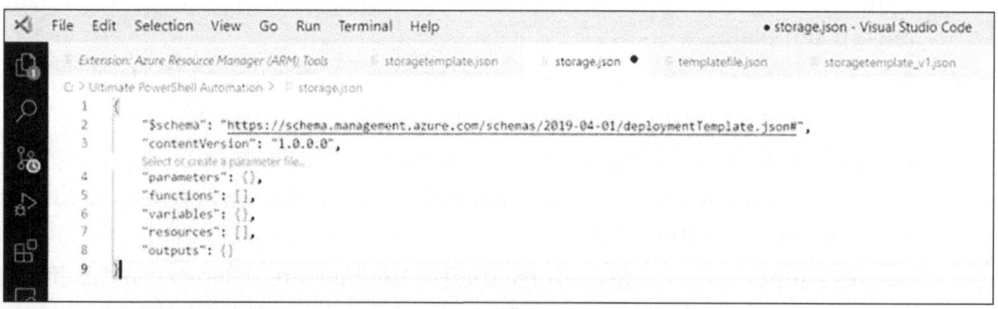

Figure 10.30: *Template details*

The following code snippet demonstrates creating a storage account in Microsoft Azure using Azure Resource Manager (ARM). The code starts with the resource type, which in this case is **`Microsoft.Storage/storageAccounts`**. This tells the ARM that we are creating a storage account. The API version used is **`2023-01-01`**.

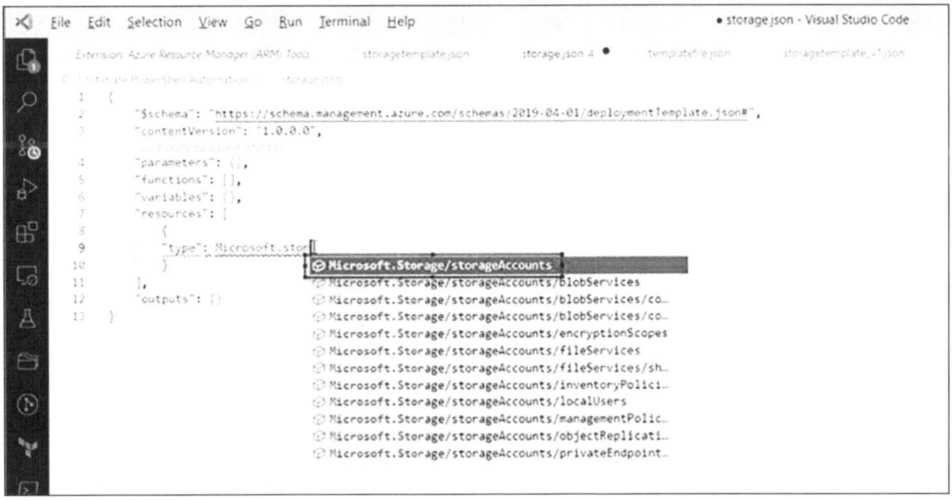

Figure 10.31: *Creating a storage account in Microsoft Azure using Azure Resource Manager (ARM)*

Next, we have the name of the storage account. It is recommended to give a descriptive name that is unique across Azure. In the given example, the name is **"pjstgavaccount"**. However, it is best to use a unique name that is easy to remember. In general, the resources are defined with best naming standards with tags and other unique identifiers.

The location of the storage account is specified next, which in this case is **CentralIndia**. The SKU (stock keeping unit) is set to **standard_LRS**, and the kind is set to StorageV2.

With these parameters set, we are ready to create the storage account in Microsoft Azure using ARM template.

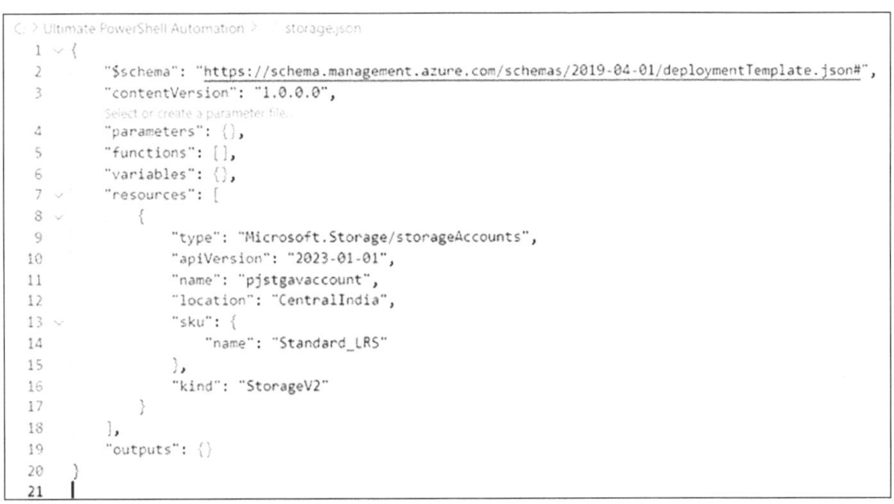

Figure 10.32: *Create the storage account in Microsoft Azure using ARM template*

The following image shows the complete code of the template file, and it is ready for deployment. Let deep dive further and see how easy it is to deploy the templates.

```
# Parameters
$resourceGroupName = "MyPowerShellRG"
$deploymentName = "StorageAccountDeploymentv1"
$templateFilePath = "C:\Ultimate PowerShell Automation\storagetemplate.
json"

# Create a new resource group
New-AzResourceGroup -Name $resourceGroupName -Location "CentralIndia"

#Test the deployment
Test-AzResourceGroupDeployment -ResourceGroupName $resourceGroupName
-TemplateFile $templateFilePath

# Deploy the ARM template
New-AzResourceGroupDeployment -ResourceGroupName $resourceGroupName `
    -Name $deploymentName `
    -TemplateFile $templateFilePath
```

After running this script, Azure PowerShell will create a new resource group, and then it will deploy the Azure resources defined in the ARM template to that resource group. The output will indicate whether the deployment was successful.

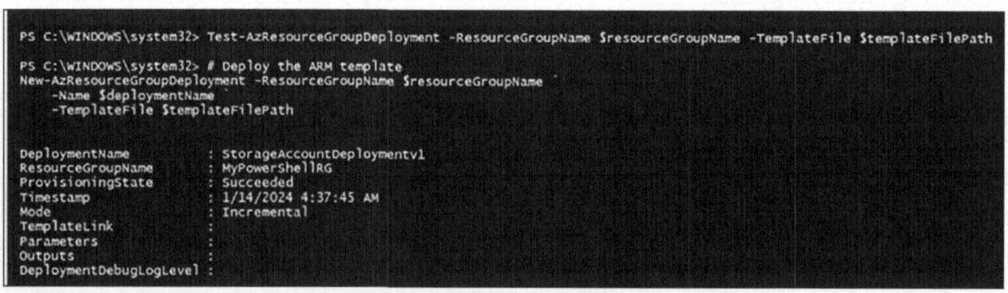

***Figure 10.33**: View the deployment output*

```
# Output the storage account endpoint
$storageAccount = Get-AzStorageAccount -ResourceGroupName
$resourceGroupName -Name $storageAccountName
$storageAccountEndpoint = $storageAccount.PrimaryEndpoints.Blob

Write-Output "Storage Account Endpoint: $storageAccountEndpoint"
```

The output indicates the deployment is successful by displaying the storage account endpoint details.

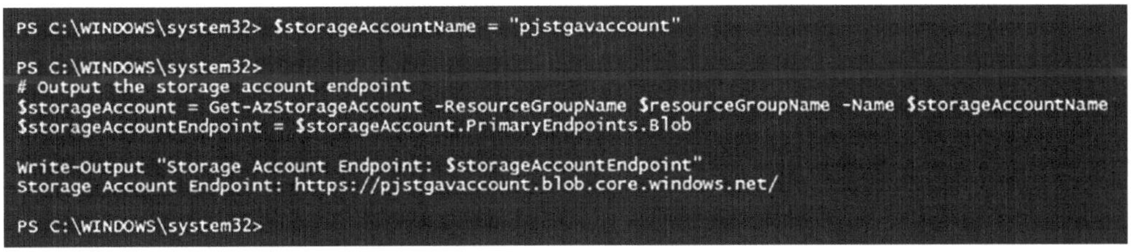

Figure 10.34: *Validate the deployment*

Navigate to the Azure portal to verify the deployment status and view the specifics of the resources deployed.

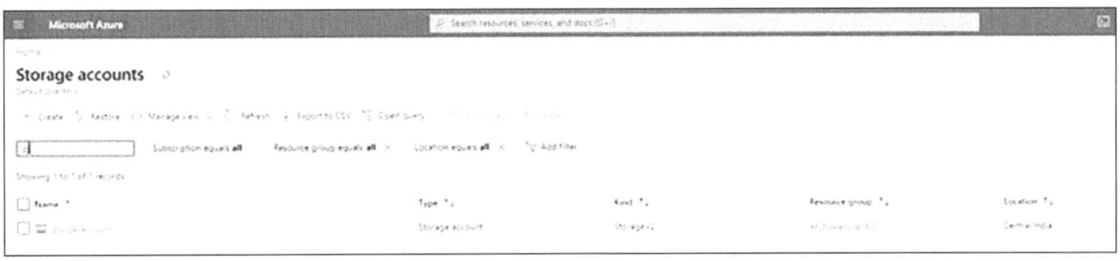

Figure 10.35: *View the deployed resources*

Using Parameters to Fine-Tune ARM Templates

Let us understand how you can use ARM templates to streamline your deployment process.

For example, when you need to deploy a storage account, you can assign a unique name to it using a parameter. This makes it easy to deploy the same template with different configurations.

Variables are also useful for simplifying and reusing your templates. They allow you to declare values that can be used throughout the template, saving you time and effort.

Functions are another powerful feature of ARM templates. You can use them to add custom methods and logic to your templates, making them more flexible and powerful. More about this will be discussed in the next example.

Finally, outputs are a great way to get specific information about your deployed resources. This allows you to check that everything is working as expected easily.

Parameters are a key feature of ARM templates that allow you to tailor your deployments to different environments. By using parameters, you can easily customize your templates for development, production, or other specific environments.

These features make ARM templates a powerful tool for streamlining your deployment process, reducing errors, and saving you time and effort.

The storage template contains the following information:

- **`$schema`:** This specifies the URL of the JSON schema that the template adheres to. In this case, it uses the Azure Resource Manager template schema from April 2019.
- **`contentVersion`:** This represents the version of the template. Here, it is set to "**`1.0.0.0`**."
- **`parameters`**: This section defines parameters that can be passed during deployment. There is one parameter named "**`storageAccountName`**," which is of type string.
- **`resources`**: This section describes the Azure resources to be deployed. It contains the following details:
    - **Resource Type**: **`Microsoft.Storage/storageAccounts`**
    - **API Version:** "**`2023-01-01`**"
    - **Resource Properties:**
        - **`name`**: Uses the parameter value for the storage account name, making it dynamic.
        - **`location`**: Specifies the deployment location as "**`CentralIndia`**."
        - **`sku`**: Defines the SKU (Stock Keeping Unit) of the storage account as "**`Standard_LRS`**" (Locally Redundant Storage).
        - **`kind`:** Specifies the kind of storage as "**`StorageV2`**" (general-purpose v2).

When this template is deployed, it will create a storage account in the "**`CentralIndia`**" region with the specified storage account name, following the constraints set by the parameters. The storage account will use the **`Standard_LRS SKU`** and be of kind StorageV2. The dynamic nature of the storage account name allows for flexibility during deployment.

***Figure 10.36**: Constraint sets in deployment*

With these parameters set, we are ready to create the storage account in Microsoft Azure using ARM template:

```
# Parameters
$resourceGroupName = "MyPowerShellRG"
$deploymentName = "StorageAccountDeploymentv1"
$templateFilePath = "C:\Ultimate PowerShell Automation\storage_parame-
ters.json"
$storageAccountName = "armstgaccount"

# Create a new resource group
New-AzResourceGroup -Name $resourceGroupName -Location "CentralIndia"

#Test the deployment

Test-AzResourceGroupDeployment -ResourceGroupName $resourceGroupName
-TemplateFile $templateFilePath `
-TemplateParameterObject @{ storageAccountName = $storageAccountName }
```

```
# Deploy the ARM template
New-AzResourceGroupDeployment -ResourceGroupName $resourceGroupName `
    -Name $deploymentName `
    -TemplateFile $templateFilePath `
    -TemplateParameterObject @{ storageAccountName = $storageAccountName }


# Monitor the deployment: The deployment process might take some time.
You can monitor the progress using:


Get-AzResourceGroupDeployment -ResourceGroupName $resourceGroupName



# Output the storage account endpoint
$storageAccount = Get-AzStorageAccount -ResourceGroupName $resource-
GroupName -Name $storageAccountName
$storageAccountEndpoint = $storageAccount.PrimaryEndpoints.Blob


Write-Output "Storage Account Endpoint: $storageAccountEndpoint"
```

Figure 10.37: *Create the storage account in Microsoft Azure using the ARM template*

You can see that the provisioned state is successful and displays the storage account endpoint at the end. This information can be useful for verifying the success of the deployment

Let us check out the Azure portal. You might want to take a look and see if the deployment script created a storage account. It is always exciting to see everything come together, isn't it?

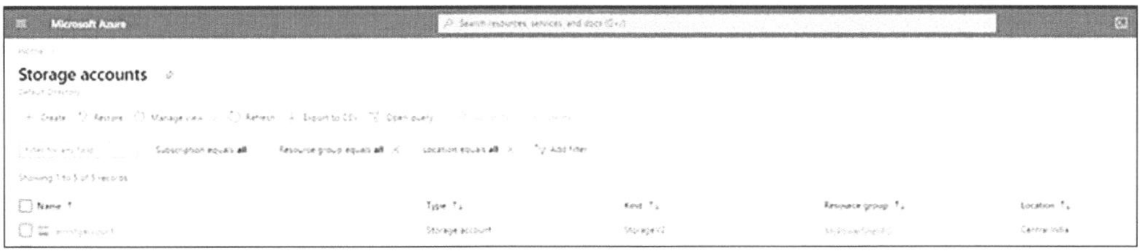

Figure 10.38: *View storage account deployed using ARM template*

Testing ARM Templates

Locally validate your ARM template using **`Test-AzResourceGroupDeployment`** cmdlet. This checks syntax errors and parameter definition accuracy.

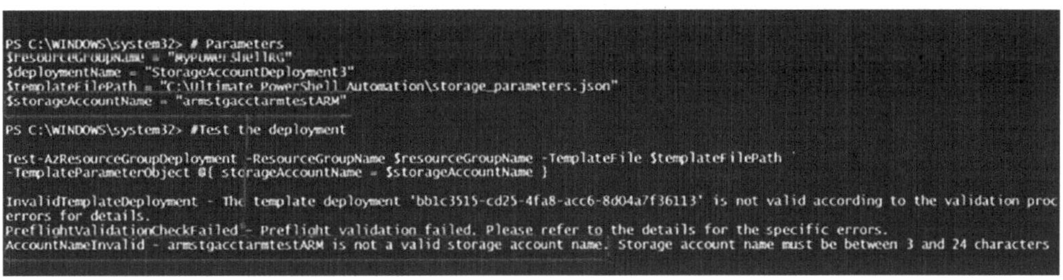

Figure 10.39: *Test ARM template deployment*

The error message shows that your storage account name, **`'automationstgdemoARM'`**, is invalid. The storage account name has certain requirements such as its name must be between 3 and 24 characters long, and should only consist of lowercase letters and numbers.

To adjust the name of the storage account, you need to change the value of **`$storageAccountName`** to a name that follows the naming rules. The name should be between 3 and 24 characters long, and must only contain lowercase letters and numbers.

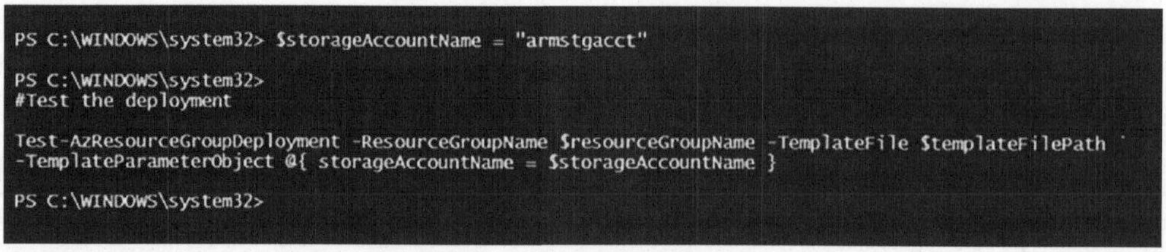

Figure 10.40: *Give valid inputs for the storage account*

Re-run the Deployment

After updating the storage account name, re-run your PowerShell script or the **`Test-AzResourceGroupDeployment`** command to test the deployment.

Figure 10.41: *Run ARM deployment with valid inputs*

We have set the storage account name to "**`armstgacct`**" for the purpose of testing and validating the usage of the ARM template using the **`Test-AzResourceGroupDeployment`** function. By ensuring that the storage account name meets the specified criteria, you will be able to resolve the "**`AccountNameInvalid`**" error and successfully deploy the ARM template.

Next, PowerShell script looks well-structured and should work for deploying the Azure Storage Account using the provided ARM template.

Monitoring the Deployment

Use "**`Get-AzResourceGroupDeployment`**" to retrieve information about the deployment progress. This command can be used to monitor the status of the deployment.

```
PS C:\WINDOWS\system32>
Get-AzResourceGroupDeployment -ResourceGroupName $resourceGroupName -DeploymentName $deploymentName


DeploymentName          : StorageAccountDeployment3
ResourceGroupName       : MyPowerShellRG
ProvisioningState       : Succeeded
Timestamp               : 1/14/2024 11:59:03 AM
Mode                    : Incremental
TemplateLink            :
Parameters              :
                          Name                 Type                       Value
                          ==================   ========================   ==========
                          storageAccountName   String                     armstgacct

Outputs                 :
DeploymentDebugLogLevel :
```

Figure 10.42: *Retrieve information about the deployment progress*

Outputting the storage account endpoint

Use this command to retrieve the storage account endpoint after the deployment and write it to the console.

```
PS C:\WINDOWS\system32>
# Output the storage account endpoint
$storageAccount = Get-AzStorageAccount -ResourceGroupName $resourceGroupName -Name $storageAccountName
$storageAccountEndpoint = $storageAccount.PrimaryEndpoints.Blob

Write-Output "Storage Account Endpoint: $storageAccountEndpoint"

Storage Account Endpoint: https://armstgacct.blob.core.windows.net/

PS C:\WINDOWS\system32> |
```

Figure 10.43: *Retrieve the storage account endpoint after the deployment*

The script essentially creates a resource group, tests and deploys an ARM template, monitors the deployment progress and outputs the storage account endpoint.

```
# Parameters
$resourceGroupName = "MyPowerShellRG"
$deploymentName = "StorageAccountDeployment3"
$templateFilePath = "C:\Ultimate PowerShell Automation\storage_parame-
ters.json"
$storageAccountName = "armstgacct"


# Create a new resource group
New-AzResourceGroup -Name $resourceGroupName -Location "CentralIndia"
```

```
#Test the deployment
Test-AzResourceGroupDeployment -ResourceGroupName $resourceGroupName
-TemplateFile $templateFilePath `
-TemplateParameterObject @{ storageAccountName = $storageAccountName }

# Deploy the ARM template
New-AzResourceGroupDeployment -ResourceGroupName $resourceGroupName `
    -Name $deploymentName `
    -TemplateFile $templateFilePath `
    -TemplateParameterObject @{ storageAccountName = $storageAccountName
}

# Monitor the deployment
Get-AzResourceGroupDeployment -ResourceGroupName $resourceGroupName
-DeploymentName $deploymentName

# Output the storage account endpoint
$storageAccount = Get-AzStorageAccount -ResourceGroupName
$resourceGroupName -Name $storageAccountName
$storageAccountEndpoint = $storageAccount.PrimaryEndpoints.Blob
Write-Output "Storage Account Endpoint: $storageAccountEndpoint"
```

To create an Azure virtual machine, you can use the following code sample which involves an ARM template file named **template.json**.

Deploying Azure Virtual Machine with ARM Template

To create an Azure virtual machine, you can use the following code sample which involves an ARM template file named template.json.

The following code creates a collection of Azure resources, including a storage account, virtual network, public IP address, network interface, and a virtual machine. Two parameters are defined for **storageName** and **vmName**, respectively. The **concat** function is utilized to generate names and IDs dynamically.

To ensure unique names for DNS-dependent resources on Azure, like storage accounts and public IPs, you can use the **uniqueString()** function. It performs a 64-bit hash of the provided strings to create a unique string. You can specify the level of uniqueness required for the result, whether it is unique for your subscription, resource group, or deployment.

```
"resources": [
  // Storage Account
  {
    "name": "[concat(parameters('storageAccountName'), uniqueString(resourceGroup().id))]",
    "type": "Microsoft.Storage/storageAccounts",
    "location": "[resourceGroup().location]",
    "apiVersion": "2023-01-01",
    "properties": {
      "accountType": "Standard_LRS"
    }
  },
```

Figure 10.44: *Deploying Azure virtual machine with ARM template*

When working in a team, it is suggested that each team member deploys in their own resource group and uses a unique prefix for their project or team to obtain a globally unique name. For instance, you can use **`[concat( parameters('storageNamePrefix'), uniqueString(resourceGroup().id))]`** as a naming convention to ensure uniqueness.

The code structure is well-organized, and comments are provided to explain each resource and property.

Note: *Retrieve the ARM template code for creating a virtual machine in Microsoft Azure using ARM template. It is available in Chapter 10 of the GitHub library as,"ARM - Create Virtual Machine in Microsoft Azure using ARM Template"*

To deploy an Azure virtual machine (VM) using Azure PowerShell with an Azure Resource Manager (ARM) template, you can follow this simple example. By now, you may be familiar with testing and deploying ARM templates. This example will help you understand the basics of deploying resources to an existing resource group. Please note that the VM creation process in this example assumes that you already have a resource group. It deploys the resources defined in your ARM template to that group.

Parameter Customization

If you are deploying to Azure using an ARM template, you can utilize the **`TemplateParameterObject`** to pass a hashtable containing the template's parameters.

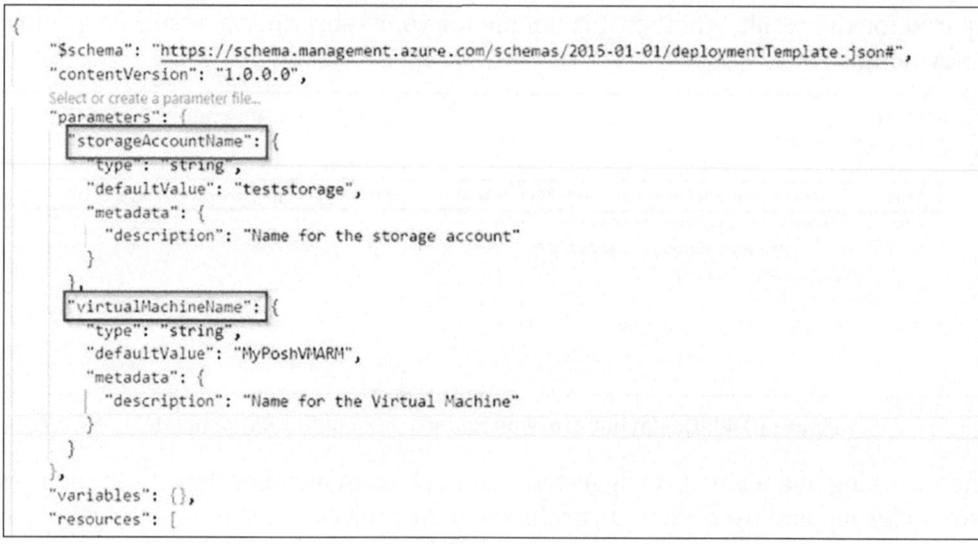

Figure 10.45: *Parameter customization with ARM template*

Customize the parameters for the storage account name (**vmstg**) and the virtual machine name (**armdemovm**) as per the specific requirements.

```
# Parameters
$resourceGroupName = "armdemoRG"
$deploymentName = "VMDeploymentv1"
$templateFilePath = "C:\Ultimate PowerShell Automation\Exported
Template-MyPowerShellRG\armtestdeployment.json"
$storageAccountName = "vmstg"
$VirtualMachineName ="armdemovm"


# Create a new resource group
New-AzResourceGroup -Name $resourceGroupName -Location "CentralIndia"

$params = @{
    storageAccountName = $storageAccountName
    VirtualMachineName = $VirtualMachineName
}



#Test the deployment
```

```
Test-AzResourceGroupDeployment -ResourceGroupName $resourceGroupName
-TemplateFile $templateFilePath `
-TemplateParameterObject $params
```

Upon execution of the following script, Azure PowerShell will generate a new resource group and proceed to deploy the Azure resources to that resource group as defined in the ARM template. The output will provide information on the success of the deployment and any errors, if encountered.

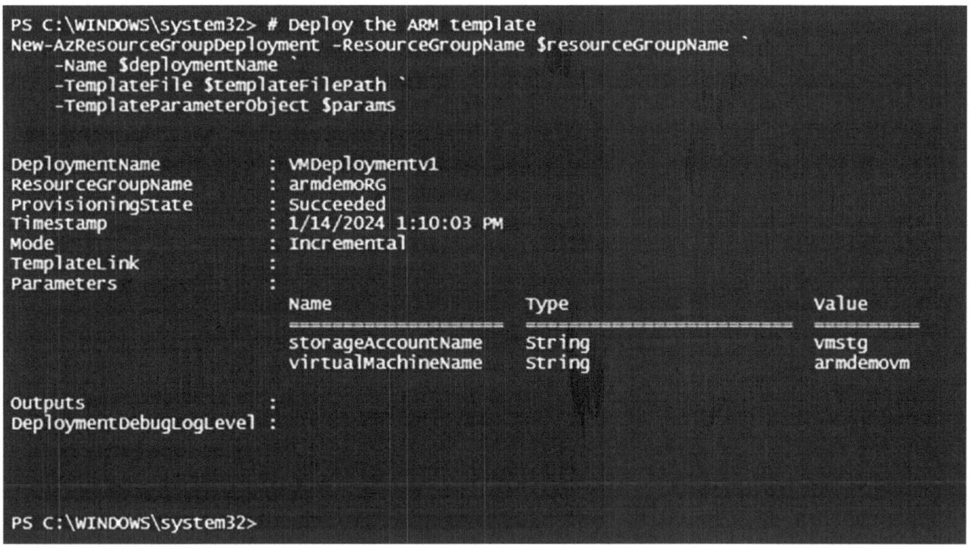

Figure 10.46: *ARM template deployment*

Navigate to the Azure portal to verify the deployment status and view the specifics of the resources deployed or retrieve the data using **`Get-AzVM`** cmdlet.

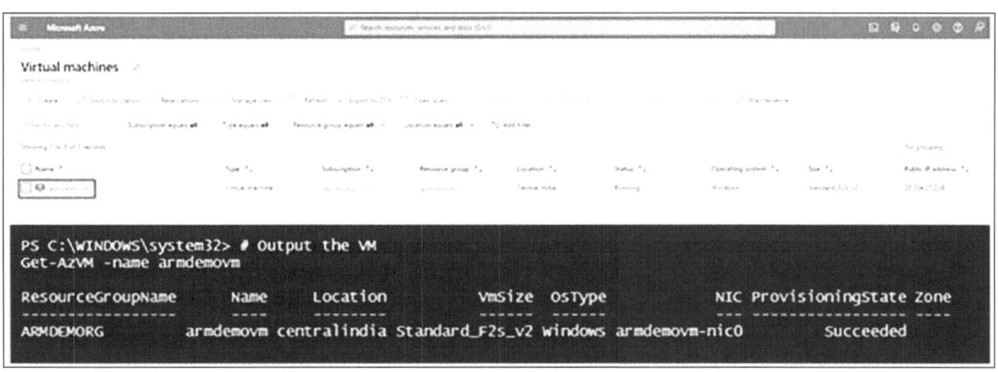

Figure 10.47: *Verify the deployment status*

ARM Templates for Infrastructure as Code

Infrastructure as Code (IAC) is the process of managing infrastructure using code. This approach enables you to automate and provision resources consistently, repeatedly, and efficiently. Azure Resource Manager (ARM) templates are a powerful implementation of IAC for Azure. Here is a breakdown of how ARM templates serve as Infrastructure as Code:

- **Declarative Syntax:**

  ARM templates use a declarative syntax. This means you can define the desired state of your Azure infrastructure without specifying the step-by-step procedures to achieve it. This approach simplifies code readability and maintenance.

- **JSON Structure**:

  ARM templates are written in JSON (JavaScript Object Notation), a lightweight data interchange format. The JSON structure of ARM templates includes sections for parameters, variables, resources, and outputs. This provides a clear organization of the infrastructure definition.

- **Version Control:**

  ARM templates can use version control systems (for example, Git). This enables collaboration among development and operations teams. Version control ensures that changes to infrastructure configurations are tracked, reviewed, and rolled back if necessary.

- **Idempotent Deployment:**

  ARM templates support idempotent deployments. This means you can repeatedly apply the same template without causing adverse effects. This characteristic supports consistency and reliability in infrastructure provisioning.

- **Parameterization:**

  Parameters in ARM templates allow you to customize deployments for different environments or scenarios. This parameterization facilitates the reuse of templates with varying configurations. It makes them adaptable to diverse use cases.

- **Resource Dependencies:**

  ARM templates define dependencies between resources. This ensures that resources are deployed in the correct order. Dependencies help in orchestrating the provisioning of complex infrastructures with interconnected components.

- **Template Functions:**

  ARM templates incorporate functions that enable dynamic calculations and configurations during deployment. Functions enhance the flexibility of templates, allowing you to create reusable and scalable solutions.

- **Incremental Updates:**

  ARM templates support incremental updates. This allows you to modify existing deployments without affecting unchanged resources. This feature is crucial for making adjustments to infrastructure configurations while minimizing downtime.

- **Integration with CI/CD:**

  ARM templates seamlessly integrate into continuous integration and continuous deployment (CI/CD) pipelines. Automated deployments through CI/CD pipelines enhance agility and speed in delivering infrastructure changes.

- **Error Handling and Rollback:**

  ARM templates include error-handling mechanisms and support rollback functionality. If an error occurs during deployment, the template can be designed to roll back changes to maintain a consistent state.

Note: *ARM templates are essential for realizing Infrastructure as Code principles in Azure. They offer a standardized, version-controlled, and automated approach to managing and provisioning cloud resources. The use of IAC practices with ARM templates contributes to enhanced efficiency, reliability, and collaboration in cloud-based infrastructure management.*

Infrastructure as Code (IaC), Terraform and ARM templates are two powerful tools worth considering. Terraform is cloud-agnostic, has a versatile language, robust state management, and a large community. On the other hand, ARM templates are great for Azure integration, easy for Azure-specific deployments, and use a familiar JSON syntax. Choosing between the two depends on your cloud strategy, integration needs, and team expertise. If you are working in an Azure-exclusive environment, ARM templates may be your best choice. However, if you are looking for a versatile solution with multi-cloud support, then Terraform's extensive community may be more appealing. Ultimately, assessing your team's proficiency and long-term goals is crucial in making the right decision.

ARM Templates versus Terraform

The following comparison table outlines the differences between Terraform and Azure Resource Manager (ARM) templates. This table provides a detailed view of the essential aspects of both tools, highlighting their strengths and areas of focus in infrastructure provisioning and management. It is worth noting that while the chapter does not cover the Terraform code, this generalized data will help you better understand the concepts and usage of ARM over other available tools in the market.

Aspect	**ARM Templates**	**Terraform**
Cloud Agnosticism	Azure-centric; designed exclusively for Azure	Offers cloud-agnostic capabilities, usable across various cloud providers
Language	Relies on JSON syntax for defining resources	Uses HashiCorp Configuration Language (HCL) or JSON
State Management	Lacks built-in state management for resources	Maintains a state file for efficient resource tracking and management
Community and Ecosystem	Relatively smaller ecosystem compared to Terraform	Boasts a large and active community; extensive registry of community-contributed modules
Learning Curve	It has lower learning curve for those already familiar with JSON	Potentially steeper learning curve due to HCL; known for readability once familiar
Integration with Azure	Native to Azure, ensuring deep integration and quicker support for new Azure features	Supports Azure but might have slightly less immediate integration and updates compared to ARM
Key Use Case	Ideal for Azure-exclusive environments requiring tight integration	Suited for multi-cloud strategies or those not tied to a single cloud provider

Table 10.4: *Comparison between ARM templates and Terraform*

Azure Inventory

It is important to understand the significance of Azure inventory. The provided PowerShell script uses a service principal name to establish a connection with Azure and execute the script from a remote machine. You can refer to the section, "*Connecting to the Azure Environment*". We will go through the script and explain each section.

```
<#

.SYNOPSIS

    This script retrieves information about Azure VMs and displays
selected properties in a formatted table.

.DESCRIPTION
```

```
    The script fetches details of the first 5 Azure VMs, such as VM name, size, resource group, OS type, and more.

    It then creates a formatted table displaying the selected VM properties.


.NOTES
    File Name      : Get-AzureVMInfo.ps1
    Author         : Prashanth Jayaram
    Prerequisite   : Azure PowerShell Module


.EXAMPLE
    .\Get-AzureVMInfo.ps1
    # Runs the script and displays information about the first 5 Azure VMs.


#>


# Clear existing Azure context
Clear-AzContext -Force


# Define service principal credentials
$clientSecret = 'E-R8Q~m4OhXhuPtwsNfsIa9MOWzwflzeuyfBVc3u' | Convert-To-SecureString -AsPlainText -Force
$connectCreds = New-Object -TypeName System.Management.Automation.PSCredential -ArgumentList 'd27561a7-ecc1-49f9-a97e-ea4c0469c6ba', $clientSecret


# Connect to Azure with service principal
Connect-AzAccount -ServicePrincipal -Credential $connectCreds -Tenant da9d7617-d9fc-461d-80ec-72cc0de2fddb


# Initialize an array to store Azure VM information
$AzureVM = @()


# Get the first 5 VMs
```

```
$vms = Get-AzVM | Select-Object -First 5

# Display total VM count
Write-Host "Total $($vms.Count)"

# Initialize variables for counting
$total = $vms.Count
$count = 1

# Iterate through each Azure VM
ForEach ($azVM in $vms) {
    # Retrieve VM details
    $vmSize = (Get-AzVM -Name $azVM.Name).HardwareProfile.VmSize
    $VmOS = Get-AzVM -Name $azVM.Name -ResourceGroupName $azVM.Resource-
GroupName -Status
    $tags = (Get-AzResource -Name $azVM.Name).Tags

    # Build a hashtable with VM properties
    $props = @{
        VMName            = $azVM.Name
        Region            = $azVM.Location
        OsType            = $azVM.StorageProfile.OsDisk.OsType
        ResourceGroupName = $azVM.ResourceGroupName
        VMSize            = $vmSize
        OsName            = $VmOS.OsName
        OsVersion         = $VmOS.OsVersion
        CPUCore           = (Get-AzVMSize -Location $azVM.Location |
Where-Object { $_.name -eq $VMSize }).NumberOfCores
        OSVer             = $azVM.StorageProfile.ImageReference.Offer + "
$($azVM.StorageProfile.ImageReference.Sku)"

    }

    # Check for LicenseType and add to properties
```

```
    if (!$azVM.LicenseType) {
        $props += @{
            LicenseType = "No_License"
        }
    } else {
        $props += @{
            LicenseType = $azVM.LicenseType
        }
    }

    # Create a PSObject with VM properties
    $ServiceObject = New-Object -TypeName PSObject -Property $props
    $AzureVM += $ServiceObject

    # Display progress
    Write-Host "Processing VM ($count/$total): ""$($azVM.Name)"""
    $count++
}

# Display selected VM properties in a formatted table
$AzureVM | Select VMName, VMSize, ResourceGroupName, OsName, OsVersion,
Region, CPUCore, LicenseType, OSType | Format-Table -AutoSize
```

The script first clears the existing Azure context to ensure a clean environment. It then defines the service principal credentials, including the client ID ('d27561a7-ecc1-49f9-a97e-ea4c0469c6ba') and client secret. A new PowerShell credential object is created using the service principal's client ID and client secret.

The script then connects to Azure using the service principal with the specified credentials and tenant ID. Now, let us examine the section where Azure VM information is retrieved.

The script initializes an array called $AzureVM to store Azure VM information. Then, it uses the Get-AzVM command to retrieve details of the first 5 Azure VMs and stores them in the $vms variable. The total count of VMs is displayed.

A loop iterates through each Azure VM and retrieves details such as VM size, OS information, and more. These VM properties are stored in a hashtable named $props.

Additionally, the script checks for the presence of LicenseType and adds it to the properties.

For each VM, a PSObject is created, and these objects are added to the $AzureVM array. Progress is displayed for each VM. Finally, the script displays the selected VM properties in a formatted table.

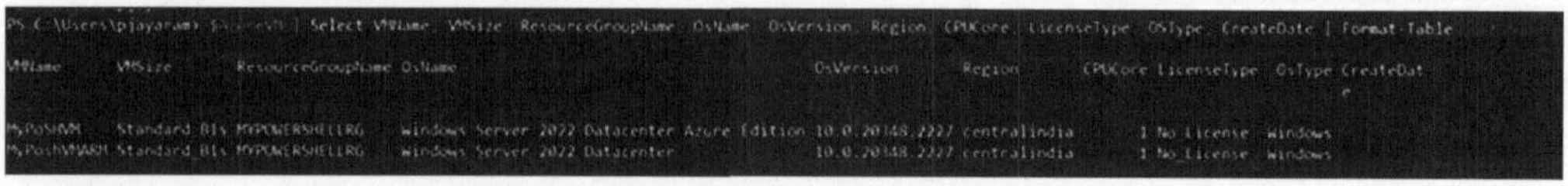

Figure 10.48: *Azure inventory example*

Learning AWS PowerShell Modules

AWS Tools for PowerShell is a handy resource for developers and administrators who want to manage their AWS services and resources directly from the familiar PowerShell environment. These tools provide numerous benefits, including:

- **Unified Management**: You can use the same PowerShell commands you already know for managing Windows, Linux, and MacOS environments to interact with your AWS resources, streamlining your workflow and reducing context switching.
- **Automation**: PowerShell's scripting capabilities empower you to automate repetitive tasks with AWS, ensuring consistency and efficiency in your infrastructure management.
- **Flexibility**: The extensive library of cmdlets covering various AWS services allows you to perform various actions, from launching EC2 instances to managing S3 buckets directly from the command line.
- **Integration**: These tools seamlessly integrate with other PowerShell modules and workflows, enabling you to build complex automation scripts that orchestrate tasks across your on-premises and cloud infrastructure.

The AWS Tools for PowerShell are available in three packages, each serving different purposes. Here is a brief overview of each:

`AWS.Tools`	It is the modern and recommended AWS PowerShell module designed to work with PowerShell 7 (and later) and .NET Core. It follows a service-driven approach, where each AWS service has its module, making it more modular and aligned with AWS service evolution.	It is cross-platform, supporting PowerShell 7 on Windows, MacOS, and Linux. It leverages the latest advancements in PowerShell and .NET Core.

`AWSPowerShell.NetCore`	This package is specifically tailored for PowerShell Core, the cross-platform edition of PowerShell, and .NET Core. It is an older version and considered somewhat legacy as AWS.Tools is the recommended module for PowerShell 7 and .NET Core.	It is suitable for PowerShell Core on Windows, MacOS, and Linux.
`AWSPowerShell`	This is the traditional AWS PowerShell module designed for Windows PowerShell, primarily up to version 5.1. It has been widely used in the past but is considered legacy, and AWS encourages users to transition to AWS.Tools for newer features and broader compatibility.	It is intended for Windows PowerShell on Windows operating systems.

Table 10.5: *AWS PowerShell packages*

Installation Commands:

- **`AWS.Tools`**: `Install-Module -Name AWS.Tools.Installer`
- **`AWSPowerShell.NetCore`**: `Install-Module -name AWSPowerShell.NetCore`
- **`AWSPowerShell`** : `Install-Module -Name AWSPowerShell`

Explore AWS.Tools :

Before you start using AWS tools for PowerShell, you need to configure your AWS credentials.

```
# Set AWS credentials
Set-AWSCredentials -AccessKey 'your-access-key' -SecretKey 'your-secret-key' -StoreAs 'MyProfile'
# Set default AWS region
Set-DefaultAWSRegion -Region 'us-east-1'
```

Let us explore a few useful operations using the AWS Tools for PowerShell.

- **Managing EC2 Instances**: Interact with EC2 instances using cmdlets such as **`Get-EC2Instance`**, **`New-EC2Instance`**, and **`Stop-EC2Instance`**.

```
# Get information about EC2 instances
Get-EC2Instance
# Launch a new EC2 instance
New-EC2Instance -ImageId 'ami-xxxxxxxx' -InstanceType 't2.micro' -Key-Name 'MyKeyPair'
```

```
# Stop an EC2 instance
Stop-EC2Instance -InstanceId 'i-xxxxxxxx'
```

- **Working with S3 Buckets:**

Perform actions on S3 buckets using cmdlets like **`Get-S3Bucket`**, **`New-S3Bucket`**, and **`Remove-S3Bucket`**.

```
# List all S3 buckets
Get-S3Bucket

# Create a new S3 bucket
New-S3Bucket -BucketName 'my-unique-bucket'

# Remove an S3 bucket
Remove-S3Bucket -BucketName 'my-unique-bucket'
```

- **Managing IAM Users**: Handle IAM users and permissions using cmdlets such as **`Get-IAMUser`**, **`New-IAMUser`**, and **`New-IAMPolicy`**.

```
# Get information about IAM users
Get-IAMUser

# Create a new IAM user
New-IAMUser -UserName 'NewUser'

# Create a new IAM policy
New-IAMPolicy -PolicyName 'MyPolicy' -PolicyDocument (Get-Content 'C:\
path\to\policy.json' | Out-String)
```

- **Managing `CloudWatch` Logs**:

Interact with **`CloudWatch`** Logs using cmdlets like **`Get-CWLLogGroup`**, **`New-CWLLogGroup`**, and **`Get-CWLLogEvents`**.

```
# List all CloudWatch Log Groups
Get-CWLLogGroup

# Create a new CloudWatch Log Group
New-CWLLogGroup -LogGroupName 'MyLogGroup'

# Get CloudWatch Log Events
Get-CWLLogEvents -LogGroupName 'MyLogGroup' -LogStreamName 'MyLogStream'
```

Learning Google PowerShell modules

Google PowerShell Module provides a comprehensive set of cmdlets for interacting with various services like Cloud Storage, Compute Engine, Cloud SQL, and many more. To install the Google Cloud PowerShell module, launch the PowerShell as an administrator and run the following command.

```
Install-Module GoogleCloud
```

Next, use the following command to Initiate the Google PowerShell Cloud with the credentials and configurations.

```
gcloud init
```

Enter the credentials in a browser window to use the cloud tools for PowerShell.

Here are a few examples of using Google cloud tools for PowerShell:

- Get buckets for the current project, for a specific project, or a specific bucket:

```
$currentProjBuckets = Get-GcsBucket

$specificProjBuckets = Get-GcsBucket -Project my-project-1

$bucket = Get-GcsBucket -Name my-bucket-name
```

- List all compute engine instances associated with a project:

```
Get-GceInstance -Project my-project-1 |

Sort Status |

Format-Table Name, Status -GroupBy Status
```

Conclusion

This chapter provided an explanation of the different ways to connect to Azure. It emphasized the importance of knowing the available tool sets, Azure automation, ARM templates, automation assets, and their properties. Additionally, this chapter elaborated on how to utilize these tools while creating runbooks. Furthermore, it explained how to implement ARM templates.

Becoming proficient in working with Azure Resource Manager (ARM) templates is crucial for improving the efficiency and effectiveness of Azure resource deployments. The declarative and repeatable nature of ARM templates simplifies the deployment process, enabling consistency and reliability. The orchestration capabilities eliminate concerns about deployment order, providing a seamless experience. Parameters can be used to customize deployments for different environments, while variables enhance template flexibility and reusability. Outputs provide valuable insights after deployment. A demonstration of the creation of a storage account and an Azure virtual machine showcased the practical application of ARM templates. Mastery of

ARM templates equips users to efficiently manage Azure resources with precision and scalability.

Switching to ARM templates can bring several benefits, transforming infrastructure management into a streamlined and efficient process. Embracing the concept of "*infrastructure as code*" where code defines and builds the infrastructure provides numerous advantages. ARM templates offer modularity, breaking down complex deployments into manageable and reusable components. This modular approach enhances scalability and simplifies maintenance as changes can be made to individual components without affecting the entire infrastructure.

Additionally, ARM templates help ensure consistency across environments, meaning that the same configuration is reproducible across different scenarios. This consistency contributes to improved reliability and reduces the likelihood of configuration errors. Furthermore, the declarative nature of ARM templates allows for clear and easily understandable code, promoting collaboration among team members.

Along with version control support, ARM templates empower teams to track changes, maintain documentation, and ensure a smooth and controlled deployment process. Overall, adopting ARM templates marks a significant shift towards efficient, scalable, and maintainable infrastructure management in the cloud computing domain.

Multiple Choice Questions

1. What is the primary purpose of ARM templates in Azure?
    a. Data storage
    b. Virtual machine management
    c. Infrastructure as code
    d. Networking configuration
2. In an ARM template, what does the **`"$schema"`** element specify?
    a. Template version
    b. Resource group name
    c. Deployment location
    d. Schema management URL
3. Which ARM template section is used to define reusable values?
    a. Parameters
    b. Resources

   c. Variables
   d. Outputs

4. What is the purpose of parameters in an ARM template?
   a. Define variables
   b. Provide input values
   c. Declare resources
   d. Specify dependencies

5. How does ARM support modularization in templates?
   a. By using variables
   b. Through nested templates
   c. With conditional statements
   d. Using parameter files

6. What does the "`apiVersion`" property specify in a resource definition within an ARM template?
   a. Azure API version
   b. ARM template version
   c. Resource provider version
   d. Virtual machine version

7. Which ARM template section is used to define the desired state of Azure resources?
   a. Outputs
   b. Resources
   c. Parameters
   d. Variables

8. What is the role of the "`contentVersion`" property in an ARM template?
   a. Azure content version
   b. Template documentation version
   c. Version of the template
   d. Content type version

9. How does ARM contribute to consistency across environments?
    a. By enforcing strict rules
    b. Through modular design
    c. By providing Azure certification
    d. Ensuring identical configurations
10. What is the significance of the "`outputs`" section in an ARM template?
    a. Defines input parameters
    b. Specifies resource dependencies
    c. Returns values after deployment
    d. Manages virtual machine settings

Answers

1. c
2. a
3. c
4. b
5. b
6. c
7. b
8. c
9. d
10. c

Questions

- How can parameters in ARM templates enhance deployment flexibility?
- What is the purpose of the Test-AzResourceGroupDeployment cmdlet in PowerShell?
- Explain the role of the outputs section in an ARM template?
- How do ARM templates contribute to infrastructure as code (IaC) principles?
- What PowerShell cmdlet is commonly used to deploy an ARM template to Azure?

Key Terms

- **PowerShell Background Jobs:** PowerShell background jobs allow the asynchronous execution of commands or scripts, freeing up the console for additional tasks, enabling parallel processing, and providing monitoring and control mechanisms.
- **Security:** In the context of PowerShell, security involves implementing measures such as access control, prevention of injection attacks, least privilege principles, secure credential storage, encryption of sensitive data, and digital signing of code to protect systems from vulnerabilities.
- **PowerShell Cmdlets:** Cmdlets, or command-lets, are lightweight PowerShell commands that perform specific tasks. Examples include `Start-Job`, `Stop-Job`, `Wait-Job`, `Get-Job`, `Receive-Job`, `Remove-Job`, and `Debug-Job`, which are essential for managing background jobs.
- **Encryption:** Encryption in PowerShell involves converting sensitive data into a secure format. `ConvertTo-SecureString` transforms a plain text string into a secure string, while `ConvertFrom-SecureString` reverses the process.
- **Remote Execution:** Remote execution in PowerShell is facilitated by cmdlets like `Invoke-Command` and `New-PSSession`, allowing the initiation and execution of scripts or commands on remote computers.
- **PowerShell Workflows:** PowerShell workflows are sequences of PowerShell commands designed to perform long-running and parallelizable tasks. They can be suspended and resumed, providing flexibility in managing complex operations.
- **WMI (Windows Management Instrumentation):** WMI is a set of specifications from Microsoft that provides a standardized way to manage network devices and systems. In PowerShell, `Get-WmiObject` is used to interact with WMI.
- **Performance:** In the context of PowerShell, performance refers to optimizing the execution of tasks. Multicore systems are leveraged for parallel processing, enhancing overall performance in tasks that can be divided into independent components.

CHAPTER 11
PowerShell and Microsoft Ecosystem

Introduction

In this chapter, you will explore how PowerShell seamlessly integrates with various Microsoft technologies and ecosystems. This integration enables administrators and developers to automate diverse tasks more efficiently across databases, cloud infrastructure, and DevOps practices.

Structure

In this chapter, we will discuss the following topics:

- PowerShell and Microsoft Ecosystem
- PowerShell for Microsoft 365
- Active Directory Using PowerShell
- SQLServer and PowerShell
- PowerShell and AzureDevOps
- Best Practices: Harnessing Functions, Modules, and Procedures
- Best Practices for PowerShell Scripting: Ensuring Clarity and Compatibility
- Best Practices for PowerShell Security

PowerShell and Microsoft Ecosystem

PowerShell is an automation tool for managing complex tasks within SQL server environments. It automates repetitive tasks and provides flexibility and control over the environment. It allows you to manage server configuration, databases, SQL Server Agent jobs, and perform complex tasks such as executing Transact-SQL statements, managing backups and restores, and SQL Server security administration. Custom scripts can be created to automate tasks, improving productivity. PowerShell is an invaluable tool for IT professionals working with SQL server environments.

PowerShell has a wide range of features, continually adding new features to make it even more powerful. It provides cmdlets that can be used to manage and automate various tasks within your environment, including Active Directory, SQL Server, Oracle, Db2, Exchange, and SharePoint. PowerShell can also manage Azure, Office 365, VMware, Hyper-V, Windows clustering, and IBM WebSphere.

With PowerShell, you can create scripts to perform complex tasks quickly and efficiently. PowerShell cmdlets are essentially small scripts that can be combined to create more complex scripts. You can create cmdlets for performing various tasks, such as creating sites, subsites, or VMs, and you can run these scripts to perform these tasks repeatedly.

PowerShell provides a lot of flexibility when it comes to managing your environment. You can use it to create scripts that perform complex tasks automatically, saving you a lot of time and effort. Although a GUI is available for some environments, PowerShell is preferred for many tasks because it provides more flexibility and repeatability.

It is important to note that PowerShell is a scripting language, not a compiled one. Therefore, it may not be suitable for every task. Some tasks may require a compiled language to be more efficient. However, PowerShell is an excellent tool for automating and managing repetitive tasks within your environment. It is a valuable tool to help you manage your environment more efficiently and effectively.

Limitations of a Scripting Language

Some tasks require a compiled language for greater efficiency or specific performance requirements.

Note: *PowerShell can extend its functionality by creating binary modules using compiled languages such as C#. This allows developers to leverage the power and efficiency of a compiled language while still integrating seamlessly with the PowerShell environment.*

You can refer to Chapter 7, Windows Administration Using PowerShell, for more details about creating a binary module.

PowerShell for Microsoft 365

The Microsoft 365 admin center is a powerful tool that simplifies the management of user accounts, licenses, and services such as Exchange Online, Teams, and SharePoint Online. This tool gives you complete control over user permissions, group memberships, and security settings. You can also manage licenses for various Microsoft products, including Microsoft Office, OneDrive, and Skype for Business. If you prefer using PowerShell to manage these services, you can benefit from its command-line and scripting language environment, which enables you to automate tasks, increase speed, and gain additional capabilities.

Here are step-by-step instructions for managing Exchange Online in Microsoft 365 using PowerShell:

1. Install the Exchange Online Management module for the current user context by using the following command:

```
Install-Module ExchangeOnlineManagement -Scope CurrentUser
```

2. Import the Exchange Online Management module into your current session with this command:

```
Import-Module ExchangeOnlineManagement
```

3. List all the Exchange Online Management module cmdlets using the following command:

```
Get-Command -Module ExchangeOnlineManagement
```

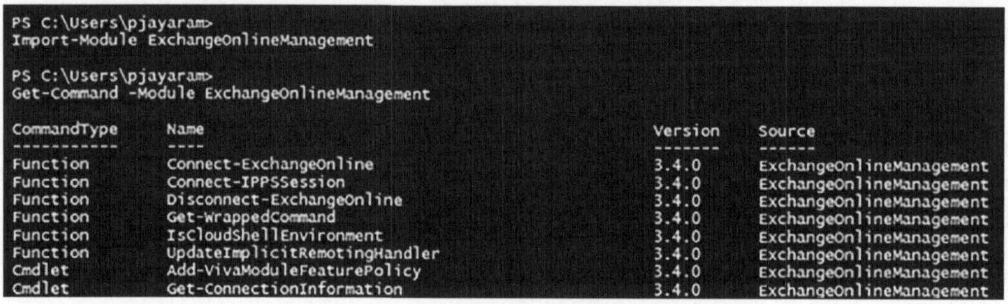

Figure 11.1: *List Exchange module cmdlets*

4. Connect to Microsoft 365 services using PowerShell with a user credential prompt. This command prompts the user for their credentials and stores them in the **`$credential`** variable:

```
$credential = Get-Credential
Connect-ExchangeOnline -Credential $credential
```

5. Retrieve a list of all mailboxes in Microsoft 365 with this command:

```
Get-Mailbox -ResultSize Unlimited
```

Alternatively, you can use the following alias in the Exchange Online Management module:

```
Get-EXOMailbox
```

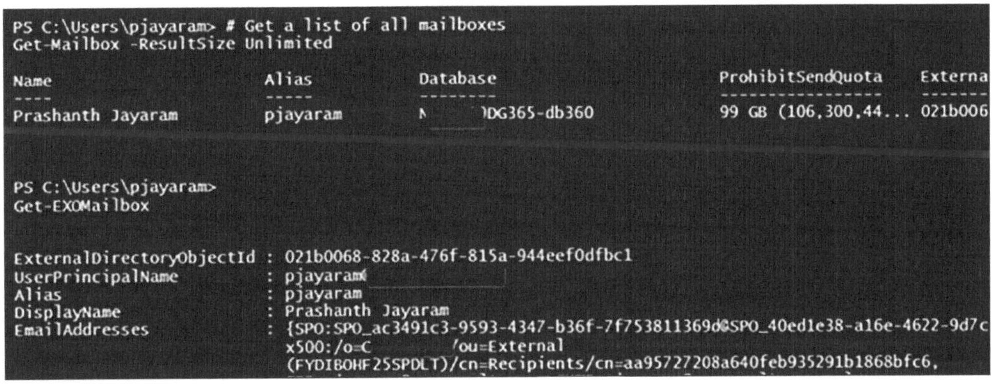

***Figure 11.2**: Use alias for Exchange Online Management module*

6. Retrieve mailbox statistics for a specific user in Microsoft 365 using the following command:

```
Get-EXOMailboxStatistics -Identity "Prashanth Jayaram"
```

7. Disconnect from Microsoft 365 without prompting for confirmation using this command:

```
Disconnect-ExchangeOnline -Confirm:$false
```

Active Directory Using PowerShell

Active Directory (AD) is a Microsoft directory service designed for Windows domain networks, providing a centralized repository for storing information about network objects, such as users, computers, groups, and resources. AD plays a pivotal role in managing and organizing these resources by offering authentication and authorization services and facilitating the deployment of policies and security settings across a network.

Using PowerShell to manage Active Directory can be advantageous in several ways. Firstly, the primary benefit of automation is that it enables the efficient management of large-scale deployments and configurations. This is particularly important in environments with many users, groups, and computers. PowerShell is a scripting language that enables administrators to create scripts and automate complex tasks. Scripts can be reused, shared, and scheduled to run at specific times, providing consistent results. PowerShell excels at handling bulk operations, where administrators can create, modify, or delete multiple user accounts, group memberships, or other AD objects in a single command, saving time and effort. PowerShell's remote management capabilities allow administrators to execute commands and scripts on remote servers and workstations, making it valuable for managing distributed environments.

PowerShell commands and scripts can be logged and audited, providing a record of changes made to Active Directory, which is crucial for security and compliance purposes.

Managing Active Directory Using PowerShell

Remote Server Administration Tools (RSAT) PowerShell modules can be used to simplify AD management. These modules enable administrators to delegate specific tasks to particular users or groups, providing more granular control over which users are authorized to perform specific Active Directory (AD) operations using PowerShell AD modules.

On a Windows Server (for versions earlier than Windows 10/11)

This command installs the RSAT feature for Active Directory PowerShell on a Windows Server. The **`-IncludeAllSubFeature`** flag also ensures that all the necessary subfeatures are installed.

```
Add-WindowsFeature -Name "RSAT-AD-PowerShell" -IncludeAllSubFeature
```

On Windows 10 or 11

This command installs the RSAT capability for Active Directory PowerShell on Windows 10 or 11. The specified capability name corresponds to the Active Directory tools.

```
Add-WindowsCapability -Online -Name "Rsat.ActiveDirectory.DSLDS.
Tools~~~~0.0.1.0"
```

To View All Active Directory cmdlets

This command imports the Active Directory PowerShell module, making the AD cmdlets available for use in the PowerShell session.

```
Import-Module ActiveDirectory
```

To view all Active Directory cmdlets

This command lists all the cmdlets available in the Active Directory module. It helps you see the specific cmdlets related to Active Directory management.

```
Get-Command -Module ActiveDirectory
```

Note: *These steps are useful when managing Active Directory from a non-DC member server or a client PC. Installing the RSAT feature or capability and importing the Active Directory module allows you to use PowerShell cmdlets for AD administration.*

Note: *To use the Active Directory module on Linux and MacOS, you cannot install it directly. However, you can establish a PowerShell remoting connection to a Windows Active Directory server and work with the AD module in a remoting session.*

If you want to learn more about this, you can refer to Chapter 9, PowerShell Remoting.

New-ADUser:

To create a new user account for "**Prashanth Jayaram**". The account includes attributes such as title, location, and password, which are securely inputted using **Read-Host -AsSecureString**. The **-Enabled $True** flag is used to enable the account.

```
# Creating a new user account
New-ADUser -Name "Prashanth Jayaram" ` -AccountPassword (Read-Host -As-
SecureString "Input User Password") `
-ChangePasswordAtLogon $True ` -Company "commvault" `
-Title "Architect" `
-State "Texas" `
-City "Dallas" `
-Description "Test Account Creation" `
-EmployeeNumber "1" `
-Department "Executives" `
-DisplayName "Prashanth Jayaram" `
-Country "us" `
 -PostalCode «90210» `
 -Enabled $True
```

Get-ADUser:

To retrieve information about the specific user "**Prashanth Jayaram**".

```
# Retrieving information about a specific user
Get-ADUser -Identity "Prashanth Jayaram"
```

Set-ADUser:

To modify the **'Title'** attribute of user "**Prashanth Jayaram**" and view the updated information in the organization tab of Active Directory Users and Computers (ADUC), execute the **Set-ADUser** cmdlet.

```
# Changing the value of the 'Title' attribute for a user
Set-ADUser -Identity "Prashanth Jayaram" -Title "Sales"
```

Remove-ADUser:

To remove the specified user "**Prashanth Jayaram**" from the Active Directory.

```
# Removing a user account
Remove-ADUser -Identity "Prashanth Jayaram"
```

To confirm that the user account has been removed, **Get-ADUser -Identity "Prashanth Jayaram"**.

```
Get-ADUser -Identity "Prashanth Jayaram"
```

Get User and List Specific Properties:

To retrieve specific properties (**Name**, **Department**, **Title**) for the user "**Prashanth Jayaram**" using **Get-ADUser**.

The **-Properties *** parameter ensures that all properties are retrieved for detailed information.

```
# Retrieve specific properties for the user "Prashanth Jayaram"
Get-ADUser -Identity "Prashanth Jayaram" -Properties * | Select-Object Name, Department, Title
```

Get All Active Directory Users in Domain:

To retrieve information for all users in the Active Directory domain using **Get-ADUser** with the **-Filter *** parameter.

```
# Retrieve information for all users in the domain
Get-ADUser -Filter *
```

Get All Users from a Specific OU

To retrieve information for all users in the specified Organizational Unit (OU) using **Get-ADUser**.

Modify the **-SearchBase** parameter with the distinguished path of the desired OU.

```
# Retrieve information for all users in a specific OU ("ADPRO Users" in this example)
Get-ADUser -SearchBase "OU=ADPRO Users,dc=ad,dc=activedirectorypro,dc=com" -Filter *
```

Get AD Users by Name

To find all users with names containing "**Prashanth Jayaram**," use the **-Filter** parameter with the -like operator.

```
# Find all users with the name containing "Prashanth Jayaram"
Get-ADUser -Filter {Name -like "*Prashanth Jayaram*"}
```

Get All Disabled User Accounts

To retrieve the names of all disabled user accounts, use the **Search-ADAccount** command with the **-AccountDisabled** parameter.

```
# Retrieve names of all disabled user accounts
Search-ADAccount -AccountDisabled | Select-Object Name
```

Disable, Enable, and Manage User Accounts

To disable the user account for "**`Prashanth Jayaram`**," use **`Disable-ADAccount`**.

```
# Disable the user account for "Prashanth Jayaram"
Disable-ADAccount -Identity "Prashanth Jayaram"
```

Enable User Account

To enable the previously disabled user account for "Prashanth Jayaram" using Enable-ADAccount.

```
# Enable the user account for "Prashanth Jayaram"
Enable-ADAccount -Identity "Prashanth Jayaram"
```

Find All Accounts with Password Set to Never Expire:

To find all user accounts with passwords set never to expire, use **`Get-ADUser`** with a filter based on the **`PasswordNeverExpires`** property.

```
# Find all accounts with passwords set never to expire
Get-ADUser -Filter * -Properties Name, PasswordNeverExpires | Where-Object {$_.PasswordNeverExpires -eq $true} | Select-Object DistinguishedName, Name, Enabled
```

Find All Locked User Accounts

Use **`Search-ADAccount`** with the **`-LockedOut`** parameter to find all locked user accounts.

```
# Find all locked user accounts
Search-ADAccount -LockedOut
```

Unlock User Account

To unlock the locked user account for "Prashanth Jayaram," use Unlock-ADAccount.

```
# Unlock the user account for "Prashanth Jayaram"
Unlock-ADAccount -Identity "Prashanth Jayaram"
```

SQLServer and PowerShell

There are two PowerShell modules available for SQL Server: SqlServer and SQLPS. The current PowerShell module to use is SqlServer. The SQLPS module is included with SQL server installation for backward compatibility but is no longer updated. The SqlServer module has updated versions of the cmdlets in SQLPS and supports the latest SQL features.

Install the SqlServer module

To install the SqlServer module, open PowerShell and run this command:

```
Install-Module SQLServer
```

Installing the module for the current user only will prevent the need for elevated permissions.

```
Install-Module SQLServer -Scope CurrentUser
```

Remove the `SqlServer` module

You can use the **`Get-Module SqlServer -ListAvailable`** command to list all installed versions of SQL server and the **`Uninstall-Module -Name SQLServer -RequiredVersion "<version number>"`** command to remove older versions.

Testing SQL Server Connectivity

The PowerShell script in this context relies on ADO.NET (ActiveX Data Objects for .Net), a comprehensive set of classes within the .NET Framework. It provides a data access layer that allows developers to interact with databases, including SQL Server.

In the script, the **`System.Data.SqlClient.SqlConnection`** is an essential ADO.NET class representing the connection to an SQL Server database. The **`System.Data.SqlClient.SqlException`**, implicitly caught in the catch block, is a specific exception class to handle SQL Server-related exceptions in ADO.NET.

The ADO.NET **`SqlConnection`** class offers several methods and properties, such as **`Open()`** and State, which allow developers to implement and manage the connection state easily. The **`Open()`** method initiates a connection to the database, while the State property tracks the current status of the connection.

Using these ADO.NET classes and methods, the script establishes a connection to an SQL Server database and checks whether the connection is successfully opened. The ADO.NET framework is a popular choice for executing database operations in .NET applications, and PowerShell can leverage it to interact with databases efficiently, making it a powerful tool for database operations.

Connected Classes and Disconnected Classes for SQL Server in .NET

Connected classes

- **`SqlConnection`**: This class establishes and manages connections to the target database via the .NET data provider for SQL server.

- **SqlCommand**: Contains the necessary details to execute T-SQL commands against the SQL server database.
- **SqlDataAdapter**: This class acts as a bridge between connected and disconnected classes. **SqlDataAdapter** is a class that bridges connected and disconnected classes in ADO.NET. It includes two methods: fill and update. Fill retrieves data from a data source and populates a DataSet or DataTable object. Update submits changes made to the DataSet or DataTable back to the database.
- **SqlBulkCopy**: This class is used to bulk load a SQL server table with data from an external source.

Disconnected classes:

- **DataTable**: This class stores data returned by a query in a tabular format, similar to how data is stored in a database table.

In summary, the PowerShell script employs several ADO.NET classes and methods to establish a connection to an SQL server database, verify its status, and execute database operations. The ADO.NET framework is a powerful and efficient tool for developers who want to interact with databases in their .NET applications.

```
try {
    # Define the connection string with SQL Server details
    $connString = "Data Source=YourInstance;Database=YourDB;User
ID=YourUser;Password=YourPassword"

    # Create a SqlConnection object
    $sqlConnection = New-Object System.Data.SqlClient.SqlConnection
$connString

    # Attempt to open the SQL connection
    $sqlConnection.Open()

    # Check if the connection state is "Open."
    if ($sqlConnection.State -eq "Open") {
        # Notify successful connection
        Write-Host "Test connection successful"

        # Close the connection since the test is successful
        $sqlConnection.Close()
```

```
    }
    else {
        # Notify that the connection is not in the "Open" state
        Write-Host "Connection not in the 'Open' state"
    }
}
catch {
    # An error occurred during the connection attempt
    Write-Host "Error connecting to the database: $_.Exception.Message"
}
```

ADO.Net Objects and `Invoke-Sqlcmd`

This script provides a basic technique for collecting data from multiple servers and storing it in a centralized SQL server database.

You need to ensure that the target SQL server has the appropriate table. You can use the provided SQL script to create the **`tbl_PoShDiskData`** table.

```
CREATE TABLE tbl_PoShDiskData
(
[SystemName] VARCHAR(40) not null,
[DeviceID] VARCHAR(40) not null,
[VolumeName] VARCHAR(40) not null,
[TotalSize] int not null,
[FreeSize] int not null
)
```

Ensure you have the correct details for the target SQL server instance. Specifically, make sure to update the connection string and input server list.

This script accepts an array of server names (**`$servers`**) and processes each server in the loop. Adjust the server names in the array according to your requirements. Additionally, it includes error handling to capture and display any errors that may occur during the processing of individual servers.

```
# Define an array of server names
$servers = @('Server1', 'Server2', 'Server3')

# Connection parameters
```

```
$params = @{
    'Server'   = '.\DemoServer'
    'Database' = 'PoshGuideDB'
}

# Connection string for the target database
$connectionString = "Data Source=.\DemoServer;Initial Catalog=PoshGuid-
eDB;Integrated Security=SSPI"

# Insert statement template
$insert = @'
    INSERT INTO [PoshGuideDB].[dbo].[tbl_PosHDiskData](SystemName, Devi-
ceID, VolumeName, TotalSize, FreeSize)
    VALUES ('{0}', '{1}', '{2}', '{3}', '{4}')
'@

# Connection object initialization
$conn = New-Object System.Data.SqlClient.SqlConnection($connection-
String)

# Iterate through each server
foreach ($server in $servers) {
    Try {
        # Open the Connection
        $conn.Open()

        # Prepare the SQL command
        $cmd = $conn.CreateCommand()

        # WMI output transformation to SQL table
        Get-WmiObject win32_logicaldisk -ComputerName $server -Filter
"Drivetype=3" | ForEach-Object {
            $cmd.CommandText = $insert -f $_.SystemName, $_.DeviceID,
$_.VolumeName, $_.TotalSize, $_.FreeSize
            $cmd.ExecuteNonQuery()
```

```
        }

        # Close the connection
        $conn.Close()
    }
    Catch {
        Write-Error "Error processing server $server: $_"
    }
}

# Query the database for all servers
Invoke-Sqlcmd @params -Query "SELECT * FROM tbl_PosHdiskData" | Format-Table -AutoSize
```

The script goes through each server as specified in the array, uses **`Get-WmiObject win32_logicaldisk`** to retrieve disk information, transforms the data into SQL insert statements, and then executes those statements to insert the data into the specified SQL server database. Finally, it queries the database to retrieve and display the data using **`Invoke-Sqlcmd`**.

PowerShell and AzureDevOps

Azure DevOps is a comprehensive platform that supports the entire DevOps process, while PowerShell is a flexible scripting language that allows for automation across the Azure ecosystem. This section demonstrates how to seamlessly integrate PowerShell scripts within Azure DevOps pipelines, unlocking many automation possibilities.

This process demonstrates how to integrate PowerShell tasks in an Azure DevOps pipeline. You can automate and execute PowerShell commands as part of your CI/CD process in Azure DevOps by pushing your PowerShell script to GitHub, creating a new pipeline with a starter code, and then editing the pipeline YAML to include PowerShell tasks.

PowerShell Tasks in an Azure DevOps Pipeline

Here is a step-by-step process that explains how to utilize PowerShell tasks in an Azure DevOps pipeline. This covers everything from pushing a simple PowerShell script to GitHub to editing the pipeline YAML to include PowerShell tasks.

Step 1: Push a PowerShell Script to GitHub

First, create a simple PowerShell script, like **`hello-world.ps1`**, that contains your desired PowerShell commands. Then, push the script to your GitHub repository in the main branch.

Step 2: Create a new pipeline

Head over to the pipelines section of the Azure DevOps project and select "**`Create a New Pipeline`**". Then, select your source repository (in this case, GitHub).

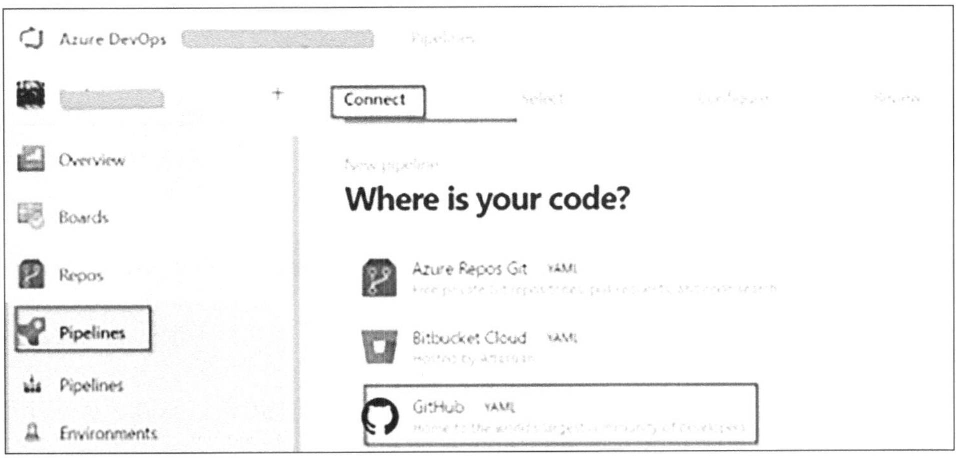

***Figure 11.3**: Azure DevOps pipeline*

Choose the "**`Starter pipeline`**" option.

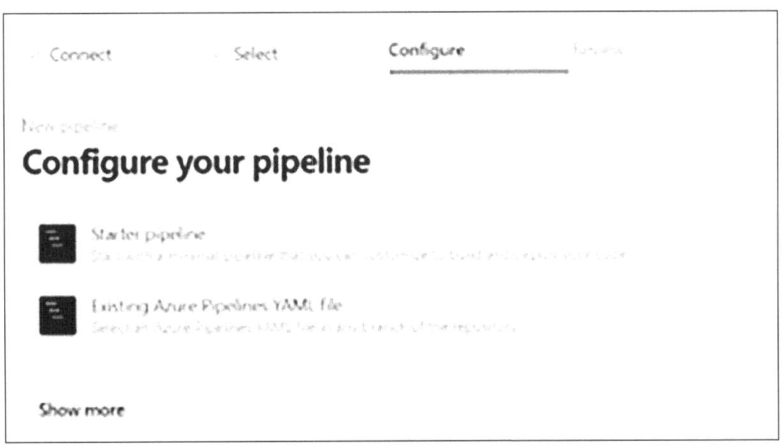

***Figure 11.4**: Configure the pipeline*

Step 3: **`Save and run`** Initial Pipeline. During the initial pipeline setup, you will create a minimal pipeline, which will act as a placeholder to generate the initial YAML file.

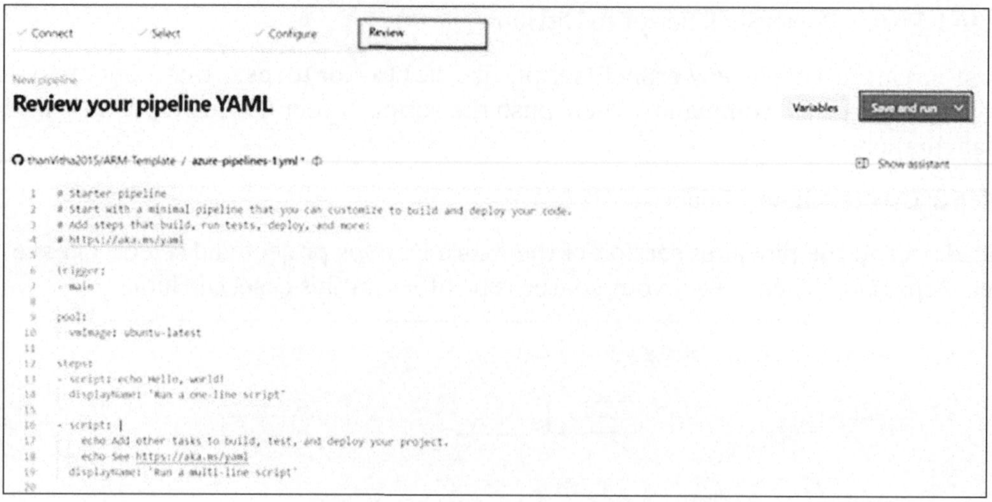

Figure 11.5: *Review YAML pipeline*

Step 4: Save your changes to the YAML file and click **`commit`** to update to the main branch.

Step 5: Edit pipeline YAML.

In the generated **`azure-pipelines.yml`** file, locate the code and add a PowerShell task.

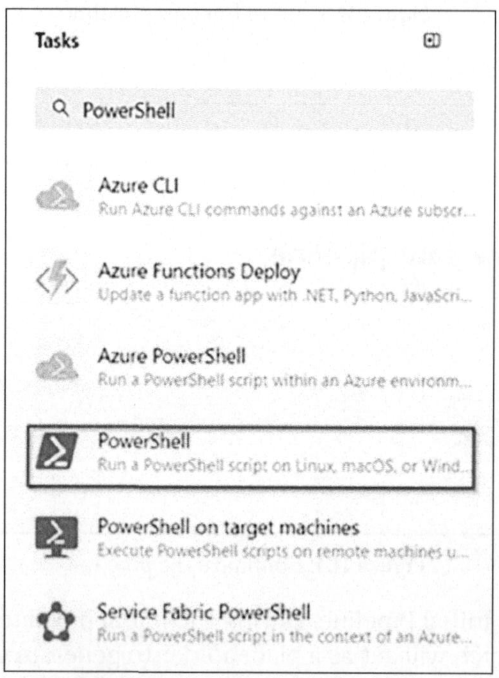

Figure 11.6: *Add PowerShell task*

To execute PowerShell commands, use the **`PowerShell@2`** task. You can add a PowerShell task by specifying the inline script or the file path of your script. Save the changes to the YAML file and commit them to the main branch.

Figure 11.7: *Run pipeline*

Step 6: Make sure to save any changes you made to the YAML file and commit them to the main branch.

Step 7: Trigger the Pipeline.

Manually trigger the pipeline or wait for an automatic trigger based on your configured triggers. Monitor the pipeline execution in Azure DevOps to see the PowerShell tasks being executed.

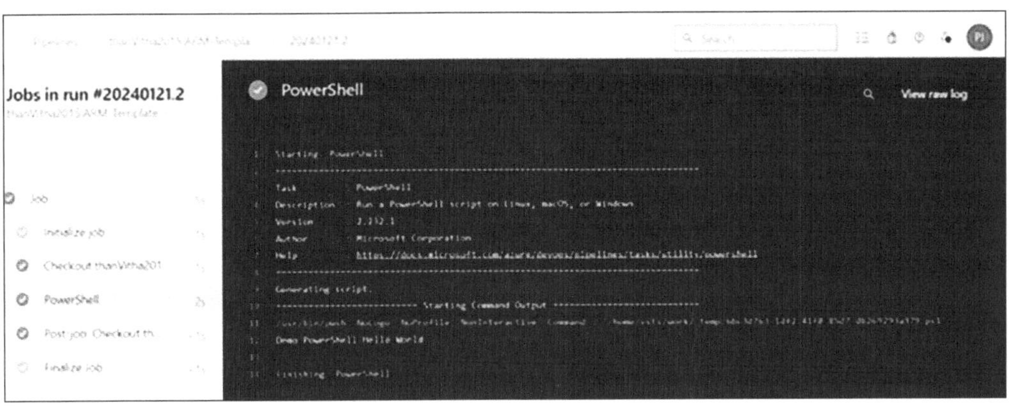

Figure 11.8: *View jobs*

Note: *PowerShell v2 uses Windows PowerShell for Windows agents and PowerShell Core for Linux agents by default.*

This example demonstrates how to use PowerShell tasks within an Azure DevOps pipeline. The pipeline can be customized to build and deploy your code.

Let us break down each section:

```
# Starter pipeline

# Start with a minimal pipeline that you can customize to build and
deploy your code.
```

```
# Add steps that build, run tests, deploy, and more:
# https://aka.ms/yaml

trigger:
- main

pool:
  vmImage: ubuntu-latest

variables:
  num1 : 2
  num2 : 3
```

- **`trigger`**: The pipeline is configured to run whenever there are changes to the main branch.
- **`pool`**: The pipeline is set to run on an Ubuntu-based agent (ubuntu-latest).
- **`variables`**: Two variables (num1 and num2) are defined with values 2 and 3, respectively.

Step 1: The **`PowerShell@2`** task executes an inline PowerShell script that writes a message to the console.

```
- Task: PowerShell@2
- Inputs:
  - targetType: 'inline'
  - script: |
    # Write your PowerShell commands here.
    Write-Host "PowerShell in AzureDevOps Pipeline"
```

Step 2: The **`PowerShell@2`** task executes a PowerShell script file named **`Hello-world.ps1`**.

```
- Task: PowerShell@2
- Inputs:
  - filePath: 'Hello-world.ps1'
```

Step 3: The **`PowerShell@2`** task executes a PowerShell script file named **`Chapter 11 - Azure DevOps - PowerShell Script.ps1`** and passes values to parameters -**`number1`** and -**`number2`** using the variables **`$(num1)`** and **`$(num2)`**.

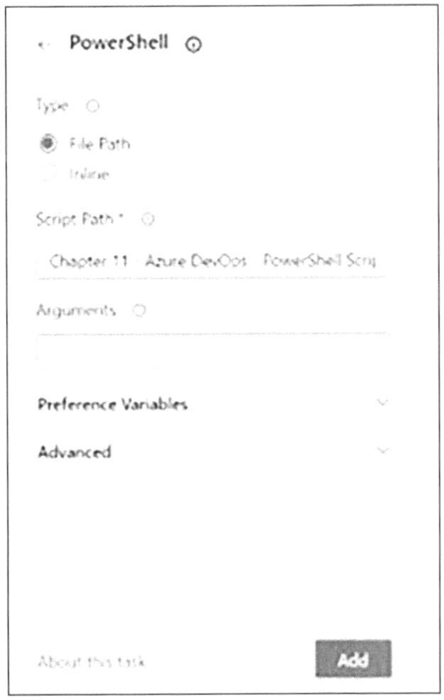

Figure 11.9: *PowerShell task configuration*

```
- Task: PowerShell@2
- Inputs:
  - filePath: 'Chapter 11 - Azure DevOps - PowerShell Script.ps1'
  - arguments: "-number1 $(num1) -number2 $(num2)"
```

This pipeline demonstrates how to use the **PowerShell@2** task to run inline PowerShell scripts and scripts from files. It also showcases the usage of variables within the pipeline. You can customize this pipeline based on your specific build and deployment requirements.

Azure Pipelines YAML Validator

This VS Code extension enables validation of Azure DevOps YAML pipelines without committing them.

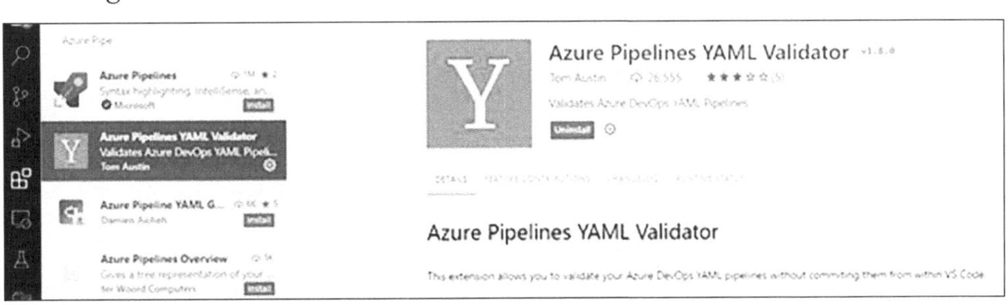

Figure 11.10: *Azure pipeline YAML validator*

To validate a YAML file in Azure pipelines, follow these steps:

Press *Ctrl+Shift+P* to open the Command Palette, then choose the **`'Azure Pipelines YAML Validator: Validate'`** command. Alternatively, use the keyboard shortcuts *Ctrl+Alt+V* on Windows or *Ctrl+Cmd+V* on Mac.

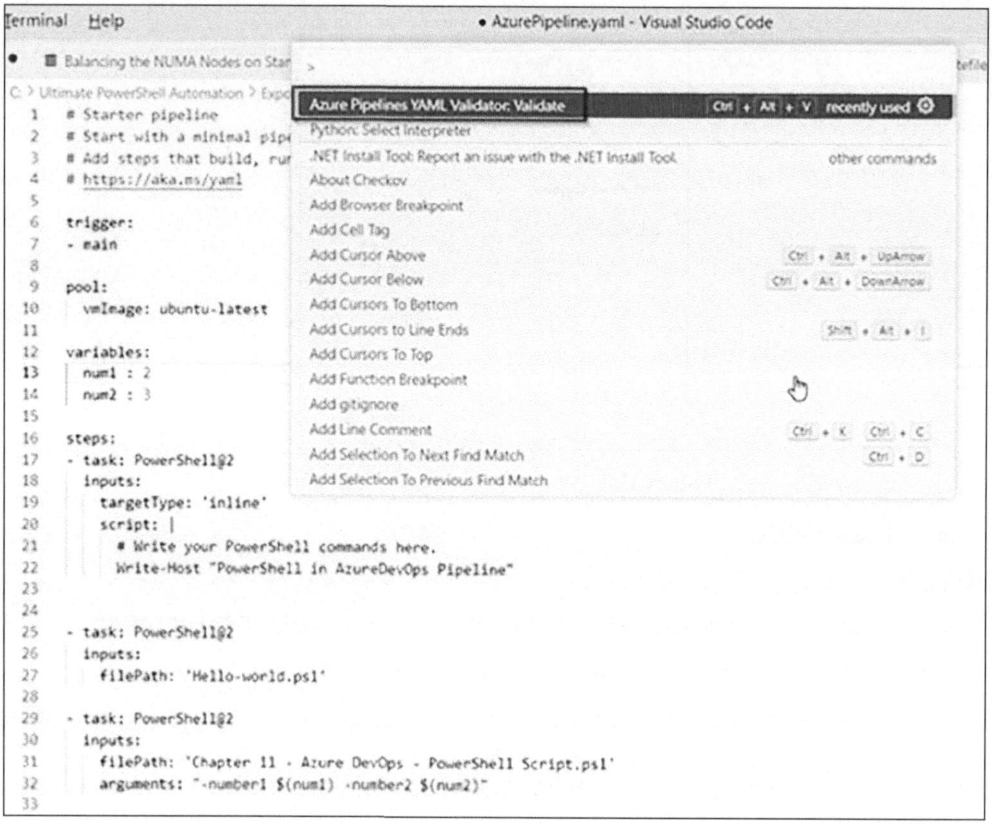

Figure 11.11: *Validate a YAML file in Azure pipelines*

This will validate your YAML file and report any issues that need to be addressed.

Figure 11.12: *Validation of the pipeline*

Best Practices: Harnessing Functions, Modules, and Procedures

When scripting in PowerShell for enterprise environments, it is crucial to adhere to best practices. The strategic use of functions, modules, and procedures enhances code structure, ensures maintainability, and fosters collaboration.

PowerShell scripts are widely used in enterprise environments to automate various tasks. It is important to follow certain best practices to ensure that the code is well-organized and easy to maintain, including:

- The strategic use of functions, modules, and procedures is one of these best practices.
- Functions help encapsulate specific tasks, promoting code modularity and clarity.
- Grouping related functions into modules creates a modular and maintainable codebase.
- Importing modules helps access encapsulated functions and streamline script execution.
- Designing functions with parameters enhances flexibility and adaptability.
- Implementing error handling within functions ensures graceful script behavior.
- Including meaningful comments and documentation enhances the clarity and readability of your code.

```
# Best Practice: Documenting functions
function New-LogEntry {
    param (
        [string]$logMessage
    )
    <#
    .SYNOPSIS
    Adds a new log entry with the specified message.

    .PARAMETER logMessage
    The message to be logged.
    #>
```

```
    # Logic to add a log entry
    # ...
}
```

These best practices can streamline script execution, improve code structure, and ensure robustness and collaboration.

Best Practices for PowerShell Scripting: Ensuring Clarity and Compatibility

When scripting in PowerShell for enterprise environments, it is crucial to follow best practices to guarantee efficient, maintainable, and scalable code. To achieve this, we can follow some recommendations that can help us maintain clarity, readability, and compatibility.

- First, leveraging the latest version of PowerShell is essential to take advantage of new features, improvements, and bug fixes. However, before using any version, we should thoroughly review its release notes and documentation to understand its changes, limitations, and potential issues.
- Second, when creating PowerShell scripts, we should aim for modularity, meaning we break the code into smaller, reusable, and testable functions. This approach can enhance code readability, simplify debugging, and facilitate maintenance.
- Third, PowerShell scripts should use a consistent naming convention for variables, functions, and parameters that are descriptive and meaningful and follow the approved naming conventions. This practice can enhance code readability and maintainability, reducing the chances of naming conflicts.

Finally, PowerShell scripts should include comments explaining the code's purpose, approach, and potential limitations or issues. This documentation can help other developers understand the code's intent and make it easier to update, debug, and maintain.

By adhering to these best practices, we can develop PowerShell scripts that are efficient, maintainable, scalable, and meet the enterprise's needs.

Keep the following tips in mind while writing PowerShell scripts to ensure they are clear, compatible, and easy to maintain:

- Use full cmdlet names instead of aliases for clarity and understanding. For example, use "**`Get-Process`**" instead of "**`ps`**".
- Use full parameter names instead of positional parameters to enhance readability. For example, use "**`Get-Service -DisplayName 'Windows Update'`**" instead of "**`Get-Service 'Windows Update'`**".

- Use advanced editors like VS Code instead of Notepad for enhanced features and compatibility.
- Write self-explanatory code sections to minimize the need for excessive comments.
- Follow the verb-noun syntax with approved verbs to maintain consistency. For example, use "**`Invoke-Action`**" instead of "**`Do-Something`**".
- Use singular English nouns in cmdlets to enhance readability. For example, use "**`Get-User`**" instead of "**`Get-Users`**".
- Specify the correct file extension when running an application. For example, use "**`Start-Process 'notepad.exe'`**" instead of "**`Start notepad`**".
- Use CIM cmdlets instead of WMI for compatibility and support for session-based connections. For example, use "**`Get-CimInstance -ClassName Win32_Process`**".
- Include the **`#Requires`** statement to ensure compatibility with specified prerequisites and the latest PowerShell version. For example, include "**`#Requires -Version 5.1`**".

By following these best practices, your PowerShell scripts will become more maintainable, understandable, and compatible across diverse environments, aligning with the latest PowerShell version for optimal results.

Best Practices for PowerShell Security

Ensuring the security of your scripts is paramount when working with PowerShell. Here are some essential security best practices for PowerShell:

1. **Script Signing**: Sign your PowerShell scripts to guarantee their integrity and authenticity. This will help prevent unauthorized changes and execution of scripts.

   ```
   #Example script for signing a script:


   Set-AuthenticodeSignature -FilePath C:\Path\To\YourScript.ps1
   -Certificate (Get-ChildItem Cert:\CurrentUser\My -CodeSigningCert)
   ```

2. **Avoid storing secrets directly**: It is not recommended to store sensitive information like passwords or API keys directly in PowerShell scripts. It is important to avoid storing passwords in plain text format or allowing users to enter them as a parameter, as this can lead to security vulnerabilities like exposing passwords to screen-scraper malware or having them saved in the command history. The best practice is to use **`PSCredential`** objects to handle passwords, as they store the password in a **`SecureString`** format, which is much more secure.

```
# Prompt for a secure string. In automation, accept it as a parameter.
$Secure = Read-Host -Prompt "Enter the secure string" -AsSecureString

#Example script for using Credential object for secure storage:
$credential = Get-Credential
```

3. **Use Credential Manager**: Use the Windows Credential Manager to store and retrieve credentials safely, reducing the risk of exposing sensitive information in scripts.

   To access the **`Credential Manager`** module in PowerShell, start by installing it. Here is an example script for retrieving credentials from Windows **`Credential Manager`**:

```
#Install Credential Manager
Install-Module -Name CredentialManager
#Example script for retrieving credentials from Windows Credential Manager:
$credential = Get-StoredCredential -Target "YourTargetName"
```

4. **Implement Execution Policies**: Set appropriate execution policies to control the level of script execution on a system. For example, setting the execution policy to "**`RemoteSigned`**" only allows locally created scripts to run without a signature.

```
# Example script for setting execution policy:
Set-ExecutionPolicy RemoteSigned
```

6. **Regularly Update PowerShell**: Keep PowerShell up-to-date with the latest security patches and updates. Regularly check for and install updates to ensure that security vulnerabilities are addressed.

```
# Example script for checking for PowerShell updates:
Install-Module -Name PowerShellGet -Force -AllowClobber -Scope CurrentUser -SkipPublisherCheck
Install-Script -Name Install-Module -Force -AllowClobber -Scope CurrentUser -SkipPublisherCheck
```

7. **Implement Constrained Language Mode**: Utilize Constrained Language Mode to restrict access to sensitive resources and enhance the security of PowerShell sessions.

```
# Example script for enabling Constrained Language Mode:
$ExecutionContext.SessionState.LanguageMode
```

8. **Audit PowerShell Usage**: Enable PowerShell script block logging and transcription to track and audit the usage of PowerShell in your environment. This helps identify potential security incidents.

```
# Example script for enabling script block logging:


Set-ItemProperty -Path 'HKLM:\SOFTWARE\Wow6432Node\Microsoft\Win-
dows\CurrentVersion\WINEVT\Channels\Microsoft-Windows-PowerShell/
Operational' -Name 'Enabled' -Value '1'
```

Always refer to the latest official Microsoft documentation for PowerShell security guidance, as security practices may evolve. Additionally, consider your organization's specific security requirements and policies when implementing these practices.

Conclusion

We covered the key points for mastering PowerShell scripting, including adopting best practices for collaboration, readability, and security. We discussed the importance of modularizing code, adhering to naming conventions and approved verbs, signing scripts, handling sensitive information carefully, and testing connectivity. We also highlighted the versatility of PowerShell in essential enterprise environments such as Active Directory (AD), Office 365, and DevOps, as well as the practical application of these best practices through a real-time example. By embracing these principles, PowerShell scripts become indispensable, contributing to streamlined operations across diverse IT landscapes.

Points to Remember

Best Practices in Scripting:

- Keep your scripts simple and linear for easy understanding.
- Use consistent indentation to enhance readability.
- Leverage functions judiciously and avoid unnecessary nesting.
- Utilize clear and intelligently named variables for better comprehension.
- Implement comment-based "`Help`" for documentation and clarity.
- Place user-defined variables at the top of the script for easy access.
- Avoid unnecessary temporary data output and retrieval.

Scripting Techniques:

- Prefer using full cmdlet names over aliases for clarity.
- Avoid partial and positional parameter names and use full names.

- Choose advanced script editors like VS Code or PowerShell ISE.
- Limit comments to ensure clarity and divide code into well-labeled sections.
- Follow the approved verb-noun syntax for cmdlets.
- Use singular English nouns in cmdlets.

Other Considerations:

- Test connectivity to external services like SQL Server before execution.
- Prefer the latest PowerShell version for enhanced features and security.
- Emphasize security by signing scripts and handling secrets cautiously.
- Specify `HelpText` for mandatory parameters to aid users.
- Utilize CIM cmdlets for improved remote management.
- Include `#Require` statements to enforce prerequisites.

Real-Time Example:

- Demonstrated using PowerShell, WMI, and SQL server for system information retrieval and storage.
- Highlighted the importance of maintaining connection strings, error handling, and WMI output transformation.
- Discussed how scripts can be organized using parameters and queries.

Multiple Choice Questions

1. What is the recommended practice for writing clear and understandable PowerShell scripts?

   a. Use as many aliases as possible for brevity.

   b. Prioritize partial and positional parameter names.

   c. Divide code into sections with clear headings.

   d. Avoid using script editors like VS Code or PowerShell ISE.

2. Which cmdlet should be preferred for output in scripts, considering versatility, and pipeline support?

   a. `Write-Host`

   b. `Write-Output`

   c. `Write-Log`

   d. `Write-Result`

3. What is the significance of specifying `HelpText` for mandatory parameters in PowerShell scripts?
    a. It is optional and does not impact script execution.
    b. It aids users when prompted for mandatory parameters without accessing documentation.
    c. It adds unnecessary complexity to the script.
    d. It is only relevant for advanced users.
4. Which method is commonly used to test connectivity to a SQL server database in PowerShell?
    a. Using a direct file import method.
    b. Leveraging the `Invoke-Command` cmdlet.
    c. Employing the `Test-SqlConnection` cmdlet.
    d. Utilizing a connection string and the basic `SqlClient` class.
5. Why is using the latest PowerShell version (N-1) rather than LTS (Long-Term Support) versions recommended?
    a. LTS versions providc morc fcatures and enhancements.
    b. N-1 versions are more stable and secure.
    c. LTS versions have better backward compatibility.
    d. N-1 versions lack critical security updates.

Answers

1. c
2. b
3. b
4. d
5. b

Key Terms

- **Cmdlet:** Lightweight command in PowerShell following a verb-noun naming convention.
- **Alias:** Symbolic name given to a cmdlet, function, file, or script, providing a shorter alternative.
- **Positional Parameter:** Parameter referenced by its exact position in the code block.
- **Script Editor:** Application for writing and editing scripts (for example, VS Code, PowerShell ISE).
- **`Write-Host`:** Cmdlet for displaying text or colors on the screen, suitable for interactive console use.
- **`Write-Output`:** Cmdlet for sending output through pipes, returning responses as objects.
- **CIM (Common Information Model):** Standards for describing management information in systems, used in PowerShell for remote access.
- **`#Require` Statement:** Ensures a script runs only when specific prerequisites are met.
- **`Invoke-Sqlcmd`:** Cmdlet for executing SQL queries and commands against SQL Server databases.
- **Security Best Practices:** Guidelines for secure PowerShell usage, including script signing, and handling of secrets.

Index

Symbols

A

R

S

T

W